Glencoe

Literature

INTERACTIVE

Novel Companion

Great Expectations
Charles Dickens

A Midsummer Night's Dream
William Shakespeare

Jane Eyre
Charlotte Brontë

The Yearling
Marjorie Kinnan Rawlings

... And the Earth Did Not Devour Him
Tomás Rivera

Animal Farm
George Orwell

COURSE 4

Photo Credits

7 Bettmann/CORBIS; **11** John Springer Collection/CORBIS; **23** Bettmann/CORBIS;
47 Leonard de Selva/CORBIS; **75 79 119 135** Bettmann/CORBIS; **147** Richard Wear/
Design Pics/CORBIS; **163** CORBIS; **167** Stapleton Collection/CORBIS; **179** CORBIS;
231 CORBIS SYGMA; **247** Underwood & Underwood/CORBIS; **271** DigitalVision;
299 Digital Vision/PunchStock; **303 315** Bettmann/CORBIS.

Acknowledgments

Grateful acknowledgment is given to authors, publishers, photographers, museums,
and agents for permission to reprint the following copyrighted material. Every effort
has been made to determine copyright owners. In case of any omissions, the Publisher
will be pleased to make suitable acknowledgments in future editions.

Send all inquiries to:
Glencoe/McGraw-Hill
8787 Orion Place
Columbus, OH 43240-4027

ISBN: 978-0-07-889153-3
MHID: 0-07-889153-1

Printed in the United States of America.

1 2 3 4 5 6 7 8 9 047 14 13 12 11 10 09 08

TABLE OF CONTENTS

TABLE OF CONTENTS

TABLE OF CONTENTS

TABLE OF CONTENTS

CHAPTERS 8–10

Welcome to the *Novel Companion*. This book is designed for you to write in. It is interactive: The book prompts, and you respond. The *Novel Companion* encourages, questions, provides space for notes, and invites you to jot down your thoughts and ideas. You can use it to circle and underline words and phrases you think are important, and to write questions that will guide your reading.

The *Novel Companion* helps you develop skills for reading, analyzing, and responding to novels, as well as to autobiographies and plays. These literary works are drawn from Glencoe's *Literature Library*. They include some of the most notable works in literature. Many are award-winning modern works; others are classics.

The *Novel Companion* is designed to follow the approach and themes in each unit of your textbook, *Glencoe Literature*. The *Novel Companion* includes two types of lessons:

- **Note-Taking Lessons** presents two methods of note-taking to help you connect major themes in *Glencoe Literature* to the other novels and works you will be reading. Using the book will help you learn these valuable note-taking methods, so you can make effective notes whenever you study.

- **Interactive Reading Lessons** are lessons based on the sequential chapter groupings in each novel. In this part of the book you'll practice identifying important ideas and themes, analyzing literary elements, applying reading strategies, completing graphic organizers, and mastering vocabulary—all skills that expert readers use to help them comprehend novels and other long works of literature.

Note to Parents and Guardians: Ask your students to show you their work periodically, and explain how it helps them study. You might want to talk to them about how the skills they are learning cross over to other subjects.

The notes and features in the interactive reading lessons will direct you through the process of reading and making meaning from each set of chapters. As you use these notes and features, you'll be practicing and mastering the strategies that good readers use whenever they read.

Get Set to Read

After reading about the novel and the author, you will begin to read the novel. You will study it in groupings of chapters, or chapter sets, in the *Novel Companion*. Each chapter set begins with an activity to connect your personal experience to the literature. You will also read background material to provide context for the chapter set content.

You're invited to interact with the information in Build Background by summarizing content or writing a caption for an image related to the content.

You are then introduced to the targeted skills for the chapter set: the Big Idea, the literary element, and the reading strategy. You will also get vocabulary for the chapter set.

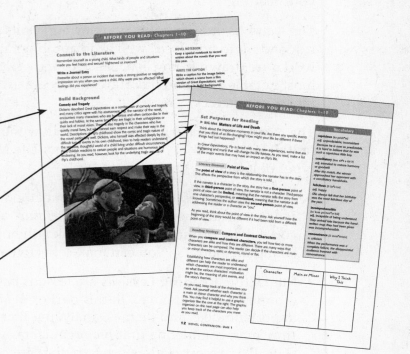

Read, Respond, Interpret

Every lesson includes an active reading graphic organizer to fill in as you read. This graphic organizer is related to either the literary element or the reading strategy for the chapter set.

Interactive reading pages include text excerpts from the novels that emphasize a literary element or a reading strategy. Questions in the margin help you interact with highlighted portions of the text.

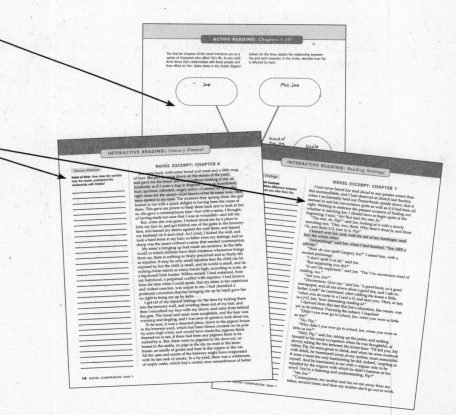

Show What You Know

After you read the chapters in the chapter set, you will answer questions about the content, including how the background information helped you as you read.

You will then demonstrate what you learned from your interactive reading of the excerpts. You will also practice using the vocabulary words you were introduced to and learn a new vocabulary word that can be used in your academic writing.

In addition, you will complete a short writing assignment and other activities related to what you read in the chapter set content. These activities will draw on what you studied in your interactive work on the excerpts from the chapters.

After you read the entire novel, you will work with related readings, connect the novel to an excerpt from *Glencoe Literature*, and finally, write an essay or story that draws upon what you learned by reading.

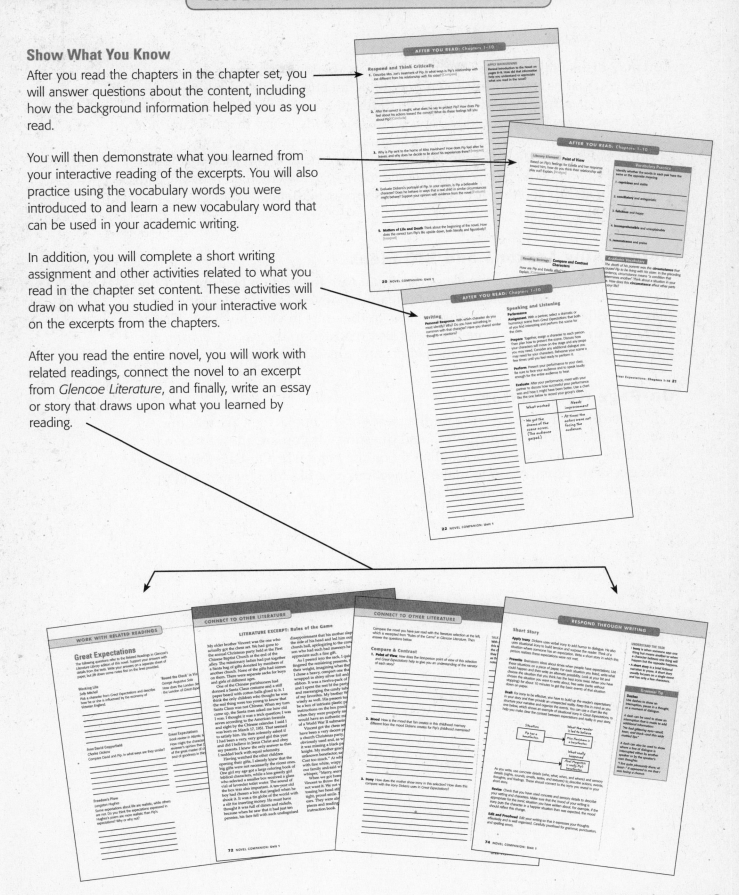

You may dislike taking notes. Perhaps you don't believe that notes are useful or maybe you just haven't been shown how to do an effective job of taking notes. The *Novel Companion* will teach you two different systems of taking notes. These systems will help you develop note-taking skills to use in school and for the rest of your life. Research shows that students who take good notes perform better on tests, and note-taking skills are crucial if you plan to attend college. When you take notes, you become more actively engaged in what you read by constantly looking for main ideas, supporting details, and key relationships.

Note-Taking Lessons and BIG Ideas

The note-taking lessons in the *Novel Companion* are focused on helping you find a connection between the main ideas of featured novels (or autobiographies or plays) and the Big Ideas, or major themes, of the units in your textbook, *Glencoe Literature*. By learning the note-taking skills presented in the *Novel Companion*, you will be able to make such connections more readily and easily.

On-Page Note-Taking

College students routinely write on the pages of the books they are reading, using the margins to jot down ideas and questions. If you are allowed to mark up your text, you can write notes directly on the page. The On-Page Note-Taking lessons prompt you to make connections to a Big Idea by marking up an excerpt using a system of symbols.

The Cornell Note-Taking System

The *Novel Companion* will also train you in the Cornell Note-Taking System, which was developed at Cornell University to help students take more effective notes. In this system, the page is divided into two columns, one wide and one narrow. This format provides a way to organize your thinking. You'll use the Cornell Note-Taking System to take notes on excerpts from the novels and how the excerpts relate to the Big Ideas. The following summarizes the steps of the system:

Record First, you will record notes in the right (wide) column as you read. Your notes may include summaries, bulleted lists, and graphic organizers.

Reduce Next, you will reduce, or condense, your notes into key words, phrases, questions, and comments in the left (narrow) column. This step will help you clarify meaning, find information within your notes, and trigger your memory when you study.

Recap Finally, you will use the bottom portion of the page to recap, or summarize, what you have learned from your notes. This step helps strengthen your grasp of what you just read before you move on to the next section of text.

A Lifelong Skill

Once you become accustomed to using the note-taking skills taught in the *Novel Companion*, you'll be able to use these skills when you read other literature, when you listen to a lecture in class, when you attend a meeting, or even as you watch a film.

Through the note-taking lessons presented in the *Novel Companion*, you'll be learning to record important information in your own words, to reduce it to key words that will help you remember your notes, and to apply your notes as you answer questions and read and write about the novels and other longer works in the program.

Read, Question, and Mark-Up

Not only will you be interacting with excerpts from the novels as you work with the literary elements and reading strategies assigned to a chapter set, but you will also be working with excerpts that relate to the Big Idea assigned to each chapter set.

You will take notes on the excerpt—right on the page. With practice, you will devise a short-hand system that works for you. In the meantime, you can use the suggested on-page mark-up system.

Record, Reduce, and Recap

You will also learn the Cornell Note-Taking System, described on the previous page. Here you will take notes on the excerpt you marked up on the On-Page Note-Taking page.

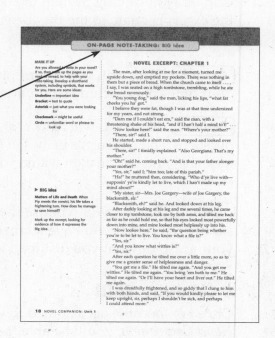

Great Expectations

Charles Dickens

Great Expectations
Charles Dickens

"I deliberated with an aching heart whether I would not get down when we changed horses and walk back, and have another evening at home, and a better parting. We changed, and I had not made up my mind. . . . We changed again, and yet again, and it was now too late and too far to go back, and I went on. And the mists had all solemnly risen now, and the world lay spread before me."

—Pip, Chapter 19

These words reveal the thoughts of one of Dickens's most famous characters as he starts a new life with great expectations as well as doubts. *Great Expectations* was Dickens's thirteenth novel, and he wrote it when he was at the height of his success as a novelist. It traces the life and experiences of Philip Pirrip, or Pip, as he comes of age in the early- to mid-nineteenth century.

New Expectations In *Great Expectations,* Pip tells his own story as an adult looking back on his younger years. When the novel begins, Pip is a poor orphan who seems destined to become a blacksmith like his brother-in-law and live out his life in the marsh area of Kent, England. An unexpected chain of events, however, thrusts him into a completely different world and way of life. Over time, Pip's new life becomes much more complicated than he imagined it would be, and he is forced to reevaluate his values and the values of the society in which he finds himself. Critic Harold Bloom says:

Great Expectations *is carefully organized so that at each new turn of events the main*

character and narrator, Philip Pirrip (Pip), learns more about himself by learning more about the complex social web in which he is enmeshed.

Class Divisions Pip's society is a complicated one indeed. The Industrial Revolution of the late 1700s and early 1800s helped England to become an especially powerful and prosperous country. During the Victorian Age (named after Queen Victoria, who reigned from 1832 to 1901), the British Empire included countries on every continent. English society as a whole benefited from advances and innovations in technology and science. Not everyone shared in the nation's wealth, however, and British society, which had always been class conscious, became even more sharply divided along class lines.

In *Great Expectations,* as in his other novels, Dickens dramatizes the moral struggles and faults of the age. Bert Hornback, the author of a book about this Dickens classic, has called it "a brilliantly conceived attack on the vices that most threaten human society: selfishness and greed." Dickens implies that a society fascinated by wealth and power is too far removed from basic moral values. The characters that he holds up as examples of moral behavior are hardworking, simple, and compassionate.

The Serial Novel While reading Dickens, it is useful to keep in mind that all his novels were published serially, or in weekly or monthly installments in magazines. To keep the reader coming back for more, Dickens ended each installment with a "cliffhanger." The chapters were then published in book form after the serial was completed. Although some novels had been published in installments before

Dickens's time, he set the standard for serials in nineteenth-century Britain with his first novel, *The Pickwick Papers* (1837).

The serial form allowed Dickens to introduce a large number of characters and develop the reader's familiarity with them. It also allowed the author to respond to the likes and dislikes of his readers as he was writing the novel. People would write to Dickens or to the magazine in which the installments were published and give him their opinions.

The Author's Vision Although his novel *David Copperfield*, published in 1850, was more autobiographical, Dickens drew on some of his own childhood perceptions of the world in his portrayal of Pip. The character of Pip was shaped by many of the personal details of Dickens's youth and young-adulthood, and *Great Expectations*

reflects Dickens's world view. According to writer Paul Pickrel, the plot:

holds the reader's interest; it is full of surprises and odd turns; its complexities all come out neatly in the end. But more than that, it is a symbolic representation of Dickens's vision of the moral universe . . . that good and evil, what we most desire and what we most loathe, are . . . intertwined. . . .

The story begins in the early 1800s, in the marsh area of Kent, England. Dickens was familiar with this area, because he lived there as a child. Later in the novel, when Pip enters young adulthood, the scene shifts to busy, industrial London. The novel shifts back and forth between these two locations as events unfold. As you read the novel, think about the values that the people in each setting hold.

A Changing Economy

The Industrial Revolution began in England in the late 1700s, when the invention of machines for weaving gave rise to a factory system. The emergence of factories changed the economy of England from one that was based on agriculture to one that was based on manufactured goods. Because of this shift, thousands of people left rural areas to take jobs in industrial cities.

Despite the prosperity and modern conveniences that resulted from the Industrial Revolution, it created many social problems. Cities grew too large too quickly, and overcrowding created filth and disease. Workers were often exploited and forced to work long hours for little pay. Even young children worked long hours under dangerous conditions in factories and mines. Reform acts addressing the concerns of working people were not passed until the early 1800s. Although the acts provided workers with some protections, working conditions were still, by

today's standards, very poor. Through his writings, Dickens drew attention to social and political problems in his country. Critic Bert Hornback writes that although the wealthy:

seemed to care absolutely nothing for the lives of the "hands" whom they employed, the nation still had a conscience—and it responded to voices like Dickens's.

Charles Dickens (1812–1870)

"_If Columbus found a new world, Dickens created one—and peopled it with men and women._**"**

—_Arthur Quiller-Couch,_ **Dickens's Fellowship Dinner, 1931**

Charles Dickens is one of the most successful and inventive English novelists of all time. Dickens wrote over 5 million words and created over 2,000 characters. His writing is rich with humor, drama, and satire, and his characters are some of the most well known in the history of literature. Dickens created eccentric, or odd, characters, often from the lower economic classes of nineteenth-century England. These characters and their worlds delighted and moved readers and helped to make Dickens the most popular writer of his time. According to critic G.K. Chesterton:

His books are full of baffled villains stalking out or cowardly bullies kicked downstairs. But the villains and the cowards are such delightful people that the reader always hopes the villain will put his head through a side window and make a last remark; or that the bully will say one more thing, even from the bottom of the stairs.

Humble Beginnings In addition to writing short stories and novels, Dickens wrote essays and journalistic pieces, and edited a weekly periodical filled with fiction, poetry, and essays. First titled _Household Words,_ the magazine was later retitled _All the Year Round._ Dickens contributed to this publication several serialized novels, including _Great Expectations,_ and writings on political and social issues.

Dickens was born on February 7, 1812, in Landport, Portsea, England. He was the second child and eldest son of eight children. Dickens's father, who worked as a clerk in the Navy Pay Office, was a spendthrift who often mismanaged the family money. In 1822 the family moved to London and soon found itself in financial crisis. The family was forced to live in poverty, and Dickens was no longer able to go to school.

Dealing with Class Issues One of the most traumatic periods of his life began in February 1824, when his father was sent to debtors prison. Young Dickens, only twelve years old, was forced to go to work for several months pasting labels on bottles. This experience was socially humiliating to him. Images of the factory haunted him for the rest of his life and provided a backdrop to much of his fiction, which often focused on class issues; the plight of the poor and oppressed; and lost, suffering children. As an adult, he championed social and political causes designed to help the poor, prisoners, and children.

Dickens became a reporter in 1832, and in 1833 he began publishing short stories and essays. In 1836 he married Catherine Hogarth. The couple had ten children, but their unhappy marriage ended in 1858.

Dickens's successful career as a novelist began in 1837 with the publication of The Pickwick Papers. Other novels include A Christmas Carol, Oliver Twist, and David Copperfield. He made readers laugh, cry, and confront social evils and institutions of his day. On his death in 1870, a London Times article praised Dickens for displaying "an extraordinary combination of intellectual and moral qualities."

Connect to the Literature

Remember yourself as a young child. What kinds of people and situations made you feel happy and secure? frightened or insecure?

Write a Journal Entry

Freewrite about a person or incident that made a strong positive or negative impression on you when you were a child. Why were you so affected? What feelings did you experience?

Build Background

Comedy and Tragedy

Dickens described *Great Expectations* as a combination of comedy and tragedy, and many critics agree with his assessment. Pip, the narrator of the novel, encounters many characters who are humorous and often cartoon-like in their quirks and foibles. At the same time, they are tragic in their unhappiness or their lack of moral vision. There is also tragedy in the characters who live quietly moral lives, but who cannot earn respect and make their way in the world. Descriptions of Pip's childhood show the comic and tragic nature of the novel particularly well. Dickens, who himself was affected deeply by the difficult turn of events in his own childhood, tries to help readers understand the sensitive, thoughtful world of a child living under difficult circumstances. Pip's childish reactions to certain people and situations are humorous and endearing. As you read, however, look for the underlying tragic aspects of Pip's childhood.

NOVEL NOTEBOOK

Keep a special notebook to record entries about the novels that you read this year.

WRITE THE CAPTION

Write a caption for the image below, which shows a scene from a film version of *Great Expectations,* using information in Build Background.

_____
_____
_____
_____
_____
_____
_____
_____
_____
_____
_____
_____
_____
_____
_____
_____
_____
_____
_____
_____
_____
_____
_____
_____
_____
_____
_____

Set Purposes for Reading

▶ **BIG Idea** **Matters of Life and Death**

Think about the important moments in your life. Are there any specific events that you think of as life-changing? How might your life be different if these things had not happened?

In *Great Expectations*, Pip is faced with many new experiences, some that are frightening and many that will change his life forever. As you read, make a list of the major events that may have an impact on Pip's life.

Literary Element Point of View

The **point of view** of a story is the relationship the narrator has to the story. This affects the perspective from which the story is told.

If the narrator is a character in the story, the story has a **first-person** point of view. In **third-person** point of view, the narrator is not a character. Third-person point of view can be **limited,** meaning that the narrator tells the story from one character's perspective, or **omniscient,** meaning that the narrator is all knowing. Sometimes the author uses the **second-person** point of view, addressing the reader or a character as "you."

As you read, think about the point of view in the story. Ask yourself how the beginning of the story would be different if it had been told from a different point of view.

Reading Strategy Compare and Contrast Characters

When you **compare and contrast characters,** you tell how two or more characters are alike and how they are different. There are many ways that characters can be compared. The reader can decide if the characters are main or minor characters, static or dynamic, round or flat.

Establishing how characters are alike and different can help the reader to understand which characters are most important, as well as what the various characters' motivation might be, the meaning of plot events, and the story's themes.

As you read, keep track of the characters you meet. Ask yourself whether each character is a main or minor character and why you think this. You may find it helpful to use a graphic organizer like the one at the right. The graphic organizer on the next page can also help you keep track of the characters you meet as you read.

Vocabulary

capricious [kə prish´əs]
adj. unpredictable; inconsistent
Because he is now so predictable, it is hard to believe that he was such a capricious little boy.

conciliatory [kən sil´ē ə tôr´ē]
adj. intended to restore harmony or goodwill
After the match, the winner approached her opponent with a conciliatory handshake.

felicitous [fi lis´ə təs]
adj. happy
She always felt that her birthday was the most felicitous day of the year.

incomprehensible
[in´kom pri hen´sə bəl]
adj. incapable of being understood
They arrived late because the hand-written map they had been given was incomprehensible.

remonstrance [ri mon´strəns]
n. criticism
When the performance was a complete failure, the disappointed audience frowned with remonstrance.

Character	Main or Minor	Why I Think This

The first ten chapters of the novel introduce you to a variety of characters who affect Pip's life. As you read, think about Pip's relationships with these people and their effect on him. Make notes in the cluster diagram below. On the lines, explain the relationship between Pip and each character. In the circles, describe how Pip is affected by each.

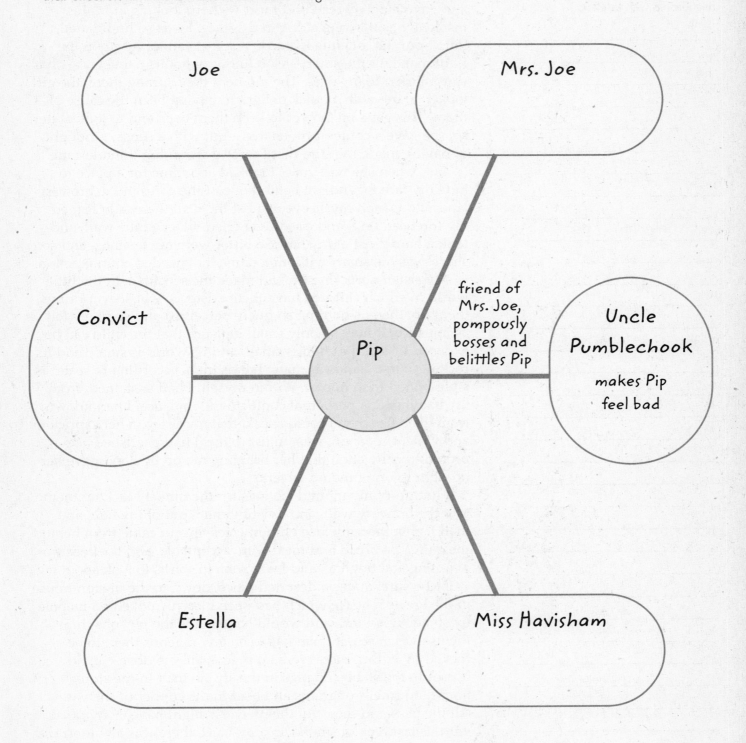

Joe

Mrs. Joe

Convict

Pip

friend of Mrs. Joe, pompously bosses and belittles Pip

Uncle Pumblechook

makes Pip feel bad

Estella

Miss Havisham

Literary Element

Point of View How does the narrator help the reader understand his relationship with Estella?

_____

_____

_____

_____

_____

_____

_____

_____

_____

_____

_____

_____

_____

_____

_____

_____

_____

_____

_____

_____

_____

_____

_____

_____

_____

_____

NOVEL EXCERPT: CHAPTER 8

She came back, with some bread and meat and a little mug of beer. She put the mug down on the stones of the yard, and gave me the bread and meat without looking at me, as insolently as if I were a dog in disgrace. I was so humiliated, hurt, spurned, offended, angry, sorry—I cannot hit upon the right name for the smart—God knows what its name was—that tears started to my eyes. The moment they sprang there, the girl looked at me with a quick delight in having been the cause of them. This gave me power to keep them back and to look at her: so, she gave a contemptuous toss—but with a sense, I thought, of having made too sure that I was so wounded—and left me.

But, when she was gone, I looked about me for a place to hide my face in, and got behind one of the gates in the brewery-lane, and leaned my sleeve against the wall there, and leaned my forehead on it and cried. As I cried, I kicked the wall, and took a hard twist at my hair; so bitter were my feelings, and so sharp was the smart without a name that needed counteraction.

My sister's bringing up had made me sensitive. In the little world in which children have their existence whosoever brings them up, there is nothing so finely perceived and so finely felt as injustice. It may be only small injustice that the child can be exposed to; but the child is small, and its world is small, and its rocking-horse stands as many hands high, according to scale, as a big-boned Irish hunter. Within myself, I had sustained, from my babyhood, a perpetual conflict with injustice. I had known, from the time when I could speak, that my sister, in her capricious and violent coercion, was unjust to me. I had cherished a profound conviction that her bringing me up by hand gave her no right to bring me up by jerks. . . .

I got rid of my injured feelings for the time by kicking them into the brewery wall, and twisting them out of my hair, and then I smoothed my face with my sleeve, and came from behind the gate. The bread and meat were acceptable, and the beer was warming and tingling, and I was soon in spirits to look about me.

To be sure, it was a deserted place, down to the pigeon-house in the brewery-yard, which had been blown crooked on its pole by some high wind, and would have made the pigeons think themselves at sea, if there had been any pigeons there to be rocked by it. But, there were no pigeons in the dove-cot, no horses in the stable, no pigs in the sty, no malt in the store-house, no smells of grains and beer in the copper or the vat. All the uses and scents of the brewery might have evaporated with its last reek of smoke. In a by-yard, there was a wilderness of empty casks, which had a certain sour remembrance of better days lingering about them; but it was too sour to be accepted as a sample of the beer that was gone—and in this respect I remember those recluses as being like most others.

Behind the furthest end of the brewery, was a rank garden with an old wall: not so high but that I could struggle up and hold on long enough to look over it, and see that the rank garden was the garden of the house, and that it was overgrown with tangled weeds, but that there was a track upon the green and yellow paths, as if some one sometimes walked there, and that Estella was walking away from me even then. But she seemed to be everywhere. For, when I yielded to the temptation presented by the casks, and began to walk on them, I saw her walking on them at the end of the yard of casks. She had her back towards me, and held her pretty brown hair spread out in her two hands, and never looked round, and passed out of my view directly. So, in the brewery itself—by which I mean the large paved lofty place in which they used to make the beer, and where the brewing utensils still were. When I first went into it, and, rather oppressed by its gloom, stood near the door looking about me, I saw her pass among the extinguished fires, and ascend some light iron stairs, and go out by a gallery high overhead, as if she were going out into the sky.

It was in this place, and at this moment, that a strange thing happened to my fancy. I thought it a strange thing then, and I thought it a stranger thing long afterwards. I turned my eyes— a little dimmed by looking up at the frosty light—towards a great wooden beam in a low nook of the building near me on my right hand, and I saw a figure hanging there by the neck. A figure all in yellow white, with but one shoe to the feet; and it hung so, that I could see that the faded trimmings of the dress were like earthy paper, and that the face was Miss Havisham's, with a movement going over the whole countenance as if she were trying to call to me. In the terror of seeing the figure, and in the terror of being certain that it had not been there a moment before, I at first ran from it, and then ran towards it. And my terror was greatest of all when I found no figure there.

Nothing less than the frosty light of the cheerful sky, the sight of people passing beyond the bars of the court-yard gate, and the reviving influence of the rest of the bread and meat and beer could have brought me round. Even with those aids, I might not have come to myself as soon as I did, but that I saw Estella approaching with the keys, to let me out. She would have some fair reason for looking down upon me, I thought, if she saw me frightened; and she should have no fair reason.

Literary Element

Point of View How does the first-person point of view help the reader understand Pip's character?

_____
_____
_____
_____
_____
_____
_____
_____
_____
_____
_____
_____
_____
_____
_____
_____
_____
_____
_____
_____
_____
_____
_____
_____
_____
_____
_____
_____

Reading Strategy

Compare and Contrast Characters What difference between Pip and Joe can you infer from this passage?

_____
_____
_____
_____
_____
_____
_____
_____
_____
_____
_____
_____
_____
_____
_____
_____
_____
_____
_____
_____
_____
_____
_____
_____
_____
_____
_____
_____
_____
_____
_____
_____

NOVEL EXCERPT: CHAPTER 7

I had never heard Joe read aloud to any greater extent than this monosyllable, and I had observed at church last Sunday when I accidentally held our Prayer-book upside down, that it seemed to suit his convenience quite as well as if it had been all right. Wishing to embrace the present occasion of finding out whether in teaching Joe, I should have to begin quite at the beginning, I said, "Ah! But read the rest, Jo."

"The rest, eh, Pip?" said Joe, looking at it with a slowly searching eye, "One, two, three. Why, here's three Js, and three Os, and three J-O, Joes in it, Pip!"

I leaned over Joe, and, with the aid of my forefinger, read him the whole letter.

"Astonishing!" said Joe, when I had finished. "You ARE a scholar."

"How do you spell Gargery, Joe?" I asked him, with a modest patronage.

"I don't spell it at all," said Joe.

"But supposing you did?"

"It *can't* be supposed," said Joe. "Tho' I'm oncommon fond of reading, too."

"Are you, Joe?"

"Oncommon. Give me," said Joe, "a good book, or a good newspaper, and sit me down afore a good fire, and I ask no better. Lord!" he continued, after rubbing his knees a little, "when you *do* come to a J and a O, and says you, 'Here, at last, is a J-O, Joe,' how interesting reading is!"

I derived from this last that Joe's education, like steam, was yet in its infancy. Pursuing the subject, I inquired:

"Didn't you ever go to school, Joe, when you were as little as me?"

"No, Pip."

"Why didn't you ever go to school, Joe, when you were as little as me?"

"Well, Pip," said Joe, taking up the poker, and settling himself to his usual occupation when he was thoughtful, of slowly raking the fire between the lower bars: "I'll tell you. My father, Pip, he were given to drink, and when he were overtook with drink, he hammered away at my mother, most onmerciful. It were a'most the only hammering he did, indeed, 'xcepting at myself. And he hammered at me with a wigour only to be equalled by the wigour with which he didn't hammer at his anwil. You're a-listening and understanding, Pip?"

"Yes, Joe."

"'Consequence, my mother and me we ran away from my father, several times; and then my mother she'd go out to work, and she'd say, 'Joe,' she'd say, 'now, please God, you shall have some schooling, child,' and she'd put me to school. But my father were that good in his hart that he couldn't a-bear to be without us. So, he'd come with a most tremenjous crowd and make such a row at the doors of the houses where we was, that they used to be obligated to have no more to do with us and to give us up to him. And then he took us home and hammered us. Which, you see, Pip," said Joe, pausing in his meditative raking of the fire, and looking at me, "were a drawback on my learning."

"Certainly, poor Joe!"

"Though mind you, Pip," said Joe, with a judicial touch or two of the poker on the top bar, "rendering unto all their doo, and maintaining equal justice betwixt man and man, my father were that good in his hart, don't you see?"

I didn't see; but I didn't say so.

"Well!" Joe pursued, "somebody must keep the pot a-biling, Pip, or the pot won't bile, don't you know?"

I saw that, and said so. . . .

Joe recited this couplet with such manifest pride and careful perspicuity that I asked him if he had made it himself.

"I made it," said Joe, "my own self. I made it in a moment. It was like striking out a horseshoe complete, in a single blow. I never was so much surprised in all my life—couldn't credit my own 'ed—to tell you the truth, hardly believed it *were* my own 'ed. As I was saying, Pip, it were my intentions to have had it cut over him; but poetry costs money, cut it how you will, small or large, and it were not done. Not to mention bearers, all the money that could be spared were wanted for my mother. She were in poor 'elth, and quite broke. She waren't long of following, poor soul, and her share of peace come round at last."

Joe's blue eyes turned a little watery; he rubbed, first one of them, and then the other, in a most uncongenial and uncomfortable manner, with the round knob on the top of the poker.

"It were but lonesome then," said Joe, "living here alone, and I got acquainted with your sister. Now, Pip"—Joe looked firmly at me, as if he knew I was not going to agree with him—"your sister is a fine figure of a woman."

I could not help looking at the fire, in an obvious state of doubt.

"Whatever family opinions, or whatever the world's opinions, on that subject may be, Pip, your sister is"—Joe tapped the top bar with the poker after every word following—"a—fine—figure—of—a—woman!"

I could think of nothing better to say than "I am glad you think so, Joe."

Reading Strategy

Compare and Contrast Characters What differences of opinion between the narrator and Joe does the narrator point out?

_____

_____

_____

_____

_____

_____

_____

_____

_____

_____

_____

_____

_____

_____

_____

_____

_____

_____

_____

_____

_____

_____

_____

_____

_____

_____

_____

_____

MARK IT UP

Are you allowed to write in your novel? If so, then mark up the pages as you read, or reread, to help with your note-taking. Develop a shorthand system, including symbols, that works for you. Here are some ideas:

Underline = important idea

Bracket = text to quote

Asterisk = just what you were looking for

Checkmark = might be useful

Circle = unfamiliar word or phrase to look up

▶ **BIG Idea**

Matters of Life and Death When Pip meets the convict, his life takes a frightening turn. How does he manage to save himself?

Mark up the excerpt, looking for evidence of how it expresses the Big Idea.

NOVEL EXCERPT: CHAPTER 1

The man, after looking at me for a moment, turned me upside down, and emptied my pockets. There was nothing in them but a piece of bread. When the church came to itself . . . , I say, I was seated on a high tombstone, trembling, while he ate the bread ravenously.

"You young dog," said the man, licking his lips, "what fat cheeks you ha' got."

I believe they were fat, though I was at that time undersized for my years, and not strong.

"Darn me if I couldn't eat em," said the man, with a threatening shake of his head, "and if I han't half a mind to't!" . . .

"Now lookee here!" said the man. "Where's your mother?"

"There, sir!" said I.

He started, made a short run, and stopped and looked over his shoulder.

"There, sir!" I timidly explained. "Also Georgiana. That's my mother."

"Oh!" said he, coming back. "And is that your father alonger your mother?"

"Yes, sir," said I; "him too; late of this parish."

"Ha!" he muttered then, considering. "Who d'ye live with—supposin' ye're kindly let to live, which I han't made up my mind about?"

"My sister, sir—Mrs. Joe Gargery—wife of Joe Gargery, the blacksmith, sir."

"Blacksmith, eh?" said he. And looked down at his leg.

After darkly looking at his leg and me several times, he came closer to my tombstone, took me by both arms, and tilted me back as far as he could hold me, so that his eyes looked most powerfully down into mine, and mine looked most helplessly up into his.

"Now lookee here," he said, "the question being whether you're to be let to live. You know what a file is?"

"Yes, sir."

"And you know what wittles is?"

"Yes, sir."

After each question he tilted me over a little more, so as to give me a greater sense of helplessness and danger.

"You get me a file." He tilted me again. "And you get me wittles." He tilted me again. "You bring 'em both to me." He tilted me again. "Or I'll have your heart and liver out." He tilted me again.

I was dreadfully frightened, and so giddy that I clung to him with both hands, and said, "If you would kindly please to let me keep upright, sir, perhaps I shouldn't be sick, and perhaps I could attend more."

Use the Cornell Note-Taking system to take notes on the excerpt at the left. Record your notes, Reduce them, and then Recap (summarize) them.

Record

_____

_____

_____

_____

_____

_____

_____

_____

_____

_____

_____

_____

_____

_____

_____

_____

_____

_____

_____

Recap

_____

_____

_____

_____

_____

Reduce

Try the following approach as you reduce your notes.

MY VIEW
Write down your thoughts on the excerpt.

_____

_____

_____

_____

_____

_____

_____

_____

_____

_____

_____

_____

_____

_____

_____

_____

_____

_____

_____

_____

Respond and Think Critically

1. Describe Mrs. Joe's treatment of Pip. In what ways is Pip's relationship with Joe different from his relationship with his sister? [Compare]

_____

_____

_____

_____

2. After the convict is caught, what does he say to protect Pip? How does Pip feel about his actions toward the convict? What do these feelings tell you about Pip? [Conclude]

_____

_____

_____

_____

3. Why is Pip sent to the home of Miss Havisham? How does Pip feel after he leaves, and why does he decide to lie about his experiences there? [Interpret]

_____

_____

_____

_____

4. Evaluate Dickens's portrayal of Pip. In your opinion, is Pip a believable character? Does he behave in ways that a real child in similar circumstances might behave? Support your opinion with evidence from the novel [Evaluate]

_____

_____

_____

_____

5. **Matters of Life and Death** Think about the beginning of the novel. How does the convict turn Pip's life upside down, both literally and figuratively? [Interpret]

_____

_____

_____

_____

APPLY BACKGROUND
Reread Introduction to the Novel on pages 8–9. How did that information help you understand or appreciate what you read in the novel?

_____

_____

_____

_____

_____

_____

_____

_____

_____

_____

_____

_____

_____

_____

_____

_____

_____

_____

_____

_____

_____

_____

_____

_____

_____

Literary Element · Point of View

Based on Pip's feelings for Estella and her response toward him, how do you think their relationship will play out? Explain. [Analyze]

_____
_____
_____
_____
_____
_____
_____
_____
_____
_____
_____

Reading Strategy · Compare and Contrast Characters

How are Pip and Estella alike? How are they different? Explain. [Compare]

_____
_____
_____
_____
_____
_____
_____
_____
_____
_____
_____
_____
_____
_____

Vocabulary Practice

Identify whether the words in each pair have the same or the opposite meaning.

1. **capricious** and stable

_____

2. **conciliatory** and antagonistic

_____

3. **felicitous** and happy

_____

4. **incomprehensible** and unexplainable

_____

5. **remonstrance** and praise

_____

Academic Vocabulary

The death of his parents was the **circumstance** that caused Pip to be living with his sister. In the preceding sentence, _circumstance_ means "a condition that determines another." Think about a situation in your life. How does this **circumstance** affect other parts of your life?

_____
_____
_____
_____
_____
_____
_____
_____
_____

Writing

Personal Response With which character do you most identify? Why? Do you have something in common with that character? Have you shared similar thoughts or reactions?

_____

_____

_____

_____

_____

_____

_____

_____

_____

_____

_____

_____

_____

_____

_____

_____

_____

_____

_____

_____

_____

_____

_____

_____

_____

_____

_____

Speaking and Listening
Performance

Assignment With a partner, select a dramatic or humorous scene from *Great Expectations* that both of you find interesting and perform the scene for the class.

Prepare Together, assign a character to each person. Then plan how to present the scene. Discuss how your characters will move on the stage and any props you may need. Consider any additional dialogue you may need for your characters. Rehearse your scene a few times until you feel ready to perform it.

Perform Present your performance to your class. Be sure to face your audience and to speak loudly enough for the entire audience to hear.

Evaluate After your performance, meet with your partner to discuss how successful your performance was and how it might have been better. Use a chart like the one below to record your group's ideas.

What worked	Needs improvement
• We got the drama of the scene across. (The audience gasped.)	• At times the actors were not facing the audience.

Connect to the Literature

If you could sample a life completely different from your own, what kind of life would you choose? Why?

Write a Paragraph

Write about a life you have always wanted to experience. In what way is this life different from your own? Why does it interest you?

Build Background

Becoming an Apprentice

Pip is to be an apprentice to Joe, which means he will work under his supervision for a specified amount of time in order to learn Joe's trade. In doing this, Pip will sign an indenture, which is a type of binding contract. In this period in history, it was common for someone as young as Pip, who is approaching fourteen, to be indentured as an apprentice. In fact, many poor families were forced to indenture their children as a means of support for the family. In Pip's case, the working relationship is an extension of the close partnership he and Joe have already been enjoying.

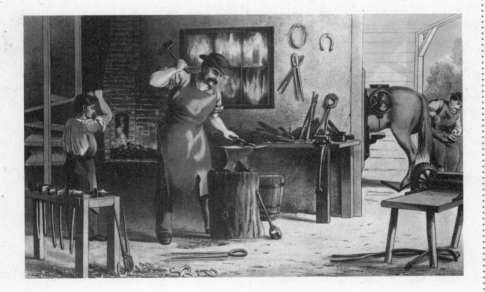

NOVEL NOTEBOOK

Keep a special notebook to record entries about the novels that you read this year.

WRITE THE CAPTION

Write a caption for the image below, in the present tense, using information in Build Background.

_____

_____

_____

_____

_____

_____

_____

_____

_____

_____

_____

_____

_____

_____

_____

_____

_____

_____

_____

_____

_____

Set Purposes for Reading

▶ **BIG Idea Dreams and Reality**

Everyone has dreams. You may have dreams of running your own business or being a movie star. Some dreams are more realistic than others. What are some of your dreams?

In *Great Expectations*, Pip has many dreams. As you read, list Pip's dreams and tell whether you think his dreams are realistic or unrealistic and why.

Literary Element Conflict

Conflict is the struggle between opposing forces in a story or drama. The conflict is what drives the plot, moving the story to its end when the conflict is resolved.

If a character is struggling against outside forces, he or she is facing **external conflict.** A character's struggle against opposing forces in the mind, such as his or her emotions or goals is **internal conflict.**

As you read, think about the conflict in the story. Ask yourself how Dickens begins to make clear Pip's internal and external conflicts. Use the graphic organizer on the next page to help you think about these conflicts.

Reading Strategy Make and Verify Predictions About Plot

Plot is the sequence of events in a narrative work. In the first stage of the plot, the **conflicts** are introduced. Next the **rising action** builds suspense, leading to the **climax,** or turning point. Finally there is a **falling action,** or **resolution.**

When you **make and verify predictions about plot,** you anticipate what will happen next in the story and then think back to your predictions as you read to determine whether you were correct. Making and verifying predictions as you read will bring you closer to the plot of the story.

As you read, keep track of any predictions you make about the characters and actions in the story. Then think about what actually happens in the story. Note if your predictions were correct. You may find it helpful to use a graphic organizer like the one at the right.

Vocabulary

clemency [klem´ən sē]
n. mercy; forgiveness
The convicted criminal begged the judge for clemency.

disconcerted [dis´kən surt´əd]
adj. confused
For weeks she had felt disconcerted by the clanging coming from the brand new pipes.

manifest [man´ə fest´]
v. to display
His talent for the arts did not manifest itself until quite late in his life.

ostentatiously [os´tən tā´shəs lē]
adv. in a showy or gaudy manner
The socialite entered the room ostentatiously waving her bejeweled hand.

trepidation [trep´ə dā´shən]
n. uneasiness
Because he was fearful of water, he entered the lake with great trepidation.

My Predictions	What Actually Happened

In Chapters 11 through 19, Pip lives in two different worlds: the world of the working class and the world of the gentleman. As you read, think about the conflicts Pip faces in each of his worlds. Then record these conflicts and label each conflict with an *I* for "internal" or an *E* for "external."

Life as a Commoner	Life as a Gentleman
does not get along with his sister—E	is in love with Estella—I

Literary Element

Conflict What is an example of Pip's internal conflict regarding Estella?

_____

_____

_____

_____

_____

_____

_____

_____

_____

_____

_____

_____

_____

_____

_____

_____

_____

_____

_____

_____

_____

_____

_____

_____

_____

_____

_____

_____

_____

_____

_____

NOVEL EXCERPT: CHAPTER 11

The ringing of a distant bell, combined with the echoing of some cry or call along the passage by which I had come, interrupted the conversation and caused Estella to say to me, "Now, boy!" On my turning round, they all looked at me with the utmost contempt, and, as I went out, I heard Sarah Pocket say, "Well I am sure! What next!" and Camilla add, with indignation, "Was there ever such a fancy! The i-de-a!"

As we were going with our candle along the dark passage, Estella stopped all of a sudden, and, facing round, said in her taunting manner with her face quite close to mine:

"Well?"

"Well, miss?" I answered, almost falling over her and checking myself.

She stood looking at me, and, of course, I stood looking at her.

"Am I pretty?"

"Yes; I think you are very pretty."

"Am I insulting?"

"Not so much so as you were last time," said I.

"Not so much so?"

"No."

She fired when she asked the last question, and she slapped my face with such force as she had, when I answered it.

"Now?" said she. "You little coarse monster, what do you think of me now?"

"I shall not tell you."

"Because you are going to tell, upstairs. Is that it?"

"No," said I, "that's not it."

"Why don't you cry again, you little wretch?"

"Because I'll never cry for you again," said I. Which was, I suppose, as false a declaration as ever was made; for I was inwardly crying for her then, and I know what I know of the pain she cost me afterwards.

We went on our way upstairs after this episode; and, as we were going up, we met a gentleman groping his way down.

"Whom have we here?" asked the gentleman, stopping and looking at me.

"A boy," said Estella.

He was a burly man of an exceedingly dark complexion, with an exceedingly large head and a corresponding large hand. He took my chin in his large hand and turned up my face to have a look at me by the light of the candle. He was prematurely bald on the top of his head, and had bushy black eyebrows that wouldn't lie down but stood up bristling. His eyes were set very deep in his head, and were disagreeably sharp and suspicious. He had a large watchchain, and strong black dots where his beard and whiskers would have been if he had let them. He was nothing to me, and I could have had no foresight then that he ever would be anything to me, but it happened that I had this opportunity of observing him well.

"Boy of the neighbourhood? Hey?" said he.

"Yes, sir," said I.

"How do *you* come here?"

"Miss Havisham sent for me, sir," I explained.

"Well! Behave yourself. I have a pretty large experience of boys, and you're a bad set of fellows. Now mind!" said he, biting the side of his great forefinger as he frowned at me, "you behave yourself!"

With those words, he released me—which I was glad of, for his hand smelt of scented soap—and went his way downstairs. I wondered whether he could be a doctor; but no, I thought; he couldn't be a doctor, or he would have a quieter and more persuasive manner. There was not much time to consider the subject, for we were soon in Miss Havisham's room, where she and everything else were just as I had left them. Estella left me standing near the door, and I stood there until Miss Havisham cast her eyes upon me from the dressing-table.

"So!" she said, without being startled or surprised; "the days have worn away, have they?"

"Yes, ma'am. To-day is—"

"There, there, there!" with the impatient movement of her fingers. "I don't want to know. Are you ready to play?"

I was obliged to answer in some confusion, "I don't think I am, ma'am."

"Not at cards again?" she demanded, with a searching look.

"Yes, ma'am; I could do that, if I was wanted."

"Since this house strikes you old and grave, boy," said Miss Havisham, impatiently, "and you are unwilling to play, are you willing to work?"

I could answer this inquiry with a better heart than I had been able to find for the other question, and I said I was quite willing.

"Then go into that opposite room," said she, pointing at the door behind me with her withered hand, "and wait there till I come."

I crossed the staircase landing, and entered the room she indicated. From that room, too, the daylight was completely excluded, and it had an airless smell that was oppressive. A fire had been lately kindled in the damp old-fashioned grate, and it was more disposed to go out than to burn up, and the reluctant smoke which hung in the room seemed colder than the clearer air—like our own marsh mist.

Literary Element

Conflict Why is Pip having a difficult time answering Miss Havisham?

_____

_____

_____

_____

_____

_____

_____

_____

_____

_____

_____

_____

_____

_____

_____

_____

_____

_____

_____

_____

_____

_____

_____

_____

_____

_____

_____

_____

Reading Strategy

Make and Verify Predictions About Plot What do you think will be the result of Joe's visit to Miss Havisham?

_____

_____

_____

_____

_____

_____

_____

_____

_____

_____

_____

_____

_____

_____

_____

_____

_____

_____

_____

_____

_____

_____

_____

_____

_____

_____

_____

_____

_____

_____

_____

_____

NOVEL EXCERPT: CHAPTER 13

It was a trial to my feelings, on the next day but one, to see Joe arraying himself in his Sunday clothes to accompany me to Miss Havisham's. However, as he thought his court-suit necessary to the occasion, it was not for me tell him that he looked far better in his working dress; the rather, because I knew he made himself so dreadfully uncomfortable entirely on my account, and that it was for me he pulled up his shirt-collar so very high behind, that it made the hair on the crown of his head stand up like a tuft of feathers. . . .

When we came to Pumblechook's, my sister bounced in and left us. As it was almost noon, Joe and I held straight on to Miss Havisham's house. Estella opened the gate as usual, and, the moment she appeared, Joe took his hat off and stood weighing it by the brim in both his hands as if he had some urgent reason in his mind for being particular to half a quarter of an ounce.

Estella took no notice of either of us, but led us the way that I knew so well. I followed next to her, and Joe came last. When I looked back at Joe in the long passage, he was still weighing his hat with the greatest care, and was coming after us in long strides on the tips of his toes.

Estella told me we were both to go in, so I took Joe by the coat-cuff and conducted him into Miss Havisham's presence. She was seated at her dressing-table, and looked round at us immediately.

"Oh!" said she to Joe. "You are the husband of the sister of this boy?"

I could hardly have imagined dear old Joe looking so unlike himself or so like some extraordinary bird; standing, as he did, speechless, with his tuft of feathers ruffled, and his mouth open as if he wanted a worm.

"You are the husband," repeated Miss Havisham, "of the sister of this boy?"

It was very aggravating; but, throughout the interview Joe persisted in addressing me instead of Miss Havisham.

"Which I meantersay, Pip," Joe now observed in a manner that was at once expressive of forcible argumentation, strict confidence, and great politeness, "as I hup and married your sister, and I were at the time what you might call (if you was anyways inclined) a single man."

"Well!" said Miss Havisham. "And you have reared the boy, with the intention of taking him for your apprentice; is that so, Mr. Gargery?"

"You know, Pip," replied Joe, "as you and me were ever friends, and it were looked for'ard to betwixt us, as being calc'lated to lead to larks. Not but what, Pip, if you had ever made objections to the business—such as its being open to black and sut, or such-like—not but what they would have been attended to, don't you see?"

"Has the boy," said Miss Havisham, "ever made any objection? Does he like the trade?"

"Which it is well beknown to yourself, Pip," returned Joe, strengthening his former mixture of argumentation, confidence, and politeness, "that it were the wish of your own hart." (I saw the idea suddenly break upon him that he would adapt his epitaph to the occasion, before he went on to say) "And there weren't no objection on your part, and Pip it were the great wish of your hart!"

It was quite in vain for me to endeavour to make him sensible that he ought to speak to Miss Havisham. The more I made faces and gestures to him to do it, the more confidential, argumentative, and polite he persisted in being to me.

"Have you brought his indentures with you?" asked Miss Havisham.

"Well, Pip, you know," replied Joe, as if that were a little unreasonable, "you yourself see me put 'em in my 'at, and therefore you know as they are here." With which he took them out, and gave them, not to Miss Havisham, but to me. I am afraid I was ashamed of the dear good fellow—I know I was ashamed of him—when I saw that Estella stood at the back of Miss Havisham's chair, and that her eyes laughed mischievously. I took the indentures out of his hand and gave them to Miss Havisham.

"You expected," said Miss Havisham, as she looked them over, "no premium with the boy?"

"Joe!" I remonstrated; for he made no reply at all. "Why don't you answer—"

"Pip," returned Joe, cutting me short as if he were hurt, "which I meantersay that were not a question requiring a answer betwixt yourself and me, and which you know the answer to be full well No. You know it to be No, Pip, and wherefore should I say it?"

Miss Havisham glanced at him as if she understood what he really was, better than I had thought possible, seeing what he was there; and took up a little bag from the table beside her.

"Pip has earned a premium here," she said, "and here it is. There are five-and-twenty guineas in this bag. Give it to your master, Pip."

As if he were absolutely out of his mind with the wonder awakened in him by her strange figure and the strange room, Joe, even at this pass, persisted in addressing me.

Reading Strategy

Make and Verify Predictions About Plot How do you think the money from Miss Havisham will affect Pip and Joe's relationship? Explain.

_____
_____
_____
_____
_____
_____
_____
_____
_____
_____
_____
_____
_____
_____
_____
_____
_____
_____
_____
_____
_____
_____

▶ **BIG Idea**

Dreams and Reality It seems that Pip's dreams are about to come true. Do you think reality will match what he dreamed of?

Mark up the excerpt, looking for evidence of how it expresses the Big Idea.

NOVEL EXCERPT: CHAPTER 19

I went circuitously to Miss Havisham's by all the back ways, and rang at the bell constrainedly, on account of the stiff long fingers of my gloves. Sarah Pocket came to the gate, and positively reeled back when she saw me so changed; her walnut-shell countenance likewise, turned from brown to green and yellow.

"You?" said she. "You, good gracious! What do you want?"

"I am going to London, Miss Pocket," said I, "and want to say good-bye to Miss Havisham."

I was not expected, for she left me locked in the yard, while she went to ask if I were to be admitted. After a very short delay, she returned and took me up, staring at me all the way.

Miss Havisham was taking exercise in the room with the long spread table, leaning on her crutch stick. The room was lighted as of yore, and at the sound of our entrance, she stopped and turned. She was then just abreast of the rotted bride-cake.

"Don't go, Sarah," she said. "Well, Pip?"

"I start for London, Miss Havisham, to-morrow," I was exceedingly careful what I said, "and I thought you would kindly not mind my taking leave of you."

"This is a gay figure, Pip," said she, making her crutch stick play round me, as if she, the fairy godmother who had changed me, were bestowing the finishing gift.

"I have come into such good fortune since I saw you last, Miss Havisham," I murmured. "And I am so grateful for it, Miss Havisham!"

"Aye, aye!" said she, looking at the discomfited and envious Sarah, with delight. "I have seen Mr. Jaggers. I have heard about it, Pip. So you go to-morrow?"

"Yes, Miss Havisham."

"And you are adopted by a rich person?"

"Yes, Miss Havisham."

"Not named?"

"No, Miss Havisham."

"And Mr. Jaggers is made your guardian?"

"Yes, Miss Havisham."

She quite gloated on these questions and answers, so keen was her enjoyment of Sarah Pocket's jealous dismay. "Well!" she went on; "you have a promising career before you. Be good—deserve it—and abide by Mr. Jaggers's instructions." She looked at me, and looked at Sarah, and Sarah's countenance wrung out of her watchful face a cruel smile. "Good-bye, Pip! you will always keep the name of Pip, you know."

"Yes, Miss Havisham."

"Good-bye, Pip!"

Use the Cornell Note-Taking system to take notes on the excerpt at the left. Record your notes, Reduce them, and then Recap (summarize) them.

Record

Reduce

Try the following approach as you reduce your notes.

ASK QUESTIONS
Write a question about the novel. Can you find the answer in your notes?

Recap

Respond and Think Critically

1. Describe the incident involving Pip and the young gentleman in Miss Havisham's garden. What prompts Pip's actions, and how does he feel about himself later? [Evaluate]

_____

_____

_____

_____

2. Why does Miss Havishan command Joe and Pip to meet with her? What does Pip's attitude toward her offer reveal about his changing sense of values? [Analyze]

_____

_____

_____

_____

3. What is the name of the mysterious stranger who visits Pip at the pub? What are Pip's expectations on learning about the reason for the man's visit? [Summarize]

_____

_____

_____

_____

4. What conflicting feelings does Pip have as he moves toward a new life? Why does he have such mixed feelings? [Interpret]

_____

_____

_____

_____

5. **Dreams and Reality** How does Pip's dream of becoming a gentleman turn into a difficult reality for Joe? [Conclude]

_____

_____

_____

_____

APPLY BACKGROUND
Reread Build Background on page 23. How did that information help you understand or appreciate what you read in the novel?

_____

_____

_____

_____

_____

_____

_____

_____

_____

_____

_____

_____

_____

_____

_____

_____

_____

_____

_____

_____

_____

_____

_____

_____

_____

_____

Literary Element **Conflict**

What internal conflict does Pip face while working as Joe's apprentice? What does this say about Pip's character? [Conclude]

_____

_____

_____

_____

_____

_____

_____

_____

_____

_____

_____

Reading Strategy **Make and Verify Predictions About Plot**

What do you think will happen to Pip in London? Why do you think this? [Analyze]

_____

_____

_____

_____

_____

_____

_____

_____

_____

_____

_____

_____

Vocabulary Practice

Respond to these questions.

1. To whom would you offer **clemency**—someone who was remorseful or someone who was unapologetic?

   _____

2. Which would make you feel more **disconcerted**—a simple problem or a difficult one?

   _____

3. Which is a better way to **manifest** an idea—to share it or to hide it?

   _____

4. Who would be more likely to act **ostentatiously**—a boastful person or a humble person?

   _____

5. Which would you approach with **trepidation**—a gentle puppy or an angry bear?

   _____

Academic Vocabulary

Pip believes that becoming a gentleman will **benefit** *him in the future.* In the preceding sentence, *benefit* is used as a verb to mean "to be useful." The word *benefit* has other meanings. For instance, *One* **benefit** *of exercise is improved health.* What do you think *benefit* means in the preceding sentence? What is the difference between the two meanings?

_____

_____

_____

_____

_____

_____

_____

_____

Writing

Personal Response How do you feel about what happens to Pip at the end of this section? Do you think he will regret making this life change? Why or why not?

_____

_____

_____

_____

_____

_____

_____

_____

_____

_____

_____

_____

_____

_____

_____

_____

_____

_____

_____

_____

_____

_____

_____

_____

_____

_____

Speaking and Listening
Speech

Assignment Pip was given the opportunity to move to London and pursue his dream of becoming a gentleman. To do so, he had to leave his old life behind. Write and deliver a speech on why it is important to take advantage of an opportunity that you are given, even thought the decision may be a difficult one.

Prepare Begin by taking notes on your ideas about the topic. Use a graphic organizer like the one below to keep your ideas organized.

Opportunity: to attend science camp	
Why it is important	Why it is a difficult decision
I'll receive science credit for school.	I'll be away from my friends all summer.

Use analogies and other logical structures to strengthen your argument. Then organize your ideas. You may wish to put your ideas on note cards and then arrange them in an order that makes sense.

Deliver Present your speech to your class. Make eye contact with your listeners and speak loudly and clearly so that everyone can hear you. Use good posture, appropriate hand gestures, and be confident.

Evaluate Write a paragraph evaluating your speech. When your classmates present, offer oral feedback on their performances.

Connect to the Literature

How do other people affect your behavior and your feelings about yourself?

Write a Journal Entry

In a journal entry, write about a person or situation that brought out the best in you. Then write about a person or situation that brought out your worst. Explain the reasons behind your different reactions.

Build Background

Dickens the Actor

Dickens was an avid theatergoer who once had ambitions of becoming an actor. In a letter to a friend, Dickens described his boyhood "rehearsals" for the stage: "I practised immensely (even such things as walking in and out, and sitting down in a chair) often four, five, six hours a day, shut up in my room or walking about in the fields." As an adult, Dickens took every opportunity to return to his first love. He acted in several amateur productions, including a production of Ben Jonson's popular play *Everyman in His Humor,* in which he played the role of Bobadil, a character given to shouting oaths. Dickens drew on his acting experience in his portrayal of Mr. Wopsle and the production of *Hamlet.*

NOVEL NOTEBOOK
Keep a special notebook to record entries about the novels that you read this year.

SUMMARIZE
Summarize in one sentence the most important idea(s) in Build Background.

_____
_____
_____
_____
_____
_____
_____
_____
_____
_____
_____
_____
_____
_____
_____
_____
_____
_____
_____
_____
_____
_____
_____
_____
_____
_____
_____

Set Purposes for Reading

▶ BIG Idea Dreams and Reality

It is sometimes possible to get so caught up in our dreams that we lose sight of reality. In your view, is it important to leave the past behind in order to make our dreams for the future come true?

As you read, think about how Pip has changed now that his dreams are coming true. Then ask yourself, is it important for Pip to think about his past as he dreams of the future?

Literary Element Mood

Mood is the emotional quality of a literary work. Elements that contribute to the mood of a literary work are language, subject matter, setting, diction, and tone, as well as rhyme and rhythm.

An author can create a mood for a character's emotions or a feeling for a setting. Using words such as *dismal* to describe a room creates a gloomy mood. Likewise, describing a character with the word *good-humored* helps the reader to imagine a jolly character.

As you read, think about the mood in the story. Ask yourself how Dickens uses language to create a mood for the settings and the characters. The graphic organizer on the next page can also help you organize your ideas about the mood of various settings.

Reading Strategy Analyze Description

A **description** is a detailed portrayal of a person, a place, an object, or an event. Writers use descriptive writing to help readers see, hear, smell, taste, or feel the subject. Description helps the characters, the events, and the settings come to life.

When you **analyze** something, you think about it critically. To **analyze description,** read a text critically, thinking about what the writer intended for your senses to experience as you read. You may also think about how the descriptive words make the actions, characters, and the place more vivid in your mind.

As you read, think about how the author uses descriptive language to portray the characters and events and to create a setting. Think about how the descriptive words appeal to your senses and make you feel as though you are in the story. You may find it helpful to use a graphic organizer like the one at the right.

Vocabulary

dexterously [deks′ trəs lē′]
adv. skillfully
The acrobat balanced dexterously upon the narrow rope high overhead.

diffidence [dif′ ə dəns]
n. shyness
Many times her diffidence was mistaken for arrogance when she simply was not comfortable speaking to strangers.

judicious [jōō dish′ əs]
adj. wise; discreet
They made the judicious decision not to eat coleslaw that had been sitting in the sun.

supplicant [sup′ lə kənt]
n. someone who begs
The supplicant bowed before the king, begging for mercy.

zealous [zel′ əs]
adj. eager
The manager appreciated the zealous attitude of the new employee.

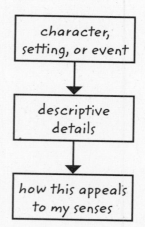

In Chapters 20 through 31, Pip finds himself with new people in a variety of new settings. Dickens uses carefully chosen details to characterize Pip's new surroundings. In the chart below, describe each setting. Then explain the mood, or atmosphere, that the details create.

Place	Details	Mood
London	large, dirty, crowded, run-down	forbidding, cold, lonely
Jaggers's office		
Bernard's Inn		
Pocket household		
Wemmick's home		
Jaggers's home		

Literary Element

Mood What is the mood in the room? What words in the passage make you feel this way?

_____

_____

_____

_____

_____

_____

_____

_____

_____

_____

_____

_____

_____

_____

_____

_____

_____

_____

_____

_____

_____

_____

_____

_____

NOVEL EXCERPT: CHAPTER 29

There was no discrepancy of years between us to remove her far from me—we were of nearly the same age, though of course the age told for more in her case than in mine—but the air of inaccessibility which her beauty and her manner gave her tormented me in the midst of my delight, and at the height of the assurance I felt that our patroness had chosen us for one another. Wretched boy!

At last we went back into the house, and there I heard, with surprise, that my guardian had come down to see Miss Havisham on business, and would come back to dinner. The old wintry branches of chandeliers in the room where the mouldering table was spread had been lighted while we were out, and Miss Havisham was in her chair and waiting for me. It was like pushing the chair itself back into the past, when we began the old slow circuit round about the ashes of the bridal feast. But, in the funereal room, with that figure of the grave fallen back in the chair fixing its eyes upon her, Estella looked more bright and beautiful than before, and I was under stronger enchantment.

The time so melted away that our early dinner-hour drew close at hand, and Estella left us to prepare herself. We had stopped near the centre of the long table, and Miss Havisham, with one of her withered arms stretched out of the chair, rested that clenched hand upon the yellow cloth. As Estella looked back over her shoulder before going out at the door, Miss Havisham kissed that hand to her, with a ravenous intensity that was of its kind quite dreadful.

Then, Estella being gone and we two left alone, she turned to me, and said in a whisper:

"Is she beautiful, graceful, well-grown? Do you admire her?"

"Everybody must who sees her, Miss Havisham."

She drew an arm round my neck, and drew my head close down to hers as she sat in the chair. "Love her, love her, love her! How does she use you?"

Before I could answer (if I could have answered so difficult a question at all), she repeated, "Love her, love her, love her! If she favours you, love her. If she wounds you, love her. If she tears your heart to pieces—and as it gets older and stronger, it will tear deeper—love her, love her, love her!"

Never had I seen such passionate eagerness as was joined to her utterance of these words. I could feel the muscles of the thin arm round my neck swell with the vehemence that possessed her.

"Hear me, Pip! I adopted her to be loved. I bred her and educated her to be loved. I developed her into what she is, that she might be loved. Love her!"

She said the word often enough, and there could be no doubt that she meant to say it; but if the often-repeated word had been hate instead of love—despair—revenge—dire death—it could not have sounded from her lips more like a curse.

"I'll tell you," said she, in the same hurried passionate whisper, "what real love is. It is blind devotion, unquestioning self-humiliation, utter submission, trust and belief against yourself and against the whole world, giving up your whole heart and soul to the smiter—as I did!"

When she came to that, and to a wild cry that followed that, I caught her round the waist. For she rose up in the chair, in her shroud of a dress, and struck at the air as if she would as soon have struck herself against the wall and fallen dead.

All this passed in a few seconds. As I drew her down into her chair, I was conscious of a scent that I knew, and turning, saw my guardian in the room.

He always carried (I have not yet mentioned it, I think) a pocket-handkerchief of rich silk and of imposing proportions which was of great value to him in his profession. I have seen him so terrify a client or a witness by ceremoniously unfolding this pocket-handkerchief as if he were immediately going to blow his nose, and then pausing, as if he knew he should not have time to do it before such client or witness committed himself, that the self-committal has followed directly, quite as a matter of course. When I saw him in the room, he had this expressive pocket-handkerchief in both hands, and was looking at us. On meeting my eye, he said plainly, by a momentary and silent pause in that attitude, "Indeed? Singular!" and then put the handkerchief to its right use with wonderful effect.

Miss Havisham had seen him as soon as I, and was (like everybody else) afraid of him. She made a strong attempt to compose herself, and stammered that he was as punctual as ever.

"As punctual as ever," he repeated, coming up to us. "(How do you do, Pip? Shall I give you a ride, Miss Havisham? Once round?) And so you are here, Pip?"

I told him when I had arrived, and how Miss Havisham had wished me to come and see Estella. To which he replied, "Ah! Very fine young lady!" Then he pushed Miss Havisham in her chair before him, with one of his large hands, and put the other in his trousers-pocket as if the pocket were full of secrets.

"Well, Pip! How often have you seen Miss Estella before?" said he, when he came to a stop.

"How often?"

"Ah! How many times? Ten thousand times?"

"Oh! Certainly not so many."

Literary Element

Mood How do Miss Havisham's actions change the mood in the room?

_____

_____

_____

_____

_____

_____

_____

_____

_____

_____

_____

_____

_____

_____

_____

_____

_____

_____

_____

_____

_____

_____

_____

_____

_____

_____

_____

_____

Reading Strategy

Analyze Description What might Dickens be intending to tell the reader through this description of Mr. Jaggers?

_____

_____

_____

_____

_____

_____

_____

_____

_____

_____

_____

_____

_____

_____

_____

_____

_____

_____

_____

_____

_____

_____

_____

_____

_____

_____

_____

_____

_____

_____

NOVEL EXCERPT: CHAPTER 26

It fell out as Wemmick had told me it would, that I had an early opportunity of comparing my guardian's establishment with that of his cashier and clerk. My guardian was in his room, washing his hands with his scented soap, when I went into the office from Walworth; and he called me to him, and gave me the invitation for myself and friends which Wemmick had prepared me to receive. "No ceremony," he stipulated, "and no dinner dress, and say tomorrow." I asked him where we should come to (for I had no idea where he lived), and I believe it was in his general objection to make anything like an admission, that he replied, "Come here, and I'll take you home with me." I embrace this opportunity of remarking that he washed his clients off, as if he were a surgeon or a dentist. He had a closet in his room, fitted up for the purpose, which smelt of the scented soap like a perfumer's shop. It had an unusually large jack-towel on a roller inside the door, and he would wash his hands, and wipe them and dry them all over this towel, whenever he came in from a police court or dismissed a client from his room. When I and my friends repaired to him at six o'clock next day, he seemed to have been engaged on a case of a darker complexion than usual, for we found him with his head butted into this closet, not only washing his hands, but laving his face and gargling his throat. And even when he had done all that, and had gone all round the jack-towel, he took out his penknife and scraped the case out of his nails before he put his coat on.

There were some people slinking about as usual when we passed out into the street, who were evidently anxious to speak with him; but there was something so conclusive in the halo of scented soap which encircled his presence that they gave it up for that day. As we walked along westward, he was recognized ever and again by some face in the crowd of the streets, and whenever that happened he talked louder to me; but he never otherwise recognized anybody, or took notice that anybody recognized him.

He conducted us to Gerrard Street, Soho, to a house on the south side of that street. Rather a stately house of its kind, but dolefully in want of painting, and with dirty windows. He took out his key and opened the door, and we all went into a stone hall, bare, gloomy, and little used. So up a dark brown staircase into a series of three dark brown rooms on the first floor. There were carved garlands on the panelled walls, and as he stood among them giving us welcome, I know what kind of loops I thought they looked like.

Dinner was laid in the best of these rooms; the second was his dressing-room; the third, his bedroom. He told us that he held the whole house, but rarely used more of it than we saw. The table was comfortably laid—no silver in the service, of course—and at the side of his chair was a capacious dumb-waiter, with a variety of bottles and decanters on it, and four dishes of fruit for dessert. I noticed throughout that he kept everything under his own hand, and distributed everything himself.

There was a bookcase in the room; I saw, from the backs of the books, that they were about evidence, criminal law, criminal biography, trials, acts of parliament, and such things. The furniture was all very solid and good, like his watch-chain. It had an official look, however, and there was nothing merely ornamental to be seen. In a corner was a little table of papers with a shaded lamp; so that he seemed to bring the office home with him in that respect too, and to wheel it out of an evening and fall to work.

As he had scarcely seen my three companions until now—for he and I had walked together—he stood on the hearth-rug, after ringing the bell, and took a searching look at them. To my surprise, he seemed at once to be principally if not solely interested in Drummle.

"Pip," said he, putting his large hand on my shoulder and moving me to the window, "I don't know one from the other. Who's the spider?"

"The spider?" said I.

"The blotchy, sprawly, sulky fellow."

"That's Bentley Drummle," I replied; "the one with the delicate face is Startop."

Not making the least account of "the one with the delicate face," he returned, "Bentley Drummle is his name, is it? I like the look of that fellow."

He immediately began to talk to Drummle, not at all deterred by his replying in his heavy reticent way, but apparently led on by it to screw discourse out of him. I was looking at the two, when there came between me and them, the housekeeper, with the first dish for the table.

She was a woman of about forty, I supposed—but I may have thought her younger than she was. Rather tall, of a lithe nimble figure, extremely pale, with large faded eyes, and a quantity of streaming hair. I cannot say whether any diseased affection of the heart caused her lips to be parted as if she were panting, and her face to bear a curious expression of suddenness and flutter, but I know that I had been to see Macbeth at the theatre a night or two before, and that her face looked to me as if it were all disturbed by fiery air, like the faces I had seen rise out of the witches' caldron.

Reading Strategy

Analyze Description What does this description of Mr. Jaggers's office tell you about him?

_____

_____

_____

_____

_____

_____

_____

_____

_____

_____

_____

_____

_____

_____

_____

_____

_____

_____

_____

_____

_____

_____

_____

_____

_____

_____

_____

_____

_____

_____

MARK IT UP

Are you allowed to write in your novel? If so, then mark up the pages as you read, or reread, to help with your note-taking. Develop a shorthand system, including symbols, that works for you. Here are some ideas:

Underline = important idea

Bracket = text to quote

Asterisk = just what you were looking for

Checkmark = might be useful

Circle = unfamiliar word or phrase to look up

▶ BIG Idea

Dreams and Reality Pip dreamed of a life in London, and now that he is there, he is coming face-to-face with reality. How does it contrast with his dreams?

Mark up the excerpt, looking for evidence of how it expresses the Big Idea.

NOVEL EXCERPT: CHAPTER 20

Of course I had no experience of a London summer day, and my spirits may have been oppressed by the hot exhausted air, and by the dust and grit that lay thick on everything. But I sat wondering and waiting in Mr. Jaggers's close room, until I really could not bear the two casts on the shelf above Mr. Jaggers's chair, and got up and went out.

When I told the clerk that I would take a turn in the air while I waited, he advised me to go round the corner and I should come into Smithfield. So, I came into Smithfield; and the shameful place, being all asmear with filth and fat and blood and foam, seemed to stick to me. So I rubbed it off with all possible speed by turning into a street where I saw the great black dome of Saint Paul's bulging at me from behind a grim stone building which a bystander said was Newgate Prison. Following the wall of the jail, I found the roadway covered with straw to deaden the noise of passing vehicles; and from this, and from the quantity of people standing about, smelling strongly of spirits and beer, I inferred that the trials were on.

While I looked about me here, an exceedingly dirty and partially drunk minister of justice asked me if I would like to step in and hear a trial or so, informing me that he could give me a front place for half-a-crown, whence I should command a full view of the Lord Chief Justice in his wig and robes— mentioning that awful personage like waxwork, and presently offering him at the reduced price of eighteenpence. As I declined the proposal on the plea of an appointment, he was so good as to take me into a yard and show me where the gallows was kept, and also where people were publicly whipped, and then he showed me the debtors' door, out of which culprits came to be hanged, heightening the interest of that dreadful portal by giving me to understand that "four on 'em" would come out at that door the day after to-morrow at eight in the morning to be killed in a row. This was horrible, and gave me a sickening idea of London, the more so as the Lord Chief Justice's proprietor wore (from his hat down to his boots and up again to his pocket-handkerchief inclusive) mildewed clothes, which had evidently not belonged to him originally, and which, I took it into my head, he had bought cheap of the executioner. Under these circumstances I thought myself well rid of him for a shilling.

I dropped into the office to ask if Mr. Jaggers had come in yet, and I found he had not, and I strolled out again. This time, I made the tour of Little Britain, and turned into Bartholomew Close; and now I became aware that other people were waiting about for Mr. Jaggers, as well as I.

Use the Cornell Note-Taking system to take notes on the excerpt at the left. Record your notes, Reduce them, and then Recap (summarize) them.

Record

Recap

Reduce

Try the following approach as you reduce your notes.

TO THE POINT
Write a few key ideas.

Respond and Think Critically

1. Describe Jaggers's work and home life. What is Pip implying about Jaggers's personality when he says that "he seemed to bully his very sandwich as he ate it"? [Interpret]

_____

_____

_____

_____

2. Briefly describe the incident that caused Miss Havisham to stop her clocks and become a recluse. What part might this incident have played in her desire to bring Estella and Pip together? [Conclude]

_____

_____

_____

_____

3. How does Pip feel when he hears that Joe is coming to visit? Why does Pip feel this way? [Infer]

_____

_____

_____

_____

4. What plans does Pip believe Miss Havisham has for him? Why does he believe this? [Analyze]

_____

_____

_____

_____

5. Dreams and Reality When Pip returns to Status House to visit Estella and Miss Havisham, he does not visit Joe. What does this say about how Pip deals with his dreams and his reality? [Evaluate]

_____

_____

_____

_____

APPLY BACKGROUND
Reread Meet the Author on page 10. How did that information help you understand or appreciate what you read in the novel?

_____

_____

_____

_____

_____

_____

_____

_____

_____

_____

_____

_____

_____

_____

_____

_____

_____

_____

_____

_____

_____

_____

_____

_____

_____

_____

_____

_____

_____

_____

Literary Element   Mood

Choose one setting in this section of the story. What words and phrases does Dickens use to create a mood for this setting? [Evaluate]

_____

_____

_____

_____

_____

_____

_____

_____

_____

_____

_____

Reading Strategy   Analyze Description

How does Dickens's description of Pip's walk through London make this setting more vivid for the reader? [Analyze]

_____

_____

_____

_____

_____

_____

_____

_____

_____

_____

_____

_____

_____

Vocabulary Practice

Choose the sentence that uses the vocabulary word correctly.

1. A. She **dexterously** tossed together the ingredients for a delicious meal.
   B. She **dexterously** tripped up the stairs as she took them two at a time.

2. A. He showed his **diffidence** as he confidently gave his speech.
   B. His **diffidence** made it hard for him to make friends.

3. A. She was considered a **judicious** person because of her wise decisions.
   B. She made a **judicious** decision to not wear her seatbelt.

4. A. The **supplicant** distributed his wealth among the poor.
   B. The **supplicant** quietly asked for more food.

5. A. She looked at the paper with **zealous** disinterest.
   B. Her **zealous** nature helped her to move quickly up the corporate ladder.

Academic Vocabulary

When Pip arrived in London, he found himself in a new **environment**, one that was completely different from the surroundings of his childhood. Using context clues, try to figure out the meaning of the word _environment_ in the sentence above. Check your guess in a dictionary.

_____

_____

_____

_____

_____

_____

_____

_____

_____

_____

Write with Style
Apply Description

Assignment Description is writing that helps readers imagine what characters see, hear, feel, taste or touch. Review the descriptions that Dickens provides in these chapters to give the reader a feeling for the mood of a setting. Write your own description of a place.

Get Ideas Think of a place that is important to you or one that makes you feel a certain mood. Make a word web. Write the name of the place you chose, such as *my father's office* in the center of the web. Next, jot down some of the things in that place, such as *desk, book case* and *chair*. Then, add the next layer to your web. Think of words that describe each of the things in the place you chose. Include both concrete and sensory details. For example, around *desk* you might write concrete details such as *wooden, stacks of books, piles of papers*, and *family photos*. Some sensory details you might include are *ornately carved, pine scent of furniture polish*, or *shiny surface*.

Give it Structure Use what you have written on your web to write a paragraph. Begin your paragraph with a sentence that makes your setting clear. Follow with sentences that include descriptive words that create a mood for your setting.

Look at Language Be sure your descriptive paragraph includes both concrete and sensory details and that all your descriptive words help to illustrate the mood you are trying to create.

EXAMPLE:
My father's office is a cozy place. The ornately carved wooden desk is covered in old leather-bound books with golden trim. The pine scent of furniture polish will always remind me of the times we sat in his chair together and he read to me from one of those books.

Connect to Content Areas
Social Studies

Assignment When Pip arrives in London, he is scared by its "immensity" and notices that it seems "rather ugly, crooked, narrow, dirty." London at this time was a center of commercial activity. During the years of the Victorian empire, the city was the capital of the powerful British Empire.

Investigate Conduct research to learn more about the conditions of London in the 1800s. Consult print or online resources to gather information about business and industry, living conditions, and daily activities.

Create Using images photocopied from books or printed from Internet sources, create a visual presentation of what London might have looked like at the time to accompany your report. Because you are presenting the image for an educational purpose and not for profit, you can use the images under the Fair Use doctrine of current copyright law. You should, however, credit each image you use with source information. Show the source information next to the image and in your report. This is a common way to cite Internet images:

Description of title of image. [online image] Available http://address/filename, Date.

Report After you have completed your research, present your findings in a report to your class. Together, discuss whether Pip's descriptions of the city are likely accurate or exaggerated.

Connect to the Literature

What kinds of life experiences cause people to feel loss?

Write a Paragraph

Describe a time in your life when you lost someone or something close or important to you. What about that person or thing did you value most? What feelings do you remember having?

Build Background

Dealing with Criminals

In the early 1800s in England, many convicts were still placed on boats and sent out of the country. In 1597 Parliament passed "An Act for the Punishment of Rogues, Vagabonds, and Sturdy Beggars." This act called for beggars to be sent to their birthplaces and jailed until they could be put to work. The act called for more serious criminals to be "conveyed unto such parts beyond the sea as shall at any time hereafter for that purpose be assigned. . . ." This allowed the transportation of criminals to British colonies in what are now the United States and Australia. A penal colony for British convicts was established in 1788 in Australia.

NOVEL NOTEBOOK

Keep a special notebook to record entries about the novels that you read this year.

WRITE THE CAPTION

Write a caption for the image below using information in Build Background.

_____
_____
_____
_____
_____
_____
_____
_____
_____
_____
_____
_____
_____
_____
_____
_____
_____
_____
_____
_____
_____
_____
_____
_____
_____
_____
_____
_____

Set Purposes for Reading

▶ BIG Idea Rewards and Sacrifices

Sometimes rewards come easily and other times they require hard work and sacrifice. Think about a time when you felt rewarded. How did your hard work and sacrifice lead to your reward?

In *Great Expectations*, Pip's expectations continue to be met. But in exchange for these rewards, he knowingly and unknowingly makes sacrifices. As you read, think about the sacrifices Pip makes and whether he feels that his rewards were worth his sacrifices.

Literary Element Irony

Irony is a contrast or discrepancy between appearance and reality, or between what is expected and what actually happens. **Situational irony** occurs when the outcome of a situation is the opposite of what is expected. **Verbal irony** occurs when a person says one thing and means another.

An author uses irony to express or show meaning without giving readers a lecture or tacking on a moral to the story. Verbal irony is often used to add humor to a story.

As you read, look for ways that Dickens uses situational and verbal irony. Ask yourself what effect the irony created, for example, did it create humor or add meaning to the story? Use the graphic organizer on the next page to help you organize moments of irony in the novel.

Reading Strategy Make Inferences About Theme

The **theme** of a story is the author's insight about life expressed as a general statement about human nature. Sometimes the theme is **stated,** or expressed directly, and other times it is **implied,** or revealed gradually through the plot, character, setting, point of view, and symbol.

When the theme is implied, you must **make inferences about the theme.** To do this, you use your reason and experience to deduce what an author is saying indirectly. You use events, dialogue, and description to help you find deeper meaning in the text. Some literary works may have more than one theme.

As you read, think about how the author shows theme though his insights by using dialogue and plot. You may find it helpful to use a graphic organizer like the one at the right.

Vocabulary

fidelity [fi del´ ə tē]
n. loyalty; faithfulness
Because he devoted is life to the company, his fidelity to it was never questioned.

melancholy [mel´ ən kol´ ē]
adj. depressed; sad
The day of the funeral was a dreary, melancholy day.

meritorious [mer´ə tôr´ē əs]
adj. noble; worthy
The completion of her first novel was a meritorious accomplishment.

predecessors [pred´ə ses´ərs]
n. someone or something that came before
The elders searched the clans history to find guidance from their predecessors.

superfluous [soo pur´ floo əs]
adj. extra; excessive
The investigator asked only for the important information and not the superfluous details of the crime.

Detail	Inference About Theme

This section of the novel represents a turning point, when Pip's expectations are forced to change because of a series of devastating disappointments. In the graphic organizer below, list three more expectations Pip held when he first learned about his anonymous benefactor. In the corresponding boxes, describe how each of his expectations had an ironic outcome.

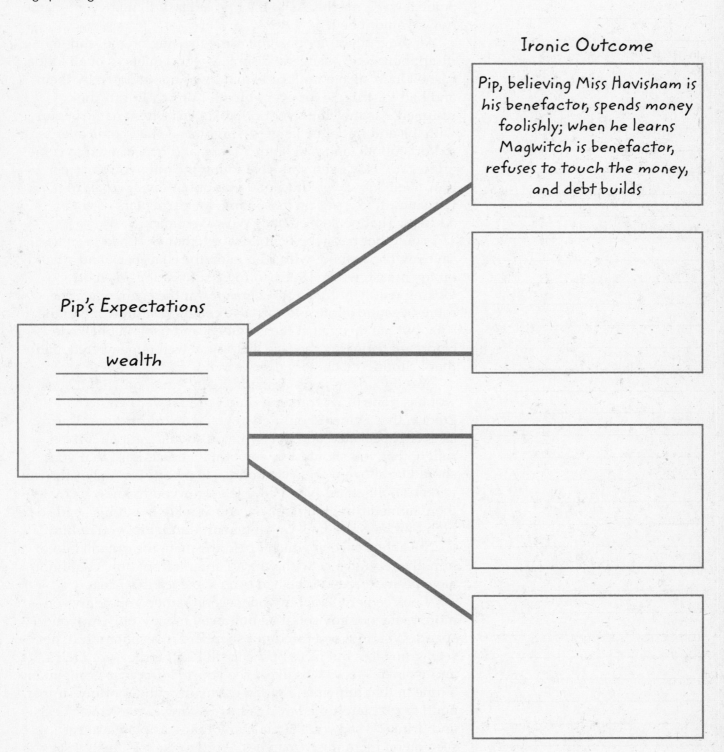

Ironic Outcome

Pip, believing Miss Havisham is his benefactor, spends money foolishly; when he learns Magwitch is benefactor, refuses to touch the money, and debt builds

Pip's Expectations

wealth

Literary Element

Irony What is ironic about how Pip has become a gentleman?

_____
_____
_____
_____
_____
_____
_____
_____
_____
_____
_____
_____
_____
_____
_____
_____
_____
_____
_____
_____
_____
_____
_____
_____
_____
_____
_____

NOVEL EXCERPT: CHAPTER 39

"Concerning a guardian," he went on. "There ought to have been some guardian, or such-like, whiles you was a minor. Some lawyer, maybe. As to the first letter of that lawyer's name now. Would it be J?"

All the truth of my position came flashing on me; and its disappointments, dangers, disgraces, consequences of all kinds, rushed in in such a multitude that I was borne down by them and had to struggle for every breath I drew. "Put it," he resumed, "as the employer of that lawyer whose name begun with a J, and might be Jaggers—put it as he had come over sea to Portsmouth, and had landed there, and had wanted to come on to you. 'However, you have found me out,' you says just now. Well! However, did I find you out? Why, I wrote from Portsmouth to a person in London, for particulars of your address. That person's name? Why, Wemmick."

I could not have spoken one word, though it had been to save my life. I stood, with a hand on the chair-back and a hand on my breast, where I seemed to be suffocating—I stood so, looking wildly at him, until I grasped at the chair, when the room began to surge and turn. He caught me, drew me to the sofa, put me up against the cushions, and bent on one knee before me, bringing the face that I now well remembered, and that I shuddered at, very near to mine.

"Yes, Pip, dear boy, I've made a gentleman on you! It's me wot has done it! I swore that time, sure as ever I earned a guinea, that guinea should go to you. I swore arterwards, sure as ever I spec'lated and got rich, you should get rich. I lived rough, that you should live smooth; I worked hard that you should be above work. What odds, dear boy? Do I tell it fur you to feel a obligation? Not a bit. I tell it fur you to know as that there hunted dunghill dog wot you kep life in got his head so high that he could make a gentleman—and, Pip, you're him!"

The abhorrence in which I held the man, the dread I had of him, the repugnance with which I shrank from him, could not have been exceeded if he had been some terrible beast.

"Look'ee here, Pip. I'm your second father. You're my son— more to me nor any son. I've put away money, only for you to spend. When I was a hired-out shepherd in a solitary hut, not seeing no faces but faces of sheep till I half forgot wot men's and women's faces wos like, I see yourn. I drops my knife many a time in that hut when I was a-eating my dinner or my supper, and I says, 'Here's the boy again, a-looking at me whiles I eats and drinks!' I see you there a many times, as plain as ever I see you on them misty marshes. 'Lord strike me dead!' I says each time—and I goes out in the air to say it under the open heavens—'but wot, if I gets liberty and money, I'll make that boy a gentleman!' And I done it. Why, look at you, dear boy! Look at these here lodgings of yourn, fit for a lord! A lord? Ah! You shall show money with lords for wagers, and beat 'em!"

In his heat and triumph, and in his knowledge that I had been nearly fainting, he did not remark on my reception of all this. It was the one grain of relief I had.

"Look'ee here!" he went on, taking my watch out of my pocket, and turning towards him a ring on my finger, while I recoiled from his touch as if he had been a snake, "a gold 'un and a beauty—*that's* a gentleman's, I hope! A diamond all set round with rubies —*that's* a gentleman's, I hope! Look at your linen; fine and beautiful! Look at your clothes; better ain't to be got! And your books, too," turning his eyes round the room, "mounting up, on their shelves, by hundreds! And you read 'em; don't you? I see you'd been a reading of 'em when I come in. Ha, ha, ha! You shall read 'em to me, dear boy! And if they're in foreign languages wot I don't understand, I shall be just as proud as if I did." . . .

"Don't you mind talking, Pip," said he, after again drawing his sleeve over his eyes and forehead, as the click came in his throat which I well remembered—and he was all the more horrible to me that he was so much in earnest; "you can't do better nor keep quiet, dear boy. You ain't looked slowly forward to this as I have; you wosn't prepared for this, as I wos. But didn't you never think it might be me?"

"Oh, no, no, no," I returned, "Never, never!"

"Well, you see it *wos* me, and single-handed. Never a soul in it but my own self and Mr. Jaggers."

"Was there no one else?" I asked.

"No," said he, with a glance of surprise. "Who else should there be? And, dear boy, how good-looking you have growed! There's bright eyes somewheres—eh? Isn't there bright eyes somewheres, wot you love the thoughts on?"

O Estella, Estella!

"They shall be yourn, dear boy, if money can buy 'em. Not that a gentleman like you, so well set up as you, can't win 'em off of his own game; but money shall back you! Let me finish wot I was a-telling you, dear boy. From that there hut and that there hiring-out, I got money left me by my master (which died, and had been the same as me), and got my liberty and went for myself. In every single thing I went for, I went for you. 'Lord strike a blight upon it,' I says, wotever it was I went for, 'if it ain't for him!' It all prospered wonderful. . . .

O, that he had never come! That he had left me at the forge— far from contented, yet, by comparison happy!

Literary Element

Irony What is ironic about the fact that Magwitch is Pip's guardian?

_____

_____

_____

_____

_____

_____

_____

_____

_____

_____

_____

_____

_____

_____

_____

_____

_____

_____

_____

_____

_____

_____

_____

_____

_____

_____

_____

_____

Reading Strategy

Make Inferences About Theme How does this passage illustrate the themes of the importance of loyalty and conscience in the novel?

_____

_____

_____

_____

_____

_____

_____

_____

_____

_____

_____

_____

_____

_____

_____

_____

_____

_____

_____

_____

_____

_____

_____

_____

_____

_____

_____

_____

_____

NOVEL EXCERPT: CHAPTER 35

Whatever my fortunes might have been, I could scarcely have recalled my sister with much tenderness. But I suppose there is a shock of regret which may exist without much tenderness. Under its influence (and perhaps to make up for the want of the softer feeling), I was seized with a violent indignation against the assailant from whom she had suffered so much; and I felt that on sufficient proof I could have revengefully pursued Orlick, or any one else, to the last extremity.

Having written to Joe to offer consolation, and to assure him that I should come to the funeral, I passed the intermediate days in the curious state of mind I have glanced at. I went down early in the morning, and alighted at the Blue Boar in good time to walk over to the forge.

It was fine summer weather again, and, as I walked along, the times when I was a little helpless creature, and my sister did not spare me, vividly returned. But they returned with a gentle tone upon them that softened even the edge of Tickler. For now, the very breath of the beans and clover whispered to my heart that the day must come when it would be well for my memory that others walking in the sunshine should be softened as they thought of me.

At last I came within sight of the house, and saw that Trabb and Co. had put in a funereal execution and taken possession. Two dismally absurd persons, each ostentatiously exhibiting a crutch done up in a black bandage—as if that instrument could possibly communicate any comfort to anybody—were posted at the front door; and in one of them I recognized a postboy discharged from the Boar for turning a young couple into a saw-pit on their bridal morning, in consequence of intoxication rendering it necessary for him to ride his horse clasped round the neck with both arms. All the children of the village, and most of the women, were admiring these sable warders and the closed windows of the house and forge; and as I came up, one of the two warders (the post-boy) knocked at the door—implying that I was far too much exhausted by grief to have strength remaining to knock for myself.

Another sable warder (a carpenter, who had once eaten two geese for a wager) opened the door, and showed me into the best parlour. Here, Mr. Trabb had taken unto himself the best table, and had got all the leaves up, and was holding a kind of black bazaar, with the aid of a quantity of black pins. At the moment of my arrival, he had just finished putting somebody's hat into black longclothes, like an African baby; so he held out his hand for mine. But I, misled by the action, and confused by the occasion, shook hands with him with every testimony of warm affection.

Poor dear Joe, entangled in a little black cloak tied in a large bow under his chin, was seated apart at the upper end of the room; where, as chief mourner, he had evidently been stationed by Trabb. When I bent down and said to him, "Dear Joe, how are you?" he said, "Pip, old chap, you knowed her when she were a fine figure of a—" and clasped my hand and said no more.

Biddy, looking very neat and modest in her black dress, went quietly here and there, and was very helpful. When I had spoken to Biddy, as I thought it not a time for talking I went and sat down near Joe, and there began to wonder in what part of the house it—she—my sister—was. The air of the parlour being faint with the smell of sweet cake, I looked about for the table of refreshments; it was scarcely visible until one had got accustomed to the gloom, but there was a cut-up plum-cake upon it, and there were cut-up oranges, and sandwiches, and biscuits, and two decanters that I knew very well as ornaments, but had never seen used in all my life—one full of port, and one of sherry. Standing at this table, I became conscious of the servile Pumblechook in a black cloak and several yards of hatband, who was alternately stuffing himself, and making obsequious movements to catch my attention. The moment he succeeded, he came over to me (breathing sherry and crumbs), and said in a subdued voice, "May I, dear sir?" and did. I then descried Mr. and Mrs. Hubble, the last-named in a decent speechless paroxysm in a corner. We were all going to "follow," and were all in course of being tied up separately (by Trabb) into ridiculous bundles.

"Which I meantersay, Pip," Joe whispered me, as we were being what Mr. Trabb called "formed" in the parlour, two and two—and it was dreadfully like a preparation for some grim kind of dance; "which I meantersay, sir, as I would in preference have carried her to the church myself, along with three or four friendly ones wot come to it with willing harts and arms, but it were considered wot the neighbours would look down on such and would be of opinions as it were wanting in respect." . . .

So, we all put our pocket-handkerchiefs to our faces, as if our noses were bleeding, and filed out two and two; Joe and I; Biddy and Pumblechook; Mr. and Mrs. Hubble. The remains of my poor sister had been brought round by the kitchen door, and, it being a point of undertaking ceremony that the six bearers must be stifled and blinded under a horrible black velvet housing with a white border, the whole looked like a blind monster with twelve human legs, shuffling and blundering along, under the guidance of two keepers—the post-boy and his comrade.

Reading Strategy

Make Inferences About Theme How does this passage change or reinforce your ideas about the themes of the novel?

MARK IT UP

Are you allowed to write in your novel? If so, then mark up the pages as you read, or reread, to help with your note-taking. Develop a shorthand system, including symbols, that works for you. Here are some ideas:

Underline = important idea

Bracket = text to quote

Asterisk = just what you were looking for

Checkmark = might be useful

Circle = unfamiliar word or phrase to look up

▶ **BIG Idea**

Rewards and Sacrifices Sometimes, even after we have been rewarded, we must still make sacrifices. What sacrifices must Pip make regarding Magwitch?

Mark up the excerpt, looking for evidence of how it expresses the Big Idea.

NOVEL EXCERPT: CHAPTER 41

"There, again!" said I, stopping before Herbert, with my open hands held out, as if they contained the desperation of the case. "I know nothing of his life. It has almost made me mad to sit here of a night and see him before me, so bound up with my fortunes and misfortunes, and yet so unknown to me, except as the miserable wretch who terrified me two days in my childhood!"

Herbert got up, and linked his arm in mine, and we slowly walked to and fro together, studying the carpet.

"Handel," said Herbert, stopping, "you feel convinced that you can take no further benefits from him, do you?"

"Fully. Surely you would, too, if you were in my place?"

"And you feel convinced that you must break with him?"

"Herbert, can you ask me?"

"And you have, and are bound to have, that tenderness for the life he has risked on your account, that you must save him, if possible, from throwing it away. Then you must get him out of England before you stir a finger to extricate yourself. That done, extricate yourself, in Heaven's name, and we'll see it out together, dear old boy."

It was a comfort to shake hands upon it, and walk up and down again, with only that done.

"Now, Herbert," said I, "with reference to gaining some knowledge of his history. There is but one way that I know of. I must ask him point-blank."

"Yes. Ask him," said Herbert, "when we sit at breakfast in the morning." For, he had said, on taking leave of Herbert, that he would come to breakfast with us.

With this project formed, we went to bed. I had the wildest dreams concerning him, and woke unrefreshed; I woke, too, to recover the fear which I had lost in the night of his being found out as a returned transport. Waking, I never lost that fear.

He came round at the appointed time, took out his jack-knife, and sat down to his meal. He was full of plans "for his gentleman's coming out strong, and like a gentleman," and urged me to begin speedily upon the pocket-book, which he had left in my possession. He considered the chambers and his own lodging as temporary residences, and advised me to look out at once for a "fashionable crib" near Hyde Park, in which he could have "a shake-down." When he had made an end of his breakfast, and was wiping his knife on his leg, I said to him, without a word of preface:

"After you were gone last night, I told my friend of the struggle that the soldiers found you engaged in on the marshes, when we came up.

You remember?"

Use the Cornell Note-Taking system to take notes on the excerpt at the left. Record your notes, Reduce them, and then Recap (summarize) them.

Record

Reduce

Try the following approach as you reduce your notes.

MY VIEW

Comment on what you learned from your own notes.

Recap

Respond and Think Critically

1. How does Pip react to driving by the prison with Estella? What does Pip's reaction indicate about his image of Estella as a person? [Conclude]

_____

_____

_____

_____

2. What news does Magwitch bring to Pip? How does Magwitch's information affect Pip? [Interpret]

_____

_____

_____

_____

3. What one financial request does Pip make of Miss Havisham? What does this request indicate about his character? [Analyze]

_____

_____

_____

_____

4. How does Pip feel about himself as a "gentleman" when he no longer has his money? What values of Pip's society is Dickens criticizing by calling attention to Pip's feelings? [Evaluate]

_____

_____

_____

_____

5. **Rewards and Sacrifices** When Pip learns that Magwitch is his benefactor, as a reward for the kindness Pip had shown him as a child, Pip turns down any further benefits. Do you agree with Pip's decision? Why or why not? [Evaluate]

_____

_____

_____

_____

APPLY BACKGROUND
Reread Build Background on page 47. How did that information help you understand or appreciate what you read in the novel?

_____

_____

_____

_____

_____

_____

_____

_____

_____

_____

_____

_____

_____

_____

_____

_____

_____

_____

_____

_____

_____

_____

_____

_____

_____

_____

_____

_____

_____

Literary Element   Irony

What are two examples in this section of the novel when you expected one thing to happen, but the opposite happened? [Compare]

_____
_____
_____
_____
_____
_____
_____
_____
_____
_____
_____
_____

Reading Strategy   Make Inferences About Theme

What themes are made clear through Pip's disappointments? [Conclude]

_____
_____
_____
_____
_____
_____
_____
_____
_____
_____
_____
_____
_____
_____

Vocabulary Practice

Complete the following sentences.

fidelity   **predecessors**
melancholy   **surperfluous**
meritorius

Michael disliked _____ things, but Roger collected many unnecessary things.

Yesterday was a _____ day, but today is bright and cheery.

Marie showed _____, but Trina was not loyal at all.

Many are concerned about what our _____ would have done, but others are more concerned about the future.

A hero is known for her _____ actions, but a coward is known for her faintheartedness.

Academic Vocabulary

It was **apparent** _that Pip was upset to discover that Magwitch was his benefactor._ In the preceding sentence, _apparent_ is used to mean "obvious or clear." Think about what Pip did that showed his discomfort, and then fill in the blank for this statement: _Because he _____

_____,

it was_ **apparent** _that Pip was upset._

Write with Style

Apply Irony

Assignment Irony can be used to add humor to dialogue. This type of irony, called *verbal irony*, occurs when a character says one thing, but he or she clearly means something else. Write a short dialogue between two people in which you use verbal irony.

Get Ideas Think of a situation in which two characters may be interacting. Decide on a relationship between the two people, for example, parent and child or two friends. Think about how these two people might interact on a regular basis.

Give it Structure Have your characters alternate speaking to each other. Develop a situation in which one or both characters will use verbal irony. You can include narrative text as a way to give context to your writing.

EXAMPLE:

"Sally, I'm sorry, but I broke the vase that belonged to your great grandmother. Are you upset?" Tony asked as he held the pieces of the heirloom vase out to her.

"That old thing? Why would I ever be upset?" Sally said, struggling to hold back the tears in her eyes.

Look at Language Be careful not to overuse verbal irony. A few uses are enough to create clear characters and a tone for your scene.

Speaking and Listening

Literature Groups

Assignment With a small group, discuss whether Pip should continue to receive financial assistance from his benefactor. try to reach a consensus—a general agreement among a group on an issue.

Prepare Before your group meets, look back at chapter 39 and skim the earlier parts of the novel to review Pip's interactions with Magwitch the convict. Then think about the pros and cons of Pip's decision to refuse further financial help from the convict. You may find a chart like the one below helpful in organizing your ideas.

Pros	Cons
Pip will be able to continue living the life of a gentleman.	Herbert will also suffer.

Discuss Respect other's viewpoints by listening attentively. Deliver your opinions in a normal tone of voice, providing clear, specific examples from your chart to support your opinions.

Report Have one group member orally state your consensus to the class or state that no consensus was reached, being sure to address the class clearly and loudly enough for all to hear.

Evaluate Write a paragraph in which you assess the effectiveness of your discussion.

Connect to the Literature

Have you ever struggled to find the answer to a difficult question? How did you feel when you finally found the answer you needed?

Share Your Thoughts

Think about a time in which you searched for the answer to a question about your life or about someone you know. Share your experience with a partner.

Build Background

Abel Magwitch

In this section of the novel, the character of Abel Magwitch plays a central role. Magwitch has already changed Pip's life once with his anonymous donation of money. In the chapters that follow, his character begins to affect Pip's life in a different way. Significantly, Dickens gave Magwitch the name Abel, which refers to the second son of Adam and Eve in the Old Testament of the Bible. According to the biblical account, Abel was a shepherd who was killed in a jealous rage by his brother Cain. Abel's innocent blood put a curse on Cain, and he became a fugitive. As you read, think about why Dickens wanted readers to associate Magwitch with the innocent, slain brother, even though Magwitch is a convict. You might also think about which characters in the novel represent Cain, the evil, murdering brother.

NOVEL NOTEBOOK
Keep a special notebook to record entries about the novels that you read this year.

SUMMARIZE
Summarize in one sentence the most important idea(s) in Build Background.

_____
_____
_____
_____
_____
_____
_____
_____
_____
_____
_____
_____
_____
_____
_____
_____
_____
_____
_____
_____
_____
_____
_____
_____
_____
_____
_____
_____
_____

Set Purposes for Reading

▶ BIG Idea Rewards and Sacrifices

We make sacrifices for many different reasons. Think about a sacrifice you have made. Did you make this sacrifice because it would help someone else? Was this a sacrifice you made because of your beliefs and values?

In the last section of the novel, Pip is faced with having to sacrifice his dreams. As you read, think about how Pip's new sacrifices help bring him even closer to meeting his old expectations.

Literary Element Motivation

Motivation is the reason that a character acts, thinks, or feels a certain way. A character's words, thoughts, and actions help to reveal his or her motivation. Motivation may be an external circumstance or an internal moral or emotional impulse.

Motivation provides a reason for characters to act the way they do. Motivation can also help point the reader to the solution to a mystery.

As you read, look for examples of the characters' motivation. Ask yourself what the characters say, think, or do that makes their motivation clear.

Reading Strategy Analyze Cause-and-Effect Relationships

A **cause** is that which makes something happen. An **effect** is what happens as a result of the cause. There may be many causes for one effect or many effects for one cause.

When you **analyze cause-and-effect relationships,** you explore the causes behind thoughts, actions, or events and examine the results of these thoughts, actions, or events. Sometimes one effect can become the cause of the next effect. Noting causes and effects as you read can help you determine the writer's intended meaning and understand the purpose of a literary work.

As you read, think about how the events of the story and the characters' thoughts and actions cause other events, thoughts, and actions. Ask yourself how the effects lead to new effects and also help you to understand the plot of the story. You may find it helpful to use a graphic organizer like the one at the right. The graphic organizer on the next page can also help you to analyze cause-and-effect relationships.

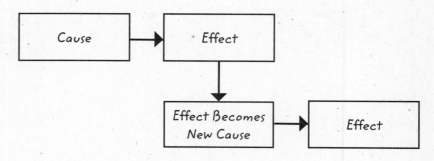

Vocabulary

acquiescence [ak´wē es´əns]
n. agreement; consent
They took her acquiescence to mean that she finally agreed, but really she was simply tired of arguing.

demeanor [di mē´nər]
n. behavior
His stern demeanor intimidated many people.

despondent [di spon´dənt]
adj. depressed
After her grandfather died, she became despondent and withdrawn.

eloquence [el´ə kwəns]
n. expressiveness
The political candidate's eloquence helped him to win many debates.

repugnance [ri pug´nəns]
n. distaste
He showed his repugnance for carrots as he disgustedly separated them from the rest of the food on his plate.

The last chapters of the novel solve many of the novel's mysteries and lead readers to a resolution. Use the ovals to record the events leading to the resolution of the novel. Use as many ovals as you need.

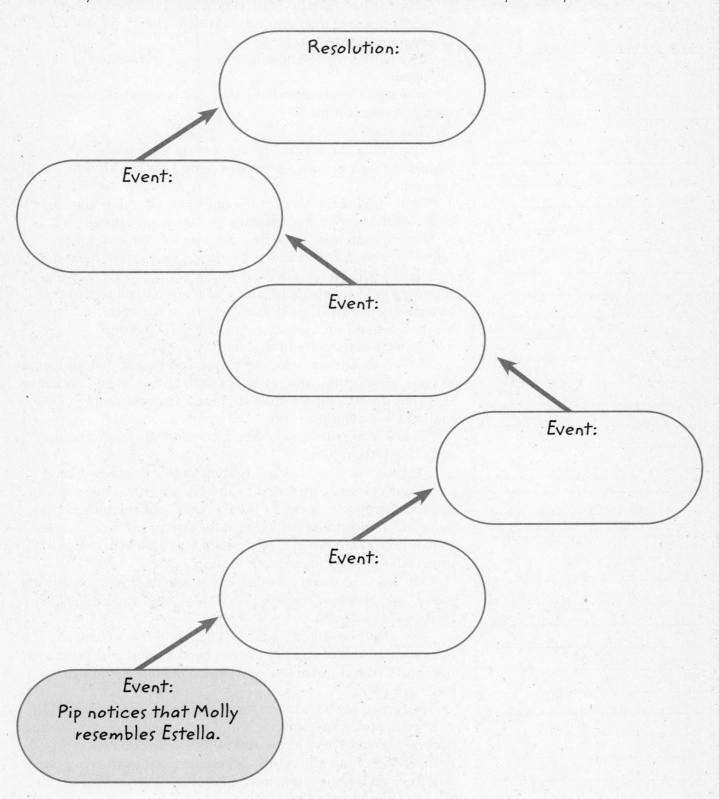

Resolution:

Event:

Event:

Event:

Event:

Event:
Pip notices that Molly resembles Estella.

Literary Element

Motivation Why does Miss Havisham want Pip's forgiveness?

_____
_____
_____
_____
_____
_____
_____
_____
_____
_____
_____
_____
_____
_____
_____
_____
_____
_____
_____
_____
_____
_____
_____
_____
_____
_____
_____
_____
_____
_____

NOVEL EXCERPT: CHAPTER 49

"I am far from happy, Miss Havisham, but I have other causes of disquiet than any you know of. They are the secrets I have mentioned."

After a little while, she raised her head and looked at the fire again.

"It is noble in you to tell me that you have other causes of unhappiness. Is it true?"

"Too true."

"Can I only serve you, Pip, by serving your friend? Regarding that as done, is there nothing I can do for you yourself?"

"Nothing. I thank you for the question. I thank you even more for the tone of the question. But there is nothing."

She presently rose from her seat, and looked about the blighted room for the means of writing. There were none there, and she took from her pocket a yellow set of ivory tablets, mounted in tarnished gold, and wrote upon them with a pencil in a case of tarnished gold that hung from her neck.

"You are still on friendly terms with Mr. Jaggers?"

"Quite. I dined with him yesterday."

"This is an authority to him to pay you that money, to lay out at your irresponsible discretion for your friend. I keep no money here; but if you would rather Mr. Jaggers knew nothing of the matter, I will send it to you."

"Thank you, Miss Havisham; I have not the least objection to receiving it from him."

She read me what she had written, and it was direct and clear, and evidently intended to absolve me from any suspicion of profiting by the receipt of the money. I took the tablets from her hand, and it trembled again, and it trembled more as she took off the chain to which the pencil was attached, and put it in mine. All this she did, without looking at me.

"My name is on the first leaf. If you can ever write under my name, 'I forgive her' though ever so long after my broken heart is dust—pray do it!"

"Oh, Miss Havisham," said I, "I can do it now. There have been sore mistakes; and my life has been a blind and thankless one; and I want forgiveness and direction far too much to be bitter with you."

She turned her face to me for the first time since she had averted it, and, to my amazement, I may even add to my terror, dropped on her knees at my feet, with her folded hands raised to me in the manner in which, when her poor heart was young and fresh and whole, they must often have been raised to heaven from her mother's side.

To see her, with her white hair and her worn face, kneeling at my feet, gave me a shock through all my frame. I entreated her to rise, and got my arms about her to help her up; but she only pressed that hand of mine which was nearest to her grasp, and hung her head over it and wept. I had never seen her shed a tear before, and in the hope that the relief might do her good, I bent over her without speaking. She was not kneeling now, but was down upon the ground.

"Oh!" she cried, despairingly. "What have I done! What have I done!"

"If you mean, Miss Havisham, what have you done to injure me, let me answer. Very little. I should have loved her under any circumstances. Is she married?"

"Yes."

It was a needless question, for a new desolation in the desolate house had told me so.

"What have I done! What have I done!" She wrung her hands, and crushed her white hair, and returned to this cry over and over again. "What have I done!"

I knew not how to answer, or how to comfort her. That she had done a grievous thing in taking an impressionable child to mould into the form that her wild resentment, spurned affection, and wounded pride found vengeance in, I knew full well. But that, in shutting out the light of day, she had shut out infinitely more; that, in seclusion, she had secluded herself from a thousand natural and healing influences; that her mind, brooding solitary, had grown diseased, as all minds do and must and will that reverse the appointed order of their Maker; I knew equally well. And could I look upon her without compassion, seeing her punishment in the ruin she was, in her profound unfitness for this earth on which she was placed, in the vanity of sorrow which had become a master mania, like the vanity of penitence, the vanity of unworthiness, and other monstrous vanities that have been curses in this world?

"Until you spoke to her the other day, and until I saw in you a looking-glass that showed me what I once felt myself, I did not know what I had done. What have I done! What have I done!" And so again, twenty, fifty times over, What had she done!

"Miss Havisham," I said, when her cry had died away, "you may dismiss me from your mind and conscience. But Estella is a different case, and if you can ever undo any scrap of what you have done amiss in keeping a part of her right nature away from her, it will be better to do that than to bemoan the past through a hundred years."

"Yes, yes, I know it. But, Pip—my dear!" There was an earnest womanly compassion for me in her new affection.

Literary Element

Motivation What is Pip's motivation for speaking to Miss Havisham about Estella?

Reading Strategy

Analyze Cause and Effect Relationships Why does Pip feel ashamed?

_____

_____

_____

_____

_____

_____

_____

_____

_____

_____

_____

_____

_____

_____

_____

_____

_____

_____

_____

_____

_____

_____

_____

_____

_____

_____

NOVEL EXCERPT: CHAPTER 57

"If you would like to hear, Joe—" I was beginning, when Joe got up and came to my sofa.

"Lookee here, old chap," said Joe, bending over me. "Ever the best of friends; ain't us, Pip?"

I was ashamed to answer him.

"Wery good, then," said Joe, as if I _had_ answered; "that's all right, that's agreed upon. Then why go into subjects, old chap, which as betwixt two sech must be for ever onnecessary? There's subjects enough as betwixt two sech, without onnecessary ones. Lord! To think of your poor sister and her rampages! And don't you remember Tickler?"

"I do indeed, Joe."

"Lookee here, old chap," said Joe. "I done what I could to keep you and Tickler in sunders, but my power were not always fully equal to my inclinations. For when your poor sister had a mind to drop into you, it were not so much," said Joe, in his favourite argumentative way, "that she dropped into me too, if I put myself in opposition to her but that she dropped into you always heavier for it. I noticed that. It ain't a grab at a man's whisker, not yet a shake or two of a man (to which your sister was quite welcome), that 'ud put a man off from getting a little child out of punishment. But when that little child is dropped into heavier for that grab of whisker or shaking, then that man naterally up and says to himself, 'Where is the good as you are a-doing? I grant you I see the 'arm,' says the man, 'but I don't see the good. I call upon you, sir, therefore, to pint out the good.'"

"The man says?" I observed, as Joe waited for me to speak.

"The man says," Joe assented. "Is he right, that man?"

"Dear Joe, he is always right."

"Well, old chap," said Joe, "then abide by your words. If he's always right (which in general he's more likely wrong), he's right when he says this: supposing ever you kep any little matter to yourself, when you was a little child, you kep it mostly because you know'd as J. Gargery's power to part you and Tickler in sunders were not fully equal to his inclinations. Therefore, think no more of it as betwixt two sech, and do not let us pass remarks upon onnecessary subjects. Biddy giv' herself a deal o' trouble with me afore I left (for I am almost awful dull), as I should view it in this light, and, viewing it in this light, as I should so put it. Both of which," said Joe, quite charmed with his logical arrangement, "being done, now this to you a true friend, say. Namely. You mustn't go a-over-doing on it, but you must have your supper and your wine-and-water, and you must be put betwixt the sheets."

The delicacy with which Joe dismissed this theme, and the sweet tact and kindness with which Biddy—who with her woman's wit had found me out so soon—had prepared him for it, made a deep impression on my mind. But whether Joe knew how poor I was, and how my great expectations had all dissolved, like our own marsh mists before the sun, I could not understand.

Another thing in Joe that I could not understand when it first began to develop itself, but which I soon arrived at a sorrowful comprehension of, was this: As I became stronger and better, Joe became a little less easy with me. In my weakness and entire dependence on him, the dear fellow had fallen into the old tone, and called me by the old names, the dear "old Pip, old chap," that now were music in my ears. I, too, had fallen into the old ways, only happy and thankful that he let me. But, imperceptibly, though I held by them fast, Joe's hold upon them began to slacken; and whereas I wondered at this, at first, I soon began to understand that the cause of it was in me, and that the fault of it was all mine.

Ah! Had I given Joe no reason to doubt my constancy, and to think that in prosperity I should grow cold to him and cast him off? Had I given Joe's innocent heart no cause to feel instinctively that as I got stronger, his hold upon me would be weaker, and that he had better loosen it in time and let me go, before I plucked myself away?

It was on the third or fourth occasion of my going out walking in the Temple Gardens, leaning on Joe's arm, that I saw this change in him very plainly. We had been sitting in the bright warm sunlight, looking at the river, and I chanced to say as we got up:

"See, Joe! I can walk quite strongly. Now, you shall see me walk back by myself."

"Which do not overdo it, Pip," said Joe; "but I shall be happy fur to see you able, sir."

The last word grated on me; but how could I remonstrate! I walked no further than the gate of the gardens, and then pretended to be weaker than I was, and asked Joe for his arm. Joe gave it me, but was thoughtful.

I, for my part, was thoughtful, too, for how best to check this growing change in Joe was a great perplexity to my remorseful thoughts. That I was ashamed to tell him exactly how I was placed, and what I had come down to, I do not seek to conceal; but I hope my reluctance was not quite an unworthy one. He would want to help me out of his little savings, I knew, and I knew that he ought not to help me, and that I must not suffer him to do it.

Reading Strategy

Analyze Cause and Effect Relationships Why does Joe's attitude toward Pip begin to change as Pip recovers?

_____
_____
_____
_____
_____
_____
_____
_____
_____
_____
_____
_____
_____
_____
_____
_____
_____
_____
_____
_____
_____
_____
_____
_____
_____
_____
_____
_____

MARK IT UP

Are you allowed to write in your novel? If so, then mark up the pages as you read, or reread, to help with your note-taking. Develop a shorthand system, including symbols, that works for you. Here are some ideas:

Underline = important idea

Bracket = text to quote

Asterisk = just what you were looking for

Checkmark = might be useful

Circle = unfamiliar word or phrase to look up

▶ **BIG Idea**

Rewards and Sacrifices What have you found out about Pip's new approach to his rewards and expectations?

Mark up the excerpt, looking for evidence of how it expresses the Big Idea.

NOVEL EXCERPT: CHAPTER 51

My narrative finished, and their questions exhausted, I then produced Miss Havisham's authority to receive the nine hundred pounds for Herbert. Mr. Jaggers's eyes retired a little deeper into his head when I handed him the tablets, but he presently handed them over to Wemmick, with instructions to draw the cheque for his signature. While that was in course of being done, I looked on at Wemmick as he wrote, and Mr. Jaggers, poising and swaying himself on his well-polished boots, looked on at me. "I am sorry, Pip," said he, as I put the cheque in my pocket, when he had signed it, "that we do nothing for *you*."

"Miss Havisham was good enough to ask me," I returned, "whether she could do nothing for me, and I told her no."

"Everybody should know his own business," said Mr. Jaggers. And I saw Wemmick's lips form the words "portable property."

"I should *not* have told her no, if I had been you," said Mr Jaggers; "but every man ought to know his own business best."

"Every man's business," said Wemmick, rather reproachfully towards me, "is portable property."

As I thought the time was now come for pursuing the theme I had at heart, I said, turning on Mr. Jaggers:

"I did ask something of Miss Havisham, however, sir. I asked her to give me some information relative to her adopted daughter, and she gave me all she possessed."

"Did she?" said Mr. Jaggers, bending forward to look at his boots and then straightening himself. "Hah! I don't think I should have done so, if I had been Miss Havisham. But *she* ought to know her own business best."

"I know more of the history of Miss Havisham's adopted child than Miss Havisham herself does, sir. I know her mother."

Mr. Jaggers looked at me inquiringly, and repeated "Mother?"

"I have seen her mother within these three days."

"Yes?" said Mr. Jaggers.

"And so have you, sir. And you have seen her still more recently."

"Yes?" said Mr. Jaggers.

"Perhaps I know more of Estella's history than even you do," said I. "I know her father, too."

A certain stop that Mr. Jaggers came to in his manner—he was too self-possessed to change his manner, but he could not help its being brought to an indefinably attentive stop—assured me that he did not know who her father was. This I had strongly suspected from Provis's account (as Herbert had repeated it) of his having kept himself dark; which I pieced on to the fact that he himself was not Mr. Jaggers's client until some four years later, and when he could have no reason for claiming his identity.

Use the Cornell Note-Taking system to take notes on the excerpt at the left. Record your notes, Reduce them, and then Recap (summarize) them.

Record

_____
_____
_____
_____
_____
_____
_____
_____
_____
_____
_____
_____
_____
_____
_____
_____
_____
_____
_____
_____
_____
_____

Recap

_____
_____
_____
_____
_____
_____

Reduce

Try the following approach as you reduce your notes.

ASK QUESTIONS

Write any questions you have about the novel. Do you have to go to an outside source to find the answers?

_____
_____
_____
_____
_____
_____
_____
_____
_____
_____
_____
_____
_____
_____
_____
_____
_____
_____
_____
_____

Respond and Think Critically

1. Describe Miss Havisham's behavior when Pip visits her. How has their relationship changed? [Compare]

_____

_____

_____

2. What happens to Magwitch? How does Pip begin to feel toward Magwitch? [Conclude]

_____

_____

_____

3. What does Joe do for Pip? How does Pip feel about himself and his actions after Joe leaves? [Analyze]

_____

_____

_____

_____

4. Why does Dickens return Pip to the countryside of his youth? What theme does this turn of events emphasize? [Infer]

_____

_____

_____

5. **Rewards and Sacrifices** Do you think that Pip's last words of the book, "I saw no shadow of another parting from her," make the sacrifices he has made seem worthwhile? Explain. [Evaluate]

_____

_____

_____

APPLY BACKGROUND
Reread Introduction to the Novel on pages 8–9. How did that information help you understand or appreciate what you read in the novel?

_____

_____

_____

_____

_____

_____

_____

_____

_____

_____

_____

_____

_____

_____

_____

_____

_____

_____

_____

_____

_____

_____

_____

_____

_____

Literary Element **Motivation**

In this section of the novel, how does Dickens show Pip's motivation to mend his relationships? [Analyze]

_____
_____
_____
_____
_____
_____
_____
_____
_____
_____
_____
_____
_____
_____

Reading Strategy **Analyze Cause and Effect Relationships**

What effect does Pip's illness have on his relationship with Joe? What does this cause Pip to learn about himself? [Conclude]

_____
_____
_____
_____
_____
_____
_____
_____
_____
_____
_____
_____
_____

Vocabulary Practice

A **synonym** is a word that has the same or nearly the same meaning as another word. Match each boldfaced vocabulary word below with its synonym. Use a thesaurus or dictionary to check your answers.

1. **acquiescence**
2. **demeanor**
3. **despondent**
4. **eloquence**
5. **repugnance**

a. forlorn
b. conduct
c. cheerfulness
d. agreement
e. aversion
f. articulateness
g. acidic

Academic Vocabulary

Many would agree that Pip had a **valid** reason to be angry with Miss Havisham. To become more familiar with the word _valid_, fill out the graphic organizer below.

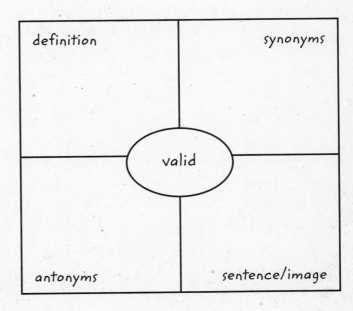

Writing

Personal Response Were you satisfied with the ending of the novel? Explain.

_____

_____

_____

_____

_____

_____

_____

_____

_____

_____

_____

_____

_____

_____

_____

_____

_____

_____

_____

_____

_____

_____

_____

_____

_____

Speaking and Listening

Speech

Assignment By the end of the novel, Pip had learned an important lesson about values and achieving goodness. He suddenly regrets being apart from Joe and Biddy. Write and deliver a speech for Pip to give to Joe in which he apologizes. In the speech, Pip should express his regrets for having stayed away from Joe for so long and for getting caught up in a world that is unworthy of Joe's values. The speech should reveal Pip's new understanding of life and the importance of true friendships.

Prepare Begin by thinking about Pip's purpose for giving this speech. Decide what tone Pip would use. Think about the emotions Pip would he be feeling and what words he would use to express those emotions. Decide it he would approach Joe formally or informally. Use a graphic organizer like the one below to keep your ideas organized.

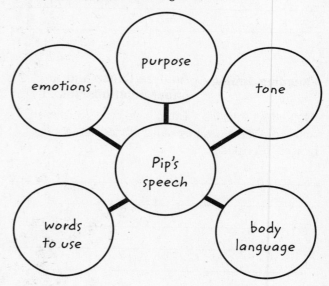

Next, keep the information you collected on you graphic organizer in mind as you write the speech.

Deliver Present Pip's speech to the class. Keep in mind that this speech is for Pip to give to Joe. Use body language that is appropriate to the emotions, tone, and purpose of your speech.

Evaluate Write a paragraph evaluating your speech. When your classmates present, offer oral feedback on their performances.

Great Expectations

The following questions refer to the Related Readings in Glencoe's *Literature Library* edition of this novel. Support your answers with details from the texts. Write your answers on a separate sheet of paper, but jot down some notes first on the lines provided.

Working Life
Sally Mitchell

Pick a character from *Great Expectations* and describe how he or she is influenced by the economy of Victorian England.

_____

_____

_____

_____

_____

from David Copperfield
Charles Dickens

Compare David and Pip. In what ways are they similar?

_____

_____

_____

_____

_____

Freedom's Plow
Langston Hughes

Some expectations about life are realistic, while others are not. Do you think the expectations expressed in Hughes's poem are more realistic than Pip's expectations? Why or why not?

_____

_____

_____

_____

_____

'Round the Clock' in Victorian London
George Augustus Sala

How does the London described by Sala compare to the London of *Great Expectations*?

_____

_____

_____

_____

Great Expectations
book review in Atlantic Monthly, *September 1861*

How might the character of Magwitch illustrate the reviewer's opinion that Dickens "follows the maxim of the great master of characterization, and seeks 'the soul of goodness in things evil'"?

_____

_____

_____

_____

_____

LITERATURE EXCERPT: Rules of the Game

My older brother Vincent was the one who actually got the chess set. We had gone to the annual Christmas party held at the First Chinese Baptist Church at the end of the alley. The missionary ladies had put together a Santa bag of gifts donated by members of another church. None of the gifts had names on them. There were separate sacks for boys and girls of different ages.

One of the Chinese parishioners had donned a Santa Claus costume and a stiff paper beard with cotton balls glued to it. I think the only children who thought he was the real thing were too young to know that Santa Claus was not Chinese. When my turn came up, the Santa man asked me how old I was. I thought it was a trick question; I was seven according to the American formula and eight by the Chinese calendar. I said I was born on March 17, 1951. That seemed to satisfy him. He then solemnly asked if I had been a very, very good girl this year and did I believe in Jesus Christ and obey my parents. I knew the only answer to that. I nodded back with equal solemnity.

Having watched the other children opening their gifts, I already knew that the big gifts were not necessarily the nicest ones. One girl my age got a large coloring book of biblical characters, while a less greedy girl who selected a smaller box received a glass vial of lavender toilet water. The sound of the box was also important. A ten-year old boy had chosen a box that jangled when he shook it. It was a tin globe of the world with a slit for inserting money. He must have thought it was full of dimes and nickels, because when he saw that it had just ten pennies, his face fell with such undisguised disappointment that his mother slapped the side of his head and led him out of the church hall, apologizing to the crowd for her son who had such bad manners he couldn't appreciate such a fine gift.

As I peered into the sack, I quickly fingered the remaining presents, testing their weight, imagining what they contained. I chose a heavy, compact one that was wrapped in shiny silver foil and a red satin ribbon. It was a twelve-pack of Life Savers and I spent the rest of the party arranging and rearranging the candy tubes in the order of my favorites. My brother Winston chose wisely as well. His present turned out to be a box of intricate plastic parts; the instructions on the box proclaimed that when they were properly assembled he would have an authentic miniature replica of a World War II submarine.

Vincent got the chess set, which would have been a very decent present to get at a church Christmas party, except it was obviously used and, as we discovered later, it was missing a black pawn and a white knight. My mother graciously thanked the unknown benefactor, saying, "Too good. Cost too much." At which point, an old lady with fine white, wispy hair nodded toward our family and said with a whistling whisper, "Merry, merry Christmas."

When we got home, my mother told Vincent to throw the chess set away. "She not want it. We not want it," she said, tossing her head stiffly to the side with a tight, proud smile. My brothers had deaf ears. They were already lining up the chess pieces and reading from the dog-eared instruction book.

Compare the novel you have just read with the literature selection at the left, which is excerpted from "Rules of the Game" in *Glencoe Literature.* Then answer the questions below.

Compare & Contrast

1. Point of View How does the first-person point of view of this selection and *Great Expectations* help to give you an understanding of the narrator of each story?

_____

_____

_____

_____

_____

_____

_____

2. Mood How is the mood that Tan creates in this childhood memory different from the mood Dickens creates for Pip's childhood memories?

_____

_____

_____

_____

_____

_____

_____

3. Irony How does the mother show irony in this selection? How does this compare with the irony Dickens uses in *Great Expectations*?

_____

_____

_____

_____

_____

_____

_____

TALK ABOUT IT

With a small group, talk about how in this selection and in *Great Expectations* the characters have expectations, but they learn that things are not always as they seem. As you discuss, take notes below.

_____

_____

_____

_____

_____

_____

_____

_____

_____

_____

_____

_____

_____

_____

_____

_____

_____

_____

_____

_____

_____

_____

_____

_____

_____

_____

_____

_____

Short Story

Apply Irony Dickens uses verbal irony to add humor to dialogue. He also uses situational irony to build tension and surprise the reader. Think of a situation where someone has an expectation. Write a short story in which this person realizes these expectations were not met.

Prewrite Brainstorm ideas about times when people have expectations. List these situations on a piece of paper. For each situation you listed, write what could happen and then write an alternate possibility. Look at your list and choose the situation that you think has the best ironic twist. When you have chosen the situation you want to write about, free write (write without stopping) for about 10 minutes to get the basic events of that situation down on paper.

Draft For irony to be effective, you have to build up the reader's expectations in your story and then provide an unexpected reality. Keep this in mind as you structure your narrative and organize the events. You can use a chart like the one below, which shows an example of situational irony in *Great Expectations,* to help you make clear the contrast between expectations and reality in your story.

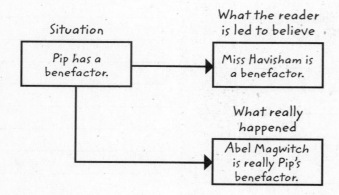

Situation

Pip has a benefactor.

What the reader is led to believe

Miss Havisham is a benefactor.

What really happened

Abel Magwitch is really Pip's benefactor.

As you write, use concrete details (who, what, when, and where) and sensory details (sights, sounds, smells, tastes, and textures) to describe actions, events, thoughts, and feelings. These should connect to the irony you reveal in your short story.

Revise Check that you have used concrete and sensory details to describe your setting and characters. Make sure that the mood of your writing is appropriate for the ironic situation you have written about. For example, if the irony puts the character in a happier situation than was expected, the mood should reflect this change.

Edit and Proofread Edit your writing so that it expresses your thoughts effectively and is well organized. Carefully proofread for grammar, punctuation, and spelling errors.

UNDERSTAND THE TASK

- **Irony** is when someone says one thing but means another or when a character believes one thing will happen but the opposite happens.

- A **short story** is a brief fictional narrative in prose. A short story usually focuses on a single event and has only a few characters.

Grammar Tip

Dashes
Use dashes to show an interruption, pause in a thought, or a moment of dialogue.

A dash can be used to show an interruption that is made to add additional information:

"He had glittering eyes—small, keen, and black—and thin wide mottled lips."

A dash can also be used to show where a line of dialogue is interrupted either by another speaker or by the speaker's own thoughts:

"I live quite pleasantly there; at least—" It appeared to me that I was losing a chance.

. . . And the Earth Did Not Devour Him

Thomás Rivera

. . . And the Earth Did Not Devour Him

Thomás Rivera

"Tierra [. . . And the Earth Did Not Devour Him] *is a novel about sorrow and sadness. This is true. But Rivera is not saying that all Chicanos live in an unfortunate world. The novel is also about a special kind of childhood—the childhood of the artist. Tierra is about a child's delicate feelings, about a child's waning innocence, about people's dreams and hopes, and about gentle transformations of the heart and soul.***"**

—*Eliud Martínez from* **Tomás Rivera: Witness and Storyteller**

Although brief and seemingly simple, Tomás Rivera's *. . . And the Earth Did Not Devour Him* is regarded as a ground-breaking work. The novel demands that readers make connections between the stories and come to their own conclusions about the identity and relationships of the characters and the meaning of nameless people's actions. As professor of Chicano studies Eliud Martínez explains:

Rivera points no accusing fingers, does not judge or indict; the incidents or his characters' stories speak for themselves. The reader draws his own conclusions. Subjectivity of selection of scenes, stories, overheard conversations, however, permit the author to comment, to lament, to express compassion, in order to touch the reader's emotions and feelings.

In the novel, Rivera tries to give voice to migrant workers like the ones he grew up with. His goal is to reveal their hopes, dreams, frustrations, and deprivations as they suffer, pray, celebrate, and remember.

The Episodic Novel *. . . And the Earth Did Not Devour Him* consists of twenty-seven episodes. Twelve of these are titled stories. Thirteen of the episodes are brief, untitled anecdotes, or short stories, that make a point. The remaining two episodes are introductory and concluding narratives that frame the novel and help unify it. Each anecdote is related by subject or theme to the story that comes before or after it. Some characters appear in more than one story; others do not. Some characters are identified; many remain nameless.

"Fragmented" Storytelling Rather than having a traditional plot with rising action, climax, and resolution, the novel presents the fragmented memories of a young boy. Some of the stories and anecdotes are told by the boy, some by a third-person narrator, and still others through the use of dialogue.

Rivera's storytelling technique has been called "fragmented" because he presents incomplete or isolated bits of information. This method allows him to cover a large range of experiences without the normal constraints of a chronologically ordered series of events. The structure of the novel seeks to mimic the way in which memory works and to present the feelings of disorientation—of feeling lost—experienced by many of the migrant workers as they struggle to make sense of a culture that is sometimes very different from their own.

Migrant Workers During World War II, many Americans enlisted in the armed forces, and so there was an increased demand for workers within the American labor force. The bracero ("manual labor") program, negotiated by the United States and Mexico in 1942, made short-term employment available to Mexicans in job areas that were previously closed to them. Over the next five years, more than 250,000 Mexican farm workers temporarily entered the United States to help harvest crops. Once the harvest season was over, the braceros returned to Mexico. At the same time, however, hundreds of thousands of other Mexican Americans—often whole families—illegally entered the United States by swimming or walking across borders into Texas, Arizona, and California.

Many of these farm workers were cruelly exploited, enduring long hours of back-breaking work, poor food, and substandard housing. Children worked in the fields beside their parents in an effort to increase the combined earnings of the family. Those who were too young to work were left with elderly family members or had to fend for themselves while their parents were at work. Few children attended school, and their health often suffered because of poor nutrition, inadequate health care, and environmental hazards. Wages of thirty cents an hour were common; however, these wages were significantly higher than those earned in Mexico for the same type of labor.

In 1954 the Eisenhower administration launched a program to try to restrain the flow of undocumented immigrants from Mexico. Over the course of the next three years, the government sent approximately 3.7 million allegedly illegal migrants back to Mexico. Often civil rights were ignored and families broken up. Authorities did not always distinguish among illegal aliens, braceros, and Mexican American citizens, and thousands of citizens were deported.

El Movimiento

Around the time that Rivera wrote . . . *And the Earth Did Not Devour Him* (1967–1968), other Chicano writers and artists were also finding expression for their ideas and opinions. As a matter of fact, production of art and literature was so great at this time that these years came to be known as a Chicano renaissance, or *El Movimiento* (The Movement). According to *The Hispanic-American Almanac*, Chicano literature written during "the decade of the 1960s was characterized by a questioning of all the commonly accepted truths in . . . society, foremost of which was the question of equality." Politically charged, *El Movimiento* was particularly concerned with civil rights, the farm labor struggle, and the Vietnam War.

Mexican American poets were among the first writers to gain prominence in the movement. Because of the nature of verse, they could easily recite their poetry before groups of students and workers. They wrote in both English and Spanish, hoping to reach the widest possible audience.

One of the most significant pieces of literature produced at this time was written by an ex-boxer from Colorado, Rodolfo "Corky" González. His poem *I Am Joaquín/ Yo Soy Joaquín* was passed hand to hand, read at rallies, and performed in the street. The poem speaks of the struggles of Mexican Americans and calls on them to maintain their unique identity and heritage. It also inspired an interest in Chicano literature at the grassroots level. New works by Chicano writers and artists flourished in the years that followed.

Rivera himself played an important role in *El Movimiento*, promoting Chicano authors and contributing to the development of a Chicano literature. His novel . . . *And the Earth Did Not Devour Him* became a landmark in the Mexican American community's search for identity.

Tomás Rivera *(1935–1984)*

> **❝***I saw a lot of suffering and much isolation of the people. Yet they lived through the whole thing, perhaps because they had no choice. I saw a lot of heroic people and I wanted to capture their feelings.***❞**
>
> —*Tomás Rivera, interview with Juan Bruce-Novoa*

If it is true that authors write best about that which they know, then it is no surprise that Tomás Rivera wrote so well about migrant farm workers. When Rivera was a boy, he and his parents, who had immigrated to Texas from Mexico, traveled north every year to pick crops in the Midwest. Rivera knew firsthand the difficulties that these workers faced and the nobility and courage with which they faced their difficulties.

Rivera was born in Crystal City, Texas, in 1935. Although his family's need to travel from place to place made it difficult for him to attend school, his parents made his education a priority. By the time Rivera graduated from high school, he was fluent in both English and Spanish. Rivera went on to attend college, earning a bachelor's degree in English, a master's degree in education administration, and a doctorate in romance languages and literature.

A Lifelong Educator After teaching English and Spanish for several years, Rivera became a university administrator. Education was extremely important to Rivera, particularly the education of Hispanic Americans. In 1979 Rivera was appointed chancellor of the University of California, Riverside. He was the university's first Chicano (Mexican American) chancellor and its youngest administrator.

In addition to his role as a university administrator, Rivera played an important role in the development of Chicano literature. He offered encouragement to Chicano authors and promoted Chicano literature and culture as areas of study in the college curriculum.

Telling Stories Rivera is most remembered, however, as an author. Although some people found it remarkable that the son of migrant farm workers would go on to write and publish stories, Rivera himself did not. As he explained in an article in *Atisbos: Journal of Chicano Research*, storytelling was important to the migrant workers with whom he grew up. He wrote:

There was always someone [in the camps] *who knew the old traditional stories. . . . Then there were always those who acted out movies, told about different parts of the world and about Aladdin and his magic lamp. An oral literature was, in that way, developed in the migrant camps. People find refuge not only in the Church or with their brothers but also by sitting in a circle, listening, telling stories and, through words, escaping to other worlds as well as inventing them.*

Rivera's body of work was relatively small— one incomplete novel in addition to . . . *And the Earth Did Not Devour Him,* several short stories, poems, and literary essays. Armed with a powerful memory and an expert eye to detail, Rivera preserved his own past in his stories. At the same time, he preserved the past of other migrant farm workers.

Connect to the Literature

Suppose you woke up one morning and could not remember what had taken place during the last year of your life. How would you feel? What would you do?

Quickwrite

Imagine what the effects of such a loss of memory might be like. Record your thoughts and feelings about losing a year. Use the questions above to help you get started.

Build Background

Fighting for the United States

Between 300,000 and 400,000 Mexican Americans served in the U.S. Armed Forces during World War II, a number far higher than their proportion of the draft-age population. Mexican Americans won seventeen Congressional Medals of Honor, the highest United States military decoration. Countless others received Distinguished Service Medals and Silver Stars for their acts of bravery. Mexican Americans also earned disinguished military records during the Korean War of the early 1950s. (During this war, the United States supported South Korea's battle against North Korean invaders. North Korea was aided by the Union of Soviet Socialist Republics and Communist China.)

In spite of their accomplishments on the battlefield, Mexican American soldiers continued to face discrimination and prejudice when they returned home. Some chapters of the American Legion refused to allow Chicanos to become members, and, like other Chicanos, many veterans were barred from Anglo restaurants, stores, and schools. In an effort to help end discrimination, Dr. Hector Garcia founded the GI Forum. The group continues to provide services to Chicanos and other Hispanics who have served in the U.S. armed forces.

NOVEL NOTEBOOK

Keep a special notebook to record entries about the novels that you read this year.

SUMMARIZE

Summarize in one sentence the most important idea(s) in Build Background.

_____
_____
_____
_____
_____
_____
_____
_____
_____
_____
_____
_____
_____
_____
_____
_____
_____
_____
_____
_____
_____
_____
_____
_____
_____
_____
_____
_____
_____

Set Purposes for Reading

▶ **BIG Idea** Looking Into Lives

As you read, think about the ways in which the immigrant farm workers' hopes and dreams are similar to yours. What particular challenges do they face that make these hopes and dreams difficult to achieve? Do you face similar challenges?

Literary Element   Anecdote

An **anecdote** is a short written or oral account of an event from a person's life. Essayists often use anecdotes to support their opinions, clarify their ideas, grab the reader's attention, or entertain. Autobiographies and biographies are often largely comprised of anecdotes.

Anecdotes enable readers to develop a deeper understanding of the character whose experience is being shared. They accomplish this by providing details about the character's environment, relationships, and motivations.

As you read, ask yourself why the author included a specific anecdote at a certain point in the novel. Consider what this anecdote reveals both about the characters involved and about the environment in which these characters live.

Reading Strategy   Activate Prior Knowledge

When you **activate prior knowledge** you consider what you already know about a person, place, idea or event in a literary work and using that knowledge to deepen your understanding of what you are reading.

Activating prior knowledge enables you to develop a broader context for the text, and it helps you understand the author's purpose more fully.

Before you read, consider what you already know about the novel's topic. As you read each chapter within the text, make note of references to historical events, people or situations and take a minute to recall what you already know about them. You may find it helpful to use a graphic organizer like the one at the right. Use the graphic organizer on the next page to help you keep track of what you know, want to know and learn as you read.

Vocabulary

beseech [bi sēch´]
v. to address a serious request to
Brian urged his parents, "I beseech you, please allow me to help the stray dog."

implore [im plôr´]
v. to beg
After the first snowfall, children often implore their parents to let them play outside in the snow.

homage [hom´ ij]
n. special honor or respect expressed publicly
In her memoir, she paid homage to the teacher who had encouraged her to be a writer.

palpitating [pal´ pə tāt´ ing]
v. beating very quickly
He was so nervous about playing in the recital that his heart was palpitating wildly.

Detail	Prior Knowledge

Because this novel has an unusual structure, you may at first have more questions than you have answers. Fill in this organizer during and after your reading to keep track of events and characters.

What I KNOW (facts and inferences about plot, characters, theme)	What I WANT to Know (questions that arise during reading)	What I LEARNED (conclusions drawn after reading and discussing)
a boy's confusion between being awake and asleep	Where are these events taking place ?	in a Mexican American community of migrant workers

Literary Element

Anecdote According to the first anecdote, why is getting an education so important to the narrator?

_____
_____
_____
_____
_____
_____
_____
_____
_____
_____
_____
_____
_____
_____
_____
_____
_____
_____
_____
_____
_____
_____
_____
_____
_____
_____
_____
_____
_____

NOVEL EXCERPT: IT'S THAT IT HURTS

But how could I even think of leaving knowing that everyone at home wanted me to go to school. Anyways, the janitor stood with his broom up in the air, ready for anything . . . And then they just told me to leave.

I'm halfway home. This cemetery is real pretty. It doesn't look anything like the one in Texas. That one is scarey, I don't like it at all. What scares me the most is when we're leaving after a burial and I look up and I read the letters on the arch over the gate that say, Don't forget me. It's like I can hear all the dead people buried there saying these words and then the sound of these words stays in my mind and sometimes even if I don't look up when I pass through the gate, I still see them. But not this one, this one is real pretty. Just lots of soft grass and trees, I guess that's why here when people bury somebody they don't even cry. I like playing here. If only they would let us fish in the little creek that runs through here, there's lots of fish. But no, you even need a license to fish and then they don't even sell us one 'cause we're from out of state.

I won't be able to go to school anymore. What am I going to tell them? They've told me over and over that our teachers are like our second parents . . . and now? And when we get back to Texas everyone will find out too. Mother and Dad will be angry; I might get more than just a whipping. And then my Uncle will find out and Grandpa. Maybe they might even send me to a reform school like the ones I've heard them talk about. There they turn you into a good person if you're bad. They're real hard on you. They leave you soft as a glove. But maybe they didn't expel me, *sure they did,* maybe not, *sure they did.* I could make like I'm going to school and stay here in the cemetery. That would be better. But then what? I could tell them that I lost my report card. And then what if I stay in the same grade? What hurt me the most is that now I won't be able to be a telephone operator like Dad wants me to. You need to finish school for that.

"Vieja, call m'ijo out here . . . look, compadre, ask your godson what he wants to be when he grows up and finishes school."

"What will you be, godson?"

"I don't know."

"Tell him! Don't be embarrassed. He's your godfather."

"What will you be, son ?"

"A telephone operator."

"Is that so?"

"Yes, compadre, he's very determined, you know that? Every time we ask him he says he wants to be an operator. I think they pay well. I told the boss the other day and he laughed. I don't think he believes that my son can do it, but that's 'cause he doesn't know him. He's smarter than anything. I just pray God helps him finish school so he can become an operator."

That movie was good. The operator was the most important one. Ever since then I suppose that's why Dad has wanted me to study for that after I finish school. But . . . maybe they didn't throw me out. What if it's not true? Maybe not. Sure, it is. What do I tell them? What do I do? Now they won't be able to ask me what I'm going to be when I grow up. Maybe not. No, yeah. What do I do? It's that it hurts and it's embarrassing at the same time. I better just stay here. No, but then Mother will get scared like she does when there's lightning and thunder. I've gotta tell them. And when my padrino comes to visit us I'll just hide. No need for him to find out. Nor for me to read to him like Dad has me do every time he comes to visit us. What I'll do when he comes is hide behind the chest or under the bed. That way Dad and Mother won't feel embarrassed. And what if I really wasn't expelled? Maybe I wasn't? No, yeah.

Why do y'all go to school so much?"

"My Dad says it's to prepare us. He says that if someday there's an opportunity, maybe they'll give it to us."

"Sure! If I were you I wouldn't worry about that. The poor can't get poorer. We can't get worst off than we already are. That's why I don't worry. The ones who have to be on their toes are the ones who are higher up. They've got something to lose. They can end up where we're at. But for us what does it matter?"

Literary Element

Anecdote In the second anecdote, consider the questioner's attitude toward education. Why might the author have placed these two anecdotes next to each other?

_____

_____

_____

_____

_____

_____

_____

_____

_____

_____

_____

_____

_____

_____

_____

_____

_____

_____

_____

_____

_____

_____

_____

_____

_____

_____

Reading Strategy

Activate Prior Knowledge What prior knowledge is required for you to fully understand this excerpt?

_____

_____

_____

_____

_____

_____

_____

_____

_____

_____

_____

_____

_____

_____

_____

_____

_____

_____

_____

_____

_____

_____

_____

_____

_____

_____

NOVEL EXCERPT: THE CHILDREN COULDN'T WAIT

She had fallen asleep right away and everyone, very mindful of not crossing their arms nor their legs nor their hands, watched her intensely. The spirit was already present in her body.

"Let's see, how may I help you this evening, brothers and sisters?"

"Well, you see, I haven't heard from my boy in two months. Yesterday a letter from the government arrived telling me that he's lost in action. I'd like to know whether or not he's alive. I feel like I'm losing my mind just thinking and thinking about it."

"Have no fear, sister. Julianito is fine. He's just fine. Don't worry about him anymore. Very soon he'll be in your arms. He'll be returning already next month."

"Thank you, thank you."

NOVEL EXCERPT: A PRAYER

Dear God, Jesus Christ, keeper of my soul. This is the third Sunday that I come to implore you, beg you, to give me word of my son. I have not heard from him. Protect him, my God, that no bullet may pierce his heart like it happened to Doña Virginia's son, may he rest in God's peace. Take care of him for me, Dear Jesus, save him from the gunfire, have pity on him who is so good. Since he was a baby, when I would nurse him to sleep, he was so gentle, very grateful, never biting me. He's very innocent, protect him, he does not wish to harm anyone, he is very noble, he is very kind, may no bullet pierce his heart.

Please, Virgin Mary, you, too, shelter him. Shield his body, cover his head, cover the eyes of the Communists and the Koreans and the Chinese so that they cannot see him, so they won't kill him. I still keep his toys from when he was a child, his little cars, little trucks, even a kite that I found the other day in the closet. Also his cards and the funnies that he has learned to read. I have put everything away until his return.

Protect him, Jesus, that they may not kill him. I have made a promise to the Virgen de San Juan to pay her homage at her shrine and to the Virgen de Guadalupe, too. He also wears a little medallion of the Virgen de San Juan del Valle and he, too, has made a promise to her; he wants to live. Take care of him, cover his heart with your hand, that no bullet may enter it. He's very noble. He was very afraid to go, he told me so. The day they took him, when he said his farewell he embraced me and he cried for a while. I could feel his heart beating and I remembered when he was little and I would nurse him and the happiness that I felt and he felt.

Take care of him for me, please, I beseech you. I promise you my life for his. Bring him back from Korea safe and sound. Cover his heart with your hands. Jesus Christ, Holy God, Virgen de Guadalupe, bring him back alive, bring me back his heart. Why have they taken him? He has done no harm. He knows nothing. He is very humble. He doesn't want to take away anybody's life. Bring him back alive, I don't want him to die.

Here is my heart for his. Here is my heart. Here in my chest, palpitating. Tear it out if blood is what you want, but tear it out of me. I sacrifice my heart for his. Here it is. Here is my heart! Through it runs his very own blood . . .

Bring him back alive and I will give you my very own heart.

Reading Strategy

Activate Prior Knowledge Briefly research one name, place or event in this excerpt with which you are unfamiliar. In the space below, explain how this information helped you understand more about the speaker's prayer.

_____
_____
_____
_____
_____
_____
_____
_____
_____
_____
_____
_____
_____
_____
_____
_____
_____
_____
_____
_____
_____
_____
_____
_____

Are you allowed to write in your novel? If so, then mark up the pages as you read, or reread, to help with your note-taking. Develop a shorthand system, including symbols, that works for you. Here are some ideas:

Underline = important idea

Bracket = text to quote

Asterisk = just what you were looking for

Checkmark = might be useful

Circle = unfamiliar word or phrase to look up

▶ **BIG Idea**

Looking Into Lives How do Don Laíto and Doña Bone show how they care about the migrant workers?

Mark up the excerpt, looking for evidence of how it expresses the Big Idea.

NOVEL EXCERPT: HAND IN HIS POCKET

Remember Don Laíto and Doña Bone? That's what everyone called them but their names were Don Hilario and Doña Bonifacia. Don't you remember? Well, I had to live with them for three weeks until school ended. At first I liked it but then later on I didn't.

Everything that people used to say about them behind their backs was true. About how they baked the bread, the pastries, how they would sometimes steal and that they were bootleggers. I saw it all. Anyways, they were good people but by the time school was about to end I was afraid of being with them in that Model-T that they had and even of sleeping in their house. And towards the end I didn't even feel like eating. That's why I'd go to the little neighborhood store to buy me some candy. And that's how I got along until my Dad, my Mother and my brothers and sisters came to get me.

I remember they were very nice to me on the first day. Don Laíto laughed a lot and you could see his gold teeth and the rotten ones, too. And every little while Doña Bone, fat as could be, would grab me and squeeze me against her and I could feel her, real fat. They fed me dinner—I say *fed* me because *they* didn't eat. Now that I'm remembering, you know, I never saw them eat. The meat that she fried for me was green and it smelled really bad when she was cooking it. But after a while it didn't smell as much. But I don't know whether this was because I got used to the smell or because Don Laíto opened the window. Just parts of it tasted bad. I ate it all because I didn't want to hurt their feelings. Everybody liked Don Laíto and Doña Bone. Even the Anglos were fond of them. They gave them canned foods, clothes, toys. And when Don Laíto and Doña Bone weren't able to sell these to us, they'd give them to us. They would also pay us visits out in the fields to sell us Mexican sweetbread, thread and needles, canned food and nopalitos, and also shoes, coats and other things that sometimes were good, sometimes pretty bad.

"Won't you buy these shoes . . . oh, come on . . . I know they're used, but they're the expensive kind . . . look how they're not worn out yet . . . these . . . I guarantee you, they last until they wear out . . . "

Use the Cornell Note-Taking system to take notes on the excerpt at the left. Record your notes, Reduce them, and then Recap (summarize) them.

Record

_____
_____
_____
_____
_____
_____
_____
_____
_____
_____
_____
_____
_____
_____
_____
_____
_____
_____
_____
_____
_____
_____

Recap

_____
_____
_____
_____
_____
_____

Reduce

Try the following approach as you reduce your notes.

ASK QUESTIONS

Write any questions you have about the novel. Do you have to go to an outside source to find the answers?

_____
_____
_____
_____
_____
_____
_____
_____
_____
_____
_____
_____
_____
_____
_____
_____
_____
_____
_____
_____
_____
_____

Respond and Think Critically

1. Why is the narrator of "It's That It Hurts" expelled from school? In your opinion, what is the "it" that hurts the narrator? [Infer]

_____

_____

_____

_____

2. Describe the couple with whom the boy in "Hand in His Pocket" lives. In your opinion, what causes the boy to slip his hand in his pocket whenever he sees a stranger? [Interpret]

_____

_____

_____

_____

3. Briefly describe at least one of the incidents in which a character is discriminated against. How does the character respond? In your opinion is the response believable? Explain. [Evaluate]

_____

_____

_____

_____

4. After reading the stories, what do you think might be troubling the boy in "The Lost Year"? What may have caused him to lose his memory? Explain. [Conclude]

_____

_____

_____

5. **Looking Into Lives** Which character in these chapters do you feel most connected to? What qualities do you and this character have in common? [Connect]

_____

_____

_____

_____

APPLY BACKGROUND
Reread Build Background on page 79. How did that information help you understand or appreciate what you read in the novel?

_____

_____

_____

_____

_____

_____

_____

_____

_____

_____

_____

_____

_____

_____

_____

_____

_____

_____

_____

_____

_____

_____

_____

Literary Element **Anecdote**

Which anecdote in this section helped you best understand the struggles that the migrant farm workers endure? [Conclude]

_____
_____
_____
_____
_____
_____
_____
_____
_____
_____
_____
_____

Reading Strategy **Activate Prior Knowledge**

How does your understanding of discrimination influence your feelings about the narrator's situation in "It's That It Hurts"? [Connect]

_____
_____
_____
_____
_____
_____
_____
_____
_____
_____
_____
_____

Vocabulary Practice

Respond to these questions.

1. In which situation would you **beseech** someone to listen to you—you are about to share some bad news or you want to explain which team played the best defensive game last night?

_____

2. In which situation should you **implore** a passerby to help you—you need directions to the local grocery store or you need directions to the emergency room of the local hospital?

_____

3. Who would you pay **homage** to—the friend who baked you cookies or the grandfather who fought valiantly in World War II?

_____

4. Which situation would most likely cause your heart to start **palpitating**—speaking in front of two hundred people or speaking to your brother on the telephone?

_____

Academic Vocabulary

The lettuce farm owner used his **authority** to control and intimidate the migrant workers. In the preceding sentence, _authority_ means "power to influence thoughts or behavior." _Authority_ also has other meanings. For instance: _Robert is a world-renowned **authority** on climate change; for years, he has studied the effects of global warming._ What do you think _authority_ means in the preceding sentence? What is the difference between the two meanings?

_____
_____
_____
_____
_____
_____

Writing

Personal Response Which story did you find the most powerful? Why?

_____

_____

_____

_____

_____

_____

_____

_____

_____

_____

_____

_____

_____

_____

_____

_____

_____

_____

_____

_____

_____

_____

_____

_____

_____

_____

_____

_____

_____

_____

_____

_____

Speaking and Listening

Oral Interpretation

Assignment With a small group of your classmates, choose one of the stories in which the characters experience discrimination, and interpret it orally for the class.

Prepare Together, reread the story aloud and discuss the kind of discrimination that is illustrated. Consider the tone of voice, pacing, and gestures you might need to bring it to life for your audience. Then divide up the scene so each group member has a chance to read. Rehearse your scene until you feel that you are ready to perform it.

Perform and Discuss Perform your scene for the class. Be sure to face your audience and speak loudly and clearly. After you perform, participate in a discussion about the choices your group made in your interpretation.

Evaluate After your performance, meet with your group to discuss how successful your performance and the subsequent discussion were and how they might have been better. Use a chart like the one below to record your group's ideas.

Good points that came up during the discussion	What worked well	What needed improvement

Connect to the Literature

Recall a time when you felt powerless, as if you were not capable of having an impact on someone or something.

Write a Journal Entry

Think about a time when your age, inexperience, or some other factor made you unable to command a situation in a way you would have liked. Write about the situation, what made you powerless, and how it felt.

Build Background

The Evolution of a Name

During the 1940s and 1950s, immigrants from Spain, Portugal, and from anywhere below the southern border of the United States were referred to simply as *Spanish*, regardless of their place of birth. As more people came to the United States from Mexico, Central America, Cuba, and other countries, a new term was added to describe the ancestry of these immigrants. *Hispanic* was widely used during the 1960s, but it was improperly applied to define the entire Spanish-speaking population as a race and culture. Furthermore, the term was coined by mainstream Americans. The use of the term *Hispanic* by the dominant American culture resulted in the stereotyping of a widely diverse group of people. During the civil rights movement of the 1960s and early 1970s, young Mexican Americans began calling themselves *Chicanos*. In the 1980s, the term *Hispanic* reappeared to refer to any person living in the United States who is of Spanish ancestry. More recently, *Latino* has become a term of choice for many Mexican Americans, Cuban Americans, and Puerto Ricans living on the the mainland.

NOVEL NOTEBOOK
Keep a special notebook to record entries about the novels that you read this year.

SUMMARIZE
Summarize in one sentence the most important idea(s) in Build Background.

_____
_____
_____
_____
_____
_____
_____
_____
_____
_____
_____
_____
_____
_____
_____
_____
_____
_____
_____
_____
_____
_____
_____
_____
_____
_____
_____
_____

Set Purposes for Reading

▶ BIG Idea Finding Common Ground

Recall a time when you needed to ally with others who shared your opinion about a topic. For example, a group of community members might join forces to stop the construction of a new housing development in their town, or students might come together to oppose a new school rule that they deem unfair. Were you able to convince others to consider your opinions?

As you read, consider how much power the farm workers have to change their situations for the better. Are they able to join together to fight for better working and living conditions? Why or why not?

Literary Element Tone

Tone refers to the author's attitude toward his or her subject matter. Tone is conveyed through elements such as word choice, rhythm, sentence structure and figures of speech.

A writer's tone may convey a variety of attitudes, such as sympathy, objectivity, seriousness, irony, sadness, bitterness, or humor. Recognizing tone can help you determine the author's purpose in writing a specific text.

As you read, think about how the author reveals his feelings and attitudes.

Reading Strategy Identify Problem and Solution

When you **identify problem and solution,** you look for obstacles, conflicts, and problems and identify how they are, or can be, solved.

This process can help you understand the purpose of a literary work and provide you with greater insight into its characters.

As you read, identify both the problems that arise in the narrator's world and the solutions that he develops for these problems. You might find it helpful to use a graphic organizer like the one at the right. The graphic organizer on the next page can also help you keep track of problems and solutions as you read.

Vocabulary

clamoring [klam′ ər ing]
v. making a sustained outcry

When the politician visited their local school, parents were clamoring to voice their frustrations about the recent school budget cuts.

sacrilege [sak′ rə lij]
n. destruction or misuse of something sacred

Destroying a statue of a religious figure is considered sacrilege in many faiths.

scapularies [skap′ yə lər ēz]
n. squares of cloth joined by shoulder tapes, often worn to show religious devotion

Individuals who wish to express their religious devotion sometimes wear scapularies under their clothes.

venial [vē′ nē əl]
adj. easily excused or forgiven, as in a venial sin

Her parents did not get too upset when they found out what she had done; the sin she committed was a venial one.

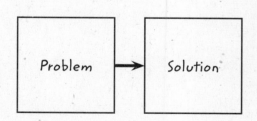

Defining a problem and evaluating its solutions are as helpful in understanding fiction as they are in solving real-life conflicts. As you read this section, fill out this problem/solution graphic organizer for one of the problems, or conflicts, a character or characters experience. Use as many boxes as you need.

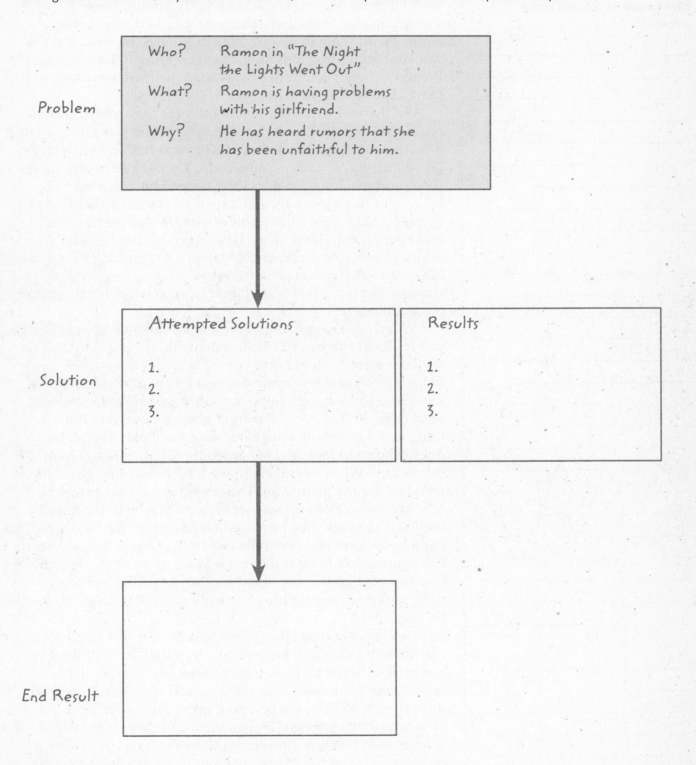

Problem

Who?   Ramon in "The Night the Lights Went Out"

What?   Ramon is having problems with his girlfriend.

Why?   He has heard rumors that she has been unfaithful to him.

Solution

Attempted Solutions

1.
2.
3.

Results

1.
2.
3.

End Result

Literary Element

Tone What attitude does the author have toward his subjects in this passage?

_____
_____
_____
_____
_____
_____
_____
_____
_____
_____
_____
_____
_____
_____
_____
_____
_____
_____
_____
_____
_____
_____
_____
_____
_____
_____
_____
_____
_____

NOVEL EXCERPT: THE NIGHT THE LIGHTS WENT OUT

"Oh, come on. You know everybody knows. I heard something else. Somebody told me that she'd been going around with some dude out there in Minnesota. And that she still kept on writing to Ramón. Kept on lying to him. Some of Ramón's friends told him everything. They were working at the same farm where she was.

And then when they saw him out here they told him right off. He was faithful to her but she wasn't. She was going around with some guy from San Antonio. He was nothing but a show-off and he was always all duded up. They say he wore orange shoes and real long coats and always had his collar turned up . . . But her, I think she liked to mess around, otherwise she wouldn't have been unfaithful. What was bad was her not breaking up with him. When he found out, Juanita hadn't returned yet from up north and he took to drinking a lot. I saw him once when he was drunk and all he would say was that he was hurting. That that was all that women left behind, nothing but pain inside."

"When I get back to Texas I'll take her away with me. I can't go on like this anymore. She'll come with me. She will. She's done me wrong. How I love her. With each swing of this hoe I hear her name. How come you feel this way when you're in love? I no sooner finish supper and I'm staring at her picture until dark. And at noon, during the lunch hour, too. But the thing is, I don't really remember how she looks. The picture doesn't seem to look like her anymore. Or she doesn't look like the picture. When the others make fun of me, I just go off to the woods. I see the picture but I just don't remember anymore how she looks, even if I see her picture. Maybe it's best to not look at it so much. She promised she'd be faithful. And she is, because her eyes and her smile keep telling me so when I picture her in my mind. Soon it'll be time to return to Texas. Each time I wake to the early crow of the roosters I feel like I'm already there and that I'm watching her walk down the street. It won't be long now."

"Well, it's not that I don't love Ramón, but this guy, he's a real smooth talker and we just talk, that's all. And all the girls just stare at him. He dresses really fine, too. It's not that I don't love Ramón, but this guy is real nice and his smile, I see it all day long . . . No, I'm not breaking up with Ramón. And, anyway, what's wrong with just talking? I don't want to get serious with this guy, I promised Ramón . . . but he just keeps on following and following me around. I don't want to get serious with him . . . I don't want to lose Ramón, I'm not getting involved with this guy. I just want him around to make the other girls jealous. No, I can't break up with Ramón because I really do love him a lot. It won't be long before we'll see each other again . . . Who said he was talking to Petra? Well, then, why is he always following me around? I'll have you know he even sends me letters every day with Don José's little boy."

" . . . I know you're going with someone else but I like talking to you. Since I got here and saw you I want to be with you more and more. Go to the dance Saturday and dance with me all night . . . Love you, Ramiro."

"They say she danced the whole night with Ramiro. I think her friends told her something about it but she just ignored them. This happened about the time when the work season was almost over and at the last dance, when they were saying good-bye, they promised to see each other back here. I don't think she even remembered Ramón at that moment. But by then Ramón already knew everything. That's why on that day, after not seeing each other in four months, he threw it all in her face. I was with him that day, I was with him when he saw her and I remember well that he was so happy to see her that he wasn't mad anymore. But then, after talking to her for a while he started getting mad all over again. They broke up right then and there."

"You do whatever you want."

"You can be sure of that."

"You're breaking up with me?"

"Yeah, and if you go to the dance tonight you better not dance with anyone else."

"And why shouldn't I? We're not going around anymore. We broke up. You can't tell me what to do."

"I don't care if we broke up or not. You're gonna pay for this. You're gonna do what I say, when I say and for as long as I say. Nobody makes a fool out of me. You're gonna pay for this one, one way or another."

"You can't tell me what to do."

"You're gonna do what I say and if you don't dance with me, you don't dance with anyone. And I mean for the entire dance."

Literary Element

Tone Create a list of at least five words or phrases in this excerpt that helped to establish the tone you identified.

_____
_____
_____
_____
_____
_____
_____
_____
_____
_____
_____
_____
_____
_____
_____
_____
_____
_____
_____
_____
_____
_____
_____
_____
_____
_____
_____
_____
_____

Identify Problem and Solution
What problem does the narrator feel
helpless to solve in this excerpt?

_____
_____
_____
_____
_____
_____
_____
_____
_____
_____
_____
_____
_____
_____
_____
_____
_____
_____
_____
_____
_____
_____
_____
_____

NOVEL EXCERPT: AND THE EARTH DID NOT DEVOUR HIM

That day started out cloudy and he could feel the morning coolness brushing his eyelashes as he and his brothers and sisters began the day's labor. Their mother had to stay home to care for her husband. Thus, he felt responsible for hurrying on his brothers and sisters. During the morning, at least for the first few hours, they endured the heat but by ten-thirty the sun had suddenly cleared the skies and pressed down against the world. They began working more slowly because of the weakness, dizziness and suffocation they felt when they worked too fast. Then they had to wipe the sweat from their eyes every little while because their vision would get blurred.

"If you start blacking out, stop working, you hear me? Or go a little slower. When we reach the edge we'll rest a bit to get our strength back. It's gonna be hot today. If only it'd stay just a bit cloudy like this morning, then nobody would complain. But no, once the sun bears down like this not even one little cloud dares to appear out of fear. And the worst of it is we'll finish up here by two and then we have to go over to that other field that's nothing but hills. It's okay at the top of the hill but down in the lower part of the slopes it gets to be real suffocating. There's no breeze there. Hardly any air goes through. Remember?"

"Yeah."

"That's where the hottest part of the day will catch us. just drink plenty of water every little while. It don't matter if the boss gets mad. Just don't get sick. And if you can't go on, tell me right away, all right? We'll go home. Y'all saw what happened to Dad when he pushed himself too hard. The sun has no mercy, it can eat you alive."

Just as they had figured, they had moved on to the other field by early afternoon. By three o'clock they were all soaked with sweat. Not one part of their clothing was dry. Every little while they would stop. At times they could barely breath, then they would black out and they would become fearful of getting sunstruck, but they kept on working.

"How do y'all feel?"

"Man, it's so hot! But we've got to keep on. 'Til six, at least. Except this water don't help our thirst any. Sure wish I had a bottle of cool water, real cool, fresh from the well, or a coke ice-cold."

"Are you crazy? That'd sure make you sunsick right now. Just don't work so fast. Let's see if we can make it until six. What do you think?"

At four o'clock the youngest became ill. He was only nine years old, but since he was paid the same as a grown up he tried to keep up with the rest. He began vomiting. He sat down, then he laid down. Terrified, the other children ran to where he lay and looked at him. It appeared that he had fainted and when they opened his eyelids they saw his eyes were rolled back. The next youngest child started crying but right away he told him to stop and help him carry his brother home. It seemed he was having cramps all over his little body. He lifted him and carried him by himself and, again, he began asking himself *why?*

"Why Dad and then my little brother? He's only nine years old. Why? He has to work like a mule buried in the earth. Dad, Mom, and my little brother here, what are they guilty of?"

Each step that he took towards the house resounded with the question, *why?* About halfway to the house he began to get furious. Then he started crying out of rage. His little brothers and sisters did not know what to do, and they, too, started crying, but out of fear. Then he started cursing. And without even realizing it, he said what he had been wanting to say for a long time. He cursed God. Upon doing this he felt that fear instilled in him by the years and by his parents. For a second he saw the earth opening up to devour him. Then he felt his footsteps against the earth, compact, more solid than ever. Then his anger swelled up again and he vented it by cursing God. He looked at his brother, he no longer looked sick. He didn't know whether his brothers and sisters had understood the graveness of his curse.

That night he did not fall asleep until very late. He felt at peace as never before. He felt as though he had become detached from everything. He no longer worried about his father nor his brother. All that he awaited was the new day, the freshness of the morning. By daybreak his father was doing better. He was on his way to recovery. And his little brother, too; the cramps had almost completely subsided. Frequently he felt a sense of surprise upon recalling what he had done the previous afternoon. He thought of telling his mother, but he decided to keep it secret. All he told her was that the earth did not devour anyone, nor did the sun.

He left for work and encountered a very cool morning. There were clouds in the sky and for the first time he felt capable of doing and undoing anything that he pleased. He looked down at the earth and kicked it hard and said.

"Not yet, you can't swallow me up yet. Someday, yes. But I'll never know it."

Reading Strategy

Identify Problem and Solution
Why is the narrator so surprised that his solution does not backfire on him?

_____

_____

_____

_____

_____

_____

_____

_____

_____

_____

_____

_____

_____

_____

_____

_____

_____

_____

_____

_____

_____

_____

_____

_____

_____

_____

_____

_____

_____

MARK IT UP

Are you allowed to write in your novel? If so, then mark up the pages as you read, or reread, to help with your note-taking. Develop a shorthand system, including symbols, that works for you. Here are some ideas:

Underline = important idea

Bracket = text to quote

Asterisk = just what you were looking for

Checkmark = might be useful

Circle = unfamiliar word or phrase to look up

▶ BIG Idea

Finding Common Ground Think about what you have learned about the immigrant farm workers' efforts to find common ground in order to fight against harsh working and living conditions.

Mark up the excerpt, looking for evidence of how it expresses the Big Idea.

NOVEL EXCERPT: FIRST COMMUNION

The priest always held First Communion during mid-spring. I'll always remember that day in my life. I remember what I was wearing and I remember my godfather and the pastries and chocolate that we had after mass, but I also remember what I saw at the cleaners that was next to the church. I think it all happened because I left so early for church. It's that I hadn't been able to sleep the night before, trying to remember all of my sins, and worse yet, trying to arrive at an exact number. Furthermore, since Mother had placed a picture of hell at the head of the bed and since the walls of the room were papered with images of the devil and since I wanted salvation from all evil, that was all I could think of.

"Remember, children, very quiet, very very quiet. You have learned your prayers well, and now you know which are the mortal sins and which are the venial sins, now you know what sacrilege is, now you know that you are God's children, but you can also be children of the devil. When you go to confession you must tell all of your sins, you must try to remember all of the sins you have committed. Because if you forget one and receive Holy Communion then that would be a sacrilege and if you commit sacrilege you will go to hell. God knows all. You cannot lie to God. You can lie to me and to the priest, but God knows everything; so if your soul is not pure of sin, then you should not receive Holy Communion. That would be a sacrilege. So everyone confess all of your sins. Recall all of your sins. Wouldn't you be ashamed if you received Holy Communion and then later remembered a sin that you had forgotten to confess? Now, let's see, let us practice confessing our sins. Who would like to start off? Let us begin with the sins that we commit with our hands when we touch our bodies. Who would like to start?"

The nun liked for us to talk about the sins of the flesh. The real truth was that we practiced a lot telling our sins, but the real truth was that I didn't understand a lot of things. What did scare me was the idea of going to hell because some months earlier I had fallen against a small basin filled with hot coals which we used as a heater in the little room where we slept. I had burned my calf. I could well imagine how it might be to burn in hell forever. That was all that I understood. So I spent that night, the eve of my First Communion, going over all the sins I had committed. But what was real hard was coming up with the exact number like the nun wanted us to. It must have been dawn by the time I finally satisfied my conscience. I had committed one hundred and fifty sins, but I was going to admit to two-hundred.

Use the Cornell Note-Taking system to take notes on the excerpt at the left. Record your notes, Reduce them, and then Recap (summarize) them.

Record

_____

_____

_____

_____

_____

_____

_____

_____

_____

_____

_____

_____

_____

_____

_____

_____

_____

_____

_____

_____

_____

_____

Recap

_____

_____

_____

_____

_____

_____

_____

Reduce

Try the following approach as you reduce your notes.

TO THE POINT
Write a few key words.

_____

_____

_____

_____

_____

_____

_____

_____

_____

_____

_____

_____

_____

_____

_____

_____

_____

_____

_____

_____

Respond and Think Critically

1. Why is the teacher surprised when the child tears a button off what may be his only shirt? In your opinion, why does the child make the sacrifice? [Infer]

_____

_____

_____

_____

2. What causes the fire that kills the children in "The Little Burnt Victims"? What is ironic about the fact that the boxing glove survives the fire intact? [Interpret]

_____

_____

_____

_____

3. Evaluate Rivera's use of dialogue in "The Night the Lights Went Out." In your opinion, would the story be improved if it were told by a single narrator? Explain. [Evaluate]

_____

_____

_____

_____

4. How might the boy in the story ". . . And the Earth Did Not Devour Him" answer the question in the Focus Activity? How does this answer compare with yours? [Connect]

_____

_____

_____

_____

5. Finding Common Ground Choose two events from this section that caused you to empathize with the narrator. What kind of impact (positive or negative) did they have on your view of the narrator's society? [Classify and Connect]

_____

_____

_____

_____

APPLY BACKGROUND
Reread Introduction to the Novel on pages 76–77. How did that information help you understand or appreciate what you read in the novel?

_____

_____

_____

_____

_____

_____

_____

_____

_____

_____

_____

_____

_____

_____

_____

_____

_____

_____

_____

_____

_____

_____

_____

_____

_____

_____

_____

_____

_____

Literary Element **Tone**

Based on what you have read so far, is the author's attitude toward the narrator the same as his attitude toward the other characters in his society? [Analyze]

_____
_____
_____
_____
_____
_____
_____
_____
_____
_____
_____

Reading Strategy **Identify Problem and Solution**

Identify a problem that arises within one of the anecdotes. Do you agree with the way the character(s) solved the problem? Why or why not? [Evaluate]

_____
_____
_____
_____
_____
_____
_____
_____
_____
_____
_____
_____

Vocabulary Practice

Write the vocabulary word that correctly completes each sentence. If none of the words fits the sentence, write "none."

clamoring   sacrilege   scapularies   venial

1. Today, he decided to _____ his normal schedule and go to the zoo instead.

2. The fans were all _____ to get the rock star's attention.

3. John's constant interrupting during class is a _____ crime. Because he asks good questions, his teachers don't usually mind.

4. Marie often wears the _____ that her mother sewed; they remind her to stay true to her faith.

5. The judicial branch functions to _____ the laws of the United States.

6. Using a deity's name in vain is considered _____ by most religions.

Academic Vocabulary

Even though the young narrator **perceives** _that he has committed a sin of the flesh on the day of his first communion, he doesn't really understand what it means._ Using context clues, try to figure out the meaning of the boldface word in the sentence above. Write your guess below. Then check it in a dictionary.

_____
_____
_____
_____
_____
_____
_____
_____
_____

Write With Style
Apply Tone

Assignment Tone is the author's attitude toward his or her subject matter. Use "It was a beautiful wedding day" as a model to write your own paragraph about an event that would be described with a different tone.

Get Ideas Review Rivera's tone in other sections of the novel to get ideas for your paragraph. For example, in "The Little Burnt Victims" Rivera uses word choice to convey a tone of objective sadness as one man explains to the other what happened to the children. Think about Rivera's word choice and sentence structure to help you decide on a tone for your paragraph.

Give It Structure Follow the structure that the author uses; to do so, pay careful attention to the kinds of details he describes in the beginning, middle, and end of his paragraph.

Look at Language Tone is conveyed through various elements of style, including word choice. Reread the paragraph "It was a beautiful wedding day" and look for words that illustrate a tone of happy anticipation such as *beautiful*, *busy fixing up*, and *decorations*. Then decide on the tone you will use. For example, if you would like to create a tone of dread, make a list of words that have a foreboding tone. You can use a thesaurus to help you with your list.

EXAMPLE:

Event: final exam day

Words that convey foreboding: stressful, dreary, ominous, dreadful

Sentence: On the morning of the final exam, clouds hung drearily in the sky.

Connect to Content Areas
Art

Assignment Explore photographs of migrant workers by Dorothea Lange, Walker Evans, or contemporary photographers from one period (1930s–1940s, 1950s–1960s, 1970s–1980s, 1990s to present). Then create a photo exhibit that includes your personal reactions to the photos and how they relate to or add to your understanding of migrant workers' lives.

Investigate First, select the photographer whose work you would like to research. Then, using either print sources or the Internet, find at least five photographs taken by this photographer. Either photocopy or download these photos, but make sure that you record where you found them. Study each photo carefully, and take notes about how they add to your understanding of migrant workers' lives. Consider using a graphic organizer like the one below.

Photo Title (or #)	Date taken	Interesting visual details	What it reveals about migrant workers

Create Organize your photo exhibit in a purposeful, coherent way that enables you to display both the photo and your written comments about the photos. Refer to the graphic organizer you completed to help you identify connections between various photos and to determine an organizational strategy for your exhibit. Make your exhibit as interesting as possible.

Report If possible, use a publishing program on the computer to help make your photo exhibit look professional.

Connect to the Literature

What are the advantages of looking forward to the future and making future plans? What disadvantages might there be in focusing on the future instead of the present?

Make a Chart

With a small group of classmates, discuss why people often concentrate on the future rather than on the present. Copy the chart and make a list of all the positive and negative factors you can think of.

	Positive Factors	Negative Factors
Focusing on the PRESENT		
Focusing on the FUTURE		

Build Background

Three Kings Day

In Mexico, January 6 is Three Kings Day. This religious holiday is typically celebrated with church services, gift giving, and special treats such as *roscas*—sweet breads decorated with red and green candies. In the nativity story of the New Testament, three kings bearing gifts travel to Bethlehem to pay homage to the infant Jesus. During their visit, the kings have a dream in which they are warned not to reveal Jesus's location to King Herod, who secretly plans to kill the infant. The three kings keep the infant's location a secret, thus protecting Jesus from harm.

NOVEL NOTEBOOK
Keep a special notebook to record entries about the novels that you read this year.

SUMMARIZE
Summarize in one sentence the most important idea(s) in Build Background.

_____

_____

_____

_____

_____

_____

_____

_____

_____

_____

_____

_____

_____

_____

_____

_____

_____

_____

_____

_____

_____

_____

_____

_____

_____

_____

_____

_____

_____

Set Purposes for Reading

▶ **BIG Idea** On the Move

Consider the ways in which you have been "on the move" during your life. Do you travel with your family? Have you moved multiple times? What impact have these moves had on your life?

As you read, think about why the farm workers need to be constantly on the move. Consider what impact that might have on their children and on their own ability to pursue their dreams of better lives.

Literary Element Theme

Theme is the main idea or message of a story, poem novel or play often expressed as a general statement about life. Some works have a **stated theme,** which is expressed directly. More commonly, works have an **implied theme,** which is revealed gradually through other elements such as plot, character, setting, point of view, and symbol.

Thomás Rivera uses an **episodic structure,** a narrative structure in which loosly related incidents and episodes are strung together. These are related in large part by the novel's themes. As you read, consider what message the author seems to want to convey. An example of one possible theme is "Respect the people around you." Use the graphic organizer on the next page to help you explore other themes of the novel.

Reading Strategy Analyze Cultural Context

When you **analyze cultural context,** you think about the time and place of a work, as well as the values of the people in that time and place, and determine how these factors affect the work.

Understanding the cultural context of a piece will help you better understand the characters, the effect of the environment on these characters, and the conflicts that the author develops.

As you read, make a list of details that show the time, place, values or attitudes. Record conclusions you draw, inferences you make, or questions you ask based on those details. You may find it helpful to use a graphic organizer like the one at the right.

Vocabulary

appease [ə pēz´]
v. to satisfy, to relieve, to soothe
In order to appease her hunger, the young girl ate a sandwich.

barrage [bə räzh´]
n. overwhelming outpouring, as of words
When she decided to run for class president, she received a barrage of support from her friends.

composure [kəm pô´zhər]
n. calm state of mind
He knew that he needed to maintain his composure during his job interview, even though he was very nervous.

discourse [dis´kôrs]
n. verbal expression in speech or writing
When trying to resolve a conflict, calm discourse is always more effective than screaming and yelling.

swindle [swind´əl]
v. to cheat
Don't let anyone swindle you out of the money you earned this summer.

Detail	Inferences/ Conclusions/ Questions

The graphic organizer below will help you think about the main ideas, or themes, that are developed in the novel. As you read the final stories and anecdotes, take notes on the subject headings of the boxes below. (You may add boxes if you wish.)

When you are finished taking notes, ask yourself the following questions: Where else in the novel are these subjects explored? What point or points might the author be making about each of these subjects?

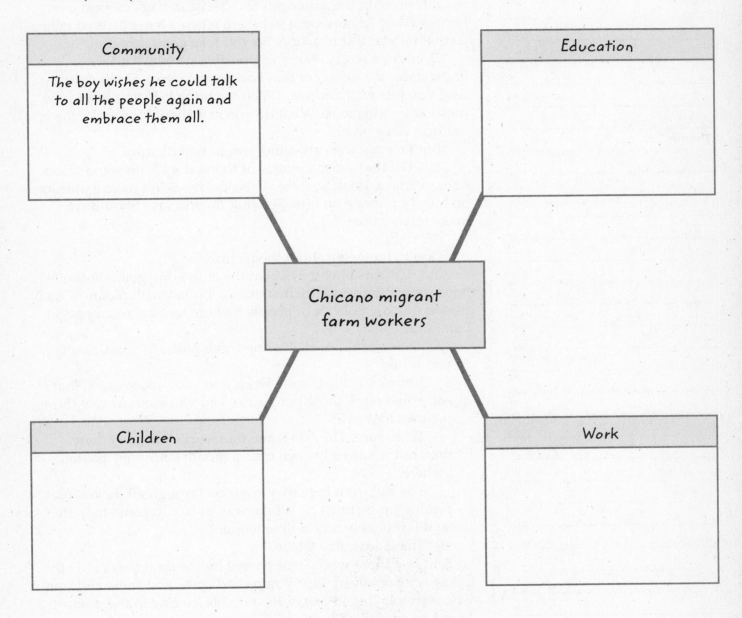

Community
The boy wishes he could talk to all the people again and embrace them all.

Education

Chicano migrant farm workers

Children

Work

Literary Element

Theme What message is the author trying to convey in this excerpt?

_____

_____

_____

_____

_____

_____

_____

_____

_____

_____

_____

_____

_____

_____

_____

_____

_____

_____

_____

_____

_____

_____

_____

_____

_____

_____

_____

_____

_____

_____

NOVEL EXCERPT: THE PORTRAIT

"All right, go ahead and write it down. But you take good care of that picture for us because it's the only one we have of our son grown up. He was going to send us one all dressed up in uniform with the American and Mexican flags crossed over his head, but he no sooner got there when a letter arrived telling us that he was lost in action. So you take good care of it."

"Don't you worry. We're responsible people. And we understand the sacrifices that you people make. Don't worry. And you just wait and see. When we bring it to you'll see how pretty it's gonna look. What do you say, should we make the uniform navy blue?"

"But he's not wearing a uniform in that picture."

"No, but that's just a matter of fixing it up with some wood fiber overlays. Look at these. This one, he didn't have a uniform on but we put one on him. So what do you say? Should we make it navy blue?"

"All right."

"Don't you worry about the picture."

And that was how they spent the entire day going house to house, street by street, their suitcases stuffed with pictures. As it turned out, a whole lot of people had ordered enlargements of that kind.

"They should be delivering those portraits soon, don't you think?"

"I think so, it's delicate work and takes more time. That's some fine work those people do. Did you see how real those pictures looked?"

"Yeah, sure. They do some fine work. You can't deny that. But it's already been over a month since they passed by here."

"Yes, but from here they went on through all the towns picking up pictures . . . all the way to San Antonio for sure. So it'll probably take a little longer."

"That's true, that's true."

And two more weeks had passed by the time they made the discovery. Some very heavy rains had come and some children who were playing in one of the tunnels leading to the dump found a sack full of pictures, all wormeaten and soaking wet. The only reason they could tell that these were pictures was because there were a lot of them and most of them the same size and with faces that could just barely be made out. Everybody caught on right away. Don Mateo was so angry that he took off to San Antonio to find the so and so who had swindled them.

"Well, you know, I stayed at Esteban's house. And every day I went with him to the market to sell produce. I helped him with everything. I had faith that I would run into that son of a gun some day soon. Then, after I'd been there for a few days, I started going out to the different barrios and I found out a lot that way. It wasn't so much the money that upset me. It was my poor vieja, crying and all because we'd lost the only picture we had of Chuy. We found it in the sack with all the other pictures but it was already ruined, you know."

"I see, but tell me, how did you find him?"

"Well, you see, to make a long story short, he came by the stand at the market one day. He stood right in front of us and bought some vegetables. It was like he was trying to remember who I was. Of course, I recognized him right off. Because when you're angry enough, you don't forget a face. I just grabbed him right then and there. Poor guy couldn't even talk. He was all scared. And I told him that I wanted that portrait of my son and that I wanted it three dimensional and that he'd best get it for me or I'd let him have it."

And I went with him to where he lived. And I put him to work right then and there. The poor guy didn't know where to begin. He had to do it all from memory."

"And how did he do it?"

"I don't know. I suppose if you're scared enough, you're capable of doing anything. Three days later he brought me the portrait all finished, just like you see it there on that table by the Virgin Mary. Now tell me, how do you like the way my boy looks?"

"Well, to be honest, I don't remember too well how Chuy looked. But he was beginning to look more and more like you, isn't that so?"

"Yes, I would say so. That's what everybody tells me now. That Chuy's a chip off the old block and that he was already looking like me. There's the portrait. Like they say, one and the same."

Literary Element

Theme In what way does the dialogue in this excerpt help convey the theme that you identified?

_____
_____
_____
_____
_____
_____
_____
_____
_____
_____
_____
_____
_____
_____
_____
_____
_____
_____
_____
_____
_____
_____
_____
_____
_____
_____

Analyze Cultural Context What do this character's thoughts tell you about how he perceives the culture around him?

_____
_____
_____
_____
_____
_____
_____
_____
_____
_____
_____
_____
_____
_____
_____
_____
_____
_____
_____
_____
_____
_____
_____
_____
_____
_____
_____
_____
_____
_____
_____

NOVEL EXCERPT: UNDER THE HOUSE

When I'd be coming back from work, at that time we had our own land with irrigation, in the early morning twilight, I'd always see these globes of light, like fireballs, bouncing off the telephone lines. They would come from the direction of Morelos, they say that's where they originate. One time I nearly made one fall down. Don Remigio taught me how to say the seven prayers that go with the seven knots. All you have to do is start praying when you see those balls of fire. After each prayer you tie a knot. This one time I got to the seventh prayer but you know, I wasn't able to tie that last knot, but the witch fell anyway, practically landing at my feet, and then she got up . . . The boy was so young and children don't understand too much at that age. And he couldn't hold out. They're not going to do anything to the boss, he's got too much pull. Can you imagine what they'd do if one of us killed one of their kids? They say that one day the boy's father took a rifle and went looking for him because he wanted to pay him back but he didn't find him . . . The woman would almost always start crying when she entered the church, and then she'd start praying. But before she was even aware of it, she would start talking in a loud voice. Then she'd start yelling, like she was having some kind of attack . . . I think Doña Cuquita is still living. I haven't seen her in a long time. She used to be very careful whenever we went to the dump. Now her I really loved. And since I never knew my grandparents. I think even Dad loved her like a grandmother because he, too, never knew his grandparents. What I liked best was for her to embrace me and tell me, "You're smarter than an eagle and more watchful than the moon" . . . Get out of there! Get away from that goddamn window! Go away! Go away . . . You know, you can't come home with me anymore. Look, I don't mind playing with you but some old ladies told mama that Mexicans steal and now mama says not to bring you home anymore. You have to turn back. But we can still play at school. I'll choose you and you choose me . . . What can I tell you! I know what I'm telling you, I'm saying that we can't get any more screwed than we already are. I know why I'm telling you. If there's another war, we won't be the ones to suffer. Don't be a damn fool. The ones who will pay for it are the ones on top, the ones who have something. Us, we're already screwed. If there's another war, hell, things might even get better for us . . . Why don't you eat sweetbread anymore? You don't like it, anymore? . . . Well, I tell you, I even went downtown and bought me a new hammer so I could be ready for when they'd come to teach us. They say that the minister, when he found out, he went straight home, took a hatchet and broke all the furniture to pieces and than he took everything outside and set it on fire. He stood there and watched everything burn to ashes . . . I don't think my viejo is going to be able to work out in the sun anymore. The boss didn't say a thing when we told him that he had gotten sick from the heat. He just shook his head. What worried him the most was that it was raining too much and the crop was getting ruined. That was the only thing he was sad about. He wasn't even sad when they had to operate on his wife because she had cancer, much less when we told him about my viejo . . . These sonofabitches are gonna cut your hair, I'll see to that, if I have to bust their noses . . . There is no devil, there isn't. The only devil is Don Rayos when he dresses up with horns and with the cape to go to the shepherds' play . . . Goddamn fool! Why don't you pay attention to what you're doing? You almost crashed with that truck! Didn't you see it? Are you blind, or what? . . . Why did the teacher cry when they came for him? Ever since he was put in her class she always just kept looking at him. And she was so young, she wasn't like the ones in Texas, little old ladies holding a paddle in their hands making sure you didn't lose your place in the book. And if you did, pow! They'd just bend you over . . . You think that was how they were burned? It's just hard to believe. But so fast? It's that fire spreads fast and once your clothes catch on fire, that's it. You remember that family that died in that fire around Christmas time? They fell asleep, never to wake up again. And then the firemen crying as they removed the bodies, the grease from the children's little burned up bodies dripping all over their boots . . . Free citizens, this is a day of magnificent and profound importance. It was in the year eighteen-hundred and seventy-two that Napoleon's troops suffered a defeat against Mexican soldiers who fought so valiantly—that was how I would begin my discourse. I always used the words "free citizens" when I was young, son, but now ever since I had the attack I can't remember too well anymore what I would say to the people. Then came the Revolution and in the end we lost. Villa made out well but I had to come out here. No one here knows what I went through. Sometimes I want to remember but, truth is, I'm not able to anymore. All my thoughts become hazy. Now, tell me, what is it that you most desire at this moment of your life? At this very moment . . . Yesterday we collected fifty pounds of copper in all. Enrique found a magnet and that makes it much easier to find the iron buried under so much junk that people throw away. Sometimes we do well but usually it's a waste of time. But at least enough to buy something to eat.

Reading Strategy

Analyze Cultural Context What do these details reveal about the relationship between the migrant farm workers and their bosses?

_____
_____
_____
_____
_____
_____
_____
_____
_____
_____
_____
_____
_____
_____
_____
_____
_____
_____
_____
_____
_____
_____
_____
_____
_____
_____
_____
_____

MARK IT UP

Are you allowed to write in your novel? If so, then mark up the pages as you read, or reread, to help with your note-taking. Develop a shorthand system, including symbols, that works for you. Here are some ideas:

Underline = important idea

Bracket = text to quote

Asterisk = just what you were looking for

Checkmark = might be useful

Circle = unfamiliar word or phrase to look up

▶ **BIG Idea**

On the Move Think about what you have learned about how the farm workers view their lives "on the move."

Mark up the excerpt, looking for evidence of how it expresses the Big Idea.

NOVEL EXCERPT: WHEN WE ARRIVE

If only it could stay like early dawn, then nobody would complain. I'm going to keep my eyes on the stars till the last one disappears. I wonder how many more people are watching the same star? And how many more might there be wondering how many are looking at the same star? It's so silent it looks like it's the stars the crickets are calling to."

"Goddamn truck. It's nothing but trouble. When we get there everybody will just have to look out for themselves. All I'm doing is dropping them off with the growers and I'm getting the hell out. Besides, we don't have a contract. They'll find themselves somebody to take them back to Texas. Somebody's bound to come by and pick them up. You can't make money off beets anymore. My best bet is to head back to Texas just as soon as I drop these people off and then see how things go hauling watermelons. The melon season's almost here. All I need now is for there not to be anyone in this goddamn town who can fix the truck. What the hell will I do then? So long as the cops don't come by and start hassling me about moving the truck from here. Boy, that town had to be the worst. We didn't even stop and still the cop caught up with us just to tell us that he didn't want us staying there. I guess he just wanted to show off in front of the town people. But we didn't even stop in their goddamn town. When we get there, as soon as I drop them off, I'll turn back. Each one to fend for himself."

"When we get there I'm gonna see about getting a good bed for my vieja. Her kidneys are really bothering her a lot nowadays. just hope we don't end up in a chicken coop like last year, with that cement floor. Even though you cover it with straw, once the cold season sets in you just can't stand it. That was why my rheumatism got so bad, I'm sure of that."

"When we arrive, when we arrive, the real truth is that I'm tired of arriving. Arriving and leaving, it's the same thing because we no sooner arrive and . . . the real truth of the matter . . . I'm tired of arriving. I really should say when we don't arrive because that's the real truth. We never arrive."

"When we arrive, when we arrive. . . "

Little by little the crickets ceased their chirping. It seemed as though they were becoming tired and the dawn gradually affirmed the presence of objects; ever so carefully and very slowly, so that no one would take notice of what was happening. And the people were becoming people. They began getting out of the trailer and they huddled around and commenced to talk about what they would do when they arrived.

Use the Cornell Note-Taking system to take notes on the excerpt at the left. Record your notes, Reduce them, and then Recap (summarize) them.

Record

_____
_____
_____
_____
_____
_____
_____
_____
_____
_____
_____
_____
_____
_____
_____
_____
_____
_____
_____
_____
_____
_____

Recap

_____
_____
_____
_____
_____
_____

Reduce

Try the following approach as you reduce your notes.

MY VIEW
Write down your thoughts on the excerpt.

_____
_____
_____
_____
_____
_____
_____
_____
_____
_____
_____
_____
_____
_____
_____
_____
_____
_____
_____

Respond and Think Critically

1. What is ironic about the priest blessing the cars for five dollars? [Analyze]

_____

_____

_____

_____

2. How and why are the migrant workers taken advantage of by the portrait salespeople? [Summarize]

_____

_____

_____

_____

3. In an interview, Tomás Rivera said that he wanted to portray the "suffering and the strength and the beauty . . . [of] the migrant worker[s], the people I had known best." In your opinion, does he succeed? Explain why or why not. [Evaluate]

_____

_____

_____

_____

4. Do the workers in "When We Arrive" tend to live in the present or the future? Which of the advantages that you listed during the Focus Activity might apply to the workers? Which disadvantages might apply? [Classify]

_____

_____

_____

_____

5. **On the Move** Do the farm workers appear hopeful or hopeless about the prospect of always being on the move from one farm to another? [Interpret]

_____

_____

_____

_____

APPLY BACKGROUND

Reread Meet the Author on page 78. How did that information help you understand or appreciate what you read in the novel?

_____

_____

_____

_____

_____

_____

_____

_____

_____

_____

_____

_____

_____

_____

_____

_____

_____

_____

_____

_____

_____

_____

_____

_____

_____

_____

_____

_____

_____

Literary Element **Theme**

Within this section, how does the novel's episodic structure contribute to your understanding of the theme? Choose two anecdotes and explain how these combine to help reveal a theme. [Synthesize]

_____
_____
_____
_____
_____
_____
_____
_____
_____
_____
_____

Reading Strategy **Analyze Cultural Context**

Do you see any similarities between your experiences or your hopes and dreams and those of the migrant farm workers that Rivera describes? [Apply]

_____
_____
_____
_____
_____
_____
_____
_____
_____
_____
_____

Vocabulary Practice

Identify whether each set of paired words have the same or the opposite meaning.

1. **appease** and enrage

   _____

2. **barrage** and bombard

   _____

3. **composure** and calmness

   _____

4. **discourse** and conversation

   _____

5. **swindle** and donate

   _____

Academic Vocabulary

Don Mateo did not realize that the portrait salesman's offer to frame his son's photo was a **scheme** *until the man had already run away with his money.* In the preceding sentence *scheme* means "a crafty or secret plan." Think about how this **scheme** will affect Don Mateo and then fill in the blank for this statement: *The salesman's* **scheme** *might cause Don Mateo to*

_____
_____ .

Writing

Write an Agency Report Imagine that you work for a 1950s government agency concerned about improving the health and welfare of Chicano migrant farm workers. Based on details in the novel, write a brief report about what life is like for the workers. In your report, be sure to include recommendations for how to improve conditions.

Jot down some notes here first.

_____

_____

_____

_____

_____

_____

_____

_____

_____

_____

_____

_____

_____

_____

_____

_____

_____

_____

_____

_____

_____

_____

_____

Speaking and Listening
Literature Group

Assignment With a small group, choose one subject and trace its development throughout the novel. Decide what points the novel makes about this subject, and share your conclusions with the rest of the class.

Prepare As a group, review the subjects presented in the Active Reading graphic organizer on page 105 and decide which one subject your group will trace through the novel. Look for stories and anecdotes that explore the subject through the use of dialogue, conflict, irony, or description.

Organize the information you collect in a graphic organizer like the one below.

Subject: Education

Chapter/ pages where it appears	Context (who, where, when, why)	Literary elements used	Author's view of subject
Page 7	Short discussion about where Utah is	Dialogue	More education is needed.

Discuss Respect others' viewpoints by listening attentively. Deliver your opinions in a normal tone of voice, providing clear, specific examples to support your conclusions about the author's view.

Report Have one person share your group's conclusions with the class, using the information on your graphic organizer to justify your conclusions. Use appropriate eye contact and speak clearly.

Evaluate Write a paragraph in which you assess your participation in the group discussion.

. . . And the Earth Did Not Devour Him

The following questions refer to the Related Readings in Glencoe's *Literature Library* edition of this novel. Support your answers with details from the texts. Write your answers on a separate sheet of paper, but jot down some notes first on the lines provided.

Voices from the Fields

Beth Atkin

Compare the lives of the children interviewed to the lives of the children in . . . *And the Earth Did Not Devour Him*. In what ways are they similar? different?

_____

_____

_____

_____

Christmas

Langston Hughes

How do the adults in "Christmas" and in . . . *And the Earth Did Not Devour Him* deal with their poverty at Christmastime? Discuss similarities you see between the families. In your opinion, do the children understand how their poverty affects their Christmas?

_____

_____

_____

_____

Children for Hire

Verena Dobnik and Ted Anthony

Compare the working conditions of the children in this article with the working conditions of the children in . . . *And the Earth Did Not Devour Him*.

_____

_____

_____

_____

_____

First Confession

Frank O'Connor

Compare and contrast Jackie's experience at his first confession with the experience of the boy in . . . *And the Earth Did Not Devour Him*. How does each character feel before the confession? What happens to change how each character feels?

_____

_____

_____

_____

_____

Aria: A Memoir of a Bilingual Childhood

Richard Rodriguez

What is the Rodriguez family's relationship to English-speaking Anglos in their community? In your opinion, how is that relationship similar to or different from the relationship between Anglos and Chicanos in . . . *And the Earth Did Not Devour Him*?

_____

_____

_____

_____

_____

LITERATURE EXCERPT: Sayonara

It was good-bye for us too, as we rushed through Japan on our way to the boat. Good-bye to the rice fields terraced up a narrow gully in the hills; to thatched roofs and paper walls; to heavy-headed grain bent to a curve; to a field of awkward lotus leaves, like big elephant ears flapping on their tall stalks; to a white road leading up a hill to a pine grove and the flicker of red of a shrine gate. Good-bye to the little towns we rattled through, with their narrow cobbled streets lined with shops, open to the passerby except for fluttering blue-toweling curtains or bright paper and cloth flag-signs. Good-bye to blue paper umbrellas in the rain and little boys chasing dragon flies.

Our real good-bye was not until the boat pulled out of the dock at Yokohama, when the crowd of Japanese leaning over the rails of the decks shot twirling strands of serpentine[5] across to those they had left behind on shore—a rain of bright fireworks. One end of these colored paper ribbons was held in the hands of those on deck; the other, by those on shore, until a brilliant multicolored web was spun between ship and shore. This and the shouts of conversation unintelligible to me, interlacing back and forth across the gap, made up a finely woven band— a tissue, intricately patterned and rich in texture which held together for a few more seconds those remaining and those departing. Then the gap of water slowly widening between dock and ship, the ribbons tautened and snapped, the broken and raveled ends twirling off idly into the water, floating away with the unfinished ends of sentences. And nothing could bridge the gap but "Sayonara!"

For *Sayonara*, literally translated, "Since it must be so," of all the good-byes I have heard is the most beautiful. Unlike the *Auf Wiedersehens* and *Au revoirs*, it does not try to cheat itself by any bravado "Till we meet again," any sedative to postpone the pain of separation. It does not evade the issue like the sturdy blinking *Farewell. Farewell* is a father's *good-bye*. It is— "Go out in the world and do well, my son." It is encouragement and admonition. It is hope and faith. But it passes over the significance of the moment; of parting it says nothing. It hides its emotion. It says too little. While *Good-bye* ("God be with you") and *Adios* say too much. They try to bridge the distance, almost to deny it. *Good-bye* is a prayer, a ringing cry. "You must not go—I cannot bear to have you go! But you shall not go alone, unwatched. God will be with you. God's hand will be over you" and even—underneath, hidden, but it is there, incorrigible—"I will be with you; I will watch you—always." It is a mother's *good-bye*. But Sayonara says neither too much nor too little. It is a simple acceptance of fact. All understanding of life lies in its limits. All emotion, smoldering, is banked up behind it. But it says nothing. It is really the unspoken good-bye, the pressure of a hand, "Sayonara."

Compare the novel you have just read to the literature selection at the left, which is excerpted from "Sayonara" by Anne Morrow Lindbergh in *Glencoe Literature.* Then answer the questions below.

Compare & Contrast

1. **Anecdote** Why do you think Lindbergh chose to share this particular anecdote about her time in Japan? How does this compare to the reason why Rivera selected particular anecdotes to share in … *And the Earth Did Not Devour Him*?

_____

_____

_____

_____

_____

_____

2. **Tone** What is the tone that Lindbergh establishes in this descriptive essay? How does this tone differ from the tone that Rivera uses to describe the farms that the migrant workers are forced to leave at the end of a season?

_____

_____

_____

_____

_____

_____

3. **Theme** Lindbergh reveals that "Sayonara" is an acceptance of fact. Upon leaving Japan, what is Lindbergh accepting? What do the migrant farm workers come to accept in Rivera's novel?

_____

_____

_____

_____

_____

_____

TALK ABOUT IT

As a class, discuss the similarities and differences between the two author's feelings about the places that they are writing about. Consider the extent to which the environment itself contributes to the author's perspectives. Take notes on the discussion.

_____

_____

_____

_____

_____

_____

_____

_____

_____

_____

_____

_____

_____

_____

_____

_____

_____

_____

_____

_____

_____

_____

_____

_____

_____

_____

_____

Research Report

Investigate Chicano Literature Rivera's novel introduces the reader to some of the themes explored in Chicano literature. In order to explore those themes further, research the life and work of one other Chicano writer, perhaps one who was part of El Movimiento. Prepare a report about this writer's life and about how Chicano themes are represented in his/her work; include an annotated recommended reading list of this author's writing.

Prewrite Write four or five questions about this author to guide the first part of your research. Answer those questions by checking secondary sources such as Web sites, encyclopedias, magazines, and books. Prepare detailed notes, identifying your sources for each fact or idea. Next, read one or two texts that your author wrote. As you read, consider the ways in which some of the themes presented in Rivera's text emerge within this author's writing as well.

As you research this authors work, organize a reading list of his or her writing. Include annotations for the entries on your list, explaining why you included each title.

Create an outline like the one below to help structure your report, adding relevant information under each outline point.

> *Tomás Rivera*
> I. *Early years*
>   a. *Childhood*
>   b. *Teen years*
> II. *Becoming a writer*
> III. *Chicano themes*

Draft Develop a thesis statement that identifies your topic and explains what you plan to say about the topic. Here is an example.

> *Example: _____ is an important figure in Chicano literature because _____ , _____ , and _____ .*

As you write, refer to your notes and outline to make sure you have included the correct information in a coherent order. You may also wish to use publishing software to include visual aids, such as a photograph, to help your readers visualize the setting you are reporting about.

Revise As you incorporate the information in your note cards, evaluate whether the information is relevant or necessary. Delete information unrelated to your thesis, and add any missing facts and ideas. If you have used any technical terms, make sure they are explained thoroughly and correctly, to avoid any misunderstandings.

Edit and Proofread Edit your writing so that it expresses your thoughts effectively and is well organized. Carefully proofread for grammar, punctuation, and spelling errors.

UNDERSTAND THE TASK

- **Primary sources** are firsthand accounts of an event, such as diaries or eyewitness news articles written at the time the event took place.
- **Secondary sources** are sources written by people who did not influence or experience the event.

Grammar Tip

Ellipses
Ellipsis points (…) are three spaced periods that indicate the omission of words within a text, such as a quotation. Ellipses are useful when you don't need to refer to the entirety of a quotation, just relevant portions:

While Hughes says that more books were written about African-Americans in the Harlem Renaissance than ever before, he claims it was white writers who benefited most: "White writers wrote about Negroes more successfully . . . than Negroes did about themselves."

The Yearling

Marjorie Kinnan Rawlings

The Yearling
Marjorie Kinnan Rawlings

❝*As a 'Southern' regionalist Marjorie Kinnan Rawlings was unique in having the insider's commitment of love for place, but also the outsider's objectivity, so that she could write of her chosen home with passion and sympathy but without the film of bias or prejudice peculiar to the place.*❞

—*Gordon E. Bigelow, critic*

In her own lifetime, Marjorie Kinnan Rawlings was best known as a regional writer—one who set her stories in a specific geographical area and presented its distinct culture through the history, speech, habits, customs, and folklore of its inhabitants. This classification frustrated the author, because she felt that regionalism should be a basic part of every piece of literature, much like the colors in a painting or the musical notes in a symphony. She believed that the truly great writer should be capable of taking material from any time or place and turning it into a universal thing of beauty.

Inspiring Readers With *The Yearling*, however, critics conceded that Rawlings had achieved something greater than regionalism. Although *The Yearling* vividly depicts a certain time and place, its message speaks to people everywhere. Lloyd Morris summed up the novel's appeal when he stated that Rawlings

plunges us deeply into the hearts and the perceptions of a child, a wise man, and a brave woman. It recreates for us those fundamental attitudes of the human spirit which make life endurable, and those inalienable experiences of love and beauty which enable us to live it without shame.

Samuel I. Bellman, one of Rawlings's biographers, agrees: "This novel elevates the writer to the rank of those special authors who at least once in their lives are capable of giving us dreams to dream by and words to shape those dreams."

Rawlings received many letters from her fans—complete strangers who wanted her to know what had touched them most about the book. For example, the curator of the Museum of Comparative Zoology in Cambridge, Massachusetts, commented on her ability to authentically evoke a boy's thoughts and feelings and to accurately portray natural history. A woman with two boyfriends reported that she had both men read *The Yearling*. She then decided to marry the one who responded more warmly to the book. Other readers cherished the novel for its descriptions of nature, its poetic qualities, or its humor. One young boy even wrote that he had always thought his father liked his sisters better than him, but that reading the novel made him realize that they had always paid more attention to their father than he had. He thought that with Jody, the novel's main character, as his inspiration, the novel would "start a better love" between him and his father. *The Yearling* carries a message that everyone can understand:

Ever' man wants life to be a fine thing, and a easy. 'Tis fine, boy, powerful fine, but 'tain't easy. Life knocks a man down and he gits up and it knocks him down again. . . . What's he to do then? . . . Why, take it for his share and go on.

A Unique Setting Both Florida coasts are well known to tourists. In contrast, few Americans are familiar with central Florida, a beautiful and unique area.

One of the qualities that make north central Florida unusual is its location. It is situated where the northern temperate zone passes into the semitropics. As a result, the area has the plant life of both zones as well as an approximation of all four seasons. During a short winter, when frosts are common and much growth is dormant, animals rest for long periods, even if they do not actually hibernate. Spring is a time of blossoming, particularly for the fruit trees. The trees bloom anywhere from late January to early March. May, sometimes the hottest month of the year, is the dividing line between spring and summer. The rains begin in June and last until mid-August. After this, the steadiness of the sun and its withering effect on plant life through October signal the presence of autumn.

The Yearling takes place in the late 1800s in the Big Scrub, a semiwilderness area located between the Oklawaha and St. Johns rivers. Measuring about fifty miles long and twenty-five miles wide, the area today falls within the Ocala National Forest.

The Baxters farm an area known as a *hammock*. Hammock soil is dark and rich, made up of centuries of leaves from live oak, palm, sweet gum, holly, ironwood, hickory, and magnolia trees.

In Chapter 14, Penny Baxter plans to search the "prairies" for his missing hogs. The term *prairies* is misleading in this context, because instead of flat, rolling land, Penny is talking about wet, flat areas around the larger lakes of the area. More like marshes, the prairies Penny searches are home to water grasses.

The uniqueness of the area's vegetation is perhaps best captured in the opening pages of Rawlings's first novel, *South Moon Under*:

The scrub rolled towards its boundaries like a dark sea. It cast itself against the narrow beach of swamp and hammock that fringed the rivers. The two types of growth did not mingle, as though an ascetic race withdrew itself from a tropical one and refused to inter-breed. The moisture along the rivers gave a footing for the lush growth of cypress in the swamp; of live oak, magnolia, hickory, ash, bay, sweet gum and holly that made up the adjoining hammock.

In *The Yearling* Rawlings emphasizes the silence of the scrub, its wildness and loneliness. Other than occasional hammock areas, the soil is so dry and sandy that, historically, few people were attracted to the area. Those who did come to live there had to be resourceful and self-supporting.

Central Florida Today

Today, the woods of central Florida remain much as they were when Marjorie Kinnan Rawlings made her home at Cross Creek. The area remains fairly isolated, even though its major industries—tourism and fruit production—have attracted attention. A few stores provide groceries and other supplies, but large-scale shopping centers have yet to infiltrate the low rolling hills of the peaceful wilderness. For every new house built, an older one sits empty, abandoned or relegated to a part-time residence. Roads meander through rural neighborhoods.

This area is home to numerous large and small lakes. Most lakes in central Florida were formed by sinkholes, cave-ins that occur when a limestone layer under the surface of the earth erodes. The waters are home to various species of plant and animal life, including palm, hickory, and pine trees; lilies, orchids, and morning glories; and alligators, foxes, and herons.

Marjorie Kinnan Rawlings (1896–1953)

"It seems to me that the earth may be borrowed but not bought. It may be used, but not owned. It gives itself in response to love and tending, offers its seasonal flowering and fruiting. But we are tenants and not possessors, lovers and not masters.**"**

—*Marjorie Kinnan Rawlings*

It is no surprise that writing about the land became a central focus in Marjorie Kinnan Rawlings's life. Born in Washington, D.C., in 1896, Rawlings's happiest memories were of weekends spent at her family's farm in Maryland and of summers spent at her maternal grandfather's farm in Michigan. She was a bright child who learned to read at an early age. Encouraged by her parents to write, she won a two-dollar prize for a story that she submitted to the children's page of the *Washington Post* when she was eleven.

A Childhood Remembered *The Yearling* has its origins in Rawlings's childhood. In an article she wrote for a Voice of America radio broadcast overseas, she said about the book's beginnings:

I remember a very special sort of April day, the day I describe in the first chapter of The Yearling. *I remember the delirious excitement I felt. And at the height of my delight, . . . I understood suddenly that . . . beyond this carefree moment life was waiting with its responsibilities. . . . As I became a writer, I thought back often to that April day and . . . I said to myself, "Sometime I shall write a story about the job of childhood, and the strange foreknowledge of maturity."*

The Writing Life As an English major at the University of Wisconsin, Rawlings was elected to the Phi Beta Kappa honorary society in recognition of her outstanding scholastic achievement. She excelled at creative writing and acting. She also served on the staffs of the yearbook and the literary magazine, where she met Charles Rawlings, her future husband.

After college, Rawlings moved to New York City. Eventually, she found work as a writer and editor for the War Work Council at the national headquarters of the YMCA, but the job was not particularly creative. In her spare time, she tried, with little luck, to sell her poems and short stories. She married Charles Rawlings a year later and moved to Louisville, Kentucky, where the couple found jobs writing for a local newspaper. Later they moved to Charles's hometown of Rochester, New York, where Rawlings wrote for the local newspapers. By 1922 she was writing feature articles and conducting celebrity interviews. Rawlings later credited her newspaper work with teaching her more about writing than she had learned in her classes. However, she continued to have little luck selling her fiction.

In 1928, Rawlings and her husband bought an orange grove in Cross Creek in north central Florida. The move gave Rawlings a new focus and inspiration. She began writing about the hard, simple life of her neighbors and the harmony in which they lived with their wild surroundings. For the next twenty-five years she created literature out of her experiences in Florida. Marjorie Kinnan Rawlings died of a cerebral hemorrhage in 1953 at the age of fifty-seven and is buried in her beloved Florida backcountry.

Connect to the Literature

Do you believe that parents should be strict with their children or lenient? Why?

Write a Journal Entry

In your journal, briefly explain which style of parenting you think is better and why.

Build Background

The Florida Farmers

Today the word *cracker* is considered offensive when used to describe a poor white person of the rural southeastern part of the United States. The term was once, however, a common label for people like the Baxters and the Forresters, hardworking farmers and hunters who depend on the land to keep them alive. The term is thought to refer to the cracked corn that the farmers and hunters used to eat or from the loud crack of the bullwhip they used to move and control cattle. According to many historical sources, these men and women came to Florida from the Appalachian Mountains. They worked in the Florida forests until the logging industry destroyed most of the large trees, after which they turned to farming to scratch out a living.

NOVEL NOTEBOOK

Keep a special notebook to record entries about the novels that you read this year.

SUMMARIZE

Summarize in one sentence the most important idea(s) in Build Background.

_____

_____

_____

_____

_____

_____

_____

_____

_____

_____

_____

_____

_____

_____

_____

_____

_____

_____

_____

_____

_____

_____

_____

_____

_____

_____

_____

Set Purposes for Reading

▶ BIG Idea Nature Inspires

Think about how nature inspires you. Do you enjoy being outside, walking in the woods or along the beach? What are some of the emotions you feel when you are out in nature?

In *The Yearling*, a young boy and his family are very connected with their natural surroundings. As you read, try to identify places where nature affects, or even inspires the characters. Make a list of these events and note if you have had any similar experiences.

Literary Element Simile

A **simile** is a **figure of speech** that uses *like* or *as* to compare seemingly unlike things. Figures of speech are a type of **figurative language,** which expresses some truth beyond the literal level.

Authors employ similes to help the reader understand an abstraction and to make it easier for the reader to grasp what is being described. A simile can help the reader see an object, person or event in a new way. It can also startle the reader and inject fresh life into a familiar idea.

If you encounter a simile as you read, ask yourself what that simile reveals about the object of the comparison.

Reading Strategy Analyze Imagery

Imagery is descriptive language that appeals to one or more of the five senses: sight, hearing, touch, taste and smell. Writers use this type of language to create "word pictures" and evoke an emotional response in readers.

To **analyze imagery**, readers consider the details that an author includes in the text and determines what effect those details have on their senses. When writers create effective imagery, the reader can better understand the text's meaning.

As you read, ask yourself how the author's vivid descriptions of the book's setting give you more insight into both the characters and the relationship between these characters and nature. You may find it helpful to use a graphic organizer like the one at the right. The graphic organizer on the next page can also help you to analyze imagery.

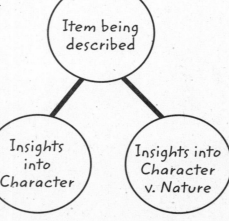

The Yearling contains many vivid examples of imagery, or descriptions that appeal to the five senses. As you read, use the cluster diagram below to take notes on imagery that you find especially interesting or effective.

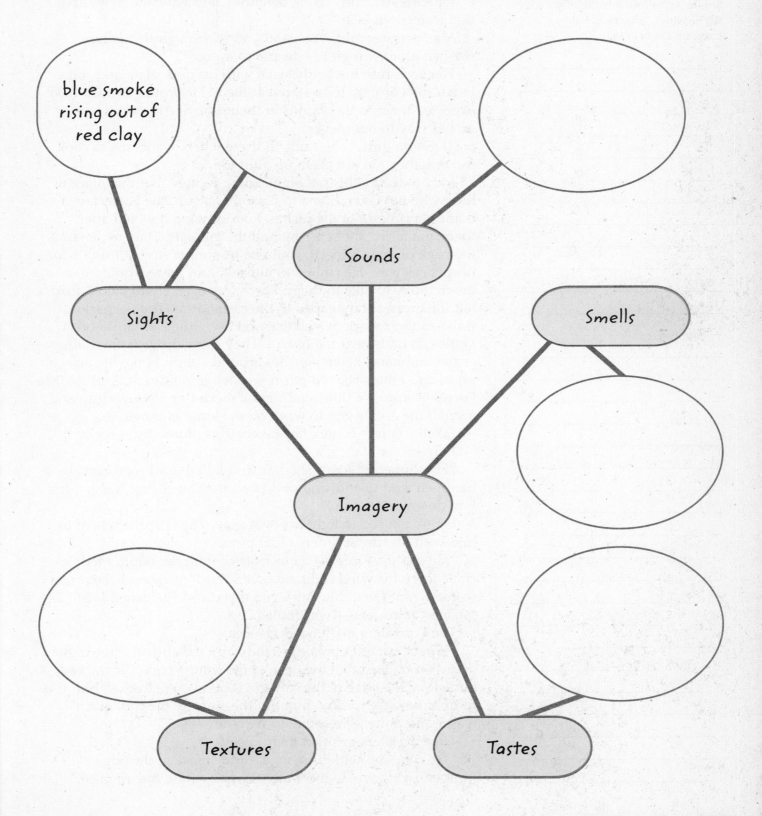

blue smoke rising out of red clay

Sights

Sounds

Smells

Imagery

Textures

Tastes

Literary Element

Simile As he recounts their fight with Big Slewfoot, what does Penny compare the bear to?

_____
_____
_____
_____
_____
_____
_____
_____
_____
_____
_____
_____
_____
_____
_____
_____
_____
_____
_____
_____
_____
_____
_____
_____
_____
_____
_____
_____

NOVEL EXCERPT: CHAPTER 7

Pa Forrester said, "Well, neighbor, let's have the news about that tormented bear."

Ma Forrester said, "Yes, and you scapers git the dishes washed afore you git too deep into it, too."

Her sons rose hurriedly, each with his own plate and some larger dish or pan. Jody stared at them. He would as soon have expected them to tie ribbons in their hair. She tweaked his ear on her way to her rocker.

"I got no girls," she said. "If these fellers wants me to cook for 'em, they kin jest clean up after me."

Jody looked at his father, pleading mutely that this piece of heresy be not taken home to Baxter's Island. The Forresters made short work of the dishes. Fodder-wing hobbled after them, gathering the scraps for all the animals. Only by feeding the pack of dogs himself, could he be sure of saving tid-bits for his pets as well. He smiled to himself, that there would be so much today to take to them. There was even enough cold food left for supper. Jody gaped at the abundance. The Forresters finished their work in a clatter, and hung the iron pots and kettles on nails near the hearth. They drew up their cowhide chairs and hand-hewn benches around Penny. Some lit corn-cob pipes and others shaved parings of tobacco from dark plugs. Ma Forrester lipped a little snuff. Buck picked up Penny's gun and a small file and began to work on the loose hammer.

"Well," Penny began, "he takened us plumb by surprise."

Jody shivered.

"He slipped in like a shadow and killed our brood-sow. Laid her open, end to end, and only ate a mouthful. Not hongry. Jest low-down and mean."

Penny paused to light his own pipe. The Forresters bent to him with blazing splinters of fat pine.

"He come as quiet as a black cloud, into the wind. Made a circle to git his wind right. So quiet, the dogs never heered nor scented him. Even this un—even this un—" he leaned to stroke the feist at his feet—"was fooled."

The Forresters exchanged glances.

"We set out after breakfast, Jody and me and all three o' the dogs. We tracked that bear acrost the south scrub. We tracked him along the edge o' the saw-grass ponds. We tracked him thu Juniper Bay. We tracked him thu the swamp, the trail gittin' hotter and hotter. We come up with him—"

The Forresters gripped their knees.

"We come up with him, men, right smack at the edge o' Juniper Creek, where the water flows swiftest and deepest."

The story, Jody thought, was even better than the hunt. He saw it all again, the shadows and the fern, the broken palmettos and the running branch water. He was bursting with the excitement of the story. He was bursting, too, with pride in his father. Penny Baxter, no bigger than a dirt-dauber, could out-hunt the best of them. And he could sit, as he sat now, weaving a spell of mystery and magic, that held these huge hairy men eager and breathless.

He made the fight an epic thing. When his gun back-fired, and old Slewfoot crushed Julia to his breast, Gabby swallowed his tobacco and rushed to the fire-place, spitting and choking. The Forresters clenched their fists, and sat precariously at the edges of their seats, and listened with their mouths open.

"Gawd," Buck breathed, "I'd o' loved to o' been there."

"And where's Slewfoot gone?" Gabby begged.

"No man knows," Penny told them.

There was silence.

Lem said at last, "You ain't never oncet mentioned that dog you got there."

"Don't press me," Penny said. "I done told you he's wuthless."

"I notice he come outen it in mighty good shape. Not a mark on him, is there?"

"No, there's nary mark on him."

"Takes a mighty clever dog to fight a bear and not git ary scratch on him."

Penny puffed on his pipe.

Lem rose and walked to him, towering over him. He cracked his knuckles. He was sweating.

"I want two things," he said hoarsely. "I want to be in at the death o' ol' Slewfoot. And I want that dog there."

"Oh my, no," Penny said mildly. "I'd not cheat you, tradin' him."

"No use lyin' to me. Name your trade."

"I'll trade you old Rip, instead."

"Think you're foxy. I got better dogs than Rip right now."

Lem went to the wall and took down from its nails a gun. It was a London Fine Twist. The double barrels shone. The stock was walnut, warm and glowing. The twin hammers were jaunty. The fittings were chased and intricate. Lem swung it to his shoulder, sighted it. He handed it to Penny.

Literary Element

Simile What effect, ultimately, do Penny's similies have on Pa Forrester?

_____

_____

_____

_____

_____

_____

_____

_____

_____

_____

_____

_____

_____

_____

_____

_____

_____

_____

_____

_____

_____

_____

_____

_____

_____

_____

_____

_____

_____

_____

Reading Strategy

Analyze imagery What tone does Rawlins establish through the imagery in this passage?

_____

_____

_____

_____

_____

_____

_____

_____

_____

_____

_____

_____

_____

_____

_____

_____

_____

_____

_____

_____

_____

_____

_____

_____

_____

_____

NOVEL EXCERPT: CHAPTER 1

Jody drew a deep breath. He threw himself on the weedy sand close to the water and abandoned himself to the magic of motion. Up, over, down, up, over, down—the flutter-mill was enchanting. The bubbling spring would rise forever from the earth, the thin current was endless. The spring was the beginning of waters sliding to the sea. Unless leaves fell, or squirrels cut sweet bay twigs to drop and block the fragile wheel, the flutter-mill might turn forever. When he was an old man, as old as his father, there seemed no reason why this rippling movement might not continue as he had begun it.

He moved a stone that was matching its corners against his sharp ribs and burrowed a little, hollowing himself a nest for his hips and shoulders. He stretched out one arm and laid his head on it. A shaft of sunlight, warm and thin like a light patchwork quilt, lay across his body. He watched the flutter-mill indolently, sunk in the sand and the sunlight. The movement was hypnotic. His eyelids fluttered with the palm-leaf paddles. Drops of silver slipping from the wheel blurred together like the tail of a shooting star. The water made a sound like kittens lapping. A rain frog sang a moment and then was still. There was an instant when the boy hung at the edge of a high bank made of the soft fluff of broom-sage, and the rain frog and the starry dripping of the flutter-mill hung with him. Instead of falling over the edge, he sank into the softness. The blue, white-tufted sky closed over him. He slept.

When he awakened, he thought he was in a place other than the branch bed. He was in another world, so that for an instant he thought he might still be dreaming. The sun was gone and all the light and shadow. There were no black holes of live oaks, no glossy green of magnolia leaves, no pattern of gold lace where the sun had sifted through the branches of the wild cherry. The world was all a gentle gray, and he lay in a mist as fine as spray from a waterfall. The mist tickled his skin. It was scarcely wet. It was at once warm and cool. He rolled over on his back and it was as though he looked up into the soft gray breast of a mourning dove.

He lay, absorbing the fine-dropped rain like a young plant. When his face was damp at last and his shirt was moist to the touch, he left his nest. He stopped short. A deer had come to the spring while he was sleeping. The fresh tracks came down the east bank and stopped at the water's edge. They were sharp and pointed, the tracks of a doe. They sank deeply into the sand, so that he knew the doe was an old one and a large.

Perhaps she was heavy with fawn. She had come down and drunk deeply from the spring, not seeing him where he slept. Then she had scented him. There was a scuffled confusion in the sand where she had wheeled in fright. The tracks up the opposite bank had long harried streaks behind them. Perhaps she had not drunk, after all, before she scented him, and turned and ran with that swift, sand-throwing flight. He hoped she was not now thirsty, wide-eyed in the scrub.

He looked about for other tracks. The squirrels had raced up and down the banks, but they were bold, always. A raccoon had been that way, with his feet like sharp-nailed hands, but he could not be sure how recently. Only his father could tell for certain the hour when any wild things had passed by. Only the doe had surely come and had been frightened. He turned back again to the flutter-mill. It was turning as steadily as though it had always been there. The palm-leaf paddles were frail but they made a brave show of strength, rippling against the shallow water. They were glistening from the slow rain.

Jody looked at the sky. He could not tell the time of day in the grayness, nor how long he may have slept. He bounded up the west bank, where open gallberry flats spread without obstructions. As he stood, hesitant whether to go or stay, the rain ended as gently as it had begun. A light breeze stirred from the southwest. The sun came out. The clouds rolled together into great white billowing feather bolsters, and across the east a rainbow arched, so lovely and so various that Jody thought he would burst with looking at it. The earth was pale green, the air itself was all but visible, golden with the rain-washed sunlight, and all the trees and grass and bushes glittered, varnished with the rain-drops.

A spring of delight boiled up within him as irresistibly as the spring of the branch. He lifted his arms and held them straight from his shoulders like a water-turkey's wings. He began to whirl around in his tracks. He whirled faster and faster until his ecstasy was a whirlpool, and when he thought he would explode with it, he became dizzy and closed his eyes and dropped to the ground and lay flat in the broom-sage. The earth whirled under him and with him. He opened his eyes and the blue April sky and the cotton clouds whirled over him. Boy and earth and trees and sky spun together. The whirling stopped, his head cleared and he got to his feet. He was light-headed and giddy, but something in him was relieved, and the April day could be borne again, like any ordinary day.

Reading Strategy

Analyze imagery What does the imagery reveal about Jody's state of mind and of his relationship to nature?

_____

_____

_____

_____

_____

_____

_____

_____

_____

_____

_____

_____

_____

_____

_____

_____

_____

_____

_____

_____

_____

_____

_____

_____

MARK IT UP

Are you allowed to write in your novel? If so, then mark up the pages as you read, or reread, to help with your note-taking. Develop a shorthand system, including symbols, that works for you. Here are some ideas:

Underline = important idea

Bracket = text to quote

Asterisk = just what you were looking for

Checkmark = might be useful

Circle = unfamiliar word or phrase to look up

▶ BIG Idea

Nature Inspires What have you learned about how nature affects Jody and Penny?

Mark up the excerpt, looking for evidence of how it expresses the Big Idea.

NOVEL EXCERPT: CHAPTER 10

The cranes were dancing a cotillion as surely as it was danced at Volusia. Two stood apart, erect and white, making a strange music that was part cry and part singing. The rhythm was irregular, like the dance. The other birds were in a circle. In the heart of the circle, several moved counter-clock-wise. The musicians made their music. The dancers raised their wings and lifted their feet, first one and then the other. They sunk their heads deep in their snowy breasts, lifted them and sunk again. They moved soundlessly, part awkwardness, part grace. The dance was solemn. Wings fluttered, rising and falling like out-stretched arms. The outer circle shuffled around and around. The group in the center attained a slow frenzy.

Suddenly all motion ceased. Jody thought the dance was over, or that the intruders had been discovered. Then the two musicians joined the circle. Two others took their places. There was a pause. The dance was resumed. The birds were reflected in the clear marsh water. Sixteen white shadows reflected the motions. The evening breeze moved across the sawgrass. It bowed and fluttered. The water rippled. The setting sun lay rosy on the white bodies. Magic birds were dancing in a mystic marsh. The grass swayed with them, and the shallow waters, and the earth fluttered under them. The earth was dancing with the cranes, and the low sun, and the wind and sky.

Jody found his own arms lifting and falling with his breath, as the cranes' wings lifted. The sun was sinking into the sawgrass. The marsh was golden. The whooping cranes were washed with gold. The far hammocks were black. Darkness came to the lily pads, and the water blackened. The cranes were whiter than any clouds, or any white bloom of oleander or of lily. Without warning, they took flight. Whether the hour-long dance was, simply, done, or whether the long nose of an alligator had lifted above the water to alarm them, Jody could not tell, but they were gone. . . .

At the house, bread was baked and waiting, and hot fat was in the iron skillet. Penny lighted a fat-wood torch and went to the lot to do his chores. Jody scaled and dressed the fish at the back stoop, where a ray of light glimmered from the fire on the hearth. Ma Baxter dipped the pieces in meal and fried them crisp and golden. The family ate without speaking.

She said, "What ails you fellers?"

They did not answer. They had no thought for what they ate nor for the woman. They were no more than conscious that she spoke to them. They had seen a thing that was unearthly. They were in a trance from the strong spell of its beauty.

Use the Cornell Note-Taking system to take notes on the excerpt at the left. Record your notes, Reduce them, and then Recap (summarize) them.

Record

Reduce

Try the following approach as you reduce your notes.

TO THE POINT
Write a few key words.

Recap

Respond and Think Critically

1. At the beginning of the novel, what is the one thing that Jody feels he is missing? What does this feeling suggest about Jody's life? [Interpret]

_____

_____

_____

_____

2. How does Penny react when Jody plays in the glen instead of doing his chores? How might Penny's experiences as a boy have influenced his attitude toward Jody? [Infer]

_____

_____

_____

_____

3. Penny and Ora have conflicting opinions about the Forresters and about Jody's contact with the family. Contrast Penny's and Ora's attitudes, and explain which attitude you think is right. Be sure to include your reasons for taking one side or the other. [Evaluate]

_____

_____

_____

_____

4. When Buck Forrester and Oliver Hutto fight over a young woman they both like, Jody is torn between his loyalty and affection for both Oliver and Fodder-wing. Jody finally decides to take Oliver's side. Why does he make this decision? Would you have made the same one? Why or why not? [Analyze]

_____

_____

_____

_____

5. **Nature Inspires** In what ways does nature influence Jody's life? [Conclude]

_____

_____

_____

_____

APPLY BACKGROUND
Reread Meet the Author on page 122. How did that information help you understand or appreciate what you read in the novel?

_____

_____

_____

_____

_____

_____

_____

_____

_____

_____

_____

_____

_____

_____

_____

_____

_____

_____

_____

_____

_____

_____

_____

_____

_____

_____

_____

_____

_____

_____

Literary Element Simile

At the end of Chapter 13, the author tells us that Jody's "thoughts were as turbulent as the current." Why is this simile appropriate at this point in the text? [Analyze]

_____

_____

_____

_____

_____

_____

_____

_____

_____

Reading Strategy Analyze Imagery

Choose one short passage in the text in which the author uses vivid imagery to help you visualize the setting. Does this imagery remind you of a place that you have been? If not, in what ways is this imagery different from what you are used to? [Connect]

_____

_____

_____

_____

_____

_____

_____

_____

_____

_____

Vocabulary Practice

A **synonym** is a word that has the same or nearly the same meaning as another word. Match each boldfaced vocabulary word below with its synonym. Use a thesaurus or dictionary to check your answers.

1. **deprecatory**
2. **indolently**
3. **prolific**
4. **rudiments**
5. **venerable**

a. languidly
b. expedient
c. dignified
d. scarce
e. critical
f. productive
g. basics

Academic Vocabulary

The Baxters rely on the land as their primary **resource** _for food._ In the preceding sentence, _resource_ means "supply" or "source." Think about how you obtain the food that you eat. What **resources** do you rely on for food every day?

_____

_____

_____

_____

_____

_____

_____

_____

_____

_____

_____

_____

Write with Style

Apply Figurative Language

Assignment Figurative language is used by authors to help readers grasp abstract thoughts and to see an object in a new way. Write a paragraph describing a setting that you are very familiar with and include at least three similes or metaphors.

Get Ideas Make a word web, placing the setting that you chose in the center of the web. On the outside of the web, jot down every sight, smell, texture, taste, and sound that you associate with that place. Connect words that connect in your mind. Then extend your web to the next level. This time think about how the central word is *like* something else that is normally completely different. Write those comparisons around it, continuing the web and the comparisons.

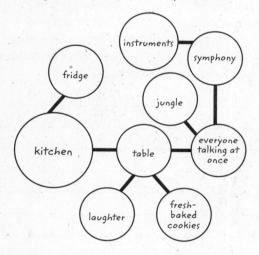

When you have finished your web, turn your three strongest comparisons into similes and metaphors you can include in your paragraph.

EXAMPLE:
At the dinner table, our conversation often sounds like a symphony of a million instruments playing simultaneously.

Give It Structure Because you are describing a place, consider how you are going to organize your paragraph. Are you going to start by describing the top of the scene and work down?

Look at Language Pay careful attention to your word choice and ask yourself whether the similes and metaphors you chose are effective.

Connect to Content Areas

Science

Assignment In *The Yearling*, Jody and his family are dependent on the nearby sinkhole for their water. Research sinkholes in order to enhance your understanding of these natural "accidents" and the setting of the story. Then prepare an informational pamphlet about sinkholes. Include a bibliography of reference materials at the end of your pamphlet.

Investigate First make a list of possible sources of information; include both print and Internet resources. Investigate what a sinkhole is and why Florida has so many. You may want to focus your investigation on ancient sinkholes, such as the one in northwest Gainesville called the Devil's Millhopper, or on record-breaking sinkholes, such as the 1981 collapse in Winter Park, Florida. Use a chart like the one below to record what you learn.

Definition	How Created	Locations	Unique Features	Unfamiliar Terms

Compare what you learn from each source. If there is contradictory information, use what you found in the most reliable source.

If you are unfamiliar with the scientific terms used in any of your sources, investigate further to clarify the meanings of those terms.

Create Besides the bibliography, your pamphlet should have an introduction, a section on each of the topics in your chart, and a graphic aid.

Report If possible, use word-processing software to make your pamphlet look professional. Create a three-panel pamphlet by setting the page layout to "landscape" and running the text in three columns.

Connect to the Literature

How do people work through the loss of a loved one or another great loss?

Discuss

As a class, discuss ways in which people can work through grief and learn to deal with their loss.

Build Background

Jody's Fawn

When Jody takes in the orphaned fawn, the deer is very young and is still walking on wobbly legs and nursing. It is not yet a yearling—an animal that is one year old. Flag, as Jody names his new pet, was probably born in late March or early April. If the fawn is like most, it weighs about six pounds. His red coat is probably dappled with small white spots, which help him blend in with his surroundings. His fur makes him indistinguishable from the red clay of the soil, and the white markings on his coat look like spots of sunlight on the leaves and branches around him. These characteristics help protect young deer from their predators.

NOVEL NOTEBOOK
Keep a special notebook to record entries about the novels that you read this year.

WRITE THE CAPTION
Write a caption for the image below, in the present tense, using information in Build Background.

_____

_____

_____

_____

_____

_____

_____

_____

_____

_____

_____

_____

_____

_____

_____

_____

_____

_____

_____

_____

_____

_____

Set Purposes for Reading

▶ **BIG Idea** **The Strength of Family**

Think about the people in your family. What makes your family special? What are some ways you would define a family? Do people have to be related by blood to be family?

In *The Yearling*, Rawlings presents the inner workings of an individual family and also introduces the reader to the idea that the definition of family can extend beyond bloodlines. Make a list of the qualities you think make up a family. Then, as you read, think about your notions of family and try to identify these in the story. You can add new ideas to your list as you read.

Literary Element   **Symbol**

A **symbol** is any person, animal, place, object or event that has meaning in itself but also stands for something else, usually on an abstract level.

Recognizing an author's use of symbols can help you understand the intended meaning or theme of a literary work.

As you read, ask yourself, What are the symbols in this section and what does each symbol reveal about the characters and themes of the novel?

Reading Strategy   **Make Generalizations**

When you **make generalizations,** you formulate a broad statement that is supported by details in a work. For example, after reading a certain number of literary works about animals or nature, one might make a generalization that many animal stories address themes regarding how humans and animals relate or about conflicts between humans and nature or the wild.

Making generalizations helps the reader make connections between the text and his or her own life. This can help the reader to better understand the text and be more invested in the story and characters.

As you read, ask yourself what statements or opinions the author seems to be making about the bigger issues she raises in the novel including conflicts with nature. What did you think about these issues before you read the book? After? You may find it helpful to use a graphic organizer like the one below and the one on the next page.

Vocabulary

implacable [im plak´ə bəl]
adj. hard-hearted; impossible to change
When a tornado appears, nature can seem like an implacable enemy.

quiescent [kwīes´ənt]
adj. being still or at rest
Watching the ocean ebb and flow always helps him to have a quiescent mind.

staunch [stônch]
adj. firm and steadfast; faithful
The company president is a staunch supporter of the local school; he helped fund two new science labs last year.

stolidly [stol´id lē]
adv. with little emotion; impassively
She responded stolidly to the false accusations that had been made against her; she didn't want others to know that she was upset.

tacit [tas´ it]
adj. not spoken; implied by or inferred from actions or statements
They made a tacit agreement in the form of a handshake.

Before Reading	After Reading

In the study of literature, conflict refers to a struggle between opposing forces. *The Yearling* contains a number of different conflicts that move the story forward, including conflict with nature. Choose at least one conflict in addition to the one provided below. Then fill out the diagrams to analyze how conflict affects the story.

Conflict: What is the problem?

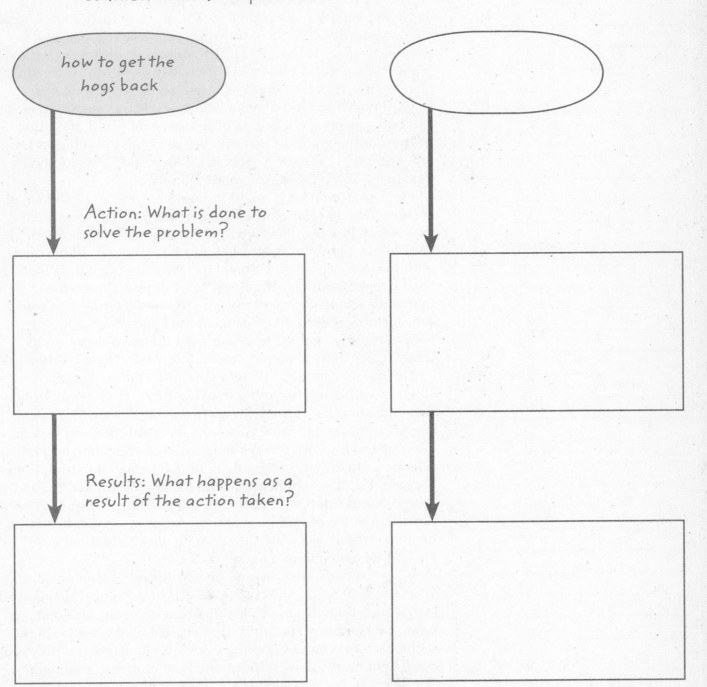

how to get the hogs back

Action: What is done to solve the problem?

Results: What happens as a result of the action taken?

Literary Element

Symbol What might the fawn symbolize in this passage?

_____
_____
_____
_____
_____
_____
_____
_____
_____
_____
_____
_____
_____
_____
_____
_____
_____
_____
_____
_____
_____
_____
_____
_____
_____
_____
_____
_____
_____

NOVEL EXCERPT: CHAPTER 15

The fawn lifted its face to his. It turned its head with a wide, wondering motion and shook him through with the stare of its liquid eyes. It was quivering. It made no effort to rise or run. Jody could not trust himself to move.

He whispered, "It's me."

The fawn lifted its nose, scenting him. He reached out one hand and laid it on the soft neck. The touch made him delirious. He moved forward on all fours until he was close beside it. He put his arms around its body. A light convulsion passed over it but it did not stir. He stroked its sides as gently as though the fawn were a china deer and he might break it. Its skin was softer than the white 'coonskin knapsack. It was sleek and clean and had a sweet scent of grass. He rose slowly and lifted the fawn from the ground. It was no heavier than old Julia. Its legs hung limply. They were surprisingly long and he had to hoist the fawn as high as possible under his arm.

He was afraid that it might kick and bleat at sight and smell of its mother. He skirted the clearing and pushed his way into the thicket. It was difficult to fight through with his burden. The fawn's legs caught in the bushes and he could not lift his own with freedom. He tried to shield its face from prickling vines. Its head bobbed with his stride. His heart thumped with the marvel of its acceptance of him. He reached the trail and walked as fast as he could until he came to the intersection with the road home. He stopped to rest and set the fawn down on its dangling legs. It wavered on them. It looked at him and bleated.

He said, enchanted, "I'll tote you time I git my breath."

He remembered his father's saying that a fawn would follow that had been first carried. He started away slowly. The fawn stared after him. He came back to it and stroked it and walked away again. It took a few wobbling steps toward him and cried piteously. It was willing to follow him. It beonged to him. It was his own. He was light-headed with his joy. He wanted to fondle it, to run and romp with it, to call to it to come to him. He dared not alarm it. He picked it up and carried it in front of him over his two arms. It seemed to him that he walked without effort. He had the strength of a Forrester.

His arms began to ache and he was forced to stop again. When he walked on, the fawn followed him at once. He allowed it to walk a little distance, then picked it up again. The distance home was nothing. He could have walked all day and into the night, carrying it and watching it follow. He was wet with sweat but a light breeze blew through the June morning, cooling him. The sky was as clear as spring water in a blue china cup. He came to the clearing. It was fresh and green after the night's rain. He could see Buck Forrester following old Caesar at the plow in the cornfield. He thought he heard him curse the horse's slowness. He fumbled with the gate latch and was finally obliged to set down the fawn to manage it. It came to him that he would walk into the house, into Penny's bedroom, with the fawn walking behind him. But at the steps, the fawn balked and refused to climb them. He picked it up and went to his father. Penny lay with closed eyes.

Jody called, "Pa! Lookit!"

Penny turned his head. Jody stood beside him, the fawn clutched hard against him. It seemed to Penny that the boy's eyes were as bright as the fawn's. His face lightened, seeing them together.

He said, "I'm proud you found him."

"Pa, he wa'n't skeert o' me. He were layin' up right where his mammy had made his bed."

"The does learns 'em that, time they're borned. You kin step on a fawn, times, they lay so still."

"Pa, I toted him, and when I set him down, right off he follered me. Like a dog, Pa."

"Ain't that fine? Let's see him better."

Jody lifted the fawn high. Penny reached out a hand and touched its nose. It bleated and reached hopefully for his fingers.

He said, "Well, leetle feller. I'm sorry I had to take away your mammy."

"You reckon he misses her?"

"No. He misses his rations and he knows that. He misses somethin' else but he don't know jest what."

Ma Baxter came into the room.

"Look, Ma, I found him."

"I see."

"Ain't he purty, Ma? Lookit them spots all in rows. Lookit them big eyes. Ain't he purty?"

Literary Element

Symbol What might the fawn symbolize in this section?

_____
_____
_____
_____
_____
_____
_____
_____
_____
_____
_____
_____
_____
_____
_____
_____
_____
_____
_____
_____
_____
_____
_____
_____
_____
_____
_____

Reading Strategy

Make Generalizations What generalizations did you make about the power of nature before you read this passage?

_____
_____
_____
_____
_____
_____
_____
_____
_____
_____
_____
_____
_____
_____
_____
_____
_____
_____
_____
_____
_____
_____
_____
_____
_____
_____
_____
_____

NOVEL EXCERPT: CHAPTER 14

He said, "When there's trouble waitin' for you, you jest as good go to meet it."

The rattler struck him from under the grape-vine without warning. Jody saw the flash, blurred as a shadow, swifter than a martin, surer than the slashing claws of a bear. He saw his father stagger backward under the force of the blow. He heard him give a cry. He wanted to step back, too. He wanted to cry out with all his voice. He stood rooted to the sand and could not make a sound. It was lightning that had struck, and not a rattler. It was a branch that broke, it was a bird that flew, it was a rabbit running—

Penny shouted, "Git back! Hold the dogs!"

The voice released him. He dropped back and clutched the dogs by the scruff of their necks. He saw the mottled shadow lift its flat head, knee-high. The head swung from side to side, following his father's slow motions. He heard the rattles hum. The dogs heard. They winded. The fur stood stiff on their bodies. Old Julia whined and twisted out of his hand. She turned and slunk down the trail. Her long tail clung to her hindquarters. Rip reared on his hind feet, barking.

As slowly as a man in a dream, Penny backed away. The rattles sung. They were not rattles—Surely it was a locust humming. Surely it was a tree-frog singing—Penny lifted his gun to his shoulder and fired. Jody quivered. The rattler coiled and writhed in its spasms. The head was buried in the sand. The contortions moved down the length of the thick body, the rattles whirred feebly and were still. The coiling flattened into slow convolutions, like a low tide ebbing. Penny turned and stared at his son.

He said, "He got me."

He lifted his right arm and gaped at it. His lips lifted dry over his teeth. His throat worked. He looked dully at two punctures in the flesh. A drop of blood oozed from each.

He said, "He was a big un."

Jody let go his hold on Rip. The dog ran to the dead snake and barked fiercely. He made sorties and at last poked the coils with one paw. He quieted and snuffed about in the sand. Penny lifted his head from his staring. His face was like hickory ashes.

He said, "Ol' Death goin' to git me yit."

He licked his lips. He turned abruptly and began to push through the scrub in the direction of the clearing. The road would be shorter going, for it was open, but he headed blindly for home in a direct line. He plowed through the low scrub oaks, the gallberries, the scrub palmettos. Jody panted behind him. His heart pounded so hard that he could not see where he was going. He followed the sound of his father's crashing across the undergrowth. Suddenly the denseness ended. A patch of higher oaks made a shaded clearing. It was strange to walk in silence.

Penny stopped short. There was a stirring ahead. A doe-deer leaped to her feet. Penny drew a deep breath, as though breathing were for some reason easier. He lifted his shotgun and leveled it at the head. It flashed over Jody's mind that his father had gone mad. This was no moment to stop for game. Penny fired. The doe turned a somersault and dropped to the sand and kicked a little and lay still. Penny ran to the body and drew his knife from its scabbard. Now Jody knew his father was insane. Penny did not cut the throat, but slashed into the belly. He laid the carcass wide open. The pulse still throbbed in the heart. Penny slashed out the liver. Kneeling, he changed his knife to his left hand. He turned his right arm and stared again at the twin punctures. They were now close. The forearm was thick-swollen and blackening. The sweat stood out on his forehead. He cut quickly across the wound. A dark blood gushed and he pressed the warm liver against the incision.

He said in a hushed voice, "I kin feel it draw—"

He pressed harder. He took the meat away and looked at it. It was a venomous green. He turned it and applied the fresh side.

He said, "Cut me out a piece o' the heart."

Jody jumped from his paralysis. He fumbled with the knife. He hacked away a portion.

Penny said, "Another."

He changed the application again and again.

He said, "Hand me the knife."

He cut a higher gash in his arm where the dark swelling rose the thickest. Jody cried out.

"Pa! You'll bleed to death!"

"I'd ruther bleed to death than swell. I seed a man die—"

The sweat poured down his cheeks.

"Do it hurt bad, Pa?"

"Like a hot knife was buried to the shoulder."

The meat no longer showed green when he withdrew it. The warm vitality of the doe's flesh was solidifying in death. He stood up.

He said quietly, "Cain't do it no more good. I'm goin' on home. You go to the Forresters and git 'em to ride to the Branch for Doc Wilson."

Reading Strategy

Make Generalizations What generalization can you make about nature after reading this passage? Does this conform to ideas about nature in other animal stories you have read?

_____

_____

_____

_____

_____

_____

_____

_____

_____

_____

_____

_____

_____

_____

_____

_____

_____

_____

_____

_____

_____

_____

_____

_____

_____

_____

_____

_____

MARK IT UP

Are you allowed to write in your novel? If so, then mark up the pages as you read, or reread, to help with your note-taking. Develop a shorthand system, including symbols, that works for you. Here are some ideas:

Underline = important idea

Bracket = text to quote

Asterisk = just what you were looking for

Checkmark = might be useful

Circle = unfamiliar word or phrase to look up

▶ **BIG Idea**

The Strength of Family Have your ideas about what makes a family changed through your reading?

Mark up the excerpt, looking for evidence of how it expresses the Big Idea.

NOVEL EXCERPT: CHAPTER 17

Jody stared at Buck and Buck stared back at him. The numbness grew into a paralysis. He felt no sorrow, only a coldness and a faintness. Fodder-wing was neither dead nor alive. He was, simply, nowhere at all.

Buck said hoarsely, "You kin come look at him."

First Buck said that Fodder-wing was gone, like candlelight, and then he said that he was here. None of it made sense. Buck turned into the house. He looked back, compelling Jody with his dull eyes. Jody lifted one leg after the other and mounted the steps. He followed Buck into the house. The Forrester men sat all together. There was a oneness about them, sitting so, motionless and heavy. They were pieces of one great dark rock, broken into separate men. Pa Forrester turned his head and looked at Jody as though he were a stranger. Then he turned it away again. Lem and Mill-wheel looked at him. The others did not stir. It seemed to Jody that they saw him from over a wall they had built against him. They were unwilling to hold the sight of him. Buck groped for his hand. He led him toward the large bedroom. He started to speak. His voice broke. He stopped and gripped Jody's shoulder.

He said, "Bear up."

Fodder-wing lay with closed eyes, small and lost in the center of the great bed. He was smaller than when he had lain sleeping on his pallet. He was covered with a sheet, turned back beneath his chin. His arms were outside the sheet, folded across his chest, the palms of the hands falling outward, twisted and clumsy, as in life. Jody was frightened. Ma Forrester sat by the side of the bed. She held her apron over her head and rocked herself back and forth. She flung down the apron.

She said, "I've lost my boy. My pore crookedy boy."

She covered herself again and swayed from side to side.

She moaned, "The Lord's hard. Oh, the Lord's hard."

Jody wanted to run away. The bony face on the pillow terrified him. It was Fodder-wing and it was not Fodder-wing. Buck drew him to the edge of the bed.

"He'll not hear, but speak to him."

Jody's throat worked. No words came. Fodder-wing seemed made of tallow, like a candle. Suddenly he was familiar.

Jody whispered, "Hey."

The paralysis broke, having spoken. His throat tightened as though a rope choked it. Fodder-wing's silence was intolerable. Now he understood. This was death. Death was a silence that gave back no answer. Fodder-wing would never speak to him again. He turned and buried his face against Buck's chest. The big arms gripped him. He stood a long time.

Use the Cornell Note-Taking system to take notes on the excerpt at the left. Record your notes, Reduce them, and then Recap (summarize) them.

Record

_____
_____
_____
_____
_____
_____
_____
_____
_____
_____
_____
_____
_____
_____
_____
_____
_____
_____
_____
_____
_____
_____
_____
_____

Recap

_____
_____
_____
_____
_____
_____
_____

Reduce

Try the following approach as you reduce your notes.

MY VIEW
Write down your thoughts on the excerpt.

_____
_____
_____
_____
_____
_____
_____
_____
_____
_____
_____
_____
_____
_____
_____
_____
_____
_____
_____
_____
_____
_____

Respond and Think Critically

1. Why did the Forresters trap and take the Baxters' hogs? Why is the loss of the hogs so serious a problem for the Baxters? [Interpret]

_____

_____

_____

_____

2. How does Jody come to terms with Fodder-wing's death? What does this response reveal about Jody? [Evaluate]

_____

_____

_____

_____

3. Evaluate the effects of the flood on the Baxter household. Why are the consequences of the flood so devastating? [Conclude]

_____

_____

_____

_____

4. Did you expect anyone from the Forrester family to help the Baxters? Why or why not? Would you have been able to overlook your hard feelings to take over Penny Baxter's chores until he recuperated? Explain your reasons. [Connect]

_____

_____

_____

_____

5. The Strength of Family In what ways do the Baxters and Forresters support each other like family in this section? [Interpret]

_____

_____

_____

_____

APPLY BACKGROUND
Reread Build Background on page 135. How did that information help you understand or appreciate what you read in the novel?

_____

_____

_____

_____

_____

_____

_____

_____

_____

_____

_____

_____

_____

_____

_____

_____

_____

_____

_____

_____

_____

_____

_____

_____

_____

_____

_____

_____

_____

_____

_____

_____

Literary Element **Symbol**

What does the sinkhole symbolize in the novel?
[Interpret]

_____

_____

_____

_____

_____

_____

_____

_____

_____

Reading Strategy **Make Generalizations**

As the Baxters' and Forresters' conflict with Old Slewfoot continues, what generalization does Rawlings seem to be making about the relationship between humans and animals? [Conclude]

_____

_____

_____

_____

_____

_____

_____

_____

_____

_____

_____

Vocabulary Practice

Studying the **etymology,** or origin and history, of a word can help you better understand and explore its meaning. Create a word map, like the one below, for each of these vocabulary words from the selection. Use a dictionary for help.

implacable   stolidly
quiescent   tacit
staunch

EXAMPLE: **scripture**
Definition: any sacred writing
Etymology: Latin _scriptura_ means book or "writing"

Sample Sentence:
Ameena follows the **scripture** of the Muslim faith.

Academic Vocabulary

The Forresters have such a rough **affect** _that Ma Baxter is surprised by the kindness they extend during Penny's recovery._ In the preceding sentence, _affect_ means "a feeling or emotion that is conveyed by body language and facial expression." _Affect_ also has other meanings. For instance: _He didn't want his decision to_ **affect** _the other students, but it did._ What do you think _affect_ means in the preceding sentence? What is the difference between the two meanings?

_____

_____

_____

_____

_____

_____

_____

_____

_____

_____

_____

Writing

Personal Response Do you think Jody was right to bring the orphaned fawn home with him? Why or why not?

_____

_____

_____

_____

_____

_____

_____

_____

_____

_____

_____

_____

_____

_____

_____

_____

_____

_____

_____

_____

_____

_____

_____

_____

_____

_____

_____

Speaking and Listening
Speech

Assignment A **eulogy** is a special speech of praise that is delivered at a funeral. Imagine that you are Jody and that the Forresters have asked you to eulogize Fodder-wing. In your speech, describe Fodder-wing's best qualities and explain why he will be missed.

Prepare Rawlings used figurative language to help deepen our understanding of her characters and settings. Following Rawling's example, incorporate similes and metaphors into your eulogy. Think about the characteristics of Fodder-wing that can be compared with something else. Make a list of these things and then extend a few of them into sentences you can use in your eulogy of Fodder-wing.

EXAMPLE:
My Aunt Emily
kind
beautiful smile
funny
courageous

When my Aunt Emily smiled, it was like her face was a beautiful flower opening to the sun.

Deliver Make sure that your speech conveys a serious, respectful tone. Make eye contact with your audience. Speak loudly and clearly so that they can understand you. Maintain good posture to reflect confidence. Use gestures as appropriate, such as in a moment of great emotion.

Evaluate Write a paragraph evaluating your eulogy. When your classmates present their eulogies, offer oral feedback on their speeches.

Connect to the Literature

Almost everyone feels like running away from his or her problems from time to time. What do you suppose makes people feel this way?

Discuss

With a group of your classmates, discuss your response to the question above. What are the disadvantages of running away? Are there any advantages? What might someone learn from the experience?

Build Background

The Florida Black Bear

The Florida black bear is an intimidating animal. Though it may look awkward, it can run very fast and climb trees with amazing ease because of its sharp, curved claws. It uses its powerful front paws to subdue its prey, and it can easily kill a small creature. Usually, male black bears are larger than females. Bears are omnivorous, that is they eat both plant and animal matter. The black bear diet includes nuts, berries, and insects, and rarely they will eat meat they may find when scavenging. The black bear has a good sense of hearing, and its sense of smell is especially keen. The common belief that they do not have good eyesight is untrue. They simply tend to depend on their other senses more. Bears are typically solitary and quiet animals that hibernate during the cold months. It is during this time that their cubs are born.

NOVEL NOTEBOOK
Keep a special notebook to record entries about the novels that you read this year.

WRITE THE CAPTION
Write a caption for the image below, in the present tense, using information in Build Background.

_____

_____

_____

_____

_____

_____

_____

_____

_____

_____

_____

_____

_____

_____

_____

_____

_____

_____

_____

_____

_____

_____

Set Purposes for Reading

▶ **BIG Idea** Life Lessons

Life lessons can change our whole perspective. What are some important life lessons you have learned? How did those lessons change the way you view the world around you?

In *The Yearling,* Jody learns an important life lesson. As you read, observe the changes in his personality and values and make a chart that lists how Jody was before and after he learned this life lesson.

Literary Element Voice

Voice refers to the distinctive use of language within a text. Each author has a unique writing voice. It is this voice that conveys the author's or narrator's personality to the reader.

Voice is determined by elements of style such as word choice and tone, however, voice is not the same as style. Voice is the language the author uses, whereas style is how language as well as many other elements are organized.

As you read, ask yourself what makes Rawlings' writing voice unique. Consider how the stylistic choices she makes contribute to your understanding of the characters and setting. These include her use of **dialect.** Dialect is a variation of a language spoken by a group of people, often within a particular region. Dialect often includes regional **idioms,** expressions with meaning different from literal meaning, such as *over the hill,* meaning "old." Use the graphic organizer on the next page to help you explore the use of dialect to show a writer's voice.

Reading Strategy Analyze Style

Style includes word choice, or **diction,** and the length and arrangement of sentences, as well as the use of figurative language and imagery.

When you **analyze style,** you analyze the expressive qualities that distinguish an author's work to determine their effect on the overall text.

As you read, notice the unique qualities of Rawlings' writing style. You may find it helpful to use a graphic organizer like the one below.

Sentence	Literary Device Used	Effect on Reader

Rawlings' use of a regional dialect makes her writing voice unique. However, that dialect can pose a challenge to a modern reader. As you read, record phrases and sentences that you have trouble deciphering. Working with your classmates, try to translate the phrases and sentences into modern English.

Regional Dialect	
Phrase	Translation
Jest as ornery dead as alive	very grouchy or hard to deal with

Literary Element

Voice What is Rawlings' attitude toward Penny in this passage? How can you tell?

_____
_____
_____
_____
_____
_____
_____
_____
_____
_____
_____
_____
_____
_____
_____
_____
_____
_____
_____
_____
_____
_____
_____
_____
_____
_____
_____
_____
_____
_____
_____
_____

NOVEL EXCERPT: CHAPTER 26

Penny said, "When I were about your size, my uncle Miles come visitin' from Georgia. And a cold day about like this he takened me in the very swamp we come through today. We was moseyin' along, not lookin' for nothin' in pertickler, and on beyond us we seed what looked like a buzzard settin' on a stump, peckin' at somethin'. Well, we got there and what do you suppose 'twas?"

"'Twasn't no buzzard?"

"'Twasn't no buzzard a-tall. 'Twas a bear cub cuffin' playful-like at his twin on the ground below him.

"My uncle Miles said, 'Now we'll jest ketch us a bear cub.' They was right gentle and he goes up to the one on the stump and ketched it. Well, when he'd ketched it, he didn't have nary thing to tote it in. And them scaper's'll gnaw on you if they ain't in a sack. Well, them up-country folks wears underwear in the winter. He takened off his breeches and he takened off his long drawers and he tied knots in the legs of 'em and he made him a sack. He puttened the cub in it and about the time he reached for his breeches to put 'em back on agin, here come a crashin' and a woofin' and a stompin' in the bresh, and the old she-bear come outen the thick right at him. Well, he takened out through the swamp and dropped the cub and the mammy gathered it up, drawers and all. But she were so clost behind him she stepped on a vine and it tripped him and throwed him flat amongst the thorns and brambles. And aunt Moll was a muddle-minded kind o' woman and she couldn't never make it out how he come home without his drawers on a cold day, and his bottom scratched. But uncle Miles allus said that wasn't nothin' to the puzzlin' the mammy bear must o' done over them drawers on her young un."

Jody laughed until he could laugh no more.

He complained, "Pa, you got all them tales in your mind and you don't tell 'em."

"Well, it takes a thing like bein' in the swamp where it happened, to call it back to me. Now in that same swamp, one very cold March, I remember comin' on another pair o' bear cubs. They was whimperin' with the cold. New-borned cubs is no bigger'n rats and plumb naked, and these uns hadn't yit growed much fur. They was huddled up in a red bay thicket and cryin' like human babies. Listen!"

The sound of hoof beats was unmistakable along the road behind them.

"Now wouldn't it be fine not to have to go clare to Fort Gates for he'p?"

The sound came closer. They stepped to the side of the road. The riders were the Forresters.

Penny said, "Looks like I mis-called myself."

Buck led the cavalcade. They streamed down the road. They were drunk as lords. They reined in.

"Now look at this! Ol' Penny Baxter and his he-cub! Hey, Penny! What the devil you doin' up here?"

Penny said, "I been on a hunt. And this un was deliberate. Me and Jody takened out after ol' Slewfoot."

"Whoops! On foot? Listen to that, boys! That's better'n a pair o' biddies rompin' on a hawk."

"And we got him," Penny said.

Buck shook himself. The whole array seemed to sober.

"Don't tell me none o' them tales. Where's he at?"

"'Bout two mile to the east, between Bear Spring and the river."

"Reckon he is. He fools around there a good bit."

"He's dead. How I know he's dead, I gutted him. Me and Jody's walkin' to Fort Gates for he'p in totin' him outen the swamp."

Buck stiffened in a drunken dignity.

"You goin' to Fort Gates for he'p gittin' out ol' Slewfoot? And the best slew-footers in the county right here beside you?"

Lem called, "What'll you give us, do we go tote him out?"

"Half the meat. I figgered on givin' it to you anyways, account of him tormentin' you so, and Buck comin' to warn me."

Buck said, "You and me's friends, Penny Baxter. I warn you and you warn me. Git up here behind me and point the way."

Mill-wheel said, "I don't know as I crave goin' into no swamp today, and clare back to Baxter's Island. I got my mind set on a frolic."

Buck said, "You ain't got no mind. Penny Baxter!"

"What you want?"

"You still figgerin' on goin' to them doin's at Volusia?"

"Could we git the bear out in time to make it, we figgered on it. We're runnin' mighty late."

"Git up here behind me and point the way. Boys, we'll git out the bear and we'll go to the doin's at Volusia. If they don't want us, they kin throw us out—if they kin."

Literary Element

Voice Rawlings chooses to include the dialect that was unique to farmers in central Florida during that time. In this excerpt, does this regional dialect make her characters more or less believable? Explain.

_____
_____
_____
_____
_____
_____
_____
_____
_____
_____
_____
_____
_____
_____
_____
_____
_____
_____
_____
_____
_____
_____
_____
_____
_____

Reading Strategy

Analyze Style In the first paragraph of this excerpt, what strategies does Rawlings use to create a mood of fear and suspense?

_____

_____

_____

_____

_____

_____

_____

_____

_____

_____

_____

_____

_____

_____

_____

_____

_____

_____

_____

_____

_____

_____

_____

_____

_____

_____

_____

_____

NOVEL EXCERPT: CHAPTER 33

The sun was setting. He was in a panic that he would not reach the clearing before dark. He exhausted himself, and was obliged to slow down to a walk. His flesh quivered. His heart pounded. He had to stop entirely and rest. Darkness overtook him half a mile from home. Even in the dusk, landmarks were familiar. The tall pines of the clearing were recognizable, blacker than the creeping night. He came to the slat fence. He felt his way along it. He opened the gate and went into the yard. He passed around the side of the house to the kitchen stoop and stepped up on it. He crept to the window on bare silent feet and peered in.

A fire burned low on the hearth. Penny sat hunched beside it, wrapped in quilts. One had covered his eyes. Jody went to the door and unlatched it and stepped inside. Penny lifted his head.

"Ory?"

"Hit's me."

He thought his father had not heard him.

"Hit's Jody."

Penny turned his head and looked at him wonderingly, as though the gaunt ragged boy with sweat and tear-streaks down the grime, with hollow eyes under matted hair, were some stranger of whom he expected that he state his business.

He said, "Jody."

Jody dropped his eyes.

"Come close."

He went to his father and stood beside him. Penny reached out for his hand and took it and turned it over and rubbed it slowly between his own. Jody felt drops on his hand like a warm rain.

"Boy—I near about give you out."

Penny felt along his arm. He looked up at him.

"You all right?"

He nodded.

"You all right—You ain't dead nor gone. You all right." A light filled his face. "Glory be."

It was unbelievable, Jody thought. He was wanted.

He said, "I had to come home."

"Why, shore you did."

"I ain't meant what I said. Hatin' you—"

The light broke into the familiar smile.

"Why, shore you ain't. 'When I was a child, I spake as a child.'"

Penny stirred in his chair.

"They's rations in the safe. In the kittle there. You hongry?"

"I ain't et but oncet. Last night."

"Not but oncet? Then now you know. Ol' Starvation—" His eyes shone in the firelight as Jody had pictured them. "Ol' Starvation— he's got a face meaner'n ol' Slewfoot, ain't he?"

"Hit's fearful."

"There's biscuits there. Open the honey. There's due to be milk in the gourd."

Jody fumbled among the dishes. He ate standing, wolfing down the food. He dipped into a dish of cooked cow-peas with his fingers, scooping them into his mouth. Penny stared at him.

He said, "I'm sorry you had to learn it that-a-way."

"Where's Ma?"

"She's drove the wagon to the Forresters to trade for seed-corn. She figgered she'd try to plant a part of a crop agin. She carried the chickens, to trade. It hurted her pride turrible, but she was obliged to go."

Jody closed the door of the cabinet.

He said, "I should of washed. I'm awful dirty."

"There's warm water on the hearth."

Jody poured water in the basin and scrubbed his face and arms and hands. The water was too dark even for his feet. He threw it out of the door and poured more, and sat on the floor and washed his feet.

Penny said, "I'd be proud to know where you been."

"I been on the river. I aimed to go to Boston."

"I see."

He looked small and shrunken inside the quilts.

Jody said, "How you makin' it, Pa? You better?"

Penny looked a long time into the embers on the hearth.

He said, "You jest as good to know the truth. I ain't scarcely wuth shootin'."

Jody said, "When I git the work done, you got to leave me go fetch ol' Doc to you."

Penny studied him.

He said, "You've done come back different. You've takened a punishment. You ain't a yearlin' no longer. Jody—"

"Yes, sir."

"I'm goin' to talk to you, man to man. You figgered I went back on you. Now there's a thing ever' man has got to know. Mebbe you know it a'ready. 'Twa'n't only me. 'Twa'n't only your yearlin' deer havin' to be destroyed. Boy, life goes back on you."

Jody looked at his father. He nodded.

Reading Strategy

Analyze Style What is personified in the highlighted passage? Why might Rawlings have chosen to use personification here?

_____

_____

_____

_____

_____

_____

_____

_____

_____

_____

_____

_____

_____

_____

_____

_____

_____

_____

_____

_____

_____

_____

_____

_____

_____

MARK IT UP

Are you allowed to write in your novel? If so, then mark up the pages as you read, or reread, to help with your note-taking. Develop a shorthand system, including symbols, that works for you. Here are some ideas:

Underline = important idea

Bracket = text to quote

Asterisk = just what you were looking for

Checkmark = might be useful

Circle = unfamiliar word or phrase to look up

▶ **BIG Idea**

Life Lessons What are some life lessons Jody has learned?

Mark up the excerpt, looking for evidence of how it expresses the Big Idea.

NOVEL EXCERPT: CHAPTER 33

I've wanted life to be easy for you. Easier'n 'twas for me. A man's heart aches, seein' his young uns face the world. Knowin' they got to git their guts tore out, the way his was tore. I wanted to spare you, long as I could. I wanted you to frolic with your yearlin'. I knowed the lonesomeness he eased for you. But ever' man's lonesome. What's he to do then? What's he to do when he gits knocked down? Why, take it for his share and go on."

Jody said, "I'm 'shamed I runned off."

Penny sat upright.

He said, "You're near enough growed to do your choosin'. Could be you'd crave to go to sea, like Oliver. There's men seems made for the land, and men seems made for the sea. But I'd be proud did you choose to live here and farm the clearin'. I'd be proud to see the day when you got a well dug, so's no woman here'd be obliged to do her washin' on a seepage hillside. You willin'?"

"I'm willin'."

"Shake hands."

He closed his eyes. The fire on the hearth had burned to embers. Jody banked them with the ashes, to assure live coals in the morning. . . .

He went to his room and closed the door. He took off his tattered shirt and breeches and climbed under the warm quilts. His bed was soft and yielding. He lay luxuriously, stretching his legs. He must be up early in the morning, to milk the cow and bring in wood and work the crops. When he worked them, Flag would not be there to play about with him. His father would no longer take the heavy part of the burden. It did not matter. He could manage alone.

He found himself listening for something. It was the sound of the yearling for which he listened, running around the house or stirring on his moss pallet in the corner of the bedroom. He would never hear him again. He wondered if his mother had thrown dirt over Flag's carcass, or if the buzzards had cleaned it. Flag—He did not believe he should ever again love anything, man or woman or his own child, as he had loved the yearling. He would be lonely all his life. But a man took it for his share and went on.

In the beginning of his sleep, he cried out, "Flag!"

It was not his own voice that called. It was a boy's voice. Somewhere beyond the sink-hole, past the magnolia, under the live oaks, a boy and a yearling ran side by side, and were gone forever.

Use the Cornell Note-Taking system to take notes on the excerpt at the left. Record your notes, Reduce them, and then Recap (summarize) them.

Record

_____
_____
_____
_____
_____
_____
_____
_____
_____
_____
_____
_____
_____
_____
_____
_____
_____
_____
_____
_____
_____
_____
_____
_____

Recap

_____
_____
_____
_____
_____
_____
_____

Reduce

Try the following approach as you reduce your notes.

MY VIEW
Comment on what you learned from your own notes.

_____
_____
_____
_____
_____
_____
_____
_____
_____
_____
_____
_____
_____
_____
_____
_____
_____
_____
_____

Respond and Think Critically

1. How do the Forresters plan on paying the Baxters for their share of the bear meat? [Recall]

_____

_____

_____

_____

2. Why does Grandma Hutto tell Oliver a lie about how the fire started in her house? [Infer]

_____

_____

_____

_____

3. When Jody meets Nellie Ginright, he decides that women come in breeds, just like dogs. Why does he make this comparison? Do you agree with him? Why or why not? [Analyze]

_____

_____

_____

_____

4. Review the questions you discussed in Connect to Literature on page 147. How would Jody have responded to the same questions had he been a member of your group? [Conclude]

_____

_____

_____

_____

5. Life Lessons In your opinion, what is the most important life lesson that Jody learned? [Conclude]

_____

_____

_____

_____

APPLY BACKGROUND
Reread Build Background on page 147. How did that information help you understand or appreciate what you read in the novel?

_____

_____

_____

_____

_____

_____

_____

_____

_____

_____

_____

_____

_____

_____

_____

_____

_____

_____

_____

_____

_____

_____

_____

_____

_____

_____

_____

Literary Element Voice

What literary techniques does Rawlings use in this novel to create her own distinct voice? [Identify]

_____
_____
_____
_____
_____
_____
_____
_____
_____
_____
_____

Reading Strategy Analyze Style

Find three idioms in this section. What is the meaning of each idiom in context? How is this different than its literal meaning? [Analyze]

_____
_____
_____
_____
_____
_____
_____
_____
_____
_____
_____
_____
_____
_____
_____

Vocabulary Practice

Respond to these questions.

1. Who would most likely treat you with **condescension** – a friendly neighbor or a know-it-all?

_____

2. Who is most likely to become **emaciated** – an explorer who has run out of food or a restaurant owner?

_____

3. Which of these is usually considered a **harbinger** of bad luck – a black cat or a shooting star?

_____

4. When would you most need to be **mollified** – after acing a test or after failing a test?

_____

5. Who would eat with more **voracity** – a young boy who just finished lunch or a young boy who just finished playing outside?

_____

Academic Vocabulary

When Jody realized that it was impossible not to **implicate** _Flag when their corn crop was eaten, he realized that he had to tell his father the truth._ Using context clues, try to figure out the meaning of the word _implicate_ in the sentence above. Write your guess below. Then check it in a dictionary.

_____
_____
_____
_____
_____
_____
_____
_____

Writing

Write an Argument Marjorie Kinnan Rawlings considered a number of different titles for the novel, including *The Sinkhole* and *Juniper Creek*, before she chose *The Yearling*. What would you have called the book if you had written it? If you think the title she chose is fitting, what do you think makes *The Yearling* an especially good title for this novel? Explain your opinions in a paragraph or two.

Jot down some notes here first.

_____

_____

_____

_____

_____

_____

_____

_____

_____

_____

_____

_____

_____

_____

_____

_____

_____

_____

_____

_____

_____

_____

_____

_____

_____

_____

Research and Report

Internet Connection

Assignment Use the Internet to research the wildlife that lives in your state. Plan an Internet Web site that shows the interactions between wildlife and the human population in your state.

Get Ideas Begin by making a list of specific research questions to answer. Start with the following questions: What are some of the problems faced by the wildlife? What problems do wild animals pose to the human population? Arrange all of your questions in a web diagram around your central topic: Wildlife.

Research As you research, use the questions below to evaluate the reliability of information on each Web site.

- *Authority* Is the site associated with a reputable organization? Does the author have credentials? Can he or she be contacted to verify information on the site?

- *Accuracy* Can the information be substantiated in another source? Are these grammatical or factual errors that make the site seem questionable?

- *Objectivity* Is the writer citing a fact or offering an opinion? Is the site associated with an organization that is biased?

- *Datedness* How often is the site updated? Can you be sure that the information isn't out of date?

As you research, record the answers to your research questions in a two-column chart. Put the questions on the left and the answers on the right. Then reorganize the questions and answers in a logical pattern in preparation for your report.

Report Plan an Internet Web site that shows the interactions between wildlife and the human population in your state. Use pictures from magazines or your own drawings to show how you would illustrate your Web site. Also include accurate and correctly formatted citations for the Web sites you consulted.

The Yearling

The following questions refer to the Related Readings in Glencoe's *Literature Library* edition of this novel. Support your answers with details from the texts. Write your answers on a separate sheet of paper, but jot down some notes first on the lines provided.

Baby Deer Do Need Your Help; Feeding Deer in Winter
Nate Trip; Jerome B. Robinson

Compare and contrast Jody's attitude toward Flag with Tripp's and Robinson's attitudes toward wild deer. In what ways are their attitudes similar? In what ways are they different?

_____

_____

_____

_____

_____

The Cub
Lois Dykeman Kleihauer

Compare Jody's progress toward manhood with that of the boy in "The Cub." What kinds of conflict do they experience that mark their initiation as adults? How do their fathers contribute to the boys' maturation processes?

_____

_____

_____

_____

_____

The Day Before Spring
Ann Haymond Zwinger

Imagine that Jody Baxter and Ann Haymond Zwinger had the chance to compare notes about spring. What similarities and differences might they find in their observations and notes?

_____

_____

_____

_____

_____

from Living with Wildlife
the California Center for Wildlife

Based on your reading of this selection, how would you evaluate the Baxters' final decision concerning Flag?

_____

_____

_____

_____

_____

from Animal Partners:
Training Animals to Help People
Patricia Curtis

What kinds of emotional support characterize Jody's and Fodder-wing's relationships with their animals? In what ways are those relationships therapeutic?

_____

_____

_____

_____

_____

LITERATURE: I Wandered Lonely as a Cloud

I wandered lonely as a cloud
That floats on high o'er vales and hills,
When all at once I saw a crowd,
A host, of golden daffodils;
5   Beside the lake, beneath the trees,
Fluttering and dancing in the breeze.

Continuous as the stars that shine
And twinkle on the milky way,
They stretched in never-ending line
10   Along the margin of a bay:
Ten thousand saw I at a glance,
Tossing their heads in sprightly[1] dance.

The waves beside them danced; but they
Outdid the sparkling waves in glee:
15   A poet could not but be gay,
In such a jocund[2] company:
I gazed—and gazed—but little thought
What wealth the show to me had brought:

For oft,[3] when on my couch I lie
20   In vacant or in pensive mood,
They flash upon that inward eye
Which is the bliss of solitude;
And then my heart with pleasure fills,
And dances with the daffodils.

---

1 *Sprightly* (sprīt' lē) means "lighthearted" or "merry."
2 *Jocund* (jok' ənd) means "cheerful" or "carefree."
3 *Oft* is an old, poetic form of "often."

Compare the novel you have just read to the literature selection at the left, "I Wandered Lonely as a Cloud" by William Wordsworth in *Glencoe Literature*. Then answer the questions below. Support your answers with details from the selections.

Compare & Contrast

1. Simile In what way could you say that Jody too "wandered lonely as a cloud"?

_____

_____

_____

_____

_____

_____

_____

2. Symbol What does nature represent, as a symbol, to Jody? To the speaker of the poem?

_____

_____

_____

_____

_____

_____

_____

_____

3. Voice What techniques does Wordsworth use to help his readers visualize the scene he is describing in his poem? How do these compare with the techniques that Rawlings used to describe the settings in *The Yearling*?

_____

_____

_____

_____

_____

_____

_____

WRITE ABOUT IT

At what points in *The Yearling* does Jody respond to nature the same way that the speaker of "I Wandered Lonely as a Cloud" does? In a short paragraph, describe two of these situations and explain the ways in which Jody's responses are similar to those presented in the poem.

_____

_____

_____

_____

_____

_____

_____

_____

_____

_____

_____

_____

_____

_____

_____

_____

_____

_____

_____

_____

_____

_____

_____

_____

Review

Convince an Audience Many student reviews of *The Yearling* on the Internet are negative. Some students today seem to find it out-of-date and therefore irrelevant. Would you continue to make it part of the school curriculum, recommend it to certain kinds of readers, or suggest that this classic be forgotten? Write a book review that answers the preceding questions.

Prewrite First, review your notes on the selection and determine what your controlling idea will be. Do you plan to recommend the book? Decide how you will present and organize your information. For example, you might begin with summary of the work, and follow up with your own opinions. You may wish to organize your information with an outline. Finally, choose an appropriate audience, such as students who might read the book for class or the school board who is determining whether or not to keep the book on the curriculum.

Draft Create your thesis, and follow it up with the logical sequence of information you outlined during the prewriting phase. As you write, remember that any claims you make must be supported with evidence, such as quotations from the selection. You may wish to create a chart like the one shown here to ensure that all of your points are well-supported. Use appeals to logic, emotion, or ethical beliefs whenever possible as you add to your support.

Claim	Evidence
Rawlings presents a timeless struggle between nature and humans.	The flood that devastates the surrounding area is similar to the recent Hurricane Katrina.

Revise As you review, make sure that you have also considered the other side of the argument. Answering the possible objections to your view will show readers that your opinion is balanced and well-considered.

Edit and Proofread Edit your writing so that it expresses your thoughts effectively and is well organized. Carefully proofread for grammar, punctuation, and spelling errors.

UNDERSTAND THE TASK

- In a **book review**, a writer presents his or her well-supported opinions about a work of literature or nonfiction. The review may also recommend that people read the book or suggest that they avoid it.

Grammar Tip

Sentence Variety

Authors can add interest to their writing by varying both the structure and the length of their sentences. They can use a combination of simple and complex sentences and of short and long sentences in order to develop a particular mood or to create suspense.

Notice how Rawlings uses sentence variety to create suspense in the following excerpt from *The Yearling*:

He clambered to his feet and up the bank and began to run down the road to the clearing, crying as he ran. His father might not be there. He might be dead.

A Midsummer Night's Dream

William Shakespeare

A Midsummer Night's Dream
William Shakespeare

" *The opening scene of* A Midsummer Night's Dream *leads the audience to expect an ordinary comedy plot.* **"**

—*René Girard*, **"Myth and Ritual in Shakespeare: A Midsummer Night's Dream"**

" *But* A Midsummer Night's Dream *does not always do exactly what we might expect, and in this way it keeps its audience guessing . . .* **"**

—*Catherine Belsey*, **"A Midsummer Night's Dream: A Modern Perspective"**

Shakespeare wrote *A Midsummer Night's Dream* toward the beginning of his career. The play describes the comic misadventures of two pairs of lovers who become lost in a dark wood and fall under the power of sprites.

A Magical Night To Shakespeare's audiences, the play's title was a clue that the play might be about romance, magic, and madness. Midsummer Night was thought to be one of the nights of the year when sprites were especially powerful. People also believed that flowers gathered on Midsummer Night could work magic and that Midsummer Night was a time when people dreamed of their true loves and sometimes went insane.

A Classical Plot Shakespeare and other Elizabethan dramatists based their comedy plots on Classical (ancient Greek and Roman) models. Often a grumpy old father blocks the love affair between a young man and a young woman. Complications and confusions follow, until finally, after some dramatic reversal, the lovers are united. Setting his first act in Athens, the birthplace of Western classical literature, Shakespeare follows just such a plot. It is not long, however, before the play moves to the woods outside Athens, and into the English concept of Midsummer Night.

This tale of frustrated love and mistaken identity makes audiences laugh at the ridiculous ease with which lovers change the object of their affection, while still believing that their feelings are completely sincere. However, although it is a comedy, *A Midsummer Night's Dream* also poses some profound and difficult questions: What is love? How and why do people fall in and out of love? How is love related to questions of identity—both of the lover and the beloved? Are lovers in control of themselves and their destinies? Which is more real, the "daylight" world of reason and law or the "nighttime" world of passion and chaos? Shakespeare leaves these questions for the audience to answer.

Drama: The Good and the Ugly Drama was tremendously popular during Shakespeare's lifetime. The queen herself, Elizabeth I, loved to watch plays—including many by Shakespeare—in her court. Companies of actors traveled throughout England, performing for eager audiences. Over a short period of time, dramatic literature developed rapidly, from the slapstick plays popular during Shakespeare's youth to the complex dramas written by Shakespeare and his contemporaries.

Yet not everyone in late sixteenth- and early seventeenth-century England loved plays and acting. Theater owners tried to avoid city authorities, many of whom disapproved of the theater because it drew large crowds, creating the potential for crime, the possible spread of disease, and the introduction of controversial ideas. Many local authorities mistrusted and persecuted visiting actors, which forced the actors to seek the protection of powerful nobles. Religious factions such as the Puritans decried acting as wicked and tried to outlaw it. In fact, the Puritans succeeded in closing down the theaters in 1642.

Many of Shakespeare's plays seem to address the issue of whether drama is mere entertainment or a vehicle for showing the truth of human experience. In the eyes of contemporary critic Alvin B. Kernan:

Shakespeare seems to have constructed in Dream *the "worst case" for theater, voicing all the attacks on drama being made in his time and deliberately showing plays, actors, and audiences at their worst.*

A Midsummer Night's Dream contains a play-within-a-play, which features comically clumsy writing, poor staging, cheap costumes, and awful acting. Furthermore, Oberon, the fairy king, can be seen as a kind of mad director, stage managing the passions of others for his own amusement or pleasure.

Yet *A Midsummer Night's Dream* allows us to laugh at human nature and observe the interaction between actors and audience. *Pyramus and Thisbe*—the play-within-a-play— may be silly, but it is funny. *A Midsummer Night's Dream* can also be seen as a tribute to the magic of illusion. After waking from their dream parts in Oberon's "play," Bottom, Lysander, Demetrius, Helena, and Hermia all express a sense of wonder and bewilderment at their recent experience.

Blank Verse and Prose

Shakespeare wrote much of *A Midsummer Night's Dream,* and most of his plays, in blank verse. This style was fairly new in the 1500s. Blank verse was first used in English drama in a play four years before Shakespeare was born. It follows a flexible rhythmic pattern consisting of an unstressed syllable followed by a stressed syllable.

Look, for example, at the lines that Hippolyta speaks to Theseus in Act 1, Scene 1:

Four days will quickly steep themselves in night;
Four nights will quickly dream away the time;

Most English verse, or poetry, falls naturally into this pattern. Prose, or ordinary, everyday language, was also becoming a popular dramatic writing style, frequently mixed with blank verse.

In *A Midsummer Night's Dream*, Shakespeare uses different writing styles to suit different characters. For example, Bottom and his friends generally speak in prose, which gives them a simple, rustic quality. For the speeches of Oberon and Titania, Shakespeare uses a much more complex form of poetry, implying the exquisite beauty and magic of the fairy kingdom.

William Shakespeare *(1564–1616)*

❝*He was not of an age, but for all time.*❞

—*Ben Jonson, poet and contemporary
of Shakespeare*

Little is known about William Shakespeare, generally acknowledged as the greatest playwright of all time. In some ways, the lack of information is ironically fitting. Whereas we can draw on personal history to understand and explain the work of most writers, in the case of Shakespeare, we must rely primarily on his work. His command of comedy and tragedy, his ability to depict the range of human character, and his profound insights into human nature add clues to the few facts that are known about his life.

Shakespeare's Childhood William Shakespeare was born in April 1564 in the English town of Stratford-upon-Avon. The son of John Shakespeare, a successful glovemaker and public official, and Mary Arden, the daughter of a gentleman, William was the oldest surviving sibling of eight children.

Shakespeare probably attended the local grammar school and studied Latin. His writings indicate that he was familiar with classical writers such as Ovid (the source for the story of *Pyramus and Thisbe*, the play-within-a-play in *A Midsummer Night's Dream*). Throughout Shakespeare's childhood, companies of touring actors visited Stratford. Although there is no evidence to prove that Shakespeare ever saw these actors perform, most scholars agree that he probably did.

Adult Life In 1582, at the age of 18, Shakespeare married Anne Hathaway, the daughter of a farmer. The couple had become parents of two daughters and a son by 1585. Sometime in the next eight years, Shakespeare left his family in Stratford and moved to London to pursue a career in the theater. Records show that by 1592, he had become a successful actor and playwright in that city.

The Actor and Writer Although an outbreak of plague forced the London theaters to close in 1592, Shakespeare continued to write, producing the long narrative poem *Venus and Adonis* and a number of comedies. By 1594 the plague was less of a threat, and theaters reopened. Shakespeare had joined a famous acting group called the Lord Chamberlain's Men, so named for their patron, or supporter, a high official in the court of Queen Elizabeth I. One of the first plays Shakespeare wrote for this company was *Romeo and Juliet*. In 1598 Shakespeare became part owner of a major new theater, the Globe.

For more than a decade, Shakespeare produced a steady stream of works, both tragedies and comedies, which were performed at the Globe, the royal court, and other London theaters. However, shortly after the Globe was destroyed by fire in 1613, he retired and returned to Stratford.

Fairly wealthy from the sales of his plays and from his shares in both the acting company and the Globe, Shakespeare was able to buy a large house and an impressive amount of property. He died in Stratford in 1616. Seven years later the first collection of his plays was published.

Connect to the Literature

Why do young people in love sometimes experience conflict with their parents?

Create a Graphic Organizer

What is the best way to resolve a conflict? Create a graphic organizer to show the six steps of problem solving listed below. Include ideas on how these steps might be applied to the question of why young people in love sometimes experience conflict with their parents.

1. identify the problem
2. determine the importance of the problem
3. identify and discuss options
4. agree on an option
5. act on your decision
6. evaluate your decision

Build Background

Borrowing from Mythology

Shakespeare borrowed the characters of Theseus and Hippolyta from Greek mythology. Theseus was the national hero of Athens. He was a friend of Heracles (Hercules) and the survivor of many adventures, including his slaying of the Minotaur, a creature half man and half bull. Hippolyta was Queen of the Amazons, a group of female warriors. Theseus took her prisoner and then married her.

NOVEL NOTEBOOK

Keep a special notebook to record entries about the novels that you read this year.

WRITE THE CAPTION

Write a caption for the image below, in the present tense, using information in Build Background.

_____
_____
_____
_____
_____
_____
_____
_____
_____
_____
_____
_____
_____
_____
_____
_____
_____
_____
_____
_____
_____
_____
_____
_____
_____
_____
_____
_____
_____

Set Purposes for Reading

▶ **BIG Idea** **The Power of Love**

Think about your definition of love and how it compares with the romances you have seen in the media. What does true love really mean? What kind of barriers prevent people from experiencing true love?

In *A Midsummer Night's Dream*, author William Shakespeare explores just how far people are willing to go to experience true love. As you read, list the barriers that prevent the characters from being with the one they love and note what these characters do to overcome these barriers?

Literary Element **Soliloquy, Aside, and Monologue**

In a **monologue,** a character speaks directly to another character or to himself or herself. In a **soliloquy,** a character speaks his or her innermost thoughts when no other characters are on stage. An **aside** is when a character says something to the audience that the other characters are not supposed to hear. Monologues and soliloquies are usually long speeches; asides are brief comments.

Playwrights cannot comment directly upon how a character is thinking or feeling, so they rely on these devices to help characters share their thoughts.

As you read, pay special attention to the monologues, soliloquies, and asides in the play. Ask yourself what these passages reveal about the characters. Use the graphic organizer on the next page to help you.

Reading Strategy **Make Inferences about Characters**

To **make inferences about characters,** we use reason and knowledge of the situation to form our own ideas about a character's motivations, personality, and social status.

A character's **motivations,** or reasons for acting in a certain way, are not always clear. Personality and social status must also often be inferred. Sometimes, the character's style of speaking—for example, rustic or poetic—will provide a clue to personality or social status.

As you read, pay attention to your understanding of a character. Are you being given this information directly, or are you making inferences based on the character's words or behaviors? You might find it helpful to use a graphic organizer like the one below.

Words / Behaviors	What They Reveal

Vocabulary

austerity [ôs ter′ ə tē]
n. condition of lacking pleasure or luxury
The family's austerity was clear to us when we entered their very humble home.

beguile [bi gīl′]
v. to trick
The speaker tried to beguile his listeners, but they recognized that many of his statements were untrue.

feign [fān]
v. to pretend
The school nurse is aware that sometimes students feign sickness to avoid taking a test.

idolatry [ī dol′ ə trē]
n. false worship
Some people argue that movie stars and rock stars should not be the objects of teenagers' idolatry.

reveling [rev′əl ing]
n. enjoying festivities
On New Year's Eve, many people spend the night reveling.

Shakespeare uses monologues, soliloquies, and asides in the play to allow his characters to share their thoughts, desires, and internal conflicts with the audience. As you encounter one of these literary devices, record information about it in the chart below.

	speaker	quote	significance
Monologue			
Soliloquy			

Literary Element

Soliloquy, Aside, and Monologue
How does the soliloquy on the next page enhance the meaning of the scene as compared with the dialogue on this page?

_____

_____

_____

_____

_____

_____

_____

_____

_____

_____

_____

_____

_____

_____

_____

_____

_____

_____

_____

_____

_____

_____

_____

_____

_____

_____

_____

_____

PLAY EXCERPT: ACT 1, SCENE 1

180   **HERMIA.** God speed, fair Helena! Whither away?

      HELENA. Call you me fair? That 'fair' again unsay.

        Demetrius loves your fair: O happy fair!

        Your eyes are lodestars,° and your tongue's sweet air

        More tuneable than lark to shepherd's ear

185   When wheat is green, when hawthorn buds appear.

        Sickness is catching. O, were favour so,

        Yours would I catch, fair Hermia, ere I go;

        My ear should catch your voice, my eye your eye,

        My tongue should catch your tongue's sweet melody.

190   Were the world mine, Demetrius being bated,°

        The rest I'd give to be to you translated.

        O, teach me how you look and with what art

        You sway the motion of Demetrius' heart.

      HERMIA. I frown upon him; yet he loves me still.

195   **HELENA.** O that your frowns would teach my smiles such skill!

      HERMIA. I give him curses; yet he gives me love.

      HELENA. O that my prayers could such affection move!

      HERMIA. The more I hate, the more he follows me.

      HELENA. The more I love, the more he hateth me.

200   **HERMIA.** His folly, Helena, is no fault of mine.

      HELENA. None but your beauty; would that fault were mine!

      HERMIA. Take comfort: he no more shall see my face;

        Lysander and myself will fly this place.

        Before the time I did Lysander see,

205   Seemed Athens as a paradise to me.

        O then, what graces in my love do dwell,

        That he hath turned a heaven unto a hell?

      LYSANDER. Helen, to you our minds we will unfold:

        Tomorrow night, when Phoebe° doth behold

210   Her silver visage in the watery glass,

        Decking with liquid pearl the bladed grass

        (A time that lovers' flights doth still conceal),

        Through Athens' gates have we devised to steal.

      HERMIA. And in the wood, where often you and I

215   Upon faint primrose beds were wont to lie,

        Emptying our bosoms of their counsel sweet,

---

183 lodestars *guiding stars*
190 bated *excepted*
209 Phoebe *Diana, goddess of the moon, associated with chastity*

There my Lysander and myself shall meet,

And thence from Athens turn away our eyes

To seek new friends and stranger companies.

220   Farewell, sweet playfellow; pray thou for us,

And good luck grant thee thy Demetrius.

Keep word, Lysander; we must starve our sight

From lovers' food till morrow deep midnight.

LYSANDER. I will, my Hermia.

[*Exit* HERMIA.]

Helena, adieu!

225   As you on him, Demetrius dote on you.

[*Exit* LYSANDER.]

HELENA. How happy some o'er other some can be!

Through Athens I am thought as fair as she.

But what of that? Demetrius thinks not so;

He will not know what all but he do know.

230   And as he errs, doting on Hermia's eyes,

So I, admiring of his qualities.

Things base and vile, holding no quantity,°

Love can transpose to form and dignity.

Love looks not with the eyes, but with the mind,

235   And therefore is winged Cupid painted blind.

Nor hath love's mind of any judgement taste;

Wings, and no eyes, figure unheedy haste;

And therefore is love said to be a child

Because in choice he is so oft beguiled.°

240   As waggish° boys in game themselves forswear,°

So the boy Love is perjured everywhere;

For, ere Demetrius looked on Hermia's eyne,°

He hailed down oaths that he was only mine,

And when this hail some heat from Hermia felt,

245   So he dissolved, and showers of oaths did melt.

I will go tell him of fair Hermia's flight:

Then to the wood will he, tomorrow night,

Pursue her; and for this intelligence,

If I have thanks it is a dear expense;

250   But herein mean I to enrich my pain,

To have his sight thither, and back again.

---

232 holding no quantity *having no value*

239 beguiled *tricked*

240 waggish *mischievous*   forswear *falsely promise*

242 eyne *eyes*

Literary Element

Soliloquy, Aside, and Monologue
What plan does Helena reveal in her soliloquy?

_____

_____

_____

_____

_____

_____

_____

_____

_____

_____

_____

_____

_____

_____

_____

_____

_____

_____

_____

_____

_____

_____

_____

_____

_____

_____

_____

_____

_____

_____

INTERACTIVE READING: Reading Strategy

Reading Strategy

Make Inferences about Characters What inferences can you make about the craftsmen based on this excerpt?

_____

_____

_____

_____

_____

_____

_____

_____

_____

_____

_____

_____

_____

_____

_____

_____

_____

_____

_____

_____

_____

_____

_____

_____

_____

_____

_____

_____

_____

_____

PLAY EXCERPT: ACT 1, SCENE 2

BOTTOM. That will ask some tears in the true performing of it. If I
20   do it, let the audience look to their eyes: I will move storms, I will
   condole,° in some measure. To the rest—yet my chief humour is
   for a tyrant. I could play Ercles° rarely, or a part to tear a cat in,° to
   make all split:

          The raging rocks
25   And shivering shocks
          Shall break the locks
            Of prison gates,
          And Phibbus'° car
          Shall shine from far,
30   And make and mar
            The foolish Fates.

   This was lofty. Now name the rest of the players.—This is Ercles'
   vein, a tyrant's vein; a lover is more condoling.

QUINCE. Francis Flute, the bellows-mender?

35 **FLUTE.** Here, Peter Quince.

QUINCE. Flute, you must take Thisbe on you.

QUINCE. What is Thisbe? A wandering knight?

QUINCE. It is the lady that Pyramus must love.

FLUTE. Nay, faith, let not me play a woman: I have a beard coming.

40 **QUINCE.** That's all one: you shall play it in a mask, and you may
   speak as small° as you will.

BOTTOM. And I may hide my face, let me play Thisbe too. I'll speak
   in a monstrous little voice: 'Thisne, Thisne!' — 'Ah, Pyramus, my
   lover dear; thy Thisbe dear, and lady dear.'

45 **QUINCE.** No, no; you must play Pyramus; and Flute, you Thisbe.

BOTTOM. Well, proceed.

QUINCE. Robin Starveling, the tailor?

STARVELING. Here, Peter Quince.

QUINCE. Robin Starveling, you must play Thisbe's mother. Tom
50   Snout, the tinker?

SNOUT. Here, Peter Quince.

QUINCE. You, Pyramus' father; myself, Thisbe's father; Snug, the
   joiner, you the lion's part; and I hope here is a play fitted.

---

21 condole _show grief_
22 Ercles _Hercules_   to tear a cat in _to rant and rave_
28 Phibbus _Phoebus, god of the sun, who was supposed to drive a chariot ('car') through the sky_
40 small _high-pitched_

SNUG. Have you the lion's part written? Pray you, if it be, give it
55   me; for I am slow of study.

QUINCE. You may do it extempore;° for it is nothing but roaring.

BOTTOM. Let me play the lion too. I will roar that I will do any
     man's heart good to hear me. I will roar that I will make the Duke
     say 'Let him roar again, let him roar again!'

60 **QUINCE.** And you should do it too terribly, you would fright the
     Duchess and the ladies that they would shriek; and that were
     enough to hang us all.

ALL. They would hang us, every mother's son.

BOTTOM. I grant you, friends, if you should fright the ladies out of
65   their wits they would have no more discretion but to hang us;
     but I will aggravate my voice so that I will roar you as gently as any
     sucking dove. I will roar you and 'twere any nightingale.

QUINCE. You can play no part but Pyramus; for Pyramus is a sweet-
     faced man, a proper man as one shall see in a summer's day, a most
70   lovely, gentlemanlike man: therefore you must needs play Pyramus.

BOTTOM. Well, I will undertake it. What beard were I best to
     play it in?

QUINCE. Why, what you will.

BOTTOM. I will discharge it in either your straw-colour beard, your
75   orange-tawny beard, your purple-in-grain beard, or your French-
     crown-colour beard, your perfect yellow.

QUINCE. Some of your French crowns° have no hair at all, and then
     you will play bare-faced. But, masters, here are your parts, and I am
     to entreat you, request you, and desire you to con° them by
80   tomorrow night, and meet me in the palace wood, a mile without
     the town, by moonlight; there will we rehearse, for if we meet in
     the city we shall be dogged with company,° and our devices
     known. In the meantime I will draw a bill of properties, such as
     our play wants. I pray you, fail me not.

85 **BOTTOM.** We will meet, and there we may rehearse most obscenely
     and courageously. Take pains, be perfect: adieu!

QUINCE. At the Duke's oak we meet.

BOTTOM. Enough; hold, or cut bowstrings.

---

56   extempore *ad lib*
77   French crown *bald*
79   con *learn*
82   be dogged with company *have people watching*

Reading Strategy

Make Inferences about Characters
What is Bottom's motivation for playing the lion? Why does he give the part up so easily?

_____
_____
_____
_____
_____
_____
_____
_____
_____
_____
_____
_____
_____
_____
_____
_____
_____
_____
_____
_____
_____
_____
_____
_____
_____
_____

MARK IT UP

Are you allowed to write in your novel? If so, then mark up the pages as you read, or reread, to help with your note-taking. Develop a shorthand system, including symbols, that works for you. Here are some ideas:

Underline = important idea

Bracket = text to quote

Asterisk = just what you were looking for

Checkmark = might be useful

Circle = unfamiliar word or phrase to look up

▶ **BIG Idea**

The Power of Love How do Hermia and Lysander feel about their love?

Mark up the excerpt, looking for evidence of how it expresses the Big Idea.

PLAY EXCERPT: ACT 1, SCENE 1

LYSANDER. How now, my love? Why is your cheek so pale?

How chance the roses there do fade so fast?

130   **HERMIA.** Belike for want of rain, which I could well

Beteem° them from the tempest of my eyes.

LYSANDER. Ay me! For aught that I could ever read,

Could ever hear by tale or history,

The course of true love never did run smooth;

135   But either it was different in blood—°

HERMIA. O cross! too high to be enthralled° to low.

LYSANDER. Or else misgraffèd° in respect of years—

HERMIA. O spite! too old to be engaged to young.

LYSANDER. Or else it stood upon the choice of friends—

140   **HERMIA.** O hell, to choose love by another's eyes!

LYSANDER. Or, if there were a sympathy in choice,

War, death, or sickness did lay siege to it,

Making it momentany as a sound,

Swift as a shadow, short as any dream,

145   Brief as the lightning in the collied° night,

That in a spleen° unfolds both heaven and earth,

And, ere a man hath power to say, 'Behold!',

The jaws of darkness do devour it up.

So quick bright things come to confusion.

150   **HERMIA.** If then true lovers have been ever crossed

It stands as an edict° in destiny.

Then let us teach our trial patience,

Because it is a customary cross,

As due to love as thoughts, and dreams, and sighs,

155   Wishes, and tears—poor fancy's followers.

---

131 beteem *grant*
135 blood *class, family background*
136 enthralled *bound*
137 misgraffèd *mismatched*
145 collied *darkened, like coal*
146 spleen *burst of temper*
151 edict *command*

Use the Cornell Note-Taking system to take notes on the excerpt at the left. Record your notes, Reduce them, and then Recap (summarize) them.

Record

_____
_____
_____
_____
_____
_____
_____
_____
_____
_____
_____
_____
_____
_____
_____
_____
_____
_____
_____
_____
_____

Recap

_____
_____
_____
_____
_____
_____

Reduce

Try the following approach as you reduce your notes.

ASK QUESTIONS

Write any questions you have about the play. Do you have to go to an outside source to find the answers?

_____
_____
_____
_____
_____
_____
_____
_____
_____
_____
_____
_____
_____
_____
_____
_____
_____
_____
_____
_____
_____
_____
_____
_____

Respond and Think Critically

1. Why is Egeus angry with his daughter? [Recall]

_____

_____

_____

_____

_____

2. Why is Helena envious of Hermia? [Summarize]

_____

_____

_____

_____

_____

3. Describe Theseus's character. What sort of leader does he seem to be?
[Analyze]

_____

_____

_____

_____

_____

_____

4. Do you think Egeus is justified in being angry with his daughter? Why or
why not? [Evaluate]

_____

_____

_____

_____

_____

5. The Power of Love Research the myth of Pyramus and Thisbe. How does
this story compare to the love stories that Shakespeare has introduced to
the reader in Act 1? [Compare]

_____

_____

_____

_____

APPLY BACKGROUND
Reread Meet the Author on
page 166. How did that information
help you understand or appreciate
what you read in the play?

_____

_____

_____

_____

_____

_____

_____

_____

_____

_____

_____

_____

_____

_____

_____

_____

_____

_____

_____

_____

_____

_____

_____

_____

_____

_____

_____

_____

_____

Literary Element   Soliloquy, Aside, and Monologue

What does Egeus threaten in his short monologue in Act 1, Scene 1 (lines 22-45)?

_____

_____

_____

_____

_____

_____

_____

_____

_____

_____

_____

_____

Reading Strategy   Make Inferences about Characters

When Hermia says in Act 1, Scene 1 (line 59), "I know not by what power I am made bold," what inference can you make about how she would usually address Theseus?

_____

_____

_____

_____

_____

_____

_____

_____

_____

_____

_____

_____

Vocabulary Practice

A **synonym** is a word that has the same or nearly the same meaning as another word. Match each boldfaced vocabulary word below with its synonym. Use a thesaurus or dictionary to check your answers.

1. **austerity**
2. **beguile**
3. **feign**
4. **idolatry**
5. **reveling**

a. false reverence
b. adherence
c. deceive
d. somberness
e. pretend
f. celebrating

Academic Vocabulary

To avoid having to marry Demetrius, Hermia develops a **scheme** with Lysander: they plan to meet in the woods at night and elope. In the preceding sentence, _scheme_ means "a secret plan." Have you ever developed a **scheme** in order to get out of a difficult situation? Did your **scheme** end up being successful? Explain.

_____

_____

_____

_____

_____

_____

_____

_____

_____

_____

_____

_____

_____

_____

_____

Writing

Write a Plan How do you go about solving your problems or conflicts? Think about a conflict you have experienced in the past week or so. Now, consider the dilemmas that Theseus, Hermia, Lysander and Helena are facing in the play.

Create your own graphic organizer that allows you to list the characters, how they are trying to solve the problem, and an alternative solution that you would suggest.

Then develop a plan for solving each character's problem. Outline your plan on a separate sheet of paper.

Jot down some notes here first.

_____
_____
_____
_____
_____
_____
_____
_____
_____
_____
_____
_____
_____
_____
_____
_____
_____
_____
_____
_____
_____

Research and Report
Visual/Media Presentation

Assignment Create a casting chart of the modern comedians who could best play each of the craftsmen's parts in a modern production of *A Midsummer Night's Dream*.

Get Ideas Divide into small groups, and make a list of comic actors in the television or movie business today who could best play each craftsman's part. Develop a list of the qualities that make each actor suitable for role that you will assign to him or her.

Research Assign each person in your group to find a photo of one of the modern actors you have agreed to include. Choose an image that best captures this actor's identity as a comic figure.

Prepare As a group, determine how you will organize your casting chart. Make sure that you include both the actor's picture and the qualities that make him/her suitable for a particular role.

Present Present your casting chart to the class, and take a class vote to decide which actor would be best cast in each part. Use appropriate eye contact and speak clearly when you present.

Connect to the Literature

How would you feel if someone you liked suddenly stopped liking you?

Write a Journal Entry

On a separate sheet of paper, jot down some of the feelings and reactions you might have toward someone whom you felt had stopped liking you.

Build Background

The Character Puck

Shakespeare did not create the character of Puck. Puck appears in many earlier works about magic and witchcraft. In some cases, he is presented as an evil goblin; in others he is merely naughty. Author Robert Burton (who lived a little later than Shakespeare) describes fire spirits who purposely mislead travelers: "We commonly call them pucks." Generally the character of Puck is not malicious, but rather intent on amusing himself at the expense of others. In *A Midsummer Night's Dream*, Puck often interferes with other characters' activities and, in doing so, changes the course of the play. He also assumes animal shapes in order to frighten or mislead people.

NOVEL NOTEBOOK

Keep a special notebook to record entries about the novels that you read this year.

WRITE THE CAPTION

Write a caption for the image below, in the present tense, using information in Build Background.

_____

_____

_____

_____

_____

_____

_____

_____

_____

_____

_____

_____

_____

_____

_____

_____

_____

_____

_____

_____

_____

_____

_____

_____

_____

_____

_____

Set Purposes for Reading

▶ BIG Idea Awkward Encounters

Awkward encounters are uncomfortable because they reveal an underlying problem or conflict. Have you ever had an awkward encounter with another person? Why was it awkward? What did you do to try to resolve the situation?

In *A Midsummer Night's Dream*, awkward encounters occur frequently. As you read, notice how the characters react during these uncomfortable meetings with other characters.

Literary Element Metaphor

A **metaphor** is a figure of speech that makes a comparison between two seemingly unlike things. Unlike a simile, a metaphor does not use the words *like* or *as*. An **extended metaphor** is a comparison that extends through an entire paragraph, stanza or selection.

Authors use metaphors to help the reader develop a more thorough understanding of a character, setting, or situation.

As you read, make note of the metaphors Shakespeare uses in his dialogue. Consider what each metaphor reveals about the things being compared.

Reading Strategy Interpret Imagery

The word pictures in a work of literature are called **imagery.** In creating effective imagery, writers use descriptions that appeal to one or more of the five senses and to suggest ideas and to evoke an emotional response in the reader. To **interpret imagery,** a reader notices the effect that sensory details have on his or her understanding of the characters, settings, or mood in the text.

As you read Act 2, pay attention to the imagery that Shakespeare uses. You might find it helpful to use a graphic organizer like the one below. The graphic organizer on the next page can help you to organize your ideas about imagery.

Imagery	My Interpretation

Vocabulary

dissemble [di sem´ bəl]
v. to pretend
She tried to dissemble ignorance, but her friends all knew she was smarter than she was willing to admit.

flout [flout]
v. to mock
He decided to flout the school rules because he felt that some of them were simply unfair.

progeny [proj´ə nē]
n. offspring
Most parents hope their progeny will grow up to be more successful than they were in their lives.

promontory [prom´ən tôr ē]
n. peak of land that juts out
The travelers carefully walked out to the edge of the promontory, hoping to spot whales in the ocean.

wanton [wont´ən]
adj. shameless
Black bears sometimes seem to show wanton cruelty toward their prey.

In Act 2, Shakespeare uses imagery related to night. As you read, identify some examples of this imagery. Write them down on the web below. Add more boxes if you need to.

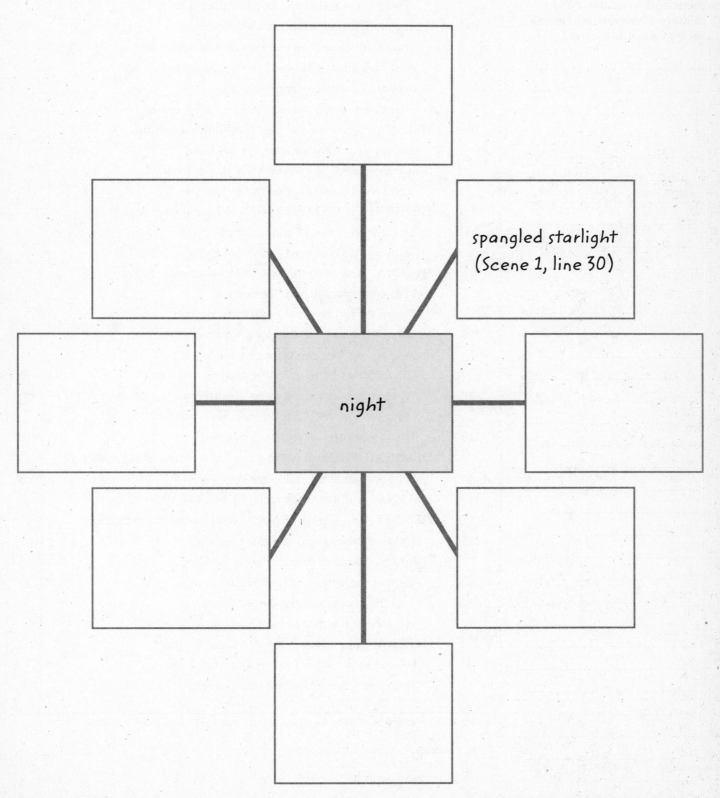

spangled starlight
(Scene 1, line 30)

night

Literary Element

Metaphor How do these metaphors reveal the contrast between Demetrius and Helen's feelings about each other?

_____

_____

_____

_____

_____

_____

_____

_____

_____

_____

_____

_____

_____

_____

_____

_____

_____

_____

_____

_____

_____

_____

_____

_____

_____

_____

_____

_____

_____

_____

_____

_____

PLAY EXCERPT: ACT 2, SCENE 1

DEMETRIUS. I love thee not, therefore pursue me not.

Where is Lysander, and fair Hermia?

190 The one I'll slay, the other slayeth me.

Thou told'st me they were stol'n unto this wood,

And here am I, and wood within this wood°

Because I cannot meet my Hermia.

Hence, get thee gone, and follow me no more.

195 **HELENA.** You draw me, you hard-heart adamant!°

But yet you draw not iron, for my heart

Is true as steel. Leave you your power to draw,

And I shall have no power to follow you.

DEMETRIUS. Do I entice you? Do I speak you fair?

200 Or rather do I not in plainest truth

Tell you I do not, nor I cannot love you?

HELENA. And even for that do I love you the more.

I am your spaniel; and, Demetrius,

The more you beat me I will fawn on you.

205 Use me but as your spaniel: spurn me, strike me,

Neglect me, lose me; only give me leave,

Unworthy as I am, to follow you.

What worser place can I beg in your love

(And yet a place of high respect with me)

210 Than to be usèd as you use your dog?

DEMETRIUS. Tempt not too much the hatred of my spirit;

For I am sick when I do look on thee.

HELENA. And I am sick when I look not on you.

DEMETRIUS. You do impeach° your modesty too much,

215 To leave the city and commit yourself

Into the hands of one that loves you not;

To trust the opportunity of night,

And the ill counsel of a desert° place,

With the rich worth of your virginity.

220 **HELENA.** Your virtue is my privilege: for that

It is not night when I do see your face,

Therefore I think I am not in the night;

---

192 wood *mad, insane while he is in a real wood. Elizabethans were fond of wordplay and puns*

195 adamant *hard stone, diamond*

214 impeach *call into question*

218 desert *lonely, deserted*

Nor doth this wood lack worlds of company,

For you, in my respect, are all the world.

225 Then how can it be said I am alone

When all the world is here to look on me?

DEMETRIUS. I'll run from thee and hide me in the brakes,°

And leave thee to the mercy of wild beasts.

HELENA. The wildest hath not such a heart as you.

230 Run when you will: the story shall be changed;

Apollo flies, and Daphne holds the chase,

The dove pursues the griffin,° the mild hind

Makes speed to catch the tiger—bootless° speed,

When cowardice pursues, and valour flies!

235 **DEMETRIUS.** I will not stay thy questions. Let me go;

Or if thou follow me, do not believe

But I shall do thee mischief in the wood.

HELENA. Ay, in the temple, in the town, the field,

You do me mischief. Fie, Demetrius,

240 Your wrongs do set a scandal on my sex!

We cannot fight for love, as men may do;

We shall be wooed, and were not made to woo.

[*Exit* DEMETRIUS.]

I'll follow thee, and make a heaven of hell,

To die upon the hand I love so well.

Literary Element

Metaphor How does Helena use metaphors to explain her pursuit of Demetrius?

_____

_____

_____

_____

_____

_____

_____

_____

_____

_____

_____

_____

_____

_____

_____

_____

_____

_____

_____

_____

_____

_____

_____

_____

_____

_____

_____

_____

_____

_____

227 brakes *undergrowth, thicket*
232 griffin *beast, half eagle, half lion*
233 bootless *useless*

Reading Strategy

Interpret Imagery What does Shakespeare express with the imagery in Titania's first monologue in this excerpt?

_____

_____

_____

_____

_____

_____

_____

_____

_____

_____

_____

_____

_____

_____

_____

_____

_____

_____

_____

_____

_____

_____

_____

_____

_____

_____

_____

_____

_____

_____

PLAY EXCERPT: ACT 2, SCENE 1

TITANIA. These are the forgeries of jealousy:
And never since the middle summer's spring
Met we on hill, in dale, forest, or mead,
By pavèd fountain or by rushy brook,
85   Or in the beachèd margent° of the sea
To dance our ringlets° to the whistling wind,
But with thy brawls thou hast disturbed our sport.
Therefore the winds, piping to us in vain,
As in revenge have sucked up from the sea
90   Contagious fogs; which, falling in the land,
Hath every pelting river made so proud
That they have overborne their continents.
The ox hath therefore stretched his yoke in vain,
The ploughman lost his sweat, and the green corn
95   Hath rotted ere his youth attained a beard.
The fold stands empty in the drownèd field,
And crows are fatted with the murrion flock;°
The nine-men's-morris° is filled up with mud,
And the quaint mazes in the wanton green
100   For lack of tread are undistinguishable.
The human mortals want their winter cheer;
No night is now with hymn or carol blessed.
Therefore the moon, the governess of floods,
Pale in her anger, washes all the air,
105   That rheumatic diseases do abound;
And thorough this distemperature° we see
The seasons alter; hoary-headed frosts
Fall in the fresh lap of the crimson rose,
And on old Hiems'° thin and icy crown
110   An odorous chaplet of sweet summer buds
Is, as in mockery, set. The spring, the summer,
The childing° autumn, angry winter change

85 beachèd margent _shore_
86 ringlets _dancing in a circle_
97 murrion flock _diseased sheep_
98 nine-men's-morris _an outdoor game_
106 distemperature _disorder_
109 old Hiems _winter_
112 childing _pregnant, fruitful_

Their wonted liveries, and the mazèd° world

By their increase now knows not which is which.

115 And this same progeny of evils comes

From our debate, from our dissension.

We are their parents and original.

OBERON. Do you amend it, then: it lies in you.

Why should Titania cross her Oberon?

120 I do but beg a little changeling boy

To be my henchman.°

TITANIA. Set your heart at rest.

The fairy land buys not the child of me.

His mother was a votress° of my order,

And in the spicèd Indian air by night

125 Full often hath she gossiped by my side,

And sat with me on Neptune's yellow sands

Marking th'embarkèd traders on the flood,

When we have laughed to see the sails conceive

And grow big-bellied with the wanton° wind;

130 Which she, with pretty and with swimming gait

Following (her womb then rich with my young squire),

Would imitate, and sail upon the land

To fetch me trifles, and return again

As from a voyage, rich with merchandise.

135 But she, being mortal, of that boy did die,

And for her sake do I rear up her boy;

And for her sake I will not part with him.

Reading Strategy

Interpret Imagery How is the imagery in Titania's second speech appropriate for the topic of that speech?

_____

_____

_____

_____

_____

_____

_____

_____

_____

_____

_____

_____

_____

_____

_____

_____

_____

_____

_____

_____

_____

_____

_____

_____

_____

_____

_____

_____

_____

_____

113 mazèd *amazed, confused*
121 henchman *page*
123 votress *member of religious order, worshipper*
129 wanton *mischievous, immoral*

▶ **BIG Idea**

Awkward Encounters What is awkward about the encounter between Helena and Lysander?

Mark up the excerpt, looking for evidence of how it expresses the Big Idea.

PLAY EXCERPT: ACT 2, SCENE 2

HELENA. But who is here?—Lysander, on the ground?

Dead, or asleep? I see no blood, no wound.

Lysander, if you live, good sir, awake!

LYSANDER. [*Waking.*]

And run through fire I will for thy sweet sake!

110   Transparent° Helena, nature shows art

That through thy bosom makes me see thy heart.

Where is Demetrius? O, how fit a word

Is that vile name to perish on my sword!

HELENA. Do not say so, Lysander, say not so.

115   What though he love your Hermia? Lord, what though?

Yet Hermia still loves you; then be content.

LYSANDER. Content with Hermia? No; I do repent

The tedious minutes I with her have spent.

Not Hermia, but Helena I love.

120   Who will not change a raven for a dove?

The will of man is by his reason swayed,

And reason says you are the worthier maid.

Things growing are not ripe until their season;

So I, being young, till now ripe not to reason.

125   And touching now the point of human skill,

Reason becomes the marshal to my will.

And leads me to your eyes, where I o'erlook

Love's stories written in love's richest book.

HELENA. Wherefore was I to this keen mockery born?

130   When at your hands did I deserve this scorn?

Is't not enough, is't not enough, young man,

That I did never, no, nor never can

Deserve a sweet look from Demetrius' eye

But you must flout° my insufficiency?

135   Good troth, you do me wrong, good sooth, you do,

In such disdainful manner me to woo!

But fare you well: perforce I must confess

I thought you lord of more true gentleness.

O, that a lady of one man refused

140   Should of another therefore be abused!

[*Exit* HELENA.]

---

110 transparent *honest, open*
134 flout *mock*

Use the Cornell Note-Taking system to take notes on the excerpt at the left. Record your notes, Reduce them, and then Recap (summarize) them.

Record

Reduce

Try the following approach as you reduce your notes.

MY VIEW
Write down your thoughts on the excerpt.

Recap

Respond and Think Critically

1. How does Oberon intend to blackmail Titania into giving him what he wants? [Recall]

_____

_____

_____

_____

2. By the end of Act 2, what is similiar about the following pairs: Lysander and Hermia, Demetrius and Helena, and Oberon and Titania? [Compare]

_____

_____

_____

_____

3. How would you describe the character of Puck? What kind of mood does he create? [Analyze]

_____

_____

_____

_____

4. How might the magical herb described by Oberon act as a metaphor for the way infatutation operates in real life? Explain. [Connect]

_____

_____

_____

_____

5. **Awkward Encounters** Describe Hermia's dream at the end of Act 2, Scene 2. Why will her ignorance about the preceding events lead to an awkward encounter? [Infer]

_____

_____

_____

_____

APPLY BACKGROUND
Reread Build Background on page 179. How did that information help you understand or appreciate what you read in the play?

_____

_____

_____

_____

_____

_____

_____

_____

_____

_____

_____

_____

_____

_____

_____

_____

_____

_____

_____

_____

_____

_____

_____

_____

_____

_____

_____

_____

Literary Element   Metaphor

Find an example of an extended metaphor in Act 2 and evaluate its effectiveness. [Evaluate]

_____
_____
_____
_____
_____
_____
_____
_____
_____
_____
_____

Reading Strategy   Interpret Imagery

What imagery presented by the sprites do you remember the best from this act? What does this imagery remind you of? [Connect]

_____
_____
_____
_____
_____
_____
_____
_____
_____
_____
_____
_____

Vocabulary Practice

A **synonym** is a word that has the same or nearly the same meaning as another word. Match each boldfaced vocabulary word below with its synonym. Use a thesaurus or dictionary to check your answers.

1. **dissemble**   a. children
2. **flout**   b. needless
3. **progeny**   c. pretend
4. **promontory**   d. mock
5. **wanton**   e. admit
                      f. cape
                      g. parents

Academic Vocabulary

Puck **alters** _the course of events in_ A Midsummer Night's Dream _when he uses his magic on Lysander._ To become more familiar with the word _alter,_ fill out the graphic organizer below.

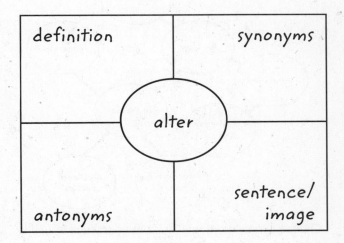

Write With Style

Apply Metaphor

Assignment Metaphors are frequently part of a poet's style. Review the metaphors used in *Midsummer Night's Dream*. Write a descriptive paragraph about a person you know well and use metaphors to make that person come alive to your reader. As an added challenge, consider using one extended metaphor throughout your paragraph.

Get Ideas Make a word web. Around the person you will describe, jot down actions, personality traits, and other items that you associate with that person. Connect words that connect in your mind. Add additional levels to your web using words from the first level. This time think about how the central word is *like* something else that is normally completely different. Write those comparisons around it, continuing the web and the comparisons.

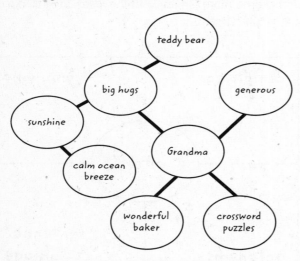

Choose two or more images from your webs to use in your descriptive paragraph. If you use an extended metaphor, choose one strong image from your word webs to develop your extended metaphor.

EXAMPLE:
My grandmother's big hugs envelope me in a burst of sunshine.

Give It Structure Present your descriptions in a logically structured paragraph.

Look at Language Be careful not to use contrasting metaphors in your paragraph. The metaphors should complement one another.

Speaking and Listening

Performance

Assignment With a group of classmates, research Foley art and create and perform a sound design for Act 2. Foley artists create sound effects with found objects.

Prepare Foley artists create sound effects with found objects. As a group, research Foley art on the Internet. Next, decide what general kinds of sounds you would need to create the appropriate magical effect for a performance of Act 2, Scene 1. Together, decide what kinds of objects you could use to generate those sounds. Identify one person who will create these sounds during your performance.

Together, assign a character to the remaining group members. Then plan how to present the scene. Discuss staging (how and where actors move "onstage") and any necessary props to accompany the Foley "soundtrack." Rehearse your performance at least once to make sure that everyone knows his or her part and that you are clear about when the sound effects should be used.

Perform Present your performance to your class. Be sure that your chosen body language and tone of voice match your character and contribute to the magical mood of the scene.

Evaluate After the performance, get together with your group and discuss how successful your performance was and how it might have been better. Use a chart like the one below to record your group's ideas.

What worked well	What needed improvement
We used the sound devices appropriately.	We needed to practice reading our lines more.

Connect to the Literature

Think of a time when you got so involved in a play or movie that you temporarily forgot that it was not real.

Share Experiences

Talk to other classmates and share examples of experiences when a play or movie made you forget the division between illusion and reality.

Build Background

Perception versus Sight

Seeing is the act of using the eyes to gain physical knowledge about the world. Perceiving is the psychological act of interpreting information received through the eyes and other senses. In Act 3, Shakespeare plays with ideas of vision, of blindness, and of different ways of interpreting what one sees. One of the things that love, or infatuation, does is to make the lover see the beloved as perfect, no matter what the actual circumstances. As you read this act, pay special attention to imagery of eyes and seeing. Analyze what Shakespeare is saying about the nature of perception.

NOVEL NOTEBOOK
Keep a special notebook to record entries about the novels that you read this year.

SUMMARIZE
Summarize in one sentence the most important idea(s) in Build Background.

_____
_____
_____
_____
_____
_____
_____
_____
_____
_____
_____
_____
_____
_____
_____
_____
_____
_____
_____
_____
_____
_____
_____
_____
_____

Set Purposes for Reading

▶ **BIG Idea** **The Power of Love**

How do individuals deal with conflicts that arise because of love? Think about relationships that you have seen, either in person or in the media. How are individuals affected when something goes awry with their relationship or when they have a conflict with the one they love?

In Act 3 of *A Midsummer Night's Dream*, author William Shakespeare explores what happens when two people who would not otherwise be together find themselves deeply in love, and ultimately, involved in conflicts because of Puck's magic spells. As you read, pay attention to how the characters try to deal with these conflicts.

Literary Element **Farce**

A **farce** is a type of comedy with stereotyped characters in ridiculous situations. Most farce incorporates exaggerated speech and action.

Farce is intended to make the audience or reader laugh, but it can also shed light on the author's perceptions of his subject.

As you read, think about why Shakespeare would have included farcical characters and situations at certain points in the play. What commentary do these characters and situations make on the other actions going on simultaneously? How do they help reveal some of the play's themes?

Reading Strategy **Identify Sequence**

Identifying sequence involves recognizing the order in which characters, plot events and, in the case of drama, movements on the stage are arranged.

Identifying sequence will help you sort out more complex arrangements of characters and plot events, and it will also help you remember the text longer. Within a play, identifying sequence will also help you keep track of the characters' movements and physical interactions.

Shakespeare intentionally creates confusion in *Midsummer Night's Dream*, and this confusion can make it difficult to keep track of characters and their actions. As you read, keep track of the sequence of events and the movement of characters in and out of the more complicated scenes. It might be helpful to use a graphic organizer like the one at the right. The graphic organizer on the next page can also help you keep track of the events in the play as they lead to the climax.

Vocabulary

bequeath [bi kwēth′]
v. to leave to or pass on to, as in a will
Brian's grandfather revealed that he would bequeath his coin collection to him once he turned 14.

chide [chīd]
v. to scold
Please don't chide me for forgetting to clean my room; I had too much homework to do last night!

entreat [en trēt′]
v. to beg
I entreat you—please help me shovel all of this snow out of my driveway!

rebuke [ri būk′]
v. to scold
After carelessly breaking her mother's prized vase, Vanessa was rebuked sharply by both of her parents.

sojourn [sō′jurn]
v. to stay somewhere for a while
My family sojourns in the French Riviera every summer.

Sequence of Events

↓

↓

↓

↓

↓

↓

The climax, or turning point, of *A Midsummer Night's Dream* comes at the end of Act 3. Describe the climax in the box at the top of the diagram below. In the other boxes, write the major events leading up to the climax. Write the events in the correct chronological order. You may add more boxes if you wish.

Climax

Titania falls in love with Bottom.

Literary Element

Farce How do the craftsmen/actors' words help define this scene as farce?

_____
_____
_____
_____
_____
_____
_____
_____
_____
_____
_____
_____
_____
_____
_____
_____
_____
_____
_____
_____
_____
_____
_____
_____
_____
_____
_____
_____
_____
_____
_____
_____

PLAY EXCERPT: ACT 3, SCENE 1

SNOUT. You can never bring in a wall. What say you, Bottom?

BOTTOM. Some man or other must present Wall; and let him have
    some plaster, or some loam, or some rough-cast about him to
    signify Wall; or let him hold his fingers thus, and through that
55   cranny shall Pyramus and Thisbe whisper.

QUINCE. If that may be, then all is well. Come, sit down every
    mother's son, and rehearse your parts. Pyramus, you begin. When
    you have spoken your speech, enter into that brake, and so
    everyone according to his cue.

[_Enter_ PUCK.]

60   **PUCK.** What hempen homespuns° have we swaggering here
    So near the cradle of the Fairy Queen?
    What, a play toward? I'll be an auditor,
    An actor too perhaps, if I see cause.

QUINCE. Speak, Pyramus! Thisbe, stand forth!

BOTTOM. [_as Pyramus._]

65   Thisbe, the flowers of odious savours sweet—

QUINCE. Odours—'odorous'!

BOTTOM. [_as Pyramus._] . . . odours savours sweet.
    So hath thy breath, my dearest Thisbe dear.
    But hark, a voice! Stay thou but here awhile,
70   And by and by I will to thee appear.

[_Exit_ BOTTOM.]

    PUCK. A stranger Pyramus than e'er played here.

[_Exit_ PUCK.]

    FLUTE. Must I speak now?

    QUINCE. Ay, marry must you; for you must understand he goes but
    to see a noise that he heard, and is to come again.

    FLUTE. [_as Thisbe._]

75   Most radiant Pyramus, most lilywhite of hue,
    Of colour like the red rose on triumphant briar,
    Most brisky juvenal, and eke° most lovely Jew,
    As true as truest horse that yet would never tire,
    I'll meet thee, Pyramus, at Ninny's tomb—

80   **QUINCE.** 'Ninus' tomb', man!—Why, you must not speak that yet;
    that you answer to Pyramus. You speak all your part at once, cues
    and all. Pyramus, enter—your cue is past. It is 'never tire'.

---

60 hempen homespuns _they are dressed in rough, homemade clothes_
77 eke _also_

FLUTE. O—

  [*as Thisbe.*]

  As true as truest horse, that yet would never tire.

[*Enter* PUCK, *and* BOTTOM *with the ass head on.*]

  BOTTOM. [*as Pyramus.*]

85 If I were fair, fair Thisbe, I were only thine.

  QUINCE. O monstrous! O strange! We are haunted! Pray, masters,

  fly, masters! Help!

[*Exit* QUINCE, SNUG, FLUTE, SNOUT, *and* STARVELING.]

  PUCK. I'll follow you: I'll lead you about a round,

  Through bog, through bush, through brake, through briar;

90 Sometime a horse I'll be, sometime a hound,

  A hog, a headless bear, sometime a fire,

  And neigh, and bark, and grunt, and roar, and burn,

  Like horse, hound, hog, bear, fire at every turn.

[*Exit* PUCK.]

  BOTTOM. Why do they run away? This is a knavery of them to make

95 me afeard.

[*Enter* SNOUT.]

  SNOUT. O Bottom, thou art changed. What do I see on thee?

  BOTTOM. What do you see? You see an ass head of your own, do you?

[*Exit* SNOUT; *enter* QUINCE.]

  QUINCE. Bless thee, Bottom, bless thee! Thou art translated!

[*Exit* QUINCE.]

  BOTTOM. I see their knavery. This is to make an ass of me, to fright

100 me, if they could; but I will not stir from this place, do what they

  can. I will walk up and down here, and will sing, that they shall

  hear I am not afraid.

  [*Sings.*] The ousel° cock° so black of hue,

  With orange-tawny bill,

105 The throstle° with his note so true,

  The wren with little quill—

---

103 ousel *blackbird*
  cock *male bird*
105 throstle *song thrush*

Literary Element

Farce Why would Bottom's transformation and his ensuing comments be considered farcical?

_____

_____

_____

_____

_____

_____

_____

_____

_____

_____

_____

_____

_____

_____

_____

_____

_____

_____

_____

_____

_____

_____

_____

_____

_____

_____

_____

_____

_____

_____

_____

_____

Reading Strategy

Identify Sequence Who remains onstage at the end of this excerpt?

_____

_____

_____

_____

_____

_____

_____

_____

_____

_____

_____

_____

_____

_____

_____

_____

_____

_____

_____

_____

_____

_____

_____

_____

_____

_____

PLAY EXCERPT: ACT 3, SCENE 2

OBERON. But we are spirits of another sort.

    I with the morning's love have oft made sport,

390   And like a forester the groves may tread

    Even till the eastern gate, all fiery-red,

    Opening on Neptune° with fair blessèd beams,

    Turns into yellow gold his salt green streams.

    But notwithstanding, haste, make no delay;

395   We may effect this business yet ere day.

[_Exit_ OBERON.]

PUCK. Up and down, up and down,

    I will lead them up and down;

    I am feared in field and town.

    Goblin, lead them up and down.

400   Here comes one.

[_Enter_ LYSANDER.]

LYSANDER. Where art thou, proud Demetrius? Speak thou now.

PUCK. Here, villain, drawn and ready! Where art thou?

LYSANDER. I will be with thee straight.

PUCK. Follow me then

    To plainer ground.

[_Exit_ LYSANDER.]

[_Enter_ DEMETRIUS.]

DEMETRIUS. Lysander, speak again.

405   Thou runaway, thou coward, art thou fled?

    Speak! In some bush? Where dost thou hide thy head?

PUCK. Thou coward, art thou bragging to the stars,

    Telling the bushes that thou look'st for wars,

    And wilt not come? Come, recreant,° come, thou child,

410   I'll whip thee with a rod. He is defiled

    That draws a sword on thee.

DEMETRIUS. Yea, art thou there?

PUCK. Follow my voice. We'll try no manhood here.

[_Exit_ PUCK and DEMETRIUS.]

[_Enter_ LYSANDER.]

---

392 Neptune _god of the sea. The morning's sunbeams turn the sea from green to 'yellow gold,' transforming it._

409 recreant _coward, villain_

LYSANDER. He goes before me, and still dares me on;

When I come where he calls, then he is gone.

415   The villain is much lighter-heeled than I;

I followed fast, but faster he did fly,

That fallen am I in dark uneven way,

And here will rest me. [*Lies down.*] Come, thou gentle day,

For if but once thou show me thy grey light

420   I'll find Demetrius and revenge this spite. [*Sleeps.*]

[*Enter* PUCK *and* DEMETRIUS.]

PUCK. Ho, ho, ho! Coward, why com'st thou not?

DEMETRIUS. Abide° me if thou dar'st, for well I wot°

Thou runn'st before me, shifting every place,

And dar'st not stand nor look me in the face.

425   Where art thou now?

PUCK. Come hither; I am here.

DEMETRIUS. Nay then, thou mock'st me. Thou shalt buy this dear

If ever I thy face by daylight see.

Now, go thy way; faintness constraineth me

To measure out my length on this cold bed.

430   By day's approach look to be visited. [*Sleeps.*]

[*Enter* HELENA.]

HELENA. O weary night, O long and tedious night,

Abate° thy hours, shine comforts from the east,

That I may back to Athens by daylight

From these that my poor company detest;

435   And sleep, that sometimes shuts up sorrow's eye,

Steal me awhile from mine own company. [*Sleeps.*]

---

422 Abide *face*
wot *know*
432 Abate *diminish, cut short*

Reading Strategy

Identify Sequence Why do you think Shakespeare moves characters on and off stage so frequently in this excerpt?

_____

_____

_____

_____

_____

_____

_____

_____

_____

_____

_____

_____

_____

_____

_____

_____

_____

_____

_____

_____

_____

_____

_____

_____

_____

_____

_____

_____

_____

_____

_____

MARK IT UP

Are you allowed to write in your novel? If so, then mark up the pages as you read, or reread, to help with your note-taking. Develop a shorthand system, including symbols, that works for you. Here are some ideas:

Underline = important idea

Bracket = text to quote

Asterisk = just what you were looking for

Checkmark = might be useful

Circle = unfamiliar word or phrase to look up

▶ **BIG Idea**

The Power of Love What have you found out about how the characters deal with romantic conflicts?

Mark up the excerpt, looking for evidence of how it expresses the Big Idea.

PLAY EXCERPT: ACT 3, SCENE 2

LYSANDER. What? Should I hurt her, strike her, kill her dead?

270 Although I hate her, I'll not harm her so.

HERMIA. What? Can you do me greater harm than hate?

Hate me? Wherefore? O me, what news, my love?

Am not I Hermia? Are not you Lysander?

I am as fair now as I was erewhile.

275 Since night you loved me; yet since night you left me.

Why then, you left me—O, the gods forbid!—

In earnest, shall I say?

LYSANDER. Ay, by my life;

And never did desire to see thee more.

Therefore be out of hope, of question, of doubt;

280 Be certain, nothing truer—'tis no jest

That I do hate thee and love Helena.

HERMIA. [*To Helena.*]

O me, you juggler, you canker-blossom,°

You thief of love! What, have you come by night

And stol'n my love's heart from him?

HELENA. Fine, i'faith!

285 Have you no modesty, no maiden shame,

No touch of bashfulness? What, will you tear

Impatient answers from my gentle tongue?

Fie, fie, you counterfeit, you puppet, you!

HERMIA. 'Puppet'? Why so?—Ay, that way goes the game.

290 Now I perceive that she hath made compare

Between our statures; she hath urged her height,

And with her personage, her tall personage,

Her height, forsooth, she hath prevailed with him.

And are you grown so high in his esteem

295 Because I am so dwarfish and so low?

How low am I, thou painted maypole? Speak!

How low am I? I am not yet so low

But that my nails can reach unto thine eyes.

HELENA. I pray you, though you mock me, gentlemen,

300 Let her not hurt me. I was never curst;

I have no gift at all in shrewishness.

I am a right maid for my cowardice;

Let her not strike me. You perhaps may think

Because she is something lower than myself

305 That I can match her.

---

282 canker-blossom *diseased flower*

Use the Cornell Note-Taking system to take notes on the excerpt at the left. Record your notes, Reduce them, and then Recap (summarize) them.

Record

_____
_____
_____
_____
_____
_____
_____
_____
_____
_____
_____
_____
_____
_____
_____
_____
_____
_____

Recap

_____
_____
_____
_____
_____
_____

Reduce

Try the following approach as you reduce your notes.

TO THE POINT
Write a few key words.

_____
_____
_____
_____
_____
_____
_____
_____
_____
_____
_____
_____
_____
_____

Respond and Think Critically

1. How does Bottom become an ass? What is the reason for this strange event? [Recall]

_____

_____

_____

_____

2. What causes Helena to become angry with Hermia? In your opinion, why does Helena refuse to believe her friend and her would-be lovers? [Infer]

_____

_____

_____

_____

_____

3. In Act 3, what emotion does Oberon show he is capable of? How does he show this? [Analyze]

_____

_____

_____

_____

_____

4. Think of characters from television or the movies who are tricksters like Puck. Why might audiences enjoy watching the antics of such characters? [Connect]

_____

_____

_____

_____

5. The Power of Love What elements of Titania's relationship with Bottom show the farcical aspects of love? [Interpret]

_____

_____

_____

_____

APPLY BACKGROUND

Reread Introduction to the Play on pages 164–165. How did that information help you understand or appreciate what you read in the play?

_____

_____

_____

_____

_____

_____

_____

_____

_____

_____

_____

_____

_____

_____

_____

_____

_____

_____

_____

_____

_____

_____

_____

_____

_____

_____

_____

_____

_____

Literary Element Farce

In your opinion, do the craftsmen's absurd preparations for their play add to or detract from the love stories in this act? [Evaluate]

_____
_____
_____
_____
_____
_____
_____
_____
_____
_____
_____
_____
_____

Reading Strategy Identify Sequence

In what way does the confusion within Act 3 help Shakespeare create a comic effect? [Analyze]

_____
_____
_____
_____
_____
_____
_____
_____
_____
_____
_____
_____
_____

Vocabulary Practice

Identify whether each set of paired words have the same or the opposite meaning.

1. **bequeath** and inherit

_____

2. **chide** and scold

_____

3. **entreat** and plead

_____

4. **rebuke** and praise

_____

5. **sojourn** and depart

_____

Academic Vocabulary

Lysander **rejects** Hermia, to her surprise and dismay, after Puck puts a spell on him. Using context clues, try to figure out the meaning of the boldfaced word in the sentence above. Write your guess below. Then check it in a dictionary.

_____
_____
_____
_____
_____
_____
_____
_____
_____
_____
_____
_____

Writing

Write a Scene Choose one of the scenes in Act 3 to rewrite using modern issues, characters, and language, but displaying the same elements of farce that Shakespeare employed. As you outline a modern version of Shakespeare's scene, try to stay true to the sequence of events that Shakespeare developed. Finally, use modern language and characters as you recreate this scene from a contemporary perspective.

Jot down some notes here first.

_____

_____

_____

_____

_____

_____

_____

_____

_____

_____

_____

_____

_____

_____

_____

_____

_____

_____

_____

_____

_____

_____

_____

_____

_____

_____

Speaking and Listening

Debate

Assignment Some critics see Bottom as a fool. Others think he is wiser than he appears. Divide into two teams. Conduct a debate about whether Bottom is a fool or wiser than he appears. Use examples from the text to support your argument.

Prepare Evidence—and how you use it—is key to a successful debate. Organize your arguments and evidence in a chart to make sure you include all the important points. Fill out a separate chart listing your opponents' potential arguments. Find evidence to counter those claims.

Your team's position: Bottom is a fool.

Argument	Evidence
Bottom lacks any self-awareness	He has no idea that he is wearing an asses' head.

Opponents' Possible Argument	Your Counter-argument
Bottom is honest with Titania about his shortcomings.	She is under a magic spell and is unable to "see" his shortcomings.

Debate Use your chart to help you defend your point with specific examples. When your opponents present their side, listen carefully so you can challenge their arguments with counter-arguments and counter-evidence. This will both weaken their argument and strengthen your own.

Evaluate Write one paragraph evaluating your individual and team performance. Write another paragraph evaluating your opponents. Conclude with a few statements about where you succeeded, what you learned, and how you might do things differently next time.

Connect to the Literature

Think of a movie or book in which characters have an unusual experience that makes them shake their heads and ask, "Did that really happen?"

Create a List

Working in a small group, list stories, novels, movies, and television shows in which a character has an amazing experience and then wakes up to realize it was just a dream. Then compare your lists with the ones compiled by other groups.

Build Background

A Mix of Settings

A curious feature of *A Midsummer Night's Dream* is the casual way in which Shakespeare mixes his settings. Whereas some of his fairies are beings from Celtic and Anglo-Saxon folklore, and the flowers and seasons he describes belong to the English countryside, Theseus and Hippolyta inhabit the world of ancient Greece. In this act, the royal lovers refer to Sparta, an ancient Greek city; Thessaly, a region of Greece; and Crete, a Greek island. Then, amusingly, Theseus mentions St. Valentine, a Christian martyr who lived and died long after the era in which Theseus would have lived.

NOVEL NOTEBOOK
Keep a special notebook to record entries about the novels that you read this year.

SUMMARIZE
Summarize in one sentence the most important idea(s) in Build Background.

_____
_____
_____
_____
_____
_____
_____
_____
_____
_____
_____
_____
_____
_____
_____
_____
_____
_____
_____
_____
_____
_____
_____
_____
_____
_____
_____
_____
_____

Set Purposes for Reading

▶ **BIG Idea** **The Power of Love**

Do you believe in a *happily ever after?* What is your view of the ideal romance?

In Act 4, Shakespeare straightens out the confusion that he established in Acts 2 and 3. In doing so, he offers a happy ending for the lovers who once again are reunited with their rightful partners. As you read, think about how this act might have played out if the lovers had not been reacquainted.

Literary Element **Foil**

A **foil** is a character who provides a strong contrast to another character, usually a main character. A foil is often known for one exaggerated trait or characteristic; that trait highlights a specific difference between the foil and the main character.

By using a foil, a writer calls attention to the strengths or weaknesses of another character.

Shakespeare's minor characters often serve as foils for the major characters. As you read, see if you can identify which of the minor characters serve as foils to some of the major characters.

Reading Strategy **Compare and Contrast Acts and Scenes**

To **compare and contrast acts and scenes** is to look for elements that reappear in different guises at different points in a play.

Playwrights carefully craft the scenes within an act to further the plot and to create artful parallels and contrasts.

In *A Midsummer Night's Dream*, Shakespeare uses **doubling,** a technique in which elements or characters in one part of the play repeat or reflect elements in another part. To compare two scenes in the play, you might find it helpful to use a graphic organizer like the one at the right. The graphic organizer on the next page can also help you to compare and contrast two acts in the play.

Vocabulary

discourse [dis′kôrs]
n. conversation
Some incredible discourse takes place on university campuses.

enmity [en′mə tē]
n. hostility
Enmity between nations can result in war.

paragon [par′ə gon′]
n. model of perfection
Mother Theresa was a paragon of good-will and charity.

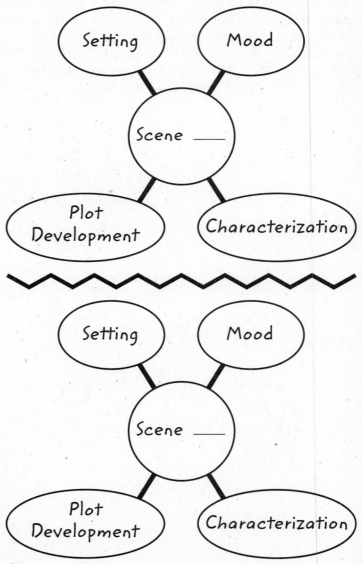

The action of *A Midsummer Night's Dream* is, in part, propelled by the contrasts between characters, scenes and acts, and these contrasts become even clearer in Act 4. As you read, identify the similarities and differences that exist between Act 3 and Act 4. Record your findings in the Venn diagram below.

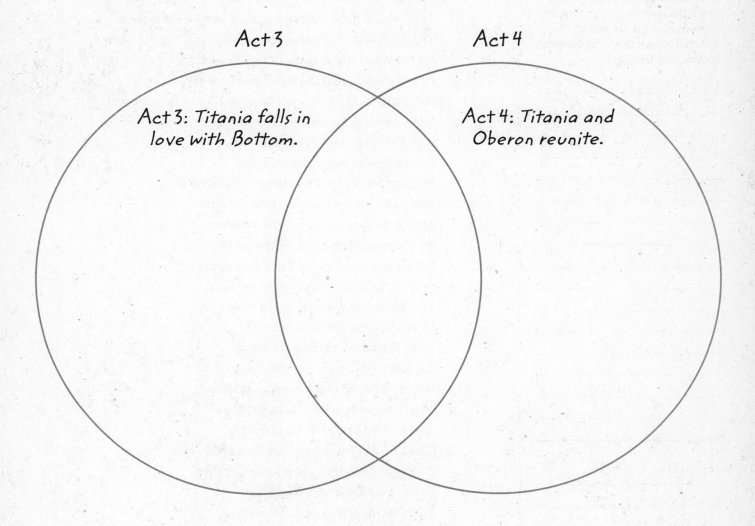

Act 3

Act 4

Act 3: Titania falls in love with Bottom.

Act 4: Titania and Oberon reunite.

Literary Element

Foil In what way does Theseus help reestablish the order and peace that were missing from the previous scenes? How does this illuminate the differences between Bottom and Theseus?

_____

_____

_____

_____

_____

_____

_____

_____

_____

_____

_____

_____

_____

_____

_____

_____

_____

_____

_____

_____

_____

_____

_____

_____

_____

_____

_____

_____

_____

_____

_____

PLAY EXCERPT: ACT 4, SCENE 1

EGEUS. Enough, enough, my lord; you have enough—

I beg the law, the law upon his head!

They would have stol'n away, they would, Demetrius,

Thereby to have defeated you and me,

155   You of your wife, and me of my consent,

Of my consent that she should be your wife.

DEMETRIUS. My lord, fair Helen told me of their stealth,

Of this their purpose hither to this wood;

And I in fury hither followed them,

160   Fair Helena in fancy following me.

But, my good lord, I wot not by what power

(But some power it is), my love to Hermia,

Melted as the snow, seems to me now

As the remembrance of an idle gaud°

165   Which in my childhood I did dote upon;

And all the faith, the virtue of my heart,

The object and the pleasure of mine eye,

Is only Helena. To her, my lord,

Was I betrothed ere I saw Hermia;

170   But like a sickness did I loathe this food.

But, as in health come to my natural taste,

Now I do wish it, love it, long for it,

And will for evermore be true to it.

THESEUS. Fair lovers, you are fortunately met.

175   Of this discourse we more will hear anon.

Egeus, I will overbear your will;°

For in the temple, by and by, with us

These couples shall eternally be knit.

And, for the morning now is something worn,

180   Our purposed hunting shall be set aside.

Away with us to Athens. Three and three,

We'll hold a feast in great solemnity.

Come, Hippolyta.

[_Exit_ THESEUS _with_ HIPPOLYTA, EGEUS, _and his train._]

DEMETRIUS. These things seem small and undistinguishable,

185   Like far-off mountains turnèd into clouds.

164   idle gaud _worthless toy_

176   overbear your will _overrule your decision_

HERMIA. Methinks I see these things with parted eye,

When everything seems double.

HELENA. So methinks;

And I have found Demetrius, like a jewel,

Mine own, and not mine own.

DEMETRIUS. Are you sure

190   That we are awake? It seems to me

That yet we sleep, we dream. Do not you think

The Duke was here, and bid us follow him?

HERMIA. Yea, and my father.

HELENA. And Hippolyta.

LYSANDER. And he did bid us follow to the temple.

195   **DEMETRIUS.** Why, then, we are awake. Let's follow him,

And by the way let us recount our dreams.

[*Exit lovers.*]

[*BOTTOM wakes.*]

BOTTOM. When my cue comes, call me, and I will answer. My next is

'Most fair Pyramus'. Heigh ho! Peter Quince? Flute the bellows-

mender? Snout the tinker? Starveling? God's my life! Stolen hence

200   and left me asleep! I have had a most rare vision. I have had a dream,

past the wit of man to say what dream it was. Man is but an ass

if he go about to expound this dream. Methought I was—there is

no man can tell what. Methought I was—and methought I had—but

man is but a patched fool if he will offer to say what methought

205   I had. The eye of man hath not heard, the ear of man hath not seen,

man's hand is not able to taste, his tongue to conceive, nor his heart

to report what my dream was! I will get Peter Quince to write a

ballad of this dream; it shall be called 'Bottom's Dream', because

it hath no bottom; and I will sing it in the latter end of a play, before

210   the Duke. Peradventure, to make it the more gracious, I shall sing

it at her death.

Literary Element

Foil How does Bottom propose to bring order to the strange dream he believes he just had? How does his proposal reflect his role as a foil to Theseus?

_____

_____

_____

_____

_____

_____

_____

_____

_____

_____

_____

_____

_____

_____

_____

_____

_____

_____

_____

_____

_____

_____

_____

_____

Reading Strategy

Compare and Contrast Acts and Scenes How is the action in this excerpt a doubling of what has happened earlier in other acts and scenes in the play?

_____

_____

_____

_____

_____

_____

_____

_____

_____

_____

_____

_____

_____

_____

_____

_____

_____

_____

_____

_____

_____

_____

_____

_____

_____

_____

_____

PLAY EXCERPT: ACT 4, SCENE 1

25   **TITANIA.** What, wilt thou hear some music, my sweet love?

      BOTTOM. I have a reasonable good ear in music. Let's have the tongs and the bones.°

      TITANIA. Or say, sweet love, what thou desir'st to eat.

      BOTTOM. Truly, a peck of provender, I could munch your good dry oats.

30   Methinks I have a great desire to a bottle of hay. Good hay, sweet hay hath no fellow.

      TITANIA. I have a venturous fairy that shall seek
The squirrel's hoard, and fetch thee new nuts.

      BOTTOM. I had rather have a handful or two of dried peas. But, I pray

35   you, let none of your people stir me; I have an exposition of° sleep come upon me.

      TITANIA. Sleep thou, and I will wind thee in my arms.
Fairies be gone, and be all ways away.

[_Exit_ FAIRIES.]

     So doth the woodbine° the sweet honeysuckle

40   Gently entwist; the female ivy so
Enrings the barky fingers of the elm.
O, how I love thee! How I dote on thee!

[_They sleep._]

[_Enter_ PUCK. OBERON _comes forward._]

      OBERON. Welcome, good Robin. Seest thou this sweet sight?
Her dotage now I do begin to pity;

45   For, meeting her of late behind the wood
Seeking sweet favours for this hateful fool,
I did upbraid her and fall out with her,
For she his hairy temples then had rounded
With coronet of fresh and fragrant flowers;

50   And that same dew, which sometime on the buds
Was wont to swell like round and orient pearls,
Stood now within the pretty flowerets' eyes
Like tears that did their own disgrace bewail.
When I had at my pleasure taunted her,

55   And she in mild terms begged my patience,
I then did ask of her her changeling child,
Which straight she gave me, and her fairy sent

26–7 tongs . . . bones _simple musical instruments_

35 exposition of _another of Bottom's mistakes; surely he means disposition to?_

39 woodbine _bindweed_

To bear him to my bower in Fairyland.

And now I have the boy, I will undo

60   This hateful imperfection of her eyes.

And, gentle Puck, take this transformèd scalp

From off the head of this Athenian swain,°

That, he awaking when the other do,

May all to Athens back again repair,

65   And think no more of this night's accidents

But as the fierce vexation of a dream.

But first I will release the Fairy Queen.

[*Squeezing a herb on* TITANIA'S *eyes.*]

Be as thou wast wont to be;

See as thou wast wont to see.

70   Dian's bud o'er Cupid's flower

Hath such force and blessèd power.

Now, my Titania, wake you, my sweet Queen!

TITANIA. [*Starting up.*]

My Oberon, what visions I have seen!

Methought I was enamoured of an ass.

75   **OBERON.** There lies your love.

TITANIA. How came these things to pass?

O, how mine eyes do loathe his visage now!

OBERON. Silence awhile: Robin, take off this head.

Titania, music call, and strike more dead

Than common sleep of all these five the sense.

80   **TITANIA.** Music, ho, music such as charmeth sleep!

[*Soft music plays.*]

PUCK. [*To* BOTTOM, *removing the ass's head.*]

Now, when thou wak'st, with thine own fool's eyes peep.

OBERON. Sound, music! Come, my Queen, take hands with me,

And rock the ground whereon these sleepers be.

[*They dance.*]

Now thou and I are new in amity,

85   And will tomorrow midnight solemnly

Dance in Duke Theseus' house triumphantly,

And bless it to all fair prosperity.

There shall the pairs of faithful lovers be

Wedded, with Theseus, all in jollity.

---

62 swain *lover*

Reading Strategy

Compare and Contrast Acts and Scenes In Act 1, Scene 1 (lines 134–142), Lysander states, "the course of true love never did run smooth." How is that theme expressed in this excerpt from Act 4, Scene 1, as compared to that scene?

_____

_____

_____

_____

_____

_____

_____

_____

_____

_____

_____

_____

_____

_____

_____

_____

_____

_____

_____

_____

_____

_____

_____

_____

_____

_____

_____

_____

_____

MARK IT UP

Are you allowed to write in your novel? If so, then mark up the pages as you read, or reread, to help with your note-taking. Develop a shorthand system, including symbols, that works for you. Here are some ideas:

Underline = important idea

Bracket = text to quote

Asterisk = just what you were looking for

Checkmark = might be useful

Circle = unfamiliar word or phrase to look up

▶ **BIG Idea**

The Power of Love How does Shakespeare resolve all of the romantic confusion of earlier acts?

Mark up the excerpt, looking for evidence of how it expresses the Big Idea.

PLAY EXCERPT: ACT 4, SCENE 1

LYSANDER. Pardon, my lord.

THESEUS. I pray you all, stand up.

    I know you two are rival enemies:

140   How comes this gentle concord in the world,

    That hatred is so far from jealousy

    To sleep by hate, and fear no enmity?

LYSANDER. My lord, I shall reply amazedly,

    Half sleep, half waking; but as yet, I swear,

145   I cannot truly say how I came here.

    But as I think (for truly would I speak)

    And now I do bethink me, so it is—

    I came with Hermia hither. Our intent

    Was to be gone from Athens, where we might

150   Without the peril of the Athenian law—

EGEUS. Enough, enough, my lord; you have enough—

    I beg the law, the law upon his head!

    They would have stol'n away, they would, Demetrius,

    Thereby to have defeated you and me,

155   You of your wife, and me of my consent,

    Of my consent that she should be your wife.

DEMETRIUS. My lord, fair Helen told me of their stealth,

    Of this their purpose hither to this wood;

    And I in fury hither followed them,

160   Fair Helena in fancy following me.

    But, my good lord, I wot not by what power

    (But some power it is), my love to Hermia,

    Melted as the snow, seems to me now

    As the remembrance of an idle gaud°

165   Which in my childhood I did dote upon;

    And all the faith, the virtue of my heart,

    The object and the pleasure of mine eye,

    Is only Helena. To her, my lord,

    Was I betrothed ere I saw Hermia;

170   But like a sickness did I loathe this food.

    But, as in health come to my natural taste,

    Now I do wish it, love it, long for it,

    And will for evermore be true to it.

---

137 couple *pair up*

164 idle gaud *worthless toy*

Use the Cornell Note-Taking system to take notes on the excerpt at the left. Record your notes, Reduce them, and then Recap (summarize) them.

Record

Recap

Reduce

Try the following approach as you reduce your notes.

TO THE POINT
Write a few key words.

Respond and Think Critically

1. How do most of the dreamers respond to the dream experience upon waking? Which character is changed permanently by the dream experience? [Summarize]

_____

_____

_____

_____

2. How does Theseus's current decision regarding Hermia and Lysander contradict his earlier statement? [Interpret]

_____

_____

_____

_____

3. The fourth act opens and ends with Bottom at center stage. What is your opinion of Bottom's character? How might he be the antithesis, or opposite, of Theseus's character? [Evaluate]

_____

_____

_____

_____

4. In this act, several characters look back at prior infatuations with disbelief. What do you think Shakespeare is saying about love and infatuation? [Analyze]

_____

_____

_____

_____

5. The Power of Love Which character was most responsible for facilitating the happy endings that occurred in this act? Why? [Analyze]

_____

_____

_____

_____

APPLY BACKGROUND
Reread Build Background on page 203. How did that information help you understand or appreciate what you read in the play?

_____

_____

_____

_____

_____

_____

_____

_____

_____

_____

_____

_____

_____

_____

_____

_____

_____

_____

_____

_____

_____

_____

_____

_____

_____

_____

_____

Literary Element   Foil

Identify one character other than Bottom that serves as a foil in the play so far. What does this foil reveal about another character? [Analyze]

_____

_____

_____

_____

_____

_____

_____

_____

_____

_____

_____

Reading Skill   Compare and Contrast Acts and Scenes

In what way did Shakespeare's use of contrast enhance your appreciation of the comedic moments in the play?

_____

_____

_____

_____

_____

_____

_____

_____

_____

_____

_____

_____

_____

Vocabulary Practice

Studying the **etymology,** or origin and history, of a word can help you better understand and explore its meaning. Create a word map, like the one below, for each of these vocabulary words from the selection. Use a dictionary for help.

discourse   enmity   paragon

EXAMPLE: **scripture**
Definition: any sacred writing or book
Etymology: Latin *scriptura* means "writing"

Sample Sentence:
Ameena follows the **scripture** of the Muslim faith.

Academic Vocabulary

In Act 4 Scene 1, Oberon decides to **facilitate** *the end of the spell that he had placed on Titania in Act 2.* In the previous sentence, *facilitate* means "to help bring about." Think about the way in which Oberon helped to bring about the end of Titania's spell, then fill in the blank. *In order to* **facilitate** *the end of Titania's spell, Oberon* _____

_____

_____

_____.

Writing

Write a Letter When Bottom is reunited with his friend, they press him for details of what happened, but he is unable to tell them much. Imagine that later Bottom calms down enough to relate his amazing experiences. Write a letter from Bottom to his friends telling about his transformation into an ass, his meeting with the fairies, and his love affair with Titania. Try to write as Bottom would (misusing long words, for example).

Jot down some notes here first.

_____
_____
_____
_____
_____
_____
_____
_____
_____
_____
_____
_____
_____
_____
_____
_____
_____
_____
_____
_____
_____
_____
_____
_____
_____

Speaking and Listening
Oral Report

Assignment Present an oral report about what Bottom's "dream" might mean, incorporating modern dream symbolism, classical mythology, English folklore, or contemporary English life.

Prepare Before you begin your research, decide what part of the topic you plan to make your focus. Next, develop a list of research questions on this topic. For example, if you focus on dream symbolism, one research question might be: "What does acquiring animal characteristics symbolize in a dream?" As you research, be sure to use a variety of reliable and authoritative sources.

Finally, organize the information you find into an outline like the one below. Use your outline as a reference while giving your report.

Bottom's Dream Explained
    I. Dream symbols
        a. Animals
        b.
    II. The meaning of these symbols
        a.
        b.

Report Assemble three or four visual aids, such as posters, graphs, or images that are relevant to the topic of dream interpretation or to Bottom's dream in particular. These should either explain the conclusions that you are presenting or add new information. Incorporate them into your outline, so you know when to refer to each one during your presentation.

Evaluate Write a paragraph in which you assess how effectively you justified your analysis of Bottom's dream, and how well you incorporated your visual aids into your presentation.

Connect to the Literature

Have you ever seen a live performance that was so badly presented it was entertaining?

Make Lists

A live theatrical performance is a two-way relationship between the performers and the audience. Make a list of ways in which the performers affect the audience. Then, next to that list, jot down typical audience reactions to the performance.

Build Background

Elizabethan Entertainment

For wealthy Elizabethans, entertainment was something quite different from today's CD/video/television center. Elizabethans, poor and rich, watched live entertainment. Nobles and members of the royalty could afford to have performers come to their homes. Sometimes they watched knights jousting in courtyards or tennis players competing in special indoor rooms. Often they watched theater. Every year, one of England's great theater companies would be chosen to appear at the court of Queen Elizabeth I. The Queen's Master of the Revels (like Theseus's Master of the Revels, Philostrate) would watch a number of performances and pick the best. Then no expense was spared for the final production. Workers painted elaborate sets and made costumes out of silk and velvet.

NOVEL NOTEBOOK

Keep a special notebook to record entries about the novels that you read this year.

SUMMARIZE

Summarize in one sentence the most important idea(s) in Build Background.

_____

_____

_____

_____

_____

_____

_____

_____

_____

_____

_____

_____

_____

_____

_____

_____

_____

_____

_____

_____

_____

_____

_____

_____

_____

_____

_____

Set Purposes for Reading

▶ BIG Idea The Power of Love

Think about any tragic love stories you have read. Why is it that, in these tragedies, like *Romeo and Juliet*, the lovers are ultimately forced to commit a final, tragic act of desperation?

In Act 5, the bumbled performance of the tragic *Pyramus and Thisbe* contrasts starkly with the happy, ordered ending of the reunited *Midsummer* lovers. As you read, think about why Shakespeare included a play within a play that presents a tragic end to romance. What does this draw the audience's attention to?

Literary Element Comedy

Comedy is a type of drama that is humorous and typically has a happy ending. Typically, a comedy moves from chaos to order to celebration.

Comedy can be divided into two categories: high and low. **High comedy** makes fun of human behavior in a witty, sophisticated matter. **Low comedy** involves physical humor and simple, often vulgar, wordplay.

Shakespeare uses many different comedic devices in *A Midsummer Night's Dream*. As you read Act 5, think about how the craftsmen's comic performance captures many of the themes presented in the play. Use the graphic organizer on the next page to help you keep track of examples of comedy in the play.

Reading Strategy Draw Conclusions About Author's Meaning

To **draw conclusions about an author's meaning** is to form an understanding of what the author is trying to say based on evidence from the text.

It requires the reader to gather evidence from the writing and to use it to support ideas suggested by the work as a whole.

Through his use of humor, Shakespeare provides commentary on the powerful emotions and confusion that love can cause. As you read, consider what the happy ending of this play reveals about the truths that Shakespeare wanted to convey. You might want to use a graphic organizer like the one at the right.

Vocabulary

amends [ə mends´]
n. something done to make up for a fault or mistake
After having a fight with a friend, it is important to make amends quickly.

audacious [ô dā´shəs]
adj. bold
The employee's audacious decision surprised his boss.

gait [gāt]
n. manner of walking
After breaking her leg, she walked with a crooked gait.

premeditated [prē med´i tāt əd]
adj. planned
It was clear that the burglary was premeditated because the burglars knew the homeowner was going to be out of town for a week.

satire [sat´īr]
n. literary work exposing human vices and shortcomings to ridicule and scorn
In a satire, an author often pokes fun at current events and human weakness.

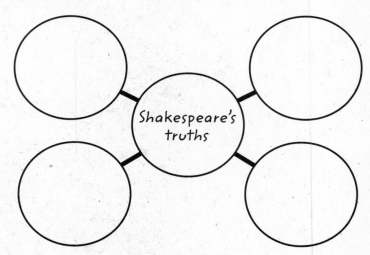

Shakespeare uses a number of different techniques to create humor in the play-within-a-play. Use the graphic organizer below to indicate examples of some of his comic devices.

ridiculous metaphor	lily lips (line 347)
excessive alliteration	
breaking the play's illusion of reality	
using the wrong word or name	
repeating a word excessively	
using puns	

Literary Element

Comedy What types of comedic devices are evident in this excerpt? Give examples of each.

_____

_____

_____

_____

_____

_____

_____

_____

_____

_____

_____

_____

_____

_____

_____

_____

_____

_____

_____

_____

_____

_____

_____

_____

PLAY EXCERPT: ACT 5, SCENE 1

SNOUT. [*as Wall.*]

In this same interlude° it doth befall

That I, one Snout by name, present a wall;

155   And such a wall as I would have you think

That had in it a crannied hole or chink,

Through which the lovers, Pyramus and Thisbe,

Did whisper often, very secretly.

This loam, this rough-cast, and this stone doth show

160   That I am that same wall; the truth is so.

And this the cranny is, right and sinister,

Through which the fearful lovers are to whisper.

THESEUS. Would you desire lime and hair to speak better?

DEMETRIUS. It is the wittiest partition that ever I heard discourse, my

165   lord.

[*Enter* BOTTOM *as Pyramus.*]

THESEUS. Pyramus draws near the wall; silence!

BOTTOM. [*as Pyramus.*]

O grim-looked night, O night with hue so black,

   O night which ever art when day is not!

O night, O night, alack, alack, alack,

170   I fear my Thisbe's promise is forgot!

And thou, O wall, O sweet, O lovely wall,

   That stand'st between her father's ground and mine,

Thou wall, O wall, O sweet and lovely wall,

   Show me thy chink, to blink through with mine eyne.

[*Wall parts his fingers.*]

175   Thanks, courteous wall; Jove shield thee well for this!

   But what see I? No Thisbe do I see.

O wicked wall, through whom I see no bliss,

   Cursed by thy stones for thus deceiving me!

THESEUS. The wall, methinks, being sensible, should curse again.°

180   **BOTTOM.** No, in truth sir, he should not. 'Deceiving me' is Thisbe's

cue. She is to enter now, and I am to spy her through the wall.

You shall see it will fall pat as I told you. Yonder she comes.

[*Enter* FLUTE *as Thisbe.*]

FLUTE. [*as Thisbe.*]

---

153 interlude *short play*

179 curse again *should curse back, since it is 'sensible' (alive)*

O wall, full often hast thou heard my moans,

For parting my fair Pyramus and me.

185 My cherry lips have often kissed thy stones,

Thy stones with lime and hair knit up in thee.

BOTTOM. [as Pyramus.]

I see a voice; now will I to the chink,

To spy and I can hear my Thisbe's face.

Thisbe!

FLUTE. [as Thisbe.]

My love! Thou art my love, I think?

BOTTOM. [as Pyramus.]

190 Think what thou wilt, I am thy lover's grace,

And like Limander° am I trusty still.

FLUTE. [as Thisbe.]

And I like Helen,° till the Fates me kill.

BOTTOM. [as Pyramus.]

Not Shafalus° to Procrus° was so true.

FLUTE. [as Thisbe.]

As Shafalus to Procrus, I to you.

BOTTOM. [as Pyramus.]

195 O, kiss me through the hole of this vile wall!

FLUTE. [as Thisbe.]

I kiss the wall's hole, not your lips at all.

BOTTOM. [as Pyramus.]

Wilt thou at Ninny's tomb meet me straightway?

FLUTE. [as Thisbe.]

Tide° life, tide death, I come without delay.

[Exit BOTTOM and FLUTE in different directions.]

SNOUT. [as Wall.]

Thus have I, Wall, my part dischargèd so;

200 And being done, thus Wall away doth go.

[Exit SNOUT.]

THESEUS. Now is the mural° down between the two neighbours.

DEMETRIUS. No remedy, my lord, when walls are so willful to hear without warning.

HIPPOLYTA. This is the silliest stuff that ever I heard.

191–2 Limander, Helen *this should be Leander and Hero, two legendary lovers*

193 Shafalus, Procrus *this should be Cephalus and Procris, other legendary lovers*

198 tide *come*

201 mural *wall*

Literary Element

Comedy Is the comedy in this excerpt high or low? Explain.

_____

_____

_____

_____

_____

_____

_____

_____

_____

_____

_____

_____

_____

_____

_____

_____

_____

_____

_____

_____

_____

_____

_____

_____

_____

_____

_____

_____

_____

Reading Strategy

Draw Conclusions about Author's Meaning What reason does Theseus give for wanting to see *Pyramus and Thisbe* performed, despite Philostrate's suggestion otherwise? What evidence leads you to this conclusion?

_____

_____

_____

_____

_____

_____

_____

_____

_____

_____

_____

_____

_____

_____

_____

_____

_____

_____

_____

_____

_____

_____

_____

_____

_____

_____

_____

_____

_____

PLAY EXCERPT: ACT 5, SCENE 1

PHILOSTRATE.   A play there is, my lord, some ten words long,

Which is as 'brief' as I have known a play,

But by ten words, my lord, it is too long,

Which makes it 'tedious'. For in all the play

65   There is not one word apt, one player fitted.

And 'tragical', my noble lord, it is,

For Pyramus therein doth kill himself,

Which when I saw rehearsed, I must confess,

Made mine eyes water; but more 'merry' tears

70   The passion of loud laughter never shed.

THESEUS.   What are they that do play it?

PHILOSTRATE.   Hard-handed men that work in Athens here,

Which never laboured in their minds till now:

And now have toiled their unbreathed° memories

75   With this same play against your nuptial.

THESEUS.   And we will hear it.

PHILOSTRATE.   No, my noble lord,

It is not for you. I have heard it over,

And it is nothing, nothing in the world,

Unless you can find sport in their intents,

80   Extremely stretched, and conned° with cruel pain,

To do you service.

THESEUS.   I will hear that play;

For never anything can be amiss

When simpleness and duty tender it.

Go bring them in; and take your places, ladies.

[*Exit* PHILOSTRATE.]

85   **HIPPOLYTA.**   I love not to see wretchedness o'ercharged,°

And duty in his service perishing.

THESEUS.   Why, gentle sweet, you shall see no such thing.

HIPPOLYTA.   He says they can do nothing in this kind.

THESEUS.   The kinder we, to give them thanks for nothing.

90   Our sport shall be to take what they mistake;

And what poor duty cannot do, noble respect

Takes it in might, not merit.°

Where I have come, great clerks have purposèd

---

74 unbreathed *unpractised*

80 conned *learnt*

85 wretchedness o'ercharged *those of little ability overstretched*

92 in might, not merit *accepts it given the ability of those that offer it*

95   To greet me with premeditated welcomes,

Where I have seen them shiver and look pale,

Make periods° in the midst of sentences,

Throttle their practised accent in their fears,

And in conclusion dumbly have broke off,

Not paying me a welcome. Trust me, sweet,

100   Out of this silence yet I picked a welcome,

And in the modesty of fearful duty

I read as much as from the rattling tongue

Of saucy and audacious eloquence.

Love, therefore, and tongue-tied simplicity

105   In least speak most, to my capacity.°

[*Enter* PHILOSTRATE.]

PHILOSTRATE. So please your grace, the Prologue is addressed.°

THESEUS. Let him approach.

[*Flourish of trumpets.*]

[*Enter* QUINCE *as Prologue.*]

QUINCE. If we offend, it is with our good will.

That you should think, we come not to offend,

110   But with good will. To show our simple skill,

That is the true beginning of our end.

Consider then, we come but in despite.

We do not come as minding to content you,

Our true intent is. All for your delight,

115   We are not here. That you should here repent you,

The actors are at hand; and by their show

You shall know all that you are like to know.

THESEUS. This fellow doth not stand upon points.°

LYSANDER. He hath rid his prologue like a rough colt; he knows not

120   the stop.° A good moral, my lord; it is not enough to speak, but to

speak true.

HIPPOLYTA. Indeed, he hath played on this prologue like a child on

a recorder—a sound, but not in government.°

THESEUS. His speech was like a tangled chain, nothing impaired, but

125   all disordered.

---

96   periods *stops*
105   capacity *understanding*
106   addressed *ready*
118   stand upon points *take notice of punctuation or detail*
120   stop *a pun on full stop, and suddenly stopping a horse when riding*
123   in government *under control*

Reading Strategy

Draw Conclusions about Author's Meaning According to this excerpt, what message might Shakespeare have been trying to send his audience?

_____

_____

_____

_____

_____

_____

_____

_____

_____

_____

_____

_____

_____

_____

_____

_____

_____

_____

_____

_____

_____

_____

_____

_____

_____

_____

_____

_____

_____

MARK IT UP

Are you allowed to write in your novel? If so, then mark up the pages as you read, or reread, to help with your note-taking. Develop a shorthand system, including symbols, that works for you. Here are some ideas:

Underline = important idea

Bracket = text to quote

Asterisk = just what you were looking for

Checkmark = might be useful

Circle = unfamiliar word or phrase to look up

▶ **BIG Idea**

The Power of Love Who is responsible for helping to craft a happy ending for the lovers?

Mark up the excerpt, looking for evidence of how it expresses the Big Idea.

PLAY EXCERPT: ACT 5, SCENE 1

OBERON. Through the house give glimmering light

370   By the dead and drowsy fire;

Every elf and fairy sprite

       Hop as light as bird from briar,

And this ditty after me

Sing, and dance it trippingly.

375 **TITANIA.** First rehearse your song by rote,

To each word a warbling note;

Hand in hand with fairy grace

Will we sing and bless this place.

[*Song and dance.*]

OBERON. Now until the break of day

380   Through this house each fairy stray.

To the best bride-bed will we,

Which by us shall blessèd be;

And the issue there create

Ever shall be fortunate.

385   So shall all the couples three

Ever true in loving be,

And the blots of nature's hand

Shall not in their issue stand.

Never mole, harelip, nor scar,

390   Nor mark prodigious,° such as are

Despisèd in nativity,

Shall upon their children be.

With this field-dew consecrate,

Every fairy take his gait,°

395   And each several chamber bless

Through this palace with sweet peace;

And the owner of it blessed

Ever shall in safety rest.

Trip away, make no stay;

400   Meet me all by break of day.

---

390 mark prodigious *birthmark that is ominous*
394 take his gait *go his way*

Use the Cornell Note-Taking system to take notes on the excerpt at the left. Record your notes, Reduce them, and then Recap (summarize) them.

Record

_____
_____
_____
_____
_____
_____
_____
_____
_____
_____
_____
_____
_____
_____
_____
_____
_____
_____
_____
_____
_____
_____

Recap

_____
_____
_____
_____
_____
_____

Reduce

Try the following approach as you reduce your notes.

MY VIEW
Comment on what you learned from your own notes.

_____
_____
_____
_____
_____
_____
_____
_____
_____
_____
_____
_____
_____
_____
_____
_____
_____
_____
_____
_____

Respond and Think Critically

1. Why does Hippolyta initially seem hesitant to watch the play? [Interpret]

_____

_____

_____

_____

2. Why does Snug, who plays the Lion, make a fuss about proclaiming his true identity? [Infer]

_____

_____

_____

_____

3. In reading the play-within-a-play, we become the audience for the drama played out by Theseus, Hippolyta, and the others. These performers, in turn, form the audience for the reenactment of _Pyramus and Thisbe_. How does observing another audience help you understand the relationship between audience and performers? [Connect]

_____

_____

_____

_____

4. Modern television shows often create comic effects by having a silly, innocent, or "clueless" character and a sarcastic, knowing, clever character play off of each other. What examples can you think of? [Connect]

_____

_____

_____

_____

5. The Power of Love Who is most responsible for the happy ending to the lovers' jumbled romances? [Analyze]

_____

_____

_____

_____

APPLY BACKGROUND
Reread Build Background on page 215. How did that information help you understand or appreciate what you read in the play?

_____

_____

_____

_____

_____

_____

_____

_____

_____

_____

_____

_____

_____

_____

_____

_____

_____

_____

_____

_____

_____

_____

_____

_____

_____

_____

_____

_____

Literary Element   Comedy

How does Shakespeare's comedy compare to the comedies you see in modern media and theater? What are the similarities and differences between the two? [Compare]

_____

_____

_____

_____

_____

_____

_____

_____

_____

_____

_____

_____

Reading Strategy   Draw Conclusions about Author's Meaning

What conclusions about the nature of romance can you support with evidence from Act 5?

_____

_____

_____

_____

_____

_____

_____

_____

_____

_____

Vocabulary Practice

Write the vocabulary word that correctly completes each sentence. If none of the words fits the sentence, write "none."

amends   audacious   gait   premeditated   satire

1. The _____ written about the President of the United States made some government officials uneasy.

2. A long time ago, large _____ wandered the earth in search of food.

3. In order to make _____ with my mom, I had to apologize for my behavior.

4. In the United States, the punishment for a _____ crime is significantly worse than for one that was not planned.

5. I can't believe you made the _____ decision to quit your job!

6. The zoo keeper left the tiger's _____ open accidentally.

7. His confident _____ made him appear stronger and tougher than he really was.

Academic Vocabulary

Theseus, Hippolyta and the others **comment** *openly and honestly about the craftsmen's performance of Pyramus and Thisbe. In the preceding sentence,* comment *means "to share opinions about." If you were watching this play-within-a-play, how would you* **comment** *on it?*

_____

_____

_____

_____

_____

_____

_____

_____

_____

Writing

Write a Blurb Imagine that you are given the job of creating the program for *A Midsummer Night's Dream*. Write a letter to the audience explaining the purpose of the play-within-a-play. Offer one or two suggestions about why Shakespeare may have included it in his comedy and, specifically, how it sheds light on the play's lovers and their antics.

Jot down some notes here first.

_____

_____

_____

_____

_____

_____

_____

_____

_____

_____

_____

_____

_____

_____

_____

_____

_____

_____

_____

_____

_____

_____

_____

Speaking and Listening

Performance

Assignment With a group of classmates, plan and present a performance of the craftsmen's play-within-a-play.

Prepare Together, assign a character to each group member. Then plan how to present the scene. Discuss staging (how and where actors move "onstage" based on both stated and implied stage directions), any necessary props, and how to best convey the humor of the scene. Costumes and sets are not necessary. Rehearse your performance at least once to make sure that everyone knows his or her part.

Perform Present your performance to your class. Be sure that your chosen body language and tone of voice match your character and contribute to the comic effect.

Evaluate After the performance, get together with your group and discuss how successful your performance was and how it might have been better. Use a chart like the one below to record your group's ideas.

What worked well	What needed improvement
We got the humor across. (Audience laughed.)	At times actors forgot exactly where they were supposed to be.

A Midsummer Night's Dream

The following questions refer to the Related Readings in Glencoe's *Literature Library* edition of this novel. Support your answers with details from the texts. Write your answers on a separate sheet of paper, but jot down some notes first on the lines provided.

Comedy

Christopher Fry

In creating characters for a comedy, Fry says, "If the characters were not qualified for tragedy there would be no comedy." How might this statement apply to the characters of Helena, Lysander, Hermia, and Demetrius in *A Midsummer Night's Dream*?

_____

_____

_____

_____

Forget the Footnotes! And Other Advice

Norrie Epstein

In your opinion, would it better to see or read *A Midsummer Night's Dream*? Justify your answer.

_____

_____

_____

_____

Based on an Original Idea by William Shakespeare

Victoria McKee

In terms of modernizing Shakespeare, with whose approach do you agree, Branagh's or McKellen's?

_____

_____

_____

_____

Allow Puck to Introduce Kids to Will

Lynne Heffley

Do you agree with Lisa Wolpe that New York City makes a good setting for a modern *Midsummer Night's Dream*? Why or why not?

_____

_____

_____

_____

How the Bard Won the West

Jennifer Lee Carrell

How do you think Shakespeare would have reacted to a nineteenth-century Western audience?

_____

_____

_____

_____

LITERATURE EXCERPT: Romeo and Juliet

SAMPSON. Nay, as they dare. I will bite my thumb° at them,
which is disgrace to them if they bear it.

40 **ABRAM.** Do you bite your thumb at us, sir?

SAMPSON. I do bite my thumb, sir.

ABRAM. Do you bite your thumb at us, sir?

SAMPSON. [*Aside to GREGORY.*] Is the law of our side if I say ay?

GREGORY. [*Aside to SAMPSON.*] No.

45 **SAMPSON.** No, sir, I do not bite my thumb at you, sir; but I
bite my thumb, sir. . . .

BENVOLIO. Part, fools!

60 Put up your swords. You know not what you do. [*Beats
down their swords.*]

[*TYBALT, LADY CAPULET's nephew, enters with his sword drawn. He
speaks first to BENVOLIO.*]

TYBALT. What, art thou drawn among these heartless hinds?°
Turn thee, Benvolio; look upon thy death.

BENVOLIO. I do but keep the peace. Put up thy sword,
Or manage it to part these men with me.

65 **TYBALT.** What, drawn, and talk of peace? I hate the word
As I hate hell, all Montagues, and thee.
Have at thee, coward!

[*BENVOLIO and TYBALT fight as men of both families enter and join the
brawl. Then an OFFICER of the town and several CITIZENS enter. They
carry clubs, battle-axes (bills), and spears (partisans).*] . . .

[*PRINCE ESCALUS enters with his TRAIN.*]

PRINCE. Rebellious subjects, enemies to peace,
Profaners of this neighbor-stained steel°—
Will they not hear? What, ho! You men, you beasts,
That quench the fire of your pernicious rage

80 With purple fountains issuing from your veins!
On pain of torture, from those bloody hands
Throw your mistemper'd° weapons to the ground
And hear the sentence of your moved° prince.

---

61 heartless hinds *cowardly servants*
77 Profaners . . . steel *Those who disrespect the law by staining weapons with neighbors' blood*
82 mistemper'd *"poorly made" or "put to bad use"*
83 moved *angry*

Compare the play you have just read to the literature selection at the left, which is excerpted from *Romeo and Juliet* in *Glencoe Literature*. Then answer the questions below. Provide details from the selections to support your answers.

Compare & Contrast

1. Foil In what way is Tybalt a foil for Benvolio in this excerpt? How does this compare to the way foils were used in *A Midsummer Night's Dream*?

_____

_____

_____

_____

2. Monologue What is the purpose of the Prince's monologue, and how does this compare with the function of monologues in *A Midsummer Night's Dream*?

_____

_____

_____

_____

3. Comedy What technique does Shakespeare use to create a comic effect during the encounter between the Montague and Capulet servants? When was this effect used in *Midsummer*?

_____

_____

_____

_____

_____

_____

_____

_____

_____

WRITE ABOUT IT

In a short paragraph, compare the characters of the Prince and either Theseus or Egeus. What do these characters have in common? In what ways are they different?

_____

_____

_____

_____

_____

_____

_____

_____

_____

_____

_____

_____

_____

_____

_____

_____

_____

_____

_____

_____

_____

_____

_____

_____

_____

_____

_____

Expository Essay

Compare and Contrast the Use of Farce Write an essay in which you compare the way that farce is used to create a comic effect in *Midsummer Night's Dream* and Anton Chekhov's *The Bear,* available in *Glencoe Literature* or on the Internet. Support your ideas with examples from the text.

Prewrite Plan carefully before you begin to write. You may wish to skim through the selections and record instances of farce in a graphic organizer like the one shown below.

A Midsummer Night's Dream	
Element of Farce	Effect
Titania falls in love with a craftsmen wearing an asses' head.	presents a ridiculous example of aphorism "love is blind."

The Bear	
Element of Farce	Effect

Once you have completed your graphic organizer, use the collected information to establish a controlling idea and general structure for your essay. What will your overall point be? In what order will you present your information?

Draft Make a list of the ways in which both authors use farce. Then, consider what effect farce has on each play. Does it help to establish characters? Develop the theme? Create or propel the major conflict? In what ways do these authors use farce for similar purposes, and it what ways do their uses of farce differ? Consider these questions as you develop your draft.

Revise Exchange papers with a classmate and evaluate each others' essays. Are any claims or viewpoints well-supported with logical assertions? Does the writer make detailed references to the text? Provide comments for your classmate and revise your own paper according to the comments you received.

Edit and Proofread Edit your writing so that it expresses your thoughts effectively and is well organized. Carefully proofread for grammar, punctuation, and spelling errors.

UNDERSTAND THE TASK

- **Farce** is a type of comedy with stereotyped characters in ridiculous situations.

Grammar Tip

Apostrophes
Look at these two sentences. Which sentence seems more informal?

Let us go to the theater tonight to see A Midsummer Night's Dream.

Let's go to the theater tonight to see A Midsummer Night's Dream.

The apostrophe in the second sentence is used to replace the letters that are omitted when two words, in this case *let* and *us*, are combined to form a **conjunction**. Conjunctions often make a statement more informal, so in this case, the use of an apostrophe helps an author create an informal mood.

Authors, poets and playwrights also use apostrophes to help create a specific rhythm in a given line or stanza. In these situations, the use of an apostrophe allows the writer to omit a syllable from a line of text.

Jane Eyre

Charlotte Brontë

Jane Eyre
Charlotte Brontë

❝*The writer has us by the hand, forces us along her road, makes us see what she sees, never leaves us for a moment or allows us to forget her. At the end we are steeped through and through with the genius, the vehemence, the indignation of Charlotte Brontë.***❞**

—*Virginia Woolf, British novelist*

How did Charlotte Brontë come to write *Jane Eyre*? According to her friend and biographer Elizabeth Gaskell, Brontë was having a debate with her sisters about the important qualities of a female protagonist. Acknowledging the tendency of authors to make their heroines beautiful, Brontë asserted she would create "a heroine as plain and small as myself, who shall be as interesting as any of yours."

Plain Jane She succeeded, creating Jane Eyre, a complex character who says of herself:

I sometimes regretted that I was not handsomer; I sometimes wished to have rosy cheeks, a straight nose, and small cherry mouth; I desired to be tall, stately and finely developed in figure; I felt it a misfortune that I was so little, so pale, and had features so irregular and so marked.

Brontë's unconventional heroine appealed to her readers. As one critic said in 1887, "Jane Eyre neither languishes in drawing-rooms nor sits dangling her ankles upon gates, but is always interesting, eloquent, vehement."

Jane Eyre is a young governess, a middle-class woman hired to teach the children of well-to-do families. When we first meet Jane, she is ten years old, without money, family, or friends. The novel charts her progress toward maturity as she contends with a social world that is hostile and indifferent to her goals and desires.

Unconventional Storytelling Brontë's novel is unconventional in ways other than her choice of heroine. Brontë tells Jane's story in the form of an autobiographical narrative. In so doing, she takes readers into Jane's inner life, a world of intense feeling and vigorous thought. At the time that the novel was published, such exploration of character and motive was new in English literature. While the popular Gothic novels of the time—stories of the supernatural set in exotic places—had explored the emotional side of experience, Brontë revealed the psychological undercurrents of everyday life. So lifelike was her depiction of Jane Eyre's personality that many readers believed Jane was a real person. As Brontë's contemporary G. H. Lewes remarked, "Reality—deep significant reality, is the characteristic of this book."

Charlotte Brontë was strongly influenced by the Romantic poets of the early 1800s, including William Wordsworth and Lord Byron. Their works stressed the importance of imagination, subjective emotion, and individual freedom. Brontë embraced these ideas, but she also believed that literature should represent life. She showed concern about the social and economic problems of her day, about the poverty of the working classes and the secondary status of women. Later in life, she wrote *Shirley*, a novel about an industrial conflict that took place in Yorkshire. *Jane Eyre* expresses Brontë's social conscience as well as her interest in the imaginative experience of the individual.

Many early readers of *Jane Eyre* also read Elizabeth Gaskell's biography of Brontë, which came out just two years after Brontë's death. Details in the biography fueled speculation about just how closely the novel mirrors Brontë's own life. While there is not an exact correspondence, the novel does incorporate incidents and characters from Brontë's life. Today the parallels between Charlotte and Jane are still part of the appeal of *Jane Eyre*, which remains one of the most popular of all English novels.

Prosperity and Poverty The novel takes place in England around the 1840s, during the Victorian era. This period takes its name from Queen Victoria, who reigned from 1837 to 1901. The period was generally a time of peace and prosperity, and by the 1840s, England had emerged as the leading industrial society of the world and the hub of a vast colonial empire. The rising middle class was amassing unprecedented wealth, but for the working population the 1840s came to be known as the "Hungry Forties," a time of poverty and economic upheaval. These class distinctions as well as the deprivations of the socially disadvantaged are evident in the plot, settings, and characters of *Jane Eyre*.

The Role of a Governess

The occupation of governess had a special appeal for middle-class women during the Victorian era. At this time, a woman who was not financially supported by a husband or other male relative had few ways to earn a living. While many women in the 1800s worked in mills and factories, the unmarried daughters of merchants, doctors, lawyers, and clergymen sought more "suitable" employment that could offer a moderately respectable lifestyle. A governess lived with the upper-middle-class or upper-class family who hired her to teach their children. In addition to securing comfortable lodgings, she earned a modest salary.

Being a governess, however, had considerable drawbacks. Although a governess maintained a ladylike appearance and was often better educated than her employers, she was not treated as an equal. At the same time, her social status was above that of the servants, who often ridiculed the governess's claims to gentility. Working long hours and being expected to remain invisible during social gatherings, governesses had little social contact with adults, male or female. They had difficulty receiving visits in their employers' homes and kept in touch with friends mainly through correspondence. Thus the life of a governess was extremely lonely. As Brontë herself commented, "A private governess has no existence, is not considered as a living and rational being except as connected with the wearisome duties she has to fulfil."

The financial situation of a governess was also precarious. The wages of first-time governesses were not much higher than those of a housekeeper or lady's maid. While their wages rose over time, governesses, unlike servants, were expected to purchase their own clothes and pay for their own travel. Thus, they were often left with only pocket money and had little extra to save.

In addition, the working life of a governess was generally short. Families favored governesses in their mid- to late-twenties. This fact, coupled with the oversupply of women seeking posts, made it harder for governesses to find work after age thirty, and many faced retirement by the age of forty. To stave off an impoverished old age, a disproportionate number of governesses ended up living in mental asylums, the cheapest lodgings they could find, or old-age homes designed specifically for these working women.

Charlotte Brontë *(1816–1855)*

"Unless I have something of my own to say, and a way of my own to say it in, I have no business to publish. . . . Unless I can have the courage to use the language of Truth in preference to the jargon of Conventionality, I ought to be silent."

—*Charlotte Brontë*

Charlotte Brontë, born in 1816, grew up in the small mill town of Haworth on the edge of the rugged moors of West Yorkshire, in northeastern England. The setting was isolated and made lonelier by the fact that Charlotte's mother had died when Charlotte was five. Charlotte, her four sisters—Maria, Elizabeth, Emily, and Anne—and their brother, Branwell, turned to each other for companionship.

Charlotte Brontë's father was a Cambridge-educated clergyman. Because the family was not well off, the Brontë girls were sent to a boarding school where they could prepare for their future employment as governesses. At the school, discipline was harsh, the food inadequate, and living conditions unhealthful. Students often became ill. Maria and Elizabeth Brontë both contracted consumption (today called tuberculosis) at the school and died at home in 1825. After this tragedy, Mr. Brontë himself educated the children at Haworth.

A Family of Storytellers Throughout their childhood and into adulthood, the close-knit Brontë children entertained themselves by creating fanciful stories. Inspired by a set of twelve wooden soldiers their father brought home, they invented imaginary worlds that were a blend of myth, history, current events, and society-page stories from newspapers and magazines. Gradually Charlotte came to focus on romantic passion and themes of temptation and betrayal in these melodramatic tales. This story-writing provided an essential outlet for Charlotte's creativity, an outlet she would painfully miss once she began her "wretched bondage" as a governess.

After unsuccessful attempts at living away from Haworth as students or teachers, Charlotte, Emily, and Anne decided to launch a school for girls in their hometown. To help them prepare for this venture, their aunt paid for them to go to a school in Belgium to study foreign languages. There, Charlotte fell deeply in love with her French teacher, a man with whom she had no hope of a future. Heartsick, she returned home.

Literary Ambitions When the sisters' school failed to attract pupils, all three turned in earnest to their long-cherished literary ambitions. Under male pseudonyms they published a joint collection of poems. Soon afterward, each sister completed a first novel. Emily's *Wuthering Heights* was published, as was Anne's novel. But Charlotte's *The Professor*, a story loosely based on her experiences in Belgium, was rejected. Charlotte's second novel was an immediate success. *Jane Eyre*, the compelling story of a self-reliant young governess, was published in 1847. Alternately referred to by critics as "a book after our own heart" and an "anti-Christian composition," *Jane Eyre* signified the triumph of Charlotte's desire to bring forth a creation entirely her own.

Brontë's enjoyment of her fame was short-lived. Her brother, Branwell, an unsuccessful artist who had become an alcoholic, died in 1848. Then, within a year, both of her sisters died of consumption. Charlotte continued to live at Haworth in order to care for her elderly father. She also continued to write. Finally, a year before her death, she married a family friend. She confided to her close friend Ellen Nussey, "What I taste of happiness is of the soberest order."

Connect to the Literature

Most people experience being left out or feeling like an outsider at some point in their lives. In your opinion, why is this experience so painful?

Discuss with a Partner

With a partner, think of some situations in which a person might feel ignored or rejected by a group of people. What kinds of feelings do people have in these situations? How can the experience of feeling like an outcast shape a person's personality? Explain.

Build Background

Talk About the Weather

The novel opens with a modest statement about the weather: "There was no possibility of taking a walk that day." It is winter; the weather is cold, dark, and rainy. Jane, taking refuge from the unfriendly Reed family, nestles on a window seat close to the glass, hidden by a heavy red curtain. There she reads a favorite book in search of comfort.

In this emblematic description of the setting, Brontë quickly conveys one of the main themes of the novel: Self-respect is vital to happiness, especially when a person is emotionally isolated. The bleak winter weather reflects not only Jane's inhospitable surroundings but also her lonely state of mind. Jane lives without the warmth of close family or friends. In this scene, she turns from people to nature, from society to her own imagination. As you read the novel, notice how Brontë continues to use the weather to represent Jane's inner self and, in addition, to establish mood and underscore the action of the story.

NOVEL NOTEBOOK

Keep a special notebook to record entries about the novels that you read this year.

SUMMARIZE

Summarize in one sentence the most important idea(s) in Build Background.

_____
_____
_____
_____
_____
_____
_____
_____
_____
_____
_____
_____
_____
_____
_____
_____
_____
_____
_____
_____
_____
_____
_____
_____
_____
_____
_____
_____
_____
_____

Set Purposes for Reading

▶ **BIG Idea** Courage and Cleverness

Think about what it means to be courageous. For people to be courageous, do they have to encounter a difficult situation, or can courage emerge even in seemingly mundane daily situations? When in your life have you demonstrated courage?

In *Jane Eyre*, Charlotte Brontë creates a character who is faced with many difficult situations. As your read, make a list of the ways in which Jane demonstrates both courage and cleverness.

Literary Element Characterization

Characterization refers to the methods a writer uses to reveal the personality of a character. In **direct characterization,** the writer makes explicit statements about a character. In **indirect characterization,** the writer reveals a character through that individual's words, thoughts, and actions and through what other characters think and say about that character.

In *Jane Eyre*, the title character is reflecting back upon events that occurred in the past. As a result, readers need to remember that the narrator's descriptions of others are memories, some of which occurred when she was only a young child. As you read, ask yourself how her situation at a given time might affect the way she remembers a particular person and how those perceptions are utilized in the author's characterization. Use the graphic organizer on the next page to help you organize information about the characters.

Reading Strategy Compare and Contrast Characters

When you **compare and contrast characters,** you look for similarities and differences in the way characters think, look, and act. You can also note similarities and differences in the way characters are presented by the author. For example, you can compare and contrast main characters, who are described in great detail, with minor characters, who are described in only a few words.

Comparing characters can give you greater insight into the major characters, the primary conflicts, and the theme of a text. You may also gain greater insights into the many tools that authors use in characterization.

As you read, consider how characters interact with others in the book and how others view them. Think also about what their behaviors tell you about them. This allows you to compare characters more fully. You may find it helpful to use a graphic organizer like the one at the right.

Vocabulary

antipathy [an tip´ə thē]
n. strong dislike
The little boy's antipathy for all vegetables constantly frustrated his parents.

ardently [ärd´ənt lē]
adv. with passion or energy
She practiced her violin ardently because she was determined to become a world-class musician.

ascertain [as´ər tān´]
v. to find out for sure
The detective knew that he had to ascertain all of the facts before trying to solve the crime.

chastisement [chas tīz´mənt]
n. punishment
Seth knew he would have to endure chastisement from his parents after he broke their prized vase.

solace [sol´is]
n. relief from grief or anxiety
When Elena gets sad or angry, she often seeks solace in her friends.

	Narrator's Comments	Unique Behaviors	Others' Comments
Character 1			
Character 2			

In Chapters 1–10, readers learn a great deal about Jane through her interactions with other characters. As you read, identify each character who is introduced and describe him or her in a short phrase. Then note the feelings Jane has toward each of these characters.

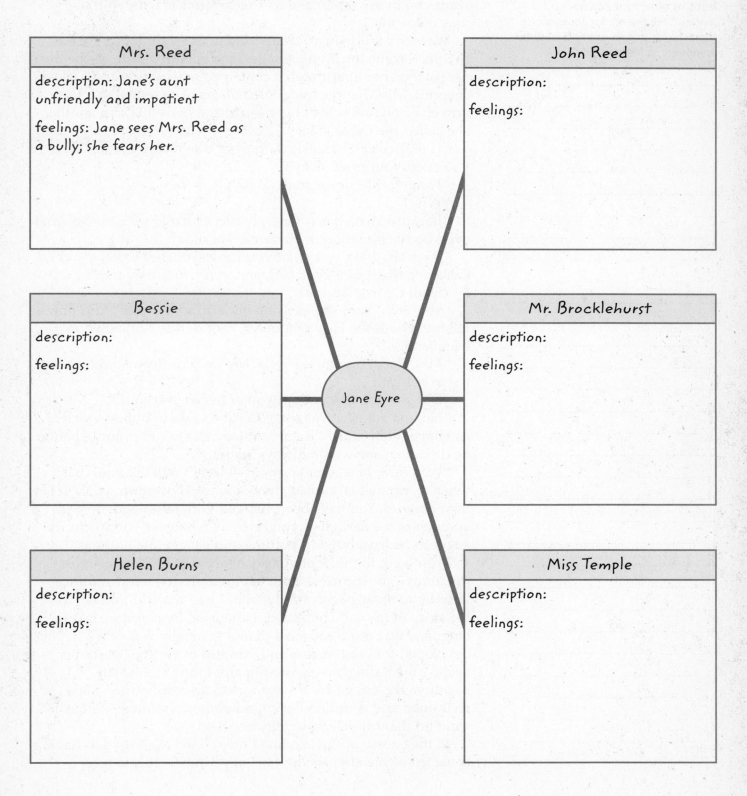

Mrs. Reed

description: Jane's aunt
unfriendly and impatient

feelings: Jane sees Mrs. Reed as a bully; she fears her.

John Reed

description:

feelings:

Bessie

description:

feelings:

Mr. Brocklehurst

description:

feelings:

Jane Eyre

Helen Burns

description:

feelings:

Miss Temple

description:

feelings:

Literary Element

Characterization What does Jane's fear that others will see her as "wicked" tell the reader about Jane's character? Is this an example of direct or indirect characterization?

_____
_____
_____
_____
_____
_____
_____
_____
_____
_____
_____
_____
_____
_____
_____
_____
_____
_____
_____
_____
_____
_____
_____
_____
_____
_____
_____
_____
_____
_____
_____
_____

NOVEL EXCERPT: CHAPTER 8

"I came on purpose to find you, Jane Eyre," said she; "I want you in my room; and as Helen Burns is with you, she may come too."

We went; following the superintendent's guidance, we had to thread some intricate passages, and mount a staircase before we reached her apartment; it contained a good fire, and looked cheerful. Miss Temple told Helen Burns to be seated in a low arm-chair on one side of the hearth, and herself taking another, she called me to her side.

"Is it all over?" she asked, looking down at my face. "Have you cried your grief away?"

"I am afraid I never shall do that."

"Why?"

"Because I have been wrongly accused; and you, ma'am, and everybody else will now think me wicked."

"We shall think you what you prove yourself to be, my child. Continue to act as a good girl, and you will satisfy me."

"Shall I, Miss Temple?"

"You will," said she, passing her arm round me. "And now tell me who is the lady whom Mr. Brocklehurst called your benefactress?"

"Mrs. Reed, my uncle's wife. My uncle is dead, and he left me to her care."

"Did she not, then, adopt you of her own accord?"

"No, ma'am; she was sorry to have to do it: but my uncle, as I have often heard the servants say, got her to promise before he died, that she would always keep me."

"Well now, Jane, you know, or at least I will tell you, that when a criminal is accused, he is always allowed to speak in his own defence. You have been charged with falsehood; defend yourself to me as well as you can. Say whatever your memory suggests as true; but add nothing and exaggerate nothing."

I resolved, in the depth of my heart, that I would be most moderate—most correct; and, having reflected a few minutes in order to arrange coherently what I had to say, I told her all the story of my sad childhood. Exhausted by emotion, my language was more subdued than it generally was when it developed that sad theme; and mindful of Helen's warnings against the indulgence of resentment, I infused into the narrative far less gall and wormwood than ordinarily. Thus restrained and simplified, it sounded more credible: I felt as I went on that Miss Temple fully believed me.

In the course of the tale I had mentioned Mr. Lloyd as having come to see me after the fit: for I never forgot the, to me, frightful episode of the red-room; in detailing which, my excitement was sure, in some degree, to break bounds; for nothing could soften in my recollection the spasm of agony which clutched my heart when Mrs. Reed spurned my wild supplication for pardon, and locked me a second time in the dark and haunted chamber.

I had finished: Miss Temple regarded me a few minutes in silence; she then said—

"I know something of Mr. Lloyd; I shall write to him; if his reply agrees with your statement, you shall be publicly cleared from every imputation: to me, Jane, you are clear now."

She kissed me, and still keeping me at her side (where I was well contented to stand, for I derived a child's pleasure from the contemplation of her face, her dress, her one or two ornaments, her white forehead, her clustered and shining curls, and beaming dark eyes), she proceeded to address Helen Burns.

"How are you to-night, Helen? Have you coughed much to-day?"

"Not quite so much I think, ma'am."

"And the pain in your chest?"

"It is a little better."

Miss Temple got up, took her hand and examined her pulse; then she returned to her own seat: as she resumed it, I heard her sigh low. She was pensive a few minutes, then rousing herself, she said cheerfully:—

"But you two are my visitors to-night; I must treat you as such." She rang her bell.

"Barbara," she said to the servant who answered it, "I have not yet had tea; bring the tray, and place cups for these two young ladies."

And a tray was soon brought. How pretty, to my eyes, did the china and bright teapot look, placed on the little round table near the fire! How fragrant was the steam of the beverage, and the scent of the toast! of which, however, I, to my dismay (for I was beginning to be hungry), discerned only a very small portion: Miss Temple discerned it too:—

"Barbara," said she, "can you not bring a little more bread and butter? There is not enough for three."

Barbara went out: she returned soon:—

"Madam, Mrs. Harden says she has sent up the usual quantity."

Mrs. Harden, be it observed, was the housekeeper: a woman after Mr. Brocklehurst's own heart, made up of equal parts of whalebone and iron.

Literary Element

Characterization After rereading this excerpt, how does your view of Miss Temple compare with the descriptions of her that Jane offers?

_____
_____
_____
_____
_____
_____
_____
_____
_____
_____
_____
_____
_____
_____
_____
_____
_____
_____
_____
_____
_____
_____
_____
_____
_____

Reading Strategy

Compare and Contrast Characters
Why might Jane envision Mr. Reed as a kinder, more benevolent figure than his wife?

_____
_____
_____
_____
_____
_____
_____
_____
_____
_____
_____
_____
_____
_____
_____
_____
_____
_____
_____
_____
_____
_____
_____
_____
_____
_____
_____
_____

NOVEL EXCERPT: CHAPTER 2

Daylight began to forsake the red-room; it was past four o'clock, and the beclouded afternoon was tending to drear twilight. I heard the rain still beating continuously on the staircase window, and the wind howling in the grove behind the hall; I grew by degrees cold as a stone, and then my courage sank. My habitual mood of humiliation, self-doubt, forlorn depression, fell damp on the embers of my decaying ire. All said I was wicked, and perhaps I might be so; what thought had I been but just conceiving of starving myself to death? That certainly was a crime: and was I fit to die? Or was the vault under the chancel of Gateshead Church an inviting bourne? In such vault I had been told did Mr. Reed lie buried; and led by this thought to recall his idea, I dwelt on it with gathering dread. I could not remember him; but I knew that he was my own uncle—my mother's brother—that he had taken me when a parentless infant to his house; and that in his last moments he had required a promise of Mrs. Reed that she would rear and maintain me as one of her own children. Mrs. Reed probably considered she had kept this promise; and so she had, I dare say, as well as her nature would permit her; but how could she really like an interloper not of her race, and unconnected with her, after her husband's death, by any tie? It must have been most irksome to find herself bound by a hard-wrung pledge to stand in the stead of a parent to a strange child she could not love, and to see an uncongenial alien permanently intruded on her own family group.

A singular notion dawned upon me. I doubted not—never doubted—that if Mr. Reed had been alive he would have treated me kindly; and now, as I sat looking at the white bed and overshadowed walls—occasionally also turning a fascinated eye towards the dimly gleaming mirror—I began to recall what I had heard of dead men, troubled in their graves by the violation of their last wishes, revisiting the earth to punish the perjured and avenge the oppressed; and I thought Mr. Reed's spirit, harassed by the wrongs of his sister's child, might quit its abode—whether in the church vault or in the unknown world of the departed—and rise before me in this chamber. I wiped my tears and hushed my sobs, fearful lest any sign of violent grief might waken a preternatural voice to comfort me, or elicit from the gloom some haloed face, bending over me with strange pity. This idea, consolatory in theory, I felt would be terrible if realised: with all my might I endeavoured to stifle it— I endeavoured to be firm. Shaking my hair from my eyes, I lifted my head and tried to look boldly round the dark room: at this moment a light gleamed on the wall. Was it, I asked myself, a ray from the moon penetrating some aperture in the blind?

No; moonlight was still, and this stirred; while I gazed, it glided up to the ceiling and quivered over my head. I can now conjecture readily that this streak of light was, in all likelihood, a gleam from a lantern, carried by some one across the lawn: but then, prepared as my mind was for horror, shaken as my nerves were by agitation, I thought the swift-darting beam was a herald of some coming vision from another world. My heart beat thick, my head grew hot; a sound filled my ears, which I deemed the rushing of wings; something seemed near me; I was oppressed, suffocated: endurance broke down; I rushed to the door and shook the lock in desperate effort. Steps came running along the outer passage; the key turned, Bessie and Abbot entered.

"Miss Eyre, are you ill?" said Bessie.

"What a dreadful noise! it went quite through me!" exclaimed Abbot.

"Take me out! Let me go into the nursery!" was my cry.

"What for! Are you hurt! Have you seen something?" again demanded Bessie.

"Oh! I saw a light, and I thought a ghost would come." I had now got hold of Bessie's hand, and she did not snatch it from me.

"She has screamed out on purpose," declared Abbot, in some disgust. "And what a scream! If she had been in great pain one would have excused it, but she only wanted to bring us all here. I know her naughty tricks."

"What is all this?" demanded another voice peremptorily; and Mrs. Reed came along the corridor, her cap flying wide, her gown rustling stormily. "Abbot and Bessie, I believe I gave orders that Jane Eyre should be left in the red-room till I came to her myself."

"Miss Jane screamed so loud, ma'am," pleaded Bessie.

"Let her go," was the only answer. "Loose Bessie's hand, child: you cannot succeed in getting out by these means, be assured. I abhor artifice, particularly in children; it is my duty to show you that tricks will not answer: you will now stay here an hour longer, and it is only on condition of perfect submission and stillness that I shall liberate you then."

"Oh aunt, have pity! Forgive me! I cannot endure it—let me be punished some other way! I shall be killed if—"

"Silence! This violence is all most repulsive:" and so, no doubt, she felt it. I was a precocious actress in her eyes: she sincerely looked on me as a compound of virulent passions, mean spirit, and dangerous duplicity.

Bessie and Abbot having retreated, Mrs. Reed, impatient of my now frantic anguish and wild sobs, abruptly thrust me back and locked me in, without farther parley. I heard her sweeping away; and soon after she was gone, I suppose I had a species of fit: unconsciousness closed the scene.

Reading Strategy

Compare and Contrast Characters
In what way does this dialogue establish a contrast between Bessie and Mrs. Reed?

_____

_____

_____

_____

_____

_____

_____

_____

_____

_____

_____

_____

_____

_____

_____

_____

_____

_____

_____

_____

_____

_____

_____

_____

_____

_____

_____

_____

MARK IT UP

Are you allowed to write in your novel? If so, then mark up the pages as you read, or reread, to help with your note-taking. Develop a shorthand system, including symbols, that works for you. Here are some ideas:

Underline = important idea

Bracket = text to quote

Asterisk = just what you were looking for

Checkmark = might be useful

Circle = unfamiliar word or phrase to look up

▶ **BIG Idea**

Courage and Cleverness How does Jane demonstrate courage, even as a child?

Mark up the excerpt, looking for evidence of how it expresses the Big Idea.

NOVEL EXCERPT: CHAPTER 4

Speak I must: I had been trodden on severely, and *must* turn: but how? What strength had I to dart retaliation at my antagonist? I gathered my energies and launched them in this blunt sentence:—

"I am not deceitful: if I were, I should say I loved *you*, but I declare I do not love you: I dislike you the worst of anybody in the world except John Reed; and this book about the liar, you may give to your girl, Georgiana, for it is she who tells lies, and not I."

Mrs. Reed's hands still lay on her work inactive: her eye of ice continued to dwell freezingly on mine.

"What more have you to say?" she asked, rather in the tone in which a person might address an opponent of adult age than such as is ordinarily used to a child.

That eye of hers, that voice stirred every antipathy I had. Shaking from head to foot, thrilled with ungovernable excitement, I continued:—

"I am glad you are no relation of mine: I will never call you aunt again as long as I live. I will never come to see you when I am grown up; and if any one asks me how I liked you, and how you treated me, I will say the very thought of you makes me sick, and that you treated me with miserable cruelty."

"How dare you affirm that, Jane Eyre?"

"How dare I, Mrs. Reed? How dare I? Because it is the *truth*. You think I have no feelings, and that I can do without one bit of love or kindness; but I cannot live so: and you have no pity. I shall remember how you thrust me back—roughly and violently thrust me back—into the red-room, and locked me up there, to my dying day; though I was in agony; though I cried out, while suffocating with distress, 'Have mercy! Have mercy, aunt Reed!' And that punishment you made me suffer because your wicked boy struck me—knocked me down for nothing. I will tell anybody who asks me questions this exact tale. People think you a good woman, but you are bad; hard-hearted. You are deceitful!"

Ere I had finished this reply, my soul began to expand, to exult, with the strangest sense of freedom, of triumph, I ever felt. It seemed as if an invisible bond had burst, and that I had struggled out into unhoped-for liberty.

Use the Cornell Note-Taking system to take notes on the excerpt at the left. Record your notes, Reduce them, and then Recap (summarize) them.

Record

_____
_____
_____
_____
_____
_____
_____
_____
_____
_____
_____
_____
_____
_____
_____
_____
_____
_____
_____
_____
_____
_____
_____
_____

Recap

_____
_____
_____
_____
_____
_____

Reduce

Try the following approach as you reduce your notes.

MY VIEW
Write down your thoughts on the excerpt.

_____
_____
_____
_____
_____
_____
_____
_____
_____
_____
_____
_____
_____
_____
_____
_____
_____
_____
_____
_____
_____
_____
_____
_____
_____
_____
_____
_____

Respond and Think Critically

1. Describe the conditions at Lowood school. What is unfair about Mr. Brocklehurst's treatment of Jane? What observation does Helen make about Jane? [Recall]

_____

_____

_____

_____

2. Why do conditions at Lowood improve? What does Jane gain from her eight years there? What is her ambition? [Summarize]

_____

_____

_____

_____

3. How are Jane and Helen Burns different in their attitude toward injustice? How would you explain this difference? [Compare]

_____

_____

_____

_____

4. Mr. Brocklehurst, the head of Lowood school, believes that hardship builds strong character. What is your opinion of this point of view? [Evaluate]

_____

_____

_____

_____

5. Courage and Cleverness What personal traits enable Jane not only to survive physically but also thrive academically at Lowood School? [Analyze]

_____

_____

_____

_____

APPLY BACKGROUND
Reread Meet the Author on page 234. How did that information help you understand or appreciate what you read in the novel?

_____

_____

_____

_____

_____

_____

_____

_____

_____

_____

_____

_____

_____

_____

_____

_____

_____

_____

_____

_____

_____

_____

_____

_____

_____

_____

_____

Literary Element | Characterization

To what extent do others' perceptions of Jane affect her own self-perception? [Analyze]

_____

_____

_____

_____

_____

_____

_____

_____

_____

_____

_____

_____

_____

Vocabulary Practice

An **antonym** is a word that has the opposite or nearly the opposite meaning of another word. Match each boldfaced vocabulary word below with its antonym. Use a thesaurus or dictionary to check your answers.

1. **antipathy**
2. **ardently**
3. **ascertain**
4. **chastisement**
5. **solace**

a. praise
b. implore
c. lazily
d. admit
e. ignore
f. chaos
g. sympathy

Academic Vocabulary

At Lowood school, Jane demonstrates that she has a great **capacity** for learning; she excels in all of her subjects. Using context clues, try to figure out the meaning of the word _capacity_ in the sentence above. Write your guess below. Then check it in a dictionary.

_____

_____

_____

_____

_____

_____

_____

_____

Reading Strategy | Compare and Contrast Characters

Why was Jane drawn to Helen Burns? What was it about Helen that made her so different from anyone Jane had ever met before? [Conclude]

_____

_____

_____

_____

_____

_____

_____

_____

_____

_____

_____

_____

Writing

Write a Character Analysis In this portion of the novel, Brontë lets the reader into Jane's mind as Jane analyzes her relations with others and describes her own personality. The author also describes Jane from the outside, through the words of other characters, such as Helen Burns, Mrs. Reed, and Mr. Brocklehurst.

Write a character analysis of Jane. To prepare review the first ten chapters, paying special attention to Chapters 2, 4, 7, and 8, to answer these questions: What challenges or trials does Jane face at Gateshead and at Lowood? What do we learn about Jane from her response to these trials? Do you see any sign of personal growth or change in Jane in these settings? What generalizations might you make about Jane from age ten to age eighteen?

Jot down some notes here first.

_____
_____
_____
_____
_____
_____
_____
_____
_____
_____
_____
_____
_____
_____
_____
_____
_____
_____
_____

Connect to Content Areas

Social Studies

Assignment In Charlotte Brontë's day, many orphans were sent to institutions like Lowood. Conduct research to find out what options exist today for children without parents. Then prepare two or three case studies, using made-up names, that present typical situations of orphans today.

Investigate First, make a list of possible sources of information, how to gain access to them, and their likely reliability. Consult library and Internet resources as well as the children's services department in your county government. Use a chart like the one below.

Source	Access	Reliability
Dr. Jenkins	ph: 555-1212	probably reliable (local child psychologist)
U.S. Department of Health and Human Services	www.hhs.gov	reliable (government site)

Take notes on what you learn from each source. If there is contradictory information, use what you found in the most reliable source. If you are unfamiliar with any of the terms you come across, investigate further to clarify the meanings of those terms.

Create Each case study that you create should reflect one option for an orphan today. Explain, in your case study, why this particular orphan might receive certain resources and describe in detail what these resources are. At the end of each case study, include a bibliography that identifies where you found the information that helped you create that profile.

Report Create your case study on a word processor so that it looks professional, and proofread for grammar and spelling errors.

Connect to the Literature

Do you believe that opposites attract in romantic relationships? Why or why not? What attributes besides physical characteristics might cause two people to be attracted to each other?

Create a Chart

Create a chart of personality traits that could be attraction factors. List at least six factors. Then rate each factor on a scale of 1 (least important) to 10 (most important).

Build Background

Writing from Experience

Many of the settings and characters in *Jane Eyre* are drawn from Charlotte Brontë's own life. The Clergy Daughters' School that Charlotte attended at the age of eight was the real-life model for the fictional Lowood Institution. Like Mr. Brocklehurst, its director, Carus Wilson, was a stern, aristocratic clergyman who believed that children were inherently wicked and should be kept in a state of humility. Another character at Lowood, the patient and wise Helen Burns, is believed to be a tribute to Charlotte's older sister Maria. The setting of Thornfield also has a counterpart in Charlotte Brontë's life. Some of its features are based on the stately family home of Charlotte's close friend Ellen Nussey, whom she met in her teens at Roe Head school.

NOVEL NOTEBOOK

Keep a special notebook to record entries about the novels that you read this year.

WRITE THE CAPTION

Write a caption for the image below, from a film version of *Jane Eyre,* using information in Build Background.

_____
_____
_____
_____
_____
_____
_____
_____
_____
_____
_____
_____
_____
_____
_____
_____
_____
_____
_____
_____
_____
_____
_____
_____
_____
_____
_____

Set Purposes for Reading

▶ **BIG Idea Journeys**

Think about the last journey that you embarked upon. What did you need to do in order to be comfortable in a new setting or an unfamiliar culture? How did you interact with the strangers that you met along the way, and in what ways did they help you on your journey?

As a young woman, Jane has already embarked on a number of journeys to unfamiliar places, and she has undertaken these journeys alone. As you read, make note of how Jane tries to familiarize herself with each new place and how she presents herself to the new people she encounters.

Literary Element **Character Archetype**

An **archetype** is an idea, a character, a story, or an image that is common to human experience across cultures and throughout the world. In their purest form, archeteypes occur in oral tradition, but they also appear in written works of literature.

Character archetypes refer to familiar individuals such as the wise leader, the rebel, the damsel in distress, the hero, the temptress, and the traitor. The Byronic hero, as Rochester could be defined, is often rebellious, alienated, gloomy, bold, dangerous, ruggedly handsome, adventurous, and moody, and he often has a guilty or shady past and a magnetic personality. The Byronic hero is named for the poet George Gordon, Lord Byron, embodied these attributes in himself and in the heroes of his poems.

As you read, consider the similarities characters in the book have to characters you commonly come across in literature, in movies and TV shows, and in real life. Use the graphic organizer on the next page to help you.

Reading Strategy **Respond to Events**

When you **respond to events,** you tell what you like, dislike, or find interesting or surprising about the events in a selection.

Reacting in a personal way to what you read helps you enjoy and remember the selection, and it also helps you connect more deeply with the characters and the conflicts they encounter.

As you read, be aware of your reactions to events that occur. Do they make you angry? Frustrated? Happy? You may find it helpful to use a graphic organizer like the one to the right.

Vocabulary

imperious [im pēr´ ē əs]
adj. commanding; dominant
The imperious president of the company refused to listen to his employees.

neophyte [nē´ ə fīt´]
n. beginner; inexperienced person
She considers herself a soccer neophyte; she just started playing a few months ago.

nonchalantly [non shə länt´ lē]
adv. coolly; without concern
The dog walked nonchalantly down the street; it didn't seem to mind the torrential rain.

quell [kwel]
v. to put to rest; to suppress
In order to quell the forest fire, the mayor called in fire departments from all the surrounding towns.

tenacious [ti nā´ shəs]
adj. persistent
The tenacious scientist spent years trying to find a cure for cancer.

Events	My Response

In these chapters, Jane gets to know her new employer, Edward Rochester of Thornfield Hall. As you read, make notes in the chart below about Rochester's appearance, manner or mood, past, and goals. Think about whether Rochester fits the archetype of a Byronic hero, as described on page 248.

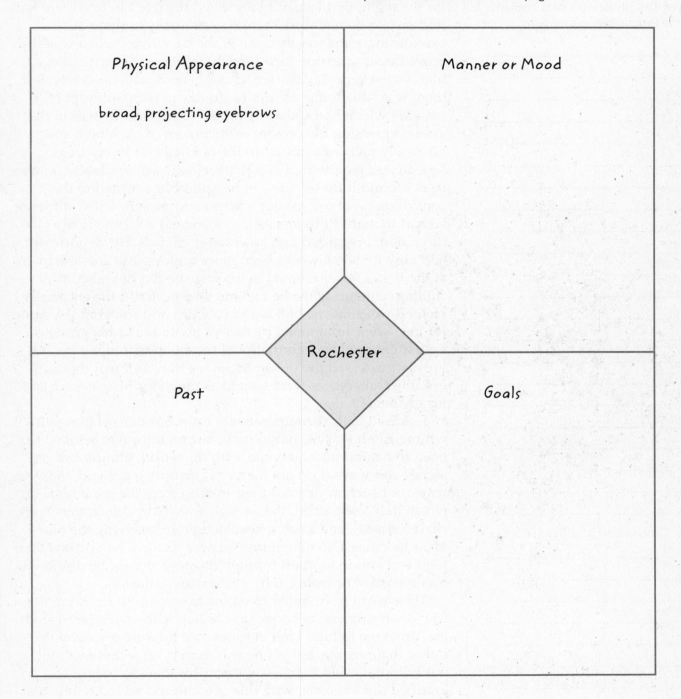

Physical Appearance

broad, projecting eyebrows

Manner or Mood

Rochester

Past

Goals

Literary Element

Character Archetype Based on this excerpt, to what extent does Rochester fit the Byronic hero archetype?

_____
_____
_____
_____
_____
_____
_____
_____
_____
_____
_____
_____
_____
_____
_____
_____
_____
_____
_____
_____
_____
_____
_____
_____
_____
_____
_____
_____
_____

NOVEL EXCERPT: CHAPTER 15

It was not till after I had withdrawn to my own chamber for the night, that I steadily reviewed the tale Mr. Rochester had told me. As he had said, there was probably nothing at all extraordinary in the substance of the narrative itself: a wealthy Englishman's passion for a French dancer, and her treachery to him, were every-day matters enough, no doubt, in society; but there was something decidedly strange in the paroxysm of emotion which had suddenly seized him, when he was in the act of expressing the present contentment of his mood, and his newly revived pleasure in the old hall and its environs. I meditated wonderingly on this incident: but gradually quitting it, as I found it for the present inexplicable, I turned to the consideration of my master's manner to myself. The confidence he had thought fit to repose in me seemed a tribute to my discretion: I regarded and accepted it as such. His deportment had now for some weeks been more uniform towards me than at the first. I never seemed in his way; he did not take fits of chilling hauteur: when he met me unexpectedly, the encounter seemed welcome; he had always a word and sometimes a smile for me: when summoned by formal invitation to his presence, I was honoured by a cordiality of reception that made me feel I really possessed the power to amuse him, and that these evening conferences were sought as much for his pleasure as for my benefit.

I, indeed, talked comparatively little; but I heard him talk with relish. It was his nature to be communicative; he liked to open to a mind unacquainted with the world, glimpses of its scenes and ways (I do not mean its corrupt scenes and wicked ways, but such as derived their interest from the great scale on which they were acted, the strange novelty by which they were characterised); and I had a keen delight in receiving the new ideas he offered, in imagining the new pictures he portrayed, or followed him in thought through the new regions he disclosed, never startled or troubled by one noxious allusion.

The ease of his manner freed me from painful restraint; the friendly frankness, as correct as cordial, with which he treated me, drew me to him. I felt at times as if he were my relation, rather than my master: yet he was imperious sometimes still; but I did not mind that; I saw it was his way. So happy, so gratified did I become with this new interest added to life, that I ceased to pine after kindred: my thin crescent-destiny seemed to enlarge; the blanks of existence were filled up; my bodily health improved; I gathered flesh and strength.

And was Mr. Rochester now ugly in my eyes? No, reader: gratitude, and many associations, all pleasurable and genial, made his face the object I best liked to see; his presence in a room was more cheering than the brightest fire. Yet I had not forgotten his faults: indeed, I could not, for he brought them frequently before me. He was proud, sardonic, harsh to inferiority of every description: in my secret soul I knew that his great kindness to me was balanced by unjust severity to many others. He was moody, too; unaccountably so: I more than once, when sent for to read to him, found him sitting in his library alone, with his head bent on his folded arms; and, when he looked up, a morose, almost a malignant scowl, blackened his features. But I believed that his moodiness, his harshness, and his former faults of morality (I say *former*, for now he seemed corrected of them) had their source in some cruel cross of fate. I believed he was naturally a man of better tendencies, higher principles, and purer tastes than such as circumstances had developed, education instilled, or destiny encouraged. I thought there were excellent materials in him; though for the present they hung together somewhat spoiled and tangled. I cannot deny that I grieved for his grief, whatever that was, and would have given much to assuage it.

Though I had now extinguished my candle and was laid down in bed, I could not sleep, for thinking of his look when he paused in the avenue, and told how his destiny had risen up before him, and dared him to be happy at Thornfield.

"Why not?" I asked myself. "What alienates him from the house? Will he leave it again soon? Mrs. Fairfax said he seldom stayed here longer than a fortnight at a time and he has now been resident eight weeks. If he does go the change will be doleful. Suppose he should be absent, spring, summer, and autumn: how joyless sunshine and fine days will seem!"

I hardly know whether I had slept or not after this musing; at any rate, I started wide awake on hearing a vague murmur, peculiar and lugubrious, which sounded, I thought, just above me. I wished I had kept my candle burning: the night was drearily dark: my spirits were depressed. I rose and sat up in bed, listening. The sound was hushed.

I tried again to sleep; but my heart beat anxiously: my inward tranquillity was broken. The clock, far down in the hall, struck two. Just then it seemed my chamber-door was touched; as if fingers had swept the panels in groping a way along the dark gallery outside. I said, "Who is there?" Nothing answered. I was chilled with fear.

Literary Element

Character Archetype The archetypal Byronic hero often possesses a degree of mystery or intrigue. What puzzles Jane about Rochester?

_____
_____
_____
_____
_____
_____
_____
_____
_____
_____
_____
_____
_____
_____
_____
_____
_____
_____
_____
_____
_____
_____
_____
_____
_____
_____
_____
_____
_____
_____

Reading Strategy

Respond to Events What interests or surprises you about this scene?

_____

_____

_____

_____

_____

_____

_____

_____

_____

_____

_____

_____

_____

_____

_____

_____

_____

_____

_____

_____

_____

_____

_____

_____

_____

_____

_____

_____

_____

_____

_____

NOVEL EXCERPT: CHAPTER 20

I put my fingers into his. "Warm and steady," was his remark: he turned the key and opened the door.

I saw a room I remembered to have seen before, the day Mrs. Fairfax showed me over the house: it was hung with tapestry; but the tapestry was now looped up in one part, and there was a door apparent, which had then been concealed. This door was open; a light shone out of the room within: I heard thence a snarling, snatching sound, almost like a dog quarrelling. Mr. Rochester, putting down his candle, said to me, "Wait a minute," and he went forward to the inner apartment. A shout of laughter greeted his entrance; noisy at first, and terminating in Grace Poole's own goblin ha! ha! _She_ then was there. He made some sort of arrangement, without speaking: though I heard a low voice address him: he came out and closed the door behind him.

"Here, Jane!" he said; and I walked round to the other side of a large bed, which with its drawn curtains concealed a considerable portion of the chamber. An easy-chair was near the bed-head: a man sat in it, dressed with the exception of his coat; he was still; his head leant back; his eyes were closed. Mr. Rochester held the candle over him; I recognised in his pale and seemingly lifeless face—the stranger, Mason: I saw too that his linen on one side, and one arm, was almost soaked in blood.

"Hold the candle," said Mr. Rochester, and I took it; he fetched a basin of water from the wash-stand: "Hold that," said he. I obeyed. He took the sponge, dipped it in and moistened the corpse-like face: he asked for my smelling-bottle, and applied it to the nostrils. Mr. Mason shortly unclosed his eyes; he groaned. Mr. Rochester opened the shirt of the wounded man, whose arm and shoulder were bandaged: he sponged away blood, trickling fast down.

"Is there immediate danger?" murmured Mr. Mason.

"Pooh! No—a mere scratch. Don't be so overcome, man: bear up! I'll fetch a surgeon for you now, myself: you'll be able to be removed by morning, I hope. Jane," he continued.

"Sir?"

"I shall have to leave you in this room with this gentleman, for an hour, or perhaps two hours; you will sponge the blood as I do when it returns: if he feels faint, you will put the glass of water on that stand to his lips, and your salts to his nose. You will not speak to him on any pretext—and—Richard—it will be at the peril of your life if you speak to her: open your lips— agitate yourself—and I'll not answer for the consequences."

Again the poor man groaned: he looked as if he dared not move: fear, either of death or of something else, appeared almost to paralyse him. Mr. Rochester put the now bloody sponge into my hand, and I proceeded to use it as he had done. He watched me a second, then saying, "Remember!—No conversation," he left the room. I experienced a strange feeling as the key grated in the lock, and the sound of his retreating step ceased to be heard.

Here then I was in the third story, fastened into one of its mystic cells; night around me; a pale and bloody spectacle under my eyes and hands; a murderess hardly separated from me by a single door: yes—that was appalling—the rest I could bear; but I shuddered at the thought of Grace Poole bursting out upon me.

I must keep to my post, however. I must watch this ghastly countenance—these blue, still lips forbidden to unclose—these eyes now shut, now opening, now wandering through the room, now fixing on me, and ever glazed with the dulness of horror. I must dip my hand again and again in the basin of blood and water, and wipe away the trickling gore. I must see the light of the unsnuffed candle wane on my employment; the shadows darken on the wrought antique tapestry round me, and grow black under the hangings of the vast old bed, and quiver strangely over the doors of a great cabinet opposite— whose front, divided into twelve panels, bore, in grim design, the heads of the twelve apostles, each inclosed in its separate panel as in a frame; while above them at the top rose an ebon crucifix and a dying Christ.

According as the shifting obscurity and flickering gleam hovered here or glanced there, it was now the bearded physician, Luke, that bent his brow; now St. John's long hair that waved; and anon the devilish face of Judas, that grew out of the panel, and seemed gathering life and threatening a revelation of the arch-traitor—of Satan himself—in his subordinate's form.

Amidst all this, I had to listen as well as watch: to listen for the movements of the wild beast or the fiend in yonder side den. But since Mr. Rochester's visit it seemed spellbound: all the night I heard but three sounds at three long intervals,—a step creak, a momentary renewal of the snarling, canine noise, and a deep human groan.

Then my own thoughts worried me. What crime was this that lived incarnate in this sequestered mansion, and could neither be expelled nor subdued by the owner? What mystery, that broke out, now in fire and now in blood, at the deadest hours of night? What creature was it, that, masked in an ordinary woman's face and shape, uttered the voice, now of a mocking demon, and anon of a carrion-seeking bird of prey?

Reading Strategy

Respond to Events What was your opinion of Mr. Rochester when he said to Jane, amidst the blood and strange circumstances, "Remember!—No conversation!"?

_____

_____

_____

_____

_____

_____

_____

_____

_____

_____

_____

_____

_____

_____

_____

_____

_____

_____

_____

_____

_____

_____

_____

_____

MARK IT UP

Are you allowed to write in your novel? If so, then mark up the pages as you read, or reread, to help with your note-taking. Develop a shorthand system, including symbols, that works for you. Here are some ideas:

Underline = important idea

Bracket = text to quote

Asterisk = just what you were looking for

Checkmark = might be useful

Circle = unfamiliar word or phrase to look up

▶ **BIG Idea**

Journeys How does Jane react to journeys that take her to new places and new people?

Mark up the excerpt, looking for evidence of how it expresses the Big Idea.

NOVEL EXCERPT: CHAPTER 11

When Mrs. Fairfax had bidden me a kind good-night, and I had fastened my door, gazed leisurely round, and in some measure effaced the eerie impression made by that wide hall, that dark and spacious staircase, and that long, cold gallery, by the livelier aspect of my little room, I remembered that after a day of bodily fatigue and mental anxiety, I was now at last in safe haven. The impulse of gratitude swelled my heart, and I knelt down at the bedside, and offered up thanks where thanks were due; not forgetting, ere I rose, to implore aid on my further path, and the power of meriting the kindness which seemed so frankly offered me before it was earned. My couch had no thorns in it that night; my solitary room no fears. At once weary and content, I slept soon and soundly: when I awoke it was broad day.

The chamber looked such a bright little place to me as the sun shone in between the gay blue chintz window curtains, showing papered walls and a carpeted floor, so unlike the bare planks and stained plaster of Lowood, that my spirits rose at the view. Externals have a great effect on the young: I thought that a fairer era of life was beginning for me, one that was to have its flowers and pleasures, as well as its thorns and toils. My faculties, roused by the change of scene, the new field offered to hope, seemed all astir. I cannot precisely define what they expected, but it was something pleasant: not perhaps that day or that month, but at an indefinite future period.

I rose; I dressed myself with care: obliged to be plain— for I had no article of attire that was not made with extreme simplicity—I was still by nature solicitous to be neat. It was not my habit to be disregardful of appearance, or careless of the impression I made: on the contrary, I ever wished to look as well as I could, and to please as much as my want of beauty would permit. I sometimes regretted that I was not handsomer: I sometimes wished to have rosy cheeks, a straight nose, and small cherry mouth; I desired to be tall, stately, and finely developed in figure; I felt it a misfortune that I was so little, so pale, and had features so irregular and so marked. And why had I these aspirations and these regrets? It would be difficult to say: I could not then distinctly say it to myself; yet I had a reason, and a logical, natural reason too. However, when I had brushed my hair very smooth, and put on my black frock—which, Quakerlike as it was, at least had the merit of fitting to a nicety—and adjusted my clean white tucker, I thought I should do respectably enough to appear before Mrs. Fairfax; and that my new pupil would not at least recoil from me with antipathy. Having opened my chamber window, and seen that I left all things straight and neat on the toilet table, I ventured forth.

CORNELL NOTE-TAKING: BIG Idea

Use the Cornell Note-Taking system to take notes on the excerpt at the left. Record your notes, Reduce them, and then Recap (summarize) them.

Record

_____
_____
_____
_____
_____
_____
_____
_____
_____
_____
_____
_____
_____
_____
_____
_____
_____
_____
_____
_____
_____
_____
_____
_____

Recap

_____
_____
_____
_____
_____

Reduce

Try the following approach as you reduce your notes.

TO THE POINT
Write a few key ideas.

_____
_____
_____
_____
_____
_____
_____
_____
_____
_____
_____
_____
_____
_____
_____
_____
_____
_____
_____
_____

Respond and Think Critically

1. How do Jane and Rochester behave toward each other when they converse? How does Jane find herself in the position of saving Rochester's life? What sort of suspicion is aroused by the event that threatens Rochester's life? [Interpret]

_____

_____

_____

2. Who is Mason? How does Rochester react when he learns of Mason's arrival? What strange incident involving Mason brings Jane to Rochester's aid again? What do all these events tell you about the relationship between Rochester and Mason? [Infer]

_____

_____

_____

3. How does Brontë create a sense of suspense, tension, and uncertainty in Chapters 11–20? [Analyze]

_____

_____

_____

4. Do you think Rochester is in love with Blanche Ingram? Do you think he has any feelings for Jane? Support your answers with examples from the novel. [Conclude]

_____

_____

_____

5. **Journeys** Based on your reading of these chapters, is Jane truly in control of her life at Thornfield, or are other people and situations controlling her? [Conclude]

_____

_____

_____

APPLY BACKGROUND
Reread Introduction to the Novel on pages 232–234. How did that information help you understand or appreciate what you read in the novel?

_____

_____

_____

_____

_____

_____

_____

_____

_____

_____

_____

_____

_____

_____

_____

_____

_____

_____

_____

_____

_____

_____

_____

_____

_____

_____

Literary Element Character Archetype

Choose one character, other than Rochester, from this section and identify an archetype that character represents. Feel free to research character archetypes on the Internet for more ideas and classifications. [Classify]

_____
_____
_____
_____
_____
_____
_____
_____
_____
_____
_____

Reading Strategy Respond to Events

Choose one situation or event in this section and tell how you felt when you read it. Describe your visceral (or "gut") reactions. [Connect]

_____
_____
_____
_____
_____
_____
_____
_____
_____
_____
_____
_____

Vocabulary Practice

Denotation is the literal, or dictionary, meaning of a word. **Connotation** is the implied, or cultural, meaning of a word. For example, the words _scrawny_ and _skeletal_ have a similar denotation, "very thin," but they have different connotations:

Negative	_More Negative_
scrawny	skeletal

Each of the vocabulary words is listed with a word that has a similar denotation. Choose the word that has a stronger connotation.

1. **imperious**   influential
2. **neophyte**   beginner
3. **nonchalantly**   apathetically
4. **quell**   squash
5. **tenacious**   stubborn

Academic Vocabulary

When Jane arrived at Thornfield, Mrs. Fairfax demonstrated that she cared a great deal about Jane's **welfare**. In the preceding sentence, _welfare_ means "well-being or happiness." List three examples from these chapters that prove Mrs. Fairfax is concerned with Jane's **welfare.**

_____
_____
_____
_____
_____
_____
_____
_____
_____
_____
_____
_____

Writing

Write Diary Entries Choose one of the following topics:

Jane
Arriving at Thornfield, Jane feels that a "fairer" era of life is beginning for her. If Jane had kept a diary of her experiences as a new governess at Thornfield Hall, what might she have written? Put yourself in Jane's place and write entries for at least three or four different days that reveal her as an archetypal character. For example, you might reflect on your tour of Thornfield Hall, your first meeting with your new pupil, the big house party, a conversation with Mr. Rochester, his intended marriage to Blanche Ingram, or one of the strange events that has occurred at Thornfield. Choose the events that best define Jane as a character archetype.

Rochester
Rochester captivates Jane with his self-possessed nature and air of mystery, but most of the descriptions of him come from Jane. If Rochester himself had kept a diary of his experiences during Jane's tenure at Thornfield Hall, what might he have written? Put yourself in Rochester's place and write entries that reveal him as a character archetype. Write entries for at least three or four different days. See above for examples of the kind of situations you might write about. Choose events that best define Rochester as a character archetype.

Jot down some notes here first.

_____
_____
_____
_____
_____
_____
_____
_____
_____
_____
_____
_____

Research and Report

Literary Criticism

Assignment Evaluate literary criticism about Charlotte Brontë's work and write a short response in which you explain whether you agree or disagree that the criticism applies to *Jane Eyre*. Present the response to the class.

Prepare Read the following quotation about Brontë's work by George Henry Lewes:

Jane herself is a creation. The delicate handling of this figure alone implies a dramatic genius of no common order. We never lose sight of her plainness; no effort is made to throw romance about her—no extraordinary goodness or cleverness appeals to your admiration; but you admire, you love her,—love her for the strong will, honest mind, loving heart, and peculiar but fascinating person. A creature of flesh and blood, with very fleshly infirmities, and very mortal excellencies; a woman, not a pattern: that is the Jane Eyre here represented.

As you read this excerpt, write notes about the ideas you agree or disagree with and list points for why you feel the way you do. Look for examples from the text to support your opinions. It will also be helpful to find the meanings of any unfamiliar words in the excerpt and keep them in your notes.

Determine your position. Craft a thesis statement about your position, and gather details from the story to support your argument.

Report When you present your response, make eye contact, speak loudly and clearly, and maintain good posture to reflect confidence. Use an appropriate tone of voice to enhance emotional and logical appeals. All this will help as you try to persuade your audience to agree with your point of view.

Evaluate Write a paragraph evaluating your report. When your classmates present, offer oral feedback on their presentations.

Connect to the Literature

When you are faced with a tough decision, how do you make up your mind? How do you figure out what is the best thing to do?

Write a Journal Entry

Describe a time when you faced a difficult "either/or" decision. What were the pros and cons of each side? Did you make a good decision? Was your decision guided by emotions, principles, the opinions of others, or some other factor?

Build Background

Gothic Novels

In this portion of the novel, Jane has embarked on a new phase of her life at Thornfield Hall, where she serves as a governess. At Thornfield, the novel takes on a more Gothic feeling. Gothic novels take place in gloomy or eerie settings, such as old castles or dark mansions, and emphasize horror, mystery, and the supernatural. Gothic novels, read mainly for entertainment, were especially popular in England in the early 1800s. While *Jane Eyre* is not a Gothic novel, it does contain Gothic features. Even in earlier chapters, there is a reference to the supernatural, when Jane, in the red-room, thinks she sees a ghost.

NOVEL NOTEBOOK

Keep a special notebook to record entries about the novels that you read this year.

SUMMARIZE

Summarize in one sentence the most important idea(s) in Build Background.

_____
_____
_____
_____
_____
_____
_____
_____
_____
_____
_____
_____
_____
_____
_____
_____
_____
_____
_____
_____
_____
_____
_____
_____
_____
_____
_____
_____
_____
_____

Set Purposes for Reading

▶ **BIG Idea** **Courage and Cleverness**

Often, it takes incredible courage to stay true to yourself and your ideals, especially when society encourages you to do otherwise. Think of a situation when you were tempted to do something you knew wasn't right. What decision did you make? Why did you make that decision?

In *Jane Eyre*, it takes great courage and cleverness for Jane to be able to stay true to her beliefs and to her sense of self; as a result, she is often in conflict with what her heart wants her to do. As you read, notice how she deals with this conflict.

Literary Element **Conflict**

Conflict is the struggle between opposing forces in a story or drama. An **external conflict** exists when a character struggles against some outside force, such as another person, nature, society, or fate. An **internal conflict** is a struggle that takes place within the mind of a character who is torn between opposing feelings or goals.

As you read, make a list of the external and internal conflicts that the characters face. Ask yourself how these conflicts can help reveal the novel's themes. Use the graphic organizer on the next page to help you think about Jane's external and internal conflicts.

Reading Strategy **Interpret Imagery**

To **interpret imagery** is to notice details in the text that appeal to your senses. Analyze how these details affect your emotions and influence your understanding of the text.

Images can also have symbolic value; they can stand for something more than their literal meaning. Studying these images and interpreting their meaning can help you to better connect with the text.

As you read, pay attention to the way that Jane describes her surroundings and her feelings. Record examples of the images that make a particular impression on you. You may find it helpful to use a graphic organizer like the one below.

Vocabulary

atone [ə tōn´]
v. to make amends
Because he regretted lying to his employer, the man knew that he would have to atone for his action.

dubious [dōō´bē əs]
adj. doubtful; questionable
The bank robber gave a dubious explanation for his actions.

feign [fān]
v. to pretend
Parents usually know when their children feign sickness to avoid going to school.

impediment [im ped´ə mənt]
n. obstacle
The war veteran was not going to let his disability be an impediment in his life.

vehemence [vē´ə məns]
n. intense emotion or force
The tornado attacked the town with a vehemence the people had never seen before.

Image	My Emotional Response	Symbolic Meaning

You have seen Jane encounter and try to reconcile a number of different conflicts during the various journeys of her life. As you read this section, record both Jane's internal and external conflicts.

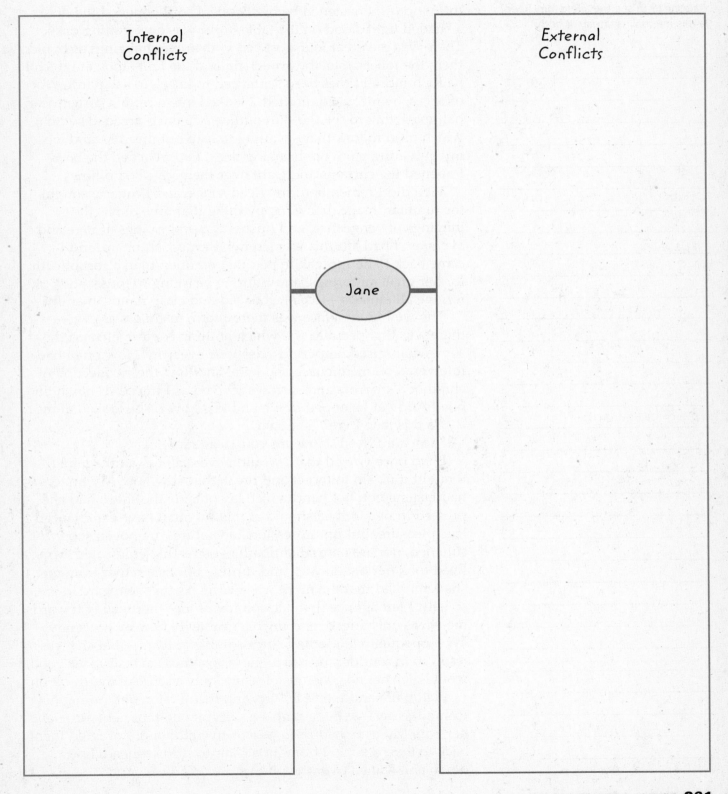

Internal
Conflicts

External
Conflicts

Jane

Literary Element

Conflict What conflict does Jane encounter when she returns to Gateshead to see the ailing Mrs. Reed? Is this internal, external, or both?

_____
_____
_____
_____
_____
_____
_____
_____
_____
_____
_____
_____
_____
_____
_____
_____
_____
_____
_____
_____
_____
_____
_____
_____
_____
_____
_____
_____
_____
_____
_____
_____
_____
_____
_____
_____

NOVEL EXCERPT: CHAPTER 21

I did not need to be guided to the well-known room: to which I had so often been summoned for chastisement or reprimand in former days. I hastened before Bessie, I softly opened the door: a shaded light stood on the table, for it was now getting dark. There was the great four-post bed with amber hangings as of old; there the toilet-table, the arm-chair, and the foot-stool: at which I had a hundred times been sentenced to kneel, to ask pardon for offences, by me, uncommitted. I looked into a certain corner near, half-expecting to see the slim outline of a once-dreaded switch; which used to lurk there, waiting to leap out imp-like and lace my quivering palm or shrinking neck. I approached the bed; I opened the curtains and leant over the high-piled pillows.

Well did I remember Mrs. Reed's face, and I eagerly sought the familiar image. It is a happy thing that time quells the longings of vengeance, and hushes the promptings of rage and aversion: I had left this woman in bitterness and hate, and I came back to her now with no other emotion than a sort of ruth for her great sufferings, and a strong yearning to forget and forgive all injuries—to be reconciled and clasp hands in amity.

The well-known face was there: stern, relentless as ever—there was that peculiar eye which nothing could melt; and the somewhat raised, imperious, despotic eyebrow. How often had it lowered on me menace and hate! and how the recollection of childhood's terrors and sorrows revived as I traced its harsh line now! And yet I stooped down and kissed her: she looked at me.

"Is this Jane Eyre?" she said.

"Yes, aunt Reed. How are you, dear aunt?"

I had once vowed that I would never call her aunt again: I thought it no sin to forget and break that vow now. My fingers had fastened on her hand which lay outside the sheet: had she pressed mine kindly, I should at that moment have experienced true pleasure. But unimpressionable natures are not so soon softened, nor are natural antipathies so readily eradicated: Mrs. Reed took her hand away, and turning her face rather from me, she remarked that the night was warm. Again she regarded me, so icily, I felt at once that her opinion of me—her feeling towards me—was unchanged, and unchangeable. I knew by her stony eye—opaque to tenderness, indissoluble to tears—that she was resolved to consider me bad to the last; because to believe me good, would give her no generous pleasure: only a sense of mortification.

I felt pain, and then I felt ire; and then I felt a determination to subdue her—to be her mistress in spite both of her nature and her will. My tears had risen, just as in childhood: I ordered them back to their source. I brought a chair to the bed-head: I sat down and leaned over the pillow.

"You sent for me," I said, "and I am here; and it is my intention to stay till I see how you get on."

"Oh, of course! You have seen my daughters?"

"Yes."

"Well, you may tell them I wish you to stay till I can talk some things over with you I have on my mind: tonight it is too late, and I have a difficulty in recalling them. But there was something I wished to say—let me see—"

The wandering look and changed utterance told what wreck had taken place in her once-vigorous frame. Turning restlessly, she drew the bed-clothes round her; my elbow, resting on a corner of the quilt, fixed it down: she was at once irritated.

"Sit up!" said she; "don't annoy me with holding the clothes fast—are you Jane Eyre?"

"I am Jane Eyre."

"I have had more trouble with that child than any one would believe. Such a burden to be left on my hands—and so much annoyance as she caused me, daily and hourly, with her incomprehensible disposition, and her sudden starts of temper, and her continual, unnatural watchings of one's movements! I declare she talked to me once like something mad, or like a fiend—no child ever spoke or looked as she did; I was glad to get her away from the house. What did they do with her at Lowood? The fever broke out there, and many of the pupils died. She, however, did not die: but I said she did—I wish she had died!"

"A strange wish, Mrs. Reed: why do you hate her so?"

"I had a dislike to her mother always; for she was my husband's only sister, and a great favourite with him: he opposed the family's disowning her when she made her low marriage; and when news came of her death, he wept like a simpleton. He would send for the baby; though I entreated him rather to put it out to nurse and pay for its maintenance, I hated it the first time I set my eyes on it—a sickly, whining, pining thing! It would wail in its cradle all night long—not screaming heartily like any other child, but whimpering and moaning. Reed pitied it; and he used to nurse it and notice it as if it had been his own: more, indeed, than he ever noticed his own at that age. He would try to make my children friendly to the little beggar: the darlings could not bear it, and he was angry with them when they showed their dislike. In his last illness, he had it brought continually to his bedside; and but an hour before he died, he bound me by vow to keep the creature. I would as soon have been charged with a pauper brat out of a workhouse: but he was weak, naturally weak. . . .

Literary Element

Conflict Given the conflicts that she had with the Reeds in the past and Jane's cool reception at Gateshead in this excerpt, do you agree with Jane's decision to return there?

_____

_____

_____

_____

_____

_____

_____

_____

_____

_____

_____

_____

_____

_____

_____

_____

_____

_____

_____

_____

_____

_____

_____

_____

_____

_____

_____

_____

Reading Strategy

Interpret Imagery Notice the references to coldness and the ocean. Why are these images appropriate in this scene?

_____
_____
_____
_____
_____
_____
_____
_____
_____
_____
_____
_____
_____
_____
_____
_____
_____
_____
_____
_____
_____
_____
_____
_____
_____
_____
_____
_____
_____
_____
_____
_____
_____
_____
_____

NOVEL EXCERPT: CHAPTER 23

. . . The thought of Mrs. O'Gall and Bitternutt Lodge struck cold to my heart; and colder the thought of all the brine and foam, destined, as it seemed, to rush between me and the master at whose side I now walked; and coldest the remembrance of the wider ocean—wealth, caste, custom intervened between me and what I naturally and inevitably loved.

"It is a long way," I again said.

"It is, to be sure; and when you get to Bitternutt Lodge, Connaught, Ireland, I shall never see you again, Jane: that's morally certain. I never go over to Ireland, not having myself much of a fancy for the country. We have been good friends, Jane; have we not?"

"Yes, sir."

"And when friends are on the eve of separation, they like to spend the little time that remains to them close to each other. Come—we'll talk over the voyage and the parting quietly, half an hour or so, while the stars enter into their shining life up in heaven yonder: here is the chestnut tree: here is the bench at its old roots. Come, we will sit there in peace to-night, though we should never more be destined to sit there together." He seated me and himself.

"It is a long way to Ireland, Janet, and I am sorry to send my little friend on such weary travels: but if I can't do better, how is it to be helped? Are you anything akin to me, do you think, Jane?"

I could risk no sort of answer by this time: my heart was full.

"Because," he said, "I sometimes have a queer feeling with regard to you—especially when you are near me, as now: it is as if I had a string somewhere under my left ribs tightly and inextricably knotted to a similar string situated in the corresponding quarter of your little frame. And if that boisterous channel, and two hundred miles or so of land come broad between us, I am afraid that cord of communion will be snapt; and then I've a nervous notion I should take to bleeding inwardly. As for you,—you'd forget me."

"That I _never_ should, sir: you know" . . .

NOVEL EXCERPT: CHAPTER 23

But what had befallen the night? The moon was not yet set, and we were all in shadow: I could scarcely see my master's face, near as I was. And what ailed the chestnut tree? it writhed and groaned; while wind roared in the laurel walk, and came sweeping over us.

"We must go in," said Mr. Rochester: "the weather changes. I could have sat with thee till morning, Jane."

"And so," thought I, "could I with you." I should have said so, perhaps, but a livid, vivid spark leapt out of a cloud at which I was looking, and there was a crack, a crash, and a close rattling peal; and I thought only of hiding my dazzled eyes against Mr. Rochester's shoulder.

The rain rushed down. He hurried me up the walk, through the grounds, and into the house; but we were quite wet before we could pass the threshold. He was taking off my shawl in the hall, and shaking the water out of my loosened hair, when Mrs. Fairfax emerged from her room. I did not observe her at first, nor did Mr. Rochester. The lamp was lit. The clock was on the stroke of twelve.

"Hasten to take off your wet things," said he: "and before you go, good-night—good-night, my darling!"

He kissed me repeatedly. When I looked up, on leaving his arms, there stood the widow, pale, grave, and amazed. I only smiled at her, and ran upstairs. "Explanation will do for another time," thought I. Still, when I reached my chamber, I felt a pang at the idea she should even temporarily misconstrue what she had seen. But joy soon effaced every other feeling; and loud as the wind blew, near and deep as the thunder crashed, fierce and frequent as the lightning gleamed, cataract-like as the rain fell during a storm of two hours' duration, I experienced no fear, and little awe. Mr. Rochester came thrice to my door in the course of it, to ask if I was safe and tranquil: and that was comfort, that was strength for anything.

Before I left my bed in the morning, little Adèle came running in to tell me that the great horse-chestnut at the bottom of the orchard had been struck by lightning in the night, and half of it split away.

Reading Strategy

Interpret Imagery Reread the descriptions of the old chestnut tree. In what way does it symbolize the relationship between Rochester and Jane?

_____

_____

_____

_____

_____

_____

_____

_____

_____

_____

_____

_____

_____

_____

_____

_____

_____

_____

_____

_____

_____

_____

_____

_____

_____

_____

_____

_____

_____

MARK IT UP

Are you allowed to write in your novel? If so, then mark up the pages as you read, or reread, to help with your note-taking. Develop a shorthand system, including symbols, that works for you. Here are some ideas:

Underline = important idea

Bracket = text to quote

Asterisk = just what you were looking for

Checkmark = might be useful

Circle = unfamiliar word or phrase to look up

▶ **BIG Idea**

Courage and Cleverness What have you learned about Jane's courage as she struggles to stay true to herself?

Mark up the excerpt, looking for evidence of how it expresses the Big Idea.

NOVEL EXCERPT: CHAPTER 27

"Mr. Rochester, . . . You will forget me before I forget you."

"You make me a liar by such language: you sully my honour. I declared I could not change: you tell me to my face I shall change soon. And what a distortion in your judgment, what a perversity in your ideas, is proved by your conduct! Is it better to drive a fellow-creature to despair than to transgress a mere human law—no man being injured by the breach? . . ."

This was true: and while he spoke my very conscience and reason turned traitors against me, and charged me with crime in resisting him. They spoke almost as loud as Feeling: and that clamoured wildly. "Oh, comply!" it said. "Think of his misery; think of his danger—look at his state when left alone; remember his headlong nature; consider the recklessness following on despair—soothe him; save him; love him; tell him you love him and will be his. Who in the world cares for *you*? or who will be injured by what you do?"

Still indomitable was the reply—"*I* care for myself. The more solitary, the more friendless, the more unsustained I am, the more I will respect myself. I will keep the law given by God; sanctioned by man. I will hold to the principles received by me when I was sane, and not mad—as I am now. Laws and principles are not for the times when there is no temptation: they are for such moments as this when body and soul rise in mutiny against their rigour; stringent are they; inviolate they shall be. If at my individual convenience I might break them, what would be their worth? They have a worth—so I have always believed; and if I cannot believe it now, it is because I am insane—quite insane: with my veins running fire, and my heart beating faster than I can count its throbs. Preconceived opinions, foregone determinations, are all I have at this hour to stand by: there I plant my foot."

I did. Mr. Rochester, reading my countenance, saw I had done so. His fury was wrought to the highest: he must yield to it for a moment, whatever followed; he crossed the floor and seized my arm, and grasped my waist. He seemed to devour me with his flaming glance: physically, I felt, at the moment, powerless as stubble exposed to the draught and glow of a furnace—mentally, I still possessed my soul, and with it the certainty of ultimate safety. The soul, fortunately, has an interpreter—often an unconscious, but still a truthful interpreter—in the eye. My eye rose to his; and while I looked in his fierce face, I gave an involuntary sigh: his grip was painful, and my over-tasked strength almost exhausted.

"Never," said he, as he ground his teeth, "never was anything at once so frail and so indomitable. . . .

Use the Cornell Note-Taking system to take notes on the excerpt at the left. Record your notes, Reduce them, and then Recap (summarize) them.

Record

_____

_____

_____

_____

_____

_____

_____

_____

_____

_____

_____

_____

_____

_____

_____

_____

_____

_____

_____

_____

_____

_____

_____

_____

_____

Recap

_____

_____

_____

_____

_____

_____

Reduce

Try the following approach as you reduce your notes.

MY VIEW

Comment on what you learned from your own notes.

_____

_____

_____

_____

_____

_____

_____

_____

_____

_____

_____

_____

_____

_____

_____

_____

_____

_____

_____

_____

_____

_____

_____

_____

Respond and Think Critically

1. What surprising revelation does Rochester make to Jane? What can you infer about Jane's feelings and beliefs from her statement "I could not, in those days, see God for his creature: of whom I had made an idol." [Infer]

_____

_____

_____

_____

2. What disastrous event happens on Jane's wedding day? Who is Bertha? How does Jane feel when she learns of Bertha's existence? What does Jane decide to do? Why? [Recall]

_____

_____

_____

_____

3. Many fiction writers use dreams to **foreshadow,** or give hints of, later events. Give three examples of this technique from Chapters 21–27. [Analyze]

_____

_____

_____

_____

4. In Victorian England, a man could not divorce his wife if she was insane. Given this fact, was Rochester justified in asking Jane to marry him? Why or why not? [Evaluate]

_____

_____

_____

_____

5. Courage and Cleverness Did Jane make the right decision in choosing to leave Mr. Rochester? [Evaluate]

_____

_____

_____

APPLY BACKGROUND
Reread Build Background on page 259. How did that information help you understand or appreciate what you read in the novel?

_____

_____

_____

_____

_____

_____

_____

_____

_____

_____

_____

_____

_____

_____

_____

_____

_____

_____

_____

_____

_____

_____

_____

_____

_____

_____

_____

_____

_____

_____

_____

_____

Literary Element | **Conflict**

In your opinion, do external or internal conflicts play a more significant role in Jane's decision to leave Thornfield? [Analyze]

_____
_____
_____
_____
_____
_____
_____
_____
_____
_____
_____
_____

Reading Strategy | **Interpret Imagery**

Though much of this novel has revolved around Jane's rebirth, both at Lowood School and at Thornfield, images of death and darkness appear frequently, even in seemingly happy scenes. Choose a passage that includes such imagery, and explain why it is appropriate in that situation. [Analyze]

_____
_____
_____
_____
_____
_____
_____
_____
_____
_____
_____

Vocabulary Practice

A **synonym** is a word that has the same or nearly the same meaning as another word. Match each boldfaced vocabulary word below with its synonym. Use a thesaurus or dictionary to check your answers.

1. **atone**	a. blameless
2. **dubious**	b. fervor
3. **feign**	c. make reparations
4. **impediment**	d. debatable
5. **vehemence**	e. penalize
	f. hindrance
	g. fake

Academic Vocabulary

To **justify** his decision to keep Bertha's presence a secret from Jane, Mr. Rochester reveals all of the details about his previous courtship and marriage. Using context clues, try to figure out the meaning of justify in the sentence above. Write your guess below. Then check it in a dictionary.

_____
_____
_____
_____
_____
_____
_____
_____
_____
_____

Write With Style

Apply Imagery

Assignment Review how Brontë uses imagery throughout *Jane Eyre.* Then write a paragraph that uses imagery to portray a conflict in your life.

Get Ideas Make a list of conflicts that you are familiar with. Consider both external conflicts (siblings, parents, friends, teachers, and so on) and internal conflicts (your desire to do something versus the knowledge that it is wrong, a pressure you place on yourself to succeed). Next, generate a list of sensory details that could help convey these conflicts. Consider including the kinds of symbolic imagery that Brontë uses, such as light and dark. Based on your prewriting work, choose the conflict that you can best convey through imagery.

Give It Structure Introduce the conflict at the start of your paragraph, then use vivid descriptions and imagery to describe this conflict. Even if this conflict has not been resolved in real life, consider including a resolution at the end of your paragraph.

Look at Language Imagery is conveyed through word choice, especially words that evoke the senses. Remember that your goal is to paint a picture of this conflict, with words, for your readers. To expand your use of imagery, it might help to use an extended simile or metaphor that describes part of the conflict.

EXAMPLE:
My brother acts like Napoleon, waving his arms and demanding that all others bow down to him and follow in his footsteps. Because he wears so much cologne, his pungent smell lingers and overtakes the whole house. It prevents me from enjoying even one moment of peaceful solitude, one moment when I can truly be myself.

Speaking and Listening

Visual/Media Presentation

Assignment Create and deliver a presentation that uses images and music to capture the mood and setting of Gothic novels.

Prepare Conduct research to determine what makes Gothic novels unique. As you identify the elements of plot, character, and theme that these novels have in common, pay attention to what kinds of mental images you associate with Gothic novels. Then, using the Internet and your own music collection, gather at least five images and five songs that you think best reflect the mood and setting of Gothic novels. As you gather these pieces, consider organizing your materials in a graphic organizer like the one below.

Image/ song title	Connection to the Gothic novel

Report Assemble your images and songs in a logical way that will appeal to your audience. As you share your information with your classmates, make sure that you discuss how each image and song reveals a unique characteristic of the Gothic novel. Make sure you speak clearly and loudly.

Evaluate Write a paragraph in which you evaluate how well your presentation captured the mood and setting of Gothic novels. Were there any images or songs that you would replace if you were to present this material again?

Connect to the Literature

People who are committed to improving the world around them must often make personal sacrifices. What do you think are some of the costs and benefits of making such a commitment?

Create a Web

In a small group, think of some individuals who have dedicated their lives to helping others or to making the world a better place. Then create a web detailing the satisfactions and sacrifices that might go with dedicating one's life to an ideal.

Build Background

Brontë Country

The scene shifts again in these next chapters as Jane finds herself in a remote moorland region, surrounded by bare, heather-clad hills. This landscape is much like that found in northern Yorkshire, where Charlotte Brontë grew up. The Brontë family has made this region of England so famous that the tourism bureau has dubbed it "Brontë Country."

Today, Brontë Country draws many visitors who travel there to see many of the area's well-known sites, including the Brontë Parsonage Museum. Formerly known as Haworth Parsonage, this site was home to the Brontë sisters for most of their lives. The museum is run by one of the world's oldest literary societies, the Brontë society, which works to preserve the powerful literary tradition that the Brontës established.

NOVEL NOTEBOOK

Keep a special notebook to record entries about the novels that you read this year.

WRITE THE CAPTION

Write a caption for the image below, in the present tense, using information in Build Background.

_____
_____
_____
_____
_____
_____
_____
_____
_____
_____
_____
_____
_____
_____
_____
_____
_____
_____
_____
_____
_____
_____
_____
_____
_____
_____
_____
_____
_____
_____
_____
_____

Set Purposes for Reading

▶ BIG Idea Journey

Think about a journey you have taken. Journeys can introduce us to new people, places and cultures, but they can also cause a significant change in the way that we perceive the world around us.

In *Jane Eyre*, the title character goes on a number of journeys to find herself and to escape from difficult situations. As you read, consider why she needs to embark on each new journey. What is she learning about life, love, and herself during these experiences?

Literary Element Plot Archetype

Plot is the sequence of events in a narrative work. Conflicts are introduced, followed by complications, which lead to the **climax,** or turning point, followed in turn by the falling action and resolution, sometimes called the **denouement,** which reveal the logical results of the climax.

A **plot archetype** is a story pattern that occurs in many cultures. Making the long journey home, completing the "impossible" task, fulfilling a quest, and outwitting the formidable enemy are all archetypal plots.

Jane Eyre contains elements of the Gothic novel plot archetype. These include gloomy settings, the sublime, temptation, the protagonist's struggle with a terrible strange person or force, and supernatural or mysterious events. As you read, notice the gloomy descriptions Jane offers us of Thornfield, as well as the mysterious events that occur under its roof. Do they seem to follow a pattern that is familiar to you?

Reading Strategy Analyze Cause-and-Effect Relationships

To analyze cause-and-effect relationships in a work of literature you look at the causes, or reasons, and their effects, or results, to see how these relationships have an impact on the story. Doing this will help you better understand the work's plot and themes.

Cause-and-effect relationships allow the writer to reveal how and why things happen. In many cases, authors want the readers to see how the characters' behaviors and choices ultimately determine the outcome of their situations.

As you continue to read *Jane Eyre*, consider why the characters are dealing with some of the more difficult challenges that they encounter. What have they done to help bring about these challenges? You may find it helpful to use a graphic organizer like the one at the right.

Vocabulary

averse [ə vurs´]
adj. opposed
Vegetarians are averse to eating meat.

despots [des´pəts]
n. rulers with absolute power
Despots often make living conditions quite difficult for the people they rule.

fetters [fet´ərs]
n. chains; restraints
She sometimes felt as if the school rules constrained her like fetters she could not break.

inexorable [i nek´sər ə bəl]
adj. relentless; inflexible
Some people hold inexorable beliefs about the way a country should be run.

stoicism [stō´ ə siz´ əm]
n. indifference to pain
He faced his illness with tremendous stoicism.

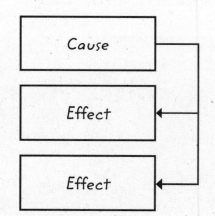

Chapter 28 introduces Jane to the Rivers family, but Brontë makes it clear that Jane might not have met them had she not been turned away by others in the village. As you read, make note of events that end up bringing about unanticipated effects for Jane and the others.

Cause

Cause		Effect
Jane is unable to find work or sufficient food in the village near Whitcross.	→	Jane ends up at Marsh End.

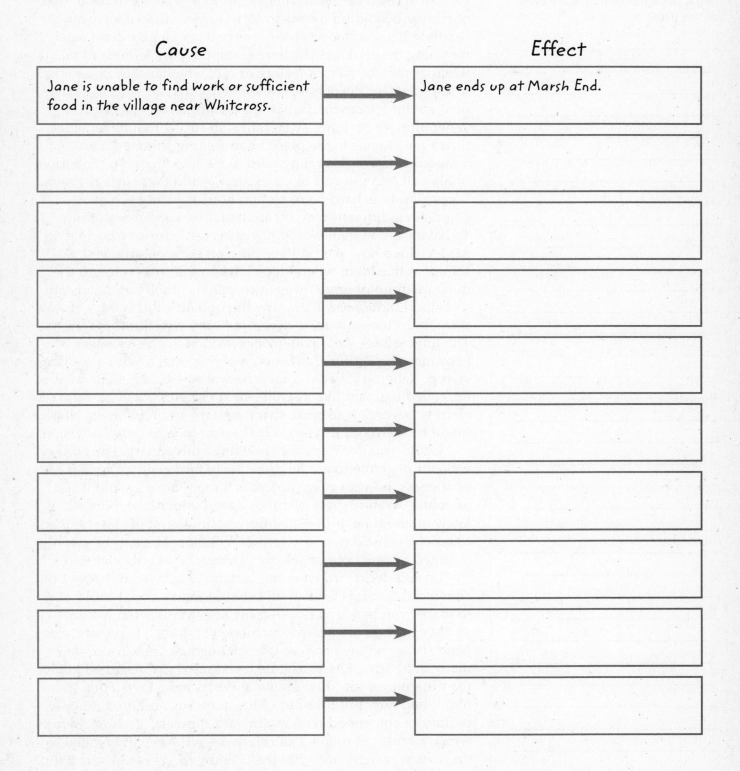

Literary Element

Plot Archetype What elements of the Gothic novel plot archetype are evident on this page?

_____
_____
_____
_____
_____
_____
_____
_____
_____
_____
_____
_____
_____
_____
_____
_____
_____
_____
_____
_____
_____
_____
_____
_____
_____
_____
_____
_____
_____
_____
_____
_____
_____
_____
_____
_____

NOVEL EXCERPT: CHAPTER 35

He laid his hand on my head as he uttered the last words. He had spoken earnestly, mildly: his look was not, indeed, that of a lover beholding his mistress; but it was that of a pastor recalling his wandering sheep—or better, of a guardian angel watching the soul for which he is responsible. All men of talent, whether they be men of feeling or not; whether they be zealots, or aspirants, or despots—provided only they be sincere—have their sublime moments: when they subdue and rule. I felt veneration for St. John—veneration so strong that its impetus thrust me at once to the point I had so long shunned. I was tempted to cease struggling with him—to rush down the torrent of his will into the gulf of his existence, and there lose my own. I was almost as hard beset by him now as I had been once before, in a different way, by another. I was a fool both times. To have yielded then would have been an error of principle; to have yielded now would have been an error of judgment. So I think at this hour, when I look back to the crisis through the quiet medium of time: I was unconscious of folly at the instant.

I stood motionless under my hierophant's touch. My refusals were forgotten—my fears overcome—my wrestlings paralysed. The Impossible—_i.e._, my marriage with St. John—was fast becoming the Possible. All was changing utterly with a sudden sweep. Religion called—Angels beckoned—God commanded—life rolled together like a scroll—death's gates opening, showed eternity beyond: it seemed, that for safety and bliss there, all here might be sacrificed in a second. The dim room was full of visions.

"Could you decide now?" asked the missionary. The inquiry was put in gentle tones: he drew me to him gently. Oh, that gentleness! how far more potent is it than force! I could resist St. John's wrath: I grew pliant as a reed under his kindness. Yet I knew all the time, if I yielded now, I should not the less be made to repent, some day, of my former rebellion. His nature was not changed by one hour of solemn prayer: it was only elevated.

"I could decide if I were but certain," I answered: "were I but convinced that it is God's will I should marry you, I could vow to marry you here and now—come afterwards what would!"

"My prayers are heard!" ejaculated St. John. He pressed his hand firmer on my head, as if he claimed me: he surrounded me with his arm, _almost_ as if he loved me (I say _almost_—I knew the difference—for I had felt what it was to be loved; but, like him, I had now put love out of the question, and thought only of duty): I contended with my inward dimness of vision, before which clouds yet rolled. I sincerely, deeply, fervently longed to do what was right; and only that. "Show me, show me the path!" I entreated of Heaven. I was excited more than I had ever been;

and whether what followed was the effect of excitement, the reader shall judge.

All the house was still; for I believe all, except St. John and myself, were now retired to rest. The one candle was dying out: the room was full of moonlight. My heart beat fast and thick: I heard its throb. Suddenly it stood still to an inexpressible feeling that thrilled it through, and passed at once to my head and extremities. The feeling was not like an electric shock; but it was quite as sharp, as strange, as startling: it acted on my senses as if their utmost activity hitherto had been but torpor; from which they were now summoned, and forced to wake. They rose expectant: eye and ear waited, while the flesh quivered on my bones.

"What have you heard? What do you see?" asked St. John. I saw nothing: but I heard a voice somewhere cry—

"Jane! Jane! Jane!" nothing more.

"Oh, God! what is it?" I gasped.

I might have said, "Where is it?" for it did not seem in the room—nor in the house—nor in the garden: it did not come out of the air—nor from under the earth—nor from overhead. I had heard it—where, or whence, for ever impossible to know! And it was the voice of a human being—a known, loved, well-remembered voice—that of Edward Fairfax Rochester; and it spoke in pain and woe wildly, eerily, urgently.

"I am coming!" I cried. "Wait for me! Oh, I will come!" I flew to the door, and looked into the passage: it was dark. I ran out into the garden: it was void.

"Where are you?" I exclaimed.

The hills beyond Marsh Glen sent the answer faintly back— "Where are you?" I listened. The wind sighed low in the firs: all was moorland loneliness and midnight hush.

"Down superstition!" I commented, as that spectre rose up black by the black yew at the gate. "This is not thy deception, not thy witchcraft: it is the work of nature. She was roused, and did—no miracle—but her best."

I broke from St. John; who had followed, and would have detained me. It was *my* time to assume ascendancy. *My* powers were in play, and in force. I told him to forbear question or remark; I desired him to leave me: I must, and would be alone. He obeyed at once. Where there is energy to command well enough, obedience never fails. I mounted to my chamber; locked myself in; fell on my knees; and prayed in my way—a different way to St. John's, but effective in its own fashion. I seemed to penetrate very near a Mighty Spirit; and my soul rushed out in gratitude at His feet. I rose from the thanksgiving—took a resolve—and lay down, unscared, enlightened—eager but for the daylight.

Literary Element

Plot Archetype What other elements of the Gothic plot archetype exists within this excerpt?

_____

_____

_____

_____

_____

_____

_____

_____

_____

_____

_____

_____

_____

_____

_____

_____

_____

_____

_____

_____

_____

_____

_____

_____

_____

_____

_____

_____

_____

Reading Strategy

Analyze Cause-and-Effect Relationships According to this passage, why does Jane feel so thankful and beholden to the Rivers family and especially to Mary and Diana?

_____
_____
_____
_____
_____
_____
_____
_____
_____
_____
_____
_____
_____
_____
_____
_____
_____
_____
_____
_____
_____
_____
_____
_____
_____
_____
_____
_____

NOVEL EXCERPT: CHAPTER 29

The recollection of about three days and nights succeeding this is very dim in my mind. I can recall some sensations felt in the interval; but few thoughts framed, and no actions performed. I knew I was in a small room; and in a narrow bed. To that bed I seemed to have grown; I lay on it motionless as a stone; and to have torn me from it would have been almost to kill me. I took no note of the lapse of time—of the change from morning to noon, from noon to evening. I observed when any one entered or left the apartment; I could even tell who they were; I could understand what was said when the speaker stood near to me; but I could not answer; to open my lips or move my limbs was actually impossible. Hannah, the servant, was my most frequent visitor. Her coming disturbed me. I had a feeling that she wished me away: that she did not understand me or my circumstances: that she was prejudiced against me. Diana and Mary appeared in the chamber once or twice a day. They would whisper sentences of this sort at my bedside:—

"It is very well we took her in."

"Yes; she would certainly have been found dead at the door in the morning, had she been left out all night. I wonder what she has gone through?"

"Strange hardships, I imagine—poor, emaciated, pallid wanderer!"

"She is not an uneducated person, I should think, by her manner of speaking; her accent was quite pure; and the clothes she took off, though splashed and wet, were little worn and fine."

"She has a peculiar face; fleshless and haggard as it is, I rather like it; and when in good health and animated, I can fancy her physiognomy would be agreeable."

Never once in their dialogues did I hear a syllable of regret at the hospitality they had extended to me; or of suspicion of, or aversion to, myself. I was comforted.

Mr. St. John came but once: he looked at me, and said my state of lethargy was the result of reaction from excessive and protracted fatigue. He pronounced it needless to send for a doctor: nature, he was sure, would manage best, left to herself. He said every nerve had been overstrained in some way, and the whole system must sleep torpid a while. There was no disease. He imagined my recovery would be rapid enough when once commenced. These opinions he delivered in a few words, in a quiet, low voice; and added, after a pause, in the tone of a man little accustomed to have expansive comment, "rather an unusual physiognomy; certainly, not indicative of vulgarity or degradation."

"Far otherwise," responded Diana. "To speak truth, St. John, my heart rather warms to the poor little soul. I wish we may be able to benefit her permanently."

"That is hardly likely," was the reply. "You will find she is some young lady who has had a misunderstanding with her friends and has probably injudiciously left them. We may, perhaps, succeed in restoring her to them, if she is not obstinate: but I trace lines of force in her face which make me sceptical of her tractability." He stood considering me some minutes; then added, "She looks sensible, but not at all handsome."

"She is so ill, St. John."

"Ill or well, she would always be plain. The grace and harmony of beauty are quite wanting in those features."

On the third day, I was better; on the fourth, I could speak, move, rise in bed, and turn. Hannah had brought me some gruel and dry toast, about, as I supposed, the dinner hour. I had eaten with relish: the food was good—void of the feverish flavour which had hitherto poisoned what I had swallowed. When she left me, I felt comparatively strong and revived: ere long satiety of repose, and desire for action stirred me. I wished to rise; but what could I put on? Only my damp and bemired apparel; in which I had slept on the ground and fallen in the marsh. I felt ashamed to appear before my benefactors so clad. I was spared the humiliation.

On a chair by the bedside were all my own things, clean and dry. My black silk frock hung against the wall. The traces of the bog were removed from it; the creases left by the wet smoothed out: it was quite decent. My very shoes and stockings were purified and rendered presentable. There were the means of washing in the room, and a comb and brush to smooth my hair. After a weary process, and resting every five minutes, I succeeded in dressing myself. My clothes hung loose on me; for I was much wasted, but I covered deficiencies with a shawl, and once more, clean and respectable-looking—no speck of dirt, no trace of the disorder I so hated, and which seemed so to degrade me, left—I crept down a stone staircase with the aid of banisters, to a narrow low passage, and found my way presently to the kitchen.

Reading Strategy

Analyze Cause-and-Effect Relationships What one other unanticipated effect is brought about by the Riverses' kindness to Jane?

MARK IT UP

Are you allowed to write in your novel? If so, then mark up the pages as you read, or reread, to help with your note-taking. Develop a shorthand system, including symbols, that works for you. Here are some ideas:

Underline = important idea

Bracket = text to quote

Asterisk = just what you were looking for

Checkmark = might be useful

Circle = unfamiliar word or phrase to look up

▶ **BIG Idea**

Journeys What struggles does Jane face during each new journey?

Mark up the excerpt, looking for evidence of how it expresses the Big Idea.

NOVEL EXCERPT: CHAPTER 28

Two days are passed. It is a summer evening; the coachman has set me down at a place called Whitcross; he could take me no farther for the sum I had given, and I was not possessed of another shilling in the world. The coach is a mile off by this time; I am alone. At this moment I discover that I forgot to take my parcel out of the pocket of the coach, where I had placed it for safety; there it remains, there it must remain; and now, I am absolutely destitute.

. . . There are great moors behind and on each hand of me; there are waves of mountains far beyond that deep valley at my feet. The population here must be thin, and I see no passengers on these roads: they stretch out east, west, north, and south— white, broad, lonely; they are all cut in the moor, and the heather grows deep and wild to their very verge. Yet a chance traveller might pass by; and I wish no eye to see me now: strangers would wonder what I am doing, lingering here at the sign-post, evidently objectless and lost. I might be questioned: I could give no answer but what would sound incredible, and excite suspicion. Not a tie holds me to human society at this moment— not a charm or hope calls me where my fellow-creatures are— none that saw me would have a kind thought or good wish for me. I have no relative but the universal mother, Nature: I will seek her breast and ask repose.

I struck straight into the heath; I held on to a hollow I saw deeply furrowing the brown moorside; I waded knee-deep in its dark growth; I turned with its turnings, and finding a moss-blackened granite crag in a hidden angle, I sat down under it. High banks of moor were about me; the crag protected my head: the sky was over that.

Some time passed before I felt tranquil even here: I had a vague dread that wild cattle might be near, or that some sportsman or poacher might discover me. If a gust of wind swept the waste, I looked up, fearing it was the rush of a bull; if a plover whistled, I imagined it a man. Finding my apprehensions unfounded, however, and calmed by the deep silence that reigned as evening declined at nightfall, I took confidence. As yet I had not thought; I had only listened, watched, dreaded; now I regained the faculty of reflection.

What was I to do? Where to go? Oh, intolerable questions, when I could do nothing and go nowhere!—when a long way must yet be measured by my weary, trembling limbs, before I could reach human habitation—when cold charity must be entreated before I could get a lodging: reluctant sympathy importuned: almost certain repulse incurred: before my tale could be listened to, or one of my wants relieved!

Use the Cornell Note-Taking system to take notes on the excerpt at the left. Record your notes, Reduce them, and then Recap (summarize) them.

Record

_____

_____

_____

_____

_____

_____

_____

_____

_____

_____

_____

_____

_____

_____

_____

_____

_____

_____

_____

_____

_____

_____

_____

_____

_____

Recap

_____

_____

_____

_____

_____

_____

Reduce

Try the following approach as you reduce your notes.

TO THE POINT
Write a few key words.

_____

_____

_____

_____

_____

_____

_____

_____

_____

_____

_____

_____

_____

_____

_____

_____

_____

_____

_____

_____

_____

_____

Respond and Think Critically

1. How does St. John help Jane? What news does he bring to Jane? What does Jane's reaction to the news reveal about her? [Infer]

_____

_____

_____

_____

2. Why does St. John ask Jane to come to India with him as his wife? How does she answer him? What do you think Jane means when she says, "If I join St. John, I abandon half myself?" [Interpret]

_____

_____

_____

_____

3. Jane comes close to changing her mind about marrying St. John. Why? What does her response to Rochester's voice suggest about her values and feelings? What conflicts seem to be troubling her? [Analyze]

_____

_____

_____

_____

4. What imagery does Brontë use to describe St. John? Give two examples. Why is this imagery appropriate? [Analyze]

_____

_____

_____

_____

5. Journeys Jane's journey from Thornfield takes her away from everything and everyone she knows. Now that you have read through Chapter 35, do you think her journey was worthwhile? Why or why not? [Evaluate]

_____

_____

_____

_____

APPLY BACKGROUND
Reread Build Background on page 271. How did that information help you understand or appreciate what you read in the novel?

_____

_____

_____

_____

_____

_____

_____

_____

_____

_____

_____

_____

_____

_____

_____

_____

_____

_____

_____

_____

_____

_____

_____

_____

_____

_____

_____

Literary Element   Plot Archetype

What aspects of the Gothic novel plot archetype in *Jane Eyre* do you recognize from other stories, television shows, or movies? Give examples. [Classify]

_____

_____

_____

_____

_____

_____

_____

_____

_____

_____

Reading Strategy   Analyze Cause-and-Effect Relationships

When St. John noticed Jane's real name on one of her drawings, it had an unexpected consequence. If you were St. John, would you have told Jane earlier that you knew who she really was? Why or why not? [Connect]

_____

_____

_____

_____

_____

_____

_____

_____

_____

_____

Vocabulary Practice

Studying the **etymology,** or origin and history, of a word can help you better understand and explore its meaning. Create a word map, like the one below, for each of these vocabulary words from the selection. Use a dictionary for help.

averse	inexorable
despots	stoicism
fetters	

EXAMPLE: **scripture**
Definition: any sacred writing
Etymology: Latin *scriptura* means book or "writing"

Sample Sentence:
Ameena follows the **scripture** of the Muslim faith.

Academic Vocabulary

Without the **assistance** *she received from the Rivers siblings, Jane might not have survived her journey from Thornfield.* In the preceding sentence, *assistance* means "help". Think about a time when you needed **assistance.** In what way did others help you?

_____

_____

_____

_____

_____

_____

_____

_____

_____

_____

_____

_____

_____

Writing

Write a Script Jane and St. John, her clergyman cousin, have a number of intense conversations that reveal much about their personalities as well as their feelings for each other. In your group, choose one of these conversations and rewrite it as a script on a separate sheet of paper. A script requires that you add stage directions, so consider how movement can help your characters convey their personalities and their feelings about the topic at hand. The stage directions should also include suggestions about particular tones of voice and attitudes that the actors should convey as they perform their lines. Make sure you follow the proper format for a script.

Jot down some notes here first.

_____

_____

_____

_____

_____

_____

_____

_____

_____

_____

_____

_____

_____

_____

_____

_____

_____

_____

_____

_____

_____

_____

_____

Research and Report

Interview

Assignment When St. John proposes a new path in life for Jane, she raises a number of objections, but St. John has an answer ready for each protest she makes. Being able to anticipate and address objections can help you in certain situations. Choose one of the following two situations and write out a mock interview in which you address potential protests or objections that might be brought up by your interviewer.

Option 1: You are eager to be hired for a particular job. You are generally well qualified, but there are certain weaknesses in your background.

Option 2: You are asking a parent or another adult to give you permission to do something special. That person needs to be sure you will behave responsibly and safely.

Prepare Once you have chosen your interview topic, write a list of relevant questions that the interviewer might ask you. Phrase these questions in mature, sensitive, respectful language. Your questions should reflect your understanding of the situation.

Interview Now, give your interview questions to a classmate. Have them ask you these questions and jot down your responses. At the end of the mock interview, ask your interviewer if you successfully convinced them that you were a strong job candidate or that you were responsible enough to gain permission to do something special, depending on the situation you chose.

Report Summarize the interview questions and your classmates' notes on your responses in a written report. If needed, extend some of your responses to fully address the objections or concerns that the "interviewer" raised. Follow a logical organization, and make sure that you use correct grammar and punctuation.

Evaluate Have the classmate who helped you conduct this mock interview read your report and evaluate how accurate it is and how convincing your arguments are.

Connect to the Literature

Have you ever heard the expression "What goes around comes around"? What does this mean? Do you subscribe to this idea? Explain.

Share Ideas with a Partner

Sometimes, a person does something bad or good. Then, later, something equally bad or good, but unrelated, happens to that person. The second event is not a result of the first, but people may view the two events as related. With a partner think of one or more examples of this phenomenon of "cosmic justice" from books, movies, television, daily life, or your imagination.

Build Background

Charlotte Brontë: Feminist?

In an early scene in the novel, Jane, just after arriving at Thornfield, reflects on her prospects in life as a woman:

> Women are supposed to be very calm generally: but women feel just as men feel; they need exercise for their faculties, and a field for their efforts as much as their brothers do; . . . and it is narrow-minded in their more privileged fellow-creatures to say that they ought to confine themselves to making pudding and knitting stockings, to playing on the piano and embroidering bags. It is thoughtless to condemn them, or laugh at them, if they seek to do more or learn more than custom has pronounced necessary for their sex.

In Brontë's day, some women were speaking out for education, voting rights, and better employment opportunities for women. While Brontë was not among these so-called "Strong-Minded Women," this statement by her main character indicates that Brontë was concerned about the status of women in her society. As you finish reading the novel, think about the outcome of the story. Has Jane fulfilled her vision of the future, as described in Chapter 12? Would you describe Charlotte Brontë as a realist or an idealist about women's roles in society?

NOVEL NOTEBOOK
Keep a special notebook to record entries about the novels that you read this year.

SUMMARIZE
Summarize in one sentence the most important idea(s) in Build Background.

_____
_____
_____
_____
_____
_____
_____
_____
_____
_____
_____
_____
_____
_____
_____
_____
_____
_____
_____
_____
_____
_____
_____
_____
_____
_____
_____
_____
_____
_____
_____

Set Purposes for Reading

▶ **BIG Idea** **Journeys**

What marks the end of a journey? Is it the moment of physically arriving in a place, the recognition that the journey has changed you in some way, or the start of another new journey?

In some senses, Jane's journey to find herself comes to an end in this section. In others, a new journey is just beginning. As you read, ask yourself what these journeys have taught Jane about herself and about the world around her.

Literary Element | Motif

A **motif** is a significant word, phrase, image description, idea, or other element that is repeated throughout a literary work and is related to the theme. Common motifs in hero stories include good and evil, light and dark, and awareness and deception.

Authors include motifs to illuminate the theme of a text. In Jane Eyre, Brontë weaves multiple motifs through her novel. The most prominent of these are the journey, light and dark, and death and rebirth.

As you read, notice how and when these motifs appear in the text. What do they reveal about the characters and the situations in which they find themselves? Use the graphic organizer on the next page to record examples of the light-and-dark motif.

Reading Strategy | Make Inferences About Theme

The **theme** of a piece of literature is a dominant idea—often a universal message about life—that the writer communicates to the reader. A work may have more than one theme. Because the author will not usually explicitly state a theme, you must **make inferences about theme** based on textual details.

Archetypal themes or universal themes, exist for different kinds of texts. In romance texts, themes such as "love will conquer all" appear frequently.

As you finish Jane Eyre, pay particular attention to the details of Rochester and Jane's new relationship. Based on these details, identify which themes Brontë wanted to present to her readers. Are any of these archetypal themes? You may find it helpful to use a graphic organizer like the one at the right.

Vocabulary

countenance [koun′ tə nəns]
n. face; expression
Though she claimed to be brave, her countenance revealed that she was indeed afraid.

desolate [des′ ə lit]
adj. alone and apart
The desolate town was located in the middle of a desert; the closest grocery store was 20 miles away.

lachrymose [lak′ rə mōs′]
adj. tearful
The boy was lachrymose for quite a while after his dog died.

relapse [rē′ laps]
v. to fall back to an earlier state
After contracting the flu at work, she was determined not to have a relapse; she washed her hands obsessively.

vainly [vān′ lē]
adv. without success
The pilot tried vainly to avoid the storm; he ended up having to fly right through it.

Detail	Inference About Theme

Though Brontë weaves the motif of light and dark through her entire novel, these images are especially prominent in Chapters 36–38. As you read, look for these references to light and dark. Then record these references on the graphic organizer below.

Light	Dark

Literary Element

Motif What references to light and dark can you find in these excerpts?

_____
_____
_____
_____
_____
_____
_____
_____
_____
_____
_____
_____
_____
_____
_____
_____
_____
_____
_____
_____
_____
_____
_____
_____
_____
_____
_____
_____
_____
_____
_____
_____

NOVEL EXCERPT: CHAPTER 37

. . . Even when within a very short distance of the manor-house, you could see nothing of it; so thick and dark grew the timber of the gloomy wood about it. Iron gates between granite pillars showed me where to enter, and passing through them, I found myself at once in the twilight of close-ranked trees. There was a grass-grown track descending the forest aisle, between hoar and knotty shafts and under branched arches. I followed it, expecting soon to reach the dwelling; but it stretched on and on, it wound far and farther: no sign of habitation or grounds was visible.

I thought I had taken a wrong direction and lost my way. The darkness of natural as well as of sylvan dusk gathered over me. I looked round in search of another road. There was none: all was interwoven stem, columnar trunk, dense, summer foliage—no opening anywhere.

I proceeded: at last my way opened, the trees thinned a little; presently I beheld a railing, then the house—scarce, by this dim light, distinguishable from the trees; so dank and green were its decaying walls. Entering a portal, fastened only by a latch, I stood amidst a space of enclosed ground, from which the wood swept away in a semicircle. There were no flowers, no garden-beds; only a broad gravel-walk girdling a grass-plat, and this set in the heavy frame of the forest. The house presented two pointed gables in its front: the windows were latticed and narrow: the front-door was narrow too, one step led up to it. The whole looked, as the host of Rochester Arms had said, "quite a desolate spot." It was as still as a church on a weekday: the pattering rain on the forest leaves was the only sound audible in its vicinage.

"Can there be life here?" I asked.

Yes: life of some kind there was; for I heard a movement—that narrow front-door was unclosing, and some shape was about to issue from the grange.

It opened slowly; a figure came out into the twilight and stood on the step; a man without a hat: he stretched forth his hand as if to feel whether it rained. Dusk as it was, I had recognised him—it was my master, Edward Fairfax Rochester, and no other.

I stayed my step, almost my breath, and stood to watch him—to examine him, myself unseen, and alas! to him invisible. . . .

NOVEL EXCERPT: CHAPTER 37

Very early the next morning, I heard him up and astir, wandering from one room to another. As soon as Mary came down I heard the question: "Is Miss Eyre here?" Then: "Which room did you put here into? Was it dry? Is she up? Go and ask if she wants anything; and when she will come down."

I came down as soon as I thought there was a prospect of breakfast. Entering the room very softly, I had a view of him before he discovered my presence. It was mournful, indeed, to witness the subjugation of that vigorous spirit to a corporeal infirmity. He sat in his chair,—still, but not at rest: expectant evidently; the lines of now habitual sadness marking his strong features. His countenance reminded one of a lamp quenched, waiting to be relit—and alas! it was not himself that could now kindle the lustre of animated expression: he was dependent on another for that office! I had meant to be gay and careless, but the powerlessness of the strong man touched my heart to the quick: still I accosted him with what vivacity I could:—

"It is a bright, sunny morning, sir," I said. "The rain is over and gone, and there is a tender shining after it: you shall have a walk soon."

I had wakened the glow: his features beamed.

"Oh, you are indeed there, my skylark! Come to me. You are not gone: not vanished? I heard one of your kind an hour ago, singing high over the wood: but its song had no music for me, any more than the rising sun had rays. All the melody on earth is concentrated in my Jane's tongue to my ear (I am glad it is not naturally a silent one): all the sunshine I can feel is in her presence."

The water stood in my eyes to hear this avowal of his dependence: just as if a royal eagle, chained to a perch, should be forced to entreat a sparrow to become its purveyor. But I would not be lachrymose: I dashed off the salt drops, and busied myself with preparing breakfast.

Most of the morning was spent in the open air. I led him out of the wet and wild wood into some cheerful fields: I described to him how brilliantly green they were; how the flowers and hedges looked refreshed; how sparklingly blue was the sky. I sought a seat for him in a hidden and lovely spot: a dry stump of a tree; nor did I refuse to let him, when seated, place me on his knee: why should I, when both he and I were happier near than apart? Pilot lay beside us: all was quiet. He broke out suddenly while clasping me in his arms:—

Literary Element

Motif What does Brontë's use of the light versus dark motif reveal about the characters' situations?

_____

_____

_____

_____

_____

_____

_____

_____

_____

_____

_____

_____

_____

_____

_____

_____

_____

_____

_____

_____

_____

_____

_____

_____

_____

_____

_____

Reading Strategy

Make Inferences About Theme In this passage, Rochester refers to "divine justice." What does he mean, and what theme might this reveal?

_____

_____

_____

_____

_____

_____

_____

_____

_____

_____

_____

_____

_____

_____

_____

_____

_____

_____

_____

_____

_____

_____

_____

_____

_____

_____

_____

NOVEL EXCERPT: CHAPTER 38

"Jane! you think me, I daresay, an irreligious dog: but my heart swells with gratitude to the beneficent God of this earth just now. He sees not as man sees, but far clearer: judges not as man judges, but far more wisely. I did wrong: I would have sullied my innocent flower—breathed guilt on its purity: the Omnipotent snatched it from me. I, in my stiff-necked rebellion, almost cursed the dispensation: instead of bending to the decree, I defied it. Divine justice pursued its course; disasters came thick on me: I was forced to pass through the valley of the shadow of death. *His* chastisements are mighty; and one smote me which has humbled me for ever. You know I was proud of my strength: but what is it now, when I must give it over to foreign guidance, as a child does its weakness? Of late, Jane—only—only of late—I began to see and acknowledge the hand of God in my doom. I began to experience remorse, repentance; the wish for reconcilement to my Maker. I began sometimes to pray: very brief prayers they were, but very sincere.

"Some days since: nay, I can number them—four; it was last Monday night, a singular mood came over me: one in which grief replaced frenzy—sorrow, sullenness. I had long had the impression that since I could nowhere find you, you must be dead. Late that night—perhaps it might be between eleven and twelve o'clock—ere I retired to my dreary rest, I supplicated God, that, if it seemed good to Him, I might soon be taken from this life, and admitted to that world to come, where there was still hope of rejoining Jane.

"I was in my own room, and sitting by the window, which was open: it soothed me to feel the balmy night-air; though I could see no stars, and only by a vague, luminous haze, knew the presence of a moon. I longed for thee, Janet! Oh, I longed for thee both with soul and flesh! I asked of God, at once in anguish and humility, if I had not been long enough desolate, afflicted, tormented; and might not soon taste bliss and peace once more. That I merited all I endured, I acknowledged—that I could scarcely endure more, I pleaded; and the alpha and omega of my heart's wishes broke involuntarily from my lips in the words—'Jane! Jane! Jane!'"

"Did you speak these words aloud?"

"I did, Jane. If any listener had heard me, he would have thought me mad: I pronounced them with such frantic energy."

"And it was last Monday night: somewhere near midnight?"

"Yes; but the time is of no consequence: what followed is the strange point. You will think me superstitious,—some superstition I have in my blood, and always had: nevertheless, this is true—true at least it is that I heard what I now relate.

"As I exclaimed 'Jane! Jane! Jane!' a voice—I cannot tell whence the voice came, but I know whose voice it was—replied, 'I am coming: wait for me;' and a moment after went whispering on the wind, the words—'Where are you?'

"I'll tell you, if I can, the idea, the picture these words opened to my mind: yet it is difficult to express what I want to express. Ferndean is buried, as you see, in a heavy wood, where sound falls dull, and dies unreverberating. 'Where are you?' seemed spoken amongst mountains; for I heard a hill-sent echo repeat the words. Cooler and fresher at the moment the gale seemed to visit my brow. I could have deemed that in some wild, lone scene, I and Jane were meeting. In spirit, I believe we must have met. You no doubt were, at that hour, in unconscious sleep, Jane: perhaps your soul wandered from its cell to comfort mine; for those were your accents—as certain as I live—they were yours!"

Reader, it was on Monday night—near midnight—that I too had received the mysterious summons: those were the very words by which I replied to it. I listened to Mr. Rochester's narrative; but made no disclosure in return. The coincidence struck me as too awful and inexplicable to be communicated or discussed. If I told anything, my tale would be such as must necessarily make a profound impression on the mind of my hearer: and that mind, yet from its sufferings too prone to gloom, needed not the deeper shade of the supernatural. I kept these things then, and pondered them in my heart.

"You cannot now wonder," continued my master, "that when you rose upon me so unexpectedly last night, I had difficulty in believing you any other than a mere voice and vision: something that would melt to silence and annihilation, as the midnight whisper and mountain echo had melted before. Now, I thank God! I knew it to be otherwise. Yes, I thank God!"

He put me off his knee, rose, and reverently lifting his hat from his brow, and bending his sightless eyes to the earth, he stood in mute devotion. Only the last words of the worship were audible.

"I thank my Maker, that in the midst of judgment he has remembered mercy. I humbly entreat my Redeemer to give me strength to lead henceforth a purer life than I have done hitherto!"

Then he stretched his hand out to be led. I took that dear hand, held it a moment to my lips, then let it pass round my shoulder: being so much lower of stature than he, I served both for his prop and guide. We entered the wood, and wended homeward.

Reading Strategy

Make Inferences About Theme What theme about love might Brontë be communicating in this passage?

_____
_____
_____
_____
_____
_____
_____
_____
_____
_____
_____
_____
_____
_____
_____
_____
_____
_____
_____
_____
_____
_____
_____
_____
_____
_____
_____
_____
_____
_____

► BIG Idea

Journeys What have you learned about the purpose of Jane's journeys?

Mark up the excerpt, looking for evidence of how it expresses the Big Idea.

NOVEL EXCERPT: CHAPTER 38

My tale draws to its close: one word respecting my experience of married life, and one brief glance at the fortunes of those whose names have most frequently recurred in this narrative, and I have done.

I have now been married ten years. I know what it is to live entirely for and with what I love best on earth. I hold myself supremely blest—blest beyond what language can express; because I am my husband's life as fully as he is mine. No woman was ever nearer to her mate than I am: ever more absolutely bone of his bone, and flesh of his flesh. I know no weariness of my Edward's society: he knows none of mine, any more than we each do of the pulsation of the heart that beats in our separate bosoms; consequently, we are ever together. To be together is for us to be at once as free as in solitude, as gay as in company. We talk, I believe, all day long: to talk to each other is but a more animated and an audible thinking. All my confidence is bestowed on him, all his confidence is devoted to me; we are precisely suited in character—perfect concord is the result.

Mr. Rochester continued blind the first two years of our union: perhaps it was that circumstance that drew us so very near—that knit us so very close! for I was then his vision, as I am still his right hand. Literally, I was (what he often called me) the apple of his eye. He saw nature—he saw books through me; and never did I weary of gazing for his behalf, and of putting into words the effect of field, tree, town, river, cloud, sunbeam— of the landscape before us; of the weather round us—and impressing by sound on his ear what light could no longer stamp on his eye. Never did I weary of reading to him; never did I weary of conducting him where he wished to go: of doing for him what he wished to be done. And there was a pleasure in my services, most full, most exquisite, even though sad— because he claimed these services without painful shame or damping humiliation. He loved me so truly, that he knew no reluctance in profiting by my attendance: he felt that I loved him so fondly, that to yield that attendance was to indulge my sweetest wishes.

One morning at the end of the two years, as I was writing a letter to his dictation, he came and bent over me, and said—

"Jane, have you a glittering ornament round your neck?"

I had a gold watch-chain: I answered "Yes."

"And have you a pale blue dress on?"

I had. He informed me then, that for some time he had fancied the obscurity clouding one eye was becoming less dense; and that now he was sure of it.

Use the Cornell Note-Taking system to take notes on the excerpt at the left. Record your notes, Reduce them, and then Recap (summarize) them.

Record

_____
_____
_____
_____
_____
_____
_____
_____
_____
_____
_____
_____
_____
_____
_____
_____
_____
_____
_____
_____
_____
_____
_____
_____
_____
_____
_____

Recap

_____
_____
_____
_____
_____
_____

Reduce

Try the following approach as you reduce your notes.

MY VIEW
Comment on what you learned from your own notes.

_____
_____
_____
_____
_____
_____
_____
_____
_____
_____
_____
_____
_____
_____
_____
_____
_____
_____
_____
_____
_____
_____
_____

Respond and Think Critically

1. How does Rochester say he felt in Jane's absence? What spiritual change has occurred in Rochester? [Paraphrase]

_____

_____

_____

_____

2. Do Jane and Rochester still feel the same way about one another? Explain. [Interpret]

_____

_____

_____

_____

3. In what way have the roles in Jane and Rochester's relationship been reversed? [Analyze]

_____

_____

_____

_____

4. Do you think the story has a fairy-tale ending? Or is the situation at the end ironic? (**Situational irony** refers to a strong or surprising contrast between what is expected to happen and what actually happens.) [Evaluate]

_____

_____

_____

_____

5. Journeys At the conclusion of the novel, at what point does Jane reveal that her journey has been successful, that she has found a situation in which she could be true to herself? [Identify]

_____

_____

_____

_____

_____

APPLY BACKGROUND
Reread Build Background on page 283. How did that information help you understand or appreciate what you read in the novel?

_____

_____

_____

_____

_____

_____

_____

_____

_____

_____

_____

_____

_____

_____

_____

_____

_____

_____

_____

_____

_____

_____

_____

_____

_____

_____

_____

_____

_____

_____

_____

Literary Element Motif

In what way does Rochester's new ability to see, even faintly, extend the motif of light and dark that Brontë established? [Analyze]

_____

_____

_____

_____

_____

_____

_____

_____

_____

_____

_____

Reading Strategy Make Inferences About Theme

Why do you think Jane chooses not to tell Rochester that she too heard his voice at Marsh End the same night that he heard hers? [Infer]

_____

_____

_____

_____

_____

_____

_____

_____

_____

_____

Vocabulary Practice

Write the vocabulary word that correctly completes each sentence. If none of the words fits the sentence, write "none."

countenance	relapse
desolate	vainly
lachrymose	

1. When her older sister left for college, she tried hard not to be _____, but it was no use. The tears came anyway.

2. I could tell, just by looking at his _____, that he was thankful for the help I had given him.

3. After hearing that he had won the _____, the governor was ecstatic.

4. The architect tried _____ to convince the city planning commision to allow him to build an apartment complex in the already-crowded town.

5. The circus performers tried _____ to find more audience members; the next three performances were sold-out as a result.

6. In order to prevent a _____, the recovering alcoholic knew that he would have to avoid places where alcohol was served.

7. The _____ island had not been habitated by humans for many years.

Academic Vocabulary

When Jane **resolves** to attend to Rochester's every need for the rest of their lives, the reader might initially be surprised that she is sacrificing herself and her abilities. Using context clues, try to figure out the meaning of the word _resolve_ in the sentence above. Write your guess below. Then check it in a dictionary.

_____

_____

_____

_____

_____

_____

_____

Writing

Personal Response Did you find the ending of the novel satisfying? Why or why not?

_____

_____

_____

_____

_____

_____

_____

_____

_____

_____

_____

_____

_____

_____

_____

_____

_____

_____

_____

_____

_____

_____

_____

_____

_____

_____

_____

_____

_____

_____

Speaking and Listening

Performance

Assignment In Chapter 24, Rochester sings a love ballad for Jane. Love songs, both happy and tragic, have been popular for centuries. Compose a song that tells the story of Jane and Rochester's love.

Prepare Select a tune you know or make up one of your own. Before you begin writing, take a moment to think about the style and scope of your song. Will it be folk, rock, rap, country-western, or some other style? Will you tell the whole story or focus on one incident or section of the novel?

Perform Present your song to the class. If you feel uncomfortable, either ask a friend to sing the song for you or speak the lyrics along with a music recording. Be sure that you sing or speak clearly enough so that everyone can understand the lyrics.

Evaluate After performing your song, critique yourself. Were the listeners able to identify what scene or situations you were singing about? Did you convey the complexity of Jane and Rochester's relationship? Did your song have a good melody, and did the words flow smoothly?

Jane Eyre

The following questions refer to the Related Readings in Glencoe's *Literature Library* edition of this novel. Support your answers with details from the text. Write your answers on a separate sheet of paper, but jot down some notes first on the lines provided.

Sonnet 116; Wedding Day in the Rockies
William Shakespeare; E.B. White

How would you compare and contrast the feelings expressed in theses two poems with the feelings that Jane and Rochester have for each other?

_____

_____

_____

_____

from Wide Sargasso Sea
Jean Rhys

Consider Bertha's description of the events surrounding the Thornfield fire in light of Brontë's description of the same events in *Jane Eyre*. Does having a different perspective change your attitude about any of the characters involved in the tragedy? Explain.

_____

_____

_____

_____

from A Stranger in a Strange Land
Juliet Barker

How do you think life in and around Haworth influenced the themes that Charlotte Brontë developed in *Jane Eyre*? Use information from this selection as well as descriptions and events from the novel to explain your answer.

_____

_____

_____

_____

Signs and Symbols
Vladimir Nabokov

In portraying the wife in his story, Nabokov says that "after all living did mean accepting the loss of one joy after another, not even joys in her case—mere possibilities of improvement." Relate this statement to one of the characters in *Jane Eyre*. Using examples from the novel, explain how the quotation describes the character you have chosen.

_____

_____

_____

_____

from The Life of Charlotte Brontë
Elizabeth Gaskell

What descriptions of Charlotte and her experiences at Roe Head correspond to Jane Eyre and her experiences at Lowood?

_____

_____

_____

_____

LITERATURE EXCERPT: The Odyssey

20   "Now!
You think you'll shuffle off and get away
after that impudence? Oh, no you don't!"
The stool he let fly hit the man's right
    shoulder
on the packed muscle under the shoulder
    blade—

25 like solid rock, for all the effect one saw.
thoughts of bloody work,° as he walked
    on,
then sat, and dropped his loaded bag again
upon the door sill. Facing the whole crowd

30 he said, and eyed them all:
                            "One word only,
my lords, and suitors of the famous queen.
One thing I have to say.
There is no pain, no burden for the heart

35 when blows come to a man, and he
    defending
his own cattle—his own cows and lambs.
Here it was otherwise. Antinous
hit me for being driven on by hunger—
how many bitter seas men cross for
    hunger!

40 If beggars interest the gods, if there are
    Furies
pent in the dark to avenge a poor man's
    wrong, then may
Antinous meet his death before his
    wedding day!"°
Then said Eupeithes'° son, Antinous:
                              "Enough.

45 Eat and be quiet where you are, or
    shamble elsewhere,
unless you want these lads to stop your
    mouth
pulling you by the heels, or hands and feet,
over the whole floor, till your back is
    peeled!"
But now the rest were mortified,° and
    someone

50 spoke from the crowd of young bucks to
    rebuke[5] him:
"A poor show, that—hitting this famished
    tramp—
bad business, if he happened to be a god.
You know they go in foreign guise, the
    gods do,
looking like strangers, turning up

55 in towns and settlements to keep an eye
on manners, good or bad."
                         But at this notion
Antinous only shrugged.
                           Telemachus,

60 after the blow his father bore, sat still
without a tear, though his heart felt the
    blow.
Slowly he shook his head from side to side,
containing murderous thoughts.
                           Penelope

65 on the higher level of her room had heard
the blow, and knew who gave it. Now she
    murmured:
"Would god you could be hit yourself,
    Antinous—
hit by Apollo's bowshot!"°

26–27 *containing thoughts of bloody work:* keeping murderous thoughts
under control. Odysseus imagines killing Antinous, but holds his
temper.

34–42 *There is . . . wedding day:* A man is not really hurt, the beggar says,
when he is injured defending his property; but when he is attacked
by being hungry, that's another matter. Odysseus's curse upon
Antinous calls upon the Furies—three female spirits who punish
wrongdoers—to bring about his death.

43 *Eupeithes* (yoo pē thēz)

49 *mortified:* deeply embarrassed, shamed, or humiliated.

50 *rebuke:* to scold sharply; criticize

68 *Apollo's bowshot:* Among other things, Apollo is the archer god
and the god of truth. His sacred silver bow can kill literally with an
arrow and figuratively with the truth.

Compare the novel you have just read to the literature selection at the left, which is excerpted from *The Odyssey* by Homer in *Glencoe Literature*. Then answer the questions below.

Compare & Contrast

1. Plot Archetype In this passage, a number of characters foreshadow Antinous' ultimate fate. As the reader, you know that within a hero myth, those who commit evil deeds or who upset the gods are usually punished. In *Jane Eyre*, Rochester and Jane both evoke God and religion frequently and understand the consequences of making the wrong decisions. How does the idea of divine supernatural, consequence play out in each literary work?

_____

_____

_____

_____

_____

_____

2. Character Archetype Which character archetype does Antinous reflect in this passage, and which character in *Jane Eyre* also fulfills this archetype?

_____

_____

_____

_____

_____

_____

3. Conflict Is the major conflict in this passage an external or internal conflict? Are the primary conflicts in *Jane Eyre* internal or external?

_____

_____

_____

_____

_____

_____

_____

TALK ABOUT IT

The Odyssey is an archetypal hero journey, and Odysseus is clearly presented as an archetypal hero. In your opinion, is Jane an archetypal hero, and could Jane's journeys follow the path of the archetypal hero's journey? Support your responses with evidence from the text.

Jot down some notes here first.

_____

_____

_____

_____

_____

_____

_____

_____

_____

_____

_____

_____

_____

_____

_____

_____

_____

_____

_____

_____

_____

_____

_____

_____

_____

_____

_____

Expository Essay

Analyze Cause-and-Effect Relationships The plot of *Jane Eyre* is moved along by a series of cause-and-effect relationships. These relationships involve not only interactions between characters but also the idea of cosmic justice—the belief that a divine power will reward individuals for good actions and will punish them for bad. Write an essay in which you analyze a cause-and-effect chain in this story and explain what it suggests about the role of cosmic justice. Use evidence from the text to support the thesis of your essay.

Prewrite To help you organize your essay, fill out a graphic organizer like the one below. Add as many rows as you need.

Cause	I have been married, and the woman to whom I was married lives.
Effect	Jane Eyre, who had been an ardent, expectant woman — almost a bride — was a cold, solitary girl again...
Effect	My daughter, flee temptation!...Mother, I will
Effect	My name is Jane Elliot.

Draft Using the cause-and-effect relationships established in your chart, determine how each one supports your thesis. You may want to use sentence frames as you draft your essay. For instance, your body paragraphs will contain statements that support your thesis, such as the following:

The scene in which _____ shows that _____ was the cause of _____ and _____.

Revise Ask a classmate to underline your thesis statement and highlight two sentences that support your thesis. If this proves difficult, you may need to make your thesis and supporting points clearer. You may even wish to include all or part of your cause-and-effect chart in your essay as a visual aid.

Edit and Proofread Edit your writing so that it expresses your thoughts effectively and is well organized. Carefully proofread for grammar, punctuation, and spelling errors.

UNDERSTAND THE TASK

- When you **analyze**, you identify the parts to find meaning in their relationships to the whole.

- A **thesis** is the main idea of a work of nonfiction, such as an essay. The thesis may be stated directly or implied.

Grammar Tip

Semicolons
Semicolons are used to connect closely related ideas. For this purpose, they are used in two specific situations. First, semicolons are used to separate main clauses that are not joined by a coordinating conjunction such as *and* or *or*:

There were two speakers at Gettysburg that day; only Lincoln's speech is remembered.

Semicolons may also be used to separate main clauses joined by a conjunctive adverb or by *for example* or *that is*:

Because of the ice storm, most students could not get to school; consequently, the principal canceled all classes for the day.

Animal Farm

George Orwell

Animal Farm

George Orwell

❝*Animal Farm is written on many levels. It is already a children's story in its own right. . . . [It] is also a lament for the fate of revolutions and the hopes contained in them. It is a moving comment on man's constant compromise with the truth.*❞

—*John Atkins,* **George Orwell**

On the publication of *Animal Farm* in 1945, George Orwell discovered with horror that booksellers were placing his novel on children's shelves. According to his housekeeper, he began traveling from bookstore to bookstore requesting that the book be shelved with adult works. This dual identity—as children's story and adult satire—has stayed with Orwell's novel for more than fifty years.

Animal Farm tells the story of Farmer Jones's animals who rise up in rebellion and take over the farm. Tired of being exploited solely for human gain, the animals—who have human characteristics such as the power of speech—vow to create a new and more just society.

Though the novel reads like a fairy tale, and Orwell subtitles it as just that, it is also a satire containing a message about world politics and especially the former Soviet Union in particular. Since the Bolshevik revolutions of the early 1900s, the former Soviet Union had captured the attention of the world with its socialist experiment. Stalin's form of government had some supporters in Britain and the United States, but Orwell was against this system.

Satire In a **satire,** the writer attacks a serious issue by presenting it in a ridiculous light or otherwise poking fun at it. Orwell uses satire to expose what he saw as the myth of Soviet socialism. Thus, the novel tells a story that people of all ages can understand, but it also tells us a second story—that of the real-life Revolution. Many critics have matched in great detail the story's characters to historical persons— for example, linking the power struggle between Napoleon and Snowball to the historical feuding between Joseph Stalin and Leon Trotsky for control of the Soviet Union. Critics also believe that Old Major represents Karl Marx, who dies before realizing his dream. Other comparisons include Moses as the Russian Orthodox church, Boxer and Clover as workers, the sheep as the general public, Squealer as Stalin's government news agency, the dogs as Stalin's military police, and Farmer Jones as Czar Nicholas II. The farm's neighbors, Pilkington and Frederick, are said to represent Great Britain and Germany, while Mollie suggests the old Russian aristocracy, which resists change.

A tremendous success when published, *Animal Farm* has since become part of school curriculums and popular literary culture. Readers and critics alike have enjoyed its imaginative premise and the engaging charm of its animal characters. Orwell's straightforward language draws readers into the farm's world, while the witty underlying satire invites serious analysis. In *George Orwell: A Personal Memoir*, T. R. Fyvel writes:

[Orwell] *turned the domestic animals on the farm into immediately recognizable and memorable and sometimes lovable characters.*

Animal Farm is more than a fairy tale. It is a commentary on the the relevance of independent thought, truth, and justice.

The Allegorical Novel An **allegory** is a narrative that can be read on more than one level. Critics often consider *Animal Farm* to be an allegory of the Russian Revolution. In the early 1900s, Russia's Czar Nicholas II faced an increasingly discontented populace. Freed from feudal serfdom in 1861, many Russian peasants were struggling to survive under an oppressive government. By 1917, amidst the tremendous suffering of World War I, a revolution began. In two major battles, the Czar's government was overthrown and replaced by the Bolshevik leadership of Vladmir Lenin. When Lenin died in 1924, his former colleagues Leon Trotsky, hero of the early Revolution, and Joseph Stalin, head of the Communist Party, struggled for power. Stalin won the battle, and he deported Trotsky into permanent exile.

Once in power, Stalin began, with despotic urgency and exalted nationalism, to move the Soviet Union into the modern industrial age. His government seized land in order to create collective farms. Stalin's Five Year Plan was an attempt to modernize Soviet industry. To counter resistance (many peasants refused to give up their land), Stalin used vicious military tactics. Rigged trials led to executions of an estimated 20 million government officials and ordinary citizens. The government controlled the flow and content of information to the people, and all but outlawed churches.

Individualism vs. Socialism

Orwell initially struggled to find a publisher for Animal Farm. Many liberal intellectuals in Europe admired the Soviet experiment with socialism. They believed socialism would produce a society in which everyone—workers and employers—was equal, and in which there were no upper, middle, or lower classes. In Orwell's words "they want[ed] to believe that, somewhere, a really Socialist country does actually exist."

Also, British publishers were hesitant to publicly criticize their Soviet allies as World War II came to a close. The book was published in 1945, after Germany surrendered.

Orwell believed that the basis for society was human decency and common sense, which conflicted with the ideals for society that were prevalent at the time: socialism, capitalism, communism, and fascism, to name a few. As an individualist who believed that his own experiences should guide his philosophy, he was often at odds with these popular ideas. He believed that governments were encroaching on the individual's freedom of choice, love of family, and tolerance for others. He emphasized honesty, individuality, and the welfare of society throughout his writings.

George Orwell *(1903–1950)*

> **❝***Liberty is telling people what they do not want to hear.***❞**
>
> —*George Orwell*

In the years since the publication of *Animal Farm* and *1984*, both of which conjure visions of modern government's dangerous power, critics have studied and analyzed George Orwell's personal life. Orwell was a man who had a reputation for standing apart and even making a virtue of his detachment. This "outsider" position often led him to oppose the crowd.

Orwell began life as Eric Arthur Blair (George Orwell was a pen name he adopted later for its "manly, English, country-sounding ring.") He spent his early years in India as a lonely boy who liked to make up stories and talk with imaginary companions. He began to "write" before he even knew how, dictating poems to his mother, and perhaps saw this outlet as an alternative to the human relationships he found so difficult. Refuge in words and ideas became increasingly important when Orwell's parents sent him, at age eight, to boarding school in England.

Political Views Later, instead of going on to university, he decided to take a job in Burma with the Indian Imperial Police. Orwell wrote about this experience in *Burmese Days* (1934) and in the essay "Shooting an Elephant." At odds with British colonial rule, Orwell said he "theoretically—and secretly, of course . . . was all for the Burmese and all against their oppressors, the British."

Returning to England to recover from a bout of the chronic lung illness that plagued him all his life, Orwell began his writing career in earnest. Over the next two decades, he wrote newspaper columns, novels, essays, and radio broadcasts, most of which grew out of his own personal experience.

Orwell's beliefs about politics were affected by his experiences fighting in the Spanish Civil War. He viewed socialists, communists, and fascists as repressive and self-serving. Orwell patriotically supported England during World War II, but remained skeptical of governments and their willingness to forsake ideals in favor of power.

The Author's Vision With each book or essay, Orwell solidified his role as the outsider willing to question any group's ideology. Orwell spoke his mind with *Animal Farm*, in which he criticized the Soviet Union despite its role as a World War II ally of Great Britain. At first, no one would publish the novel, but when *Animal Farm* finally appeared in 1945 it was a success. It was later adapted both as an animated film and as a play.

In explaining how he came to write *Animal Farm*, Orwell says he once saw a little boy whipping a horse:

It struck me that if only such animals became aware of their strength we should have no power over them, and that men exploit animals in much the same way as the rich exploit the [worker].

Orwell said it was the first book in which he consciously tried to blend artistic and political goals. Orwell's final novel, *1984*, continued that effort with a grim portrayal of a world totally under government control.

Orwell pursued his writing career faithfully, although it was not always easy. In his final days he made the statement, "Writing . . . is a horrible, exhausting struggle . . . One would never undertake such a thing if one were not driven . . ."

Connect to the Literature

Why do you think revolutions occur? What circumstances would lead people to overthrow the daily political and economical structure of their lives?

Make a List

With a partner, identify two or three revolutions that occurred more than ten years ago. What circumstances, if any, do these revolutions have in common? What sorts of goals were the revolutionaries seeking to accomplish? In retrospect were the revolutions successful?

Build Background

Karl Marx and the Soviet Revolution

Many of the ideals behind the Soviet revolution were based on the writings and teachings of Karl Marx. A German intellectual who lived in the mid-1800s, Marx believed that societies are divided into two segments, a working class and an owner class. The working class creates all the products, while the owner class enjoys all the benefits of these products. This class division leads to inequality and oppression of the working class. Marx's objective was to create a classless society in which the work is shared by all for the benefit of all, and he believed revolution was the way to achieve this goal.

In leading workers toward revolution, Marx used slogans like "From each according to his abilities, to each according to his needs." He also urged people to give up their religion, which he believed gave them false hope for a better life in heaven. The character of Old Major in *Animal Farm* is sometimes interpreted as a representation of Karl Marx. Major's speech in the novel's opening chapter reflects many Marxist ideas, from the opening "Comrades," a typical form of address in the former Soviet Union, to the revolutionary song he teaches the other animals.

NOVEL NOTEBOOK
Keep a special notebook to record entries about the novels that you read this year.

WRITE THE CAPTION
Write a caption for the image below, using information in Build Background.

_____
_____
_____
_____
_____
_____
_____
_____
_____
_____
_____
_____
_____
_____
_____
_____
_____
_____
_____
_____
_____
_____
_____
_____
_____
_____
_____

Set Purposes for Reading

▶ **BIG Idea** Our World and Beyond

Have you ever considered what the world would be like if humans weren't in charge? Who would take over? What kind of government, if any, would they establish? What changes would they make, and what institutions would they want to maintain?

In *Animal Farm*, animals on a farm rebel against their owner and develop their own system of rule. As you read, consider what the animals' interactions reveal about the nature of leadership and government. Keep a list of opinions the author seems to be sharing about power (where does it come from? who deserves it?) and equality (can it exist?).

Literary Element   Allegory

An **allegory** is a literary work in which all or most of the characters, setting, and events stand for ideas, qualities or figures beyond themselves. An allegory is a kind of **fable**; a fable teaches a lesson, or **moral**, about human behavior.

Allegories are often written so that an author can share his or her opinion about a historical event or situation. **Historical allusions** are references to well-known characters, places or situations from history. In *Animal Farm*, Orwell makes allusions to the Russian Revolution and the individuals who were involved in and affected by the Revolution.

As you read, draw conclusions about which historical individuals each of the main characters stands for.

Reading Strategy   Evaluate Details

When you **evaluate details,** you look carefully at each element of plot, character, and setting, and ask why the author might have chosen those particular details.

Next, determine whether the author successfully used these details to develop believable characters, settings and action. This is particularly important when the author is describing an extraordinary situation, as Orwell does in *Animal Farm*.

As you read, ask yourself how the details that Orwell includes about his characters and situations help contribute to his message about government and leadership. You may find it helpful to use a graphic organizer like the one at right. The graphic organizer on the next page can also help you evaluate details about characters.

Vocabulary

cannibalism [kan´ə bə liz´əm]
n. practice of eating one's own kind
In the wild, some animals have to resort to cannibalism in order to survive.

cryptic [krip´tik]
adj. intended to be mysterious or obscure
The computer specialist was unable to decipher the cryptic program that had somehow found its way onto my computer.

gambol [gam´bəl]
v. to skip about in play
Kids like to gambol on the playground with their friends.

ignominious [ig´nə min´ē əs]
adj. shameful; dishonorable
After being defeated 10-1 in the finals, the soccer team made an ignominious retreat from the field.

indefatigable [in´di fat´ə gə bəl]
adj. untiring
After she happily shoveled snow for hours without a break, I was sure that she was indefatigable.

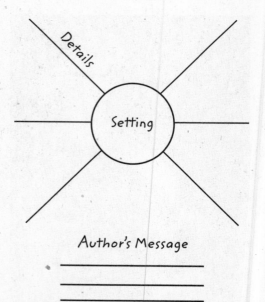

Details

Setting

Author's Message

_____
_____
_____

As you read, think about the purpose of each of Orwell's major characters. Complete the chart by noting details that describe each character and by drawing a conclusion about which individuals or groups within the Russian Revolution that character is supposed to represent.

Character	Characteristics, Actions, and Purpose	Historical Allusion
Old Major	gets the revolution started; inspires hope for real change	Karl Marx

Literary Element

Allegory The animals are initially resistant to the idea of a revolution. Do you think Snowball and Napoleon's justifications for why it has to take place are convincing? Would similar arguments work for humans considering revolution?

_____
_____
_____
_____
_____
_____
_____
_____
_____
_____
_____
_____
_____
_____
_____
_____
_____
_____
_____
_____
_____
_____
_____
_____
_____
_____
_____

NOVEL EXCERPT: CHAPTER 2

Three nights later old Major died peacefully in his sleep. His body was buried at the foot of the orchard.

This was early in March. During the next three months there was much secret activity. Major's speech had given to the more intelligent animals on the farm a completely new outlook on life. They did not know when the Rebellion predicted by Major would take place, they had no reason for thinking that it would be within their own lifetime, but they saw clearly that it was their duty to prepare for it. The work of teaching and organising the others fell naturally upon the pigs, who were generally recognised as being the cleverest of the animals. Pre-eminent among the pigs were two young boars named Snowball and Napoleon, whom Mr. Jones was breeding up for sale. Napoleon was a large, rather fierce-looking Berkshire boar, the only Berkshire on the farm, not much of a talker, but with a reputation for getting his own way. Snowball was a more vivacious pig than Napoleon, quicker in speech and more inventive, but was not considered to have the same depth of character. All the other male pigs on the farm were porkers. The best known among them was a small fat pig named Squealer, with very round cheeks, twinkling eyes, nimble movements, and a shrill voice. He was a brilliant talker, and when he was arguing some difficult point he had a way of skipping from side to side and whisking his tail which was somehow very persuasive. The others said of Squealer that he could turn black into white.

These three had elaborated old Major's teachings into a complete system of thought, to which they gave the name of Animalism. Several nights a week, after Mr. Jones was asleep, they held secret meetings in the barn and expounded the principles of Animalism to the others. At the beginning they met with much stupidity and apathy. Some of the animals talked of the duty of loyalty to Mr. Jones, whom they referred to as "Master," or made elementary remarks such as "Mr. Jones feeds us. If he were gone, we should starve to death." Others asked such questions as "Why should we care what happens after we are dead?" or "If this Rebellion is to happen anyway, what difference does it make whether we work for it or not?", and the pigs had great difficulty in making them see that this was contrary to the spirit of Animalism. The stupidest questions of all were asked by Mollie, the white mare. The very first question she asked Snowball was: "Will there still be sugar after the Rebellion?"

"No," said Snowball firmly. "We have no means of making sugar on this farm. Besides, you do not need sugar. You will have all the oats and hay you want."

"And shall I still be allowed to wear ribbons in my mane?" asked Mollie.

"Comrade," said Snowball, "those ribbons that you are so devoted to are the badge of slavery. Can you not understand that liberty is worth more than ribbons?"

Mollie agreed, but she did not sound very convinced.

The pigs had an even harder struggle to counteract the lies put about by Moses, the tame raven. Moses, who was Mr. Jones's especial pet, was a spy and a tale-bearer, but he was also a clever talker. He claimed to know of the existence of a mysterious country called Sugarcandy Mountain, to which all animals went when they died. It was situated somewhere up in the sky, a little distance beyond the clouds, Moses said. In Sugarcandy Mountain it was Sunday seven days a week, clover was in season all the year round, and lump sugar and linseed cake grew on the hedges. The animals hated Moses because he told tales and did no work, but some of them believed in Sugarcandy Mountain, and the pigs had to argue very hard to persuade them that there was no such place.

Their most faithful disciples were the two cart-horses, Boxer and Clover. These two had great difficulty in thinking anything out for themselves, but having once accepted the pigs as their teachers, they absorbed everything that they were told, and passed it on to the other animals by simple arguments. They were unfailing in their attendance at the secret meetings in the barn, and led the singing of *Beasts of England*, with which the meetings always ended. Now, as it turned out, the Rebellion was achieved much earlier and more easily than anyone had expected. In past years Mr. Jones, although a hard master, had been a capable farmer, but of late he had fallen on evil days. He had become much disheartened after losing money in a lawsuit, and had taken to drinking more than was good for him. For whole days at a time he would lounge in his Windsor chair in the kitchen, reading the newspapers, drinking, and occasionally feeding Moses on crusts of bread soaked in beer. His men were idle and dishonest, the fields were full of weeds, the buildings wanted roofing, the hedges were neglected, and the animals were underfed.

Literary Element

Allegory Why is this an appropriate time for the animals to take over Manor Farm? What does this tell you about what is necessary for a revolution to be successful?

_____

_____

_____

_____

_____

_____

_____

_____

_____

_____

_____

_____

_____

_____

_____

_____

_____

_____

_____

_____

_____

_____

_____

_____

_____

_____

_____

_____

_____

_____

Reading Strategy

Evaluate Details What details does Orwell use to remind the reader that the main characters are still animals, despite their newfound freedom?

_____
_____
_____
_____
_____
_____
_____
_____
_____
_____
_____
_____
_____
_____
_____
_____
_____
_____
_____
_____
_____
_____
_____
_____
_____
_____
_____
_____

NOVEL EXCERPT: CHAPTER 2

But they woke at dawn as usual, and suddenly remembering the glorious thing that had happened, they all raced out into the pasture together. A little way down the pasture there was a knoll that commanded a view of most of the farm. The animals rushed to the top of it and gazed round them in the clear morning light. Yes, it was theirs—everything that they could see was theirs! In the ecstasy of that thought they gambolled round and round, they hurled themselves into the air in great leaps of excitement. They rolled in the dew, they cropped mouthfuls of the sweet summer grass, they kicked up clods of the black earth and snuffed its rich scent. Then they made a tour of inspection of the whole farm and surveyed with speechless admiration the ploughland, the hayfield, the orchard, the pool, the spinney. It was as though they had never seen these things before, and even now they could hardly believe that it was all their own.

Then they filed back to the farm buildings and halted in silence outside the door of the farmhouse. That was theirs too, but they were frightened to go inside. After a moment, however, Snowball and Napoleon butted the door open with their shoulders and the animals entered in single file, walking with the utmost care for fear of disturbing anything. They tiptoed from room to room, afraid to speak above a whisper and gazing with a kind of awe at the unbelievable luxury, at the beds with their feather mattresses, the looking-glasses, the horsehair sofa, the Brussels carpet, the lithograph of Queen Victoria over the drawing-room mantelpiece. They were just coming down the stairs when Mollie was discovered to be missing. Going back, the others found that she had remained behind in the best bedroom. She had taken a piece of blue ribbon from Mrs. Jones's dressing-table, and was holding it against her shoulder and admiring herself in the glass in a very foolish manner. The others reproached her sharply, and they went outside. Some hams hanging in the kitchen were taken out for burial, and the barrel of beer in the scullery was stove in with a kick from Boxer's hoof, otherwise nothing in the house was touched. A unanimous resolution was passed on the spot that the farmhouse should be preserved as a museum. All were agreed that no animal must ever live there.

The animals had their breakfast, and then Snowball and Napoleon called them together again.

"Comrades," said Snowball, "it is half-past six and we have a long day before us. Today we begin the hay harvest. But there is another matter that must be attended to first."

The pigs now revealed that during the past three months they had taught themselves to read and write from an old spelling book which had belonged to Mr. Jones's children and which had been thrown on the rubbish heap. Napoleon sent for pots of black and white paint and led the way down to the five-barred gate that gave on to the main road. Then Snowball (for it was Snowball who was best at writing) took a brush between the two knuckles of his trotter, painted out MANOR FARM from the top bar of the gate and in its place painted ANIMAL FARM. This was to be the name of the farm from now onwards. After this they went back to the farm buildings, where Snowball and Napoleon sent for a ladder which they caused to be set against the end wall of the big barn. They explained that by their studies of the past three months the pigs had succeeded in reducing the principles of Animalism to Seven Commandments. These Seven Commandments would now be inscribed on the wall; they would form an unalterable law by which all the animals on Animal Farm must live for ever after. With some difficulty (for it is not easy for a pig to balance himself on a ladder) Snowball climbed up and set to work, with Squealer a few rungs below him holding the paint-pot. The Commandments were written on the tarred wall in great white letters that could be read thirty yards away. They ran thus:

THE SEVEN COMMANDMENTS

1. *Whatever goes upon two legs is an enemy.*
2. *Whatever goes upon four legs, or has wings, is a friend.*
3. *No animal shall wear clothes.*
4. *No animal shall sleep in a bed.*
5. *No animal shall drink alcohol.*
6. *No animal shall kill any other animal.*
7. *All animals are equal.*

It was very neatly written, and except that "friend" was written "freind" and one of the "S's" was the wrong way round, the spelling was correct all the way through. Snowball read it aloud for the benefit of the others. All the animals nodded in complete agreement, and the cleverer ones at once began to learn the Commandments by heart.

"Now, Comrades," cried Snowball, throwing down the paint-brush, "to the hayfield! Let us make it a point of honour to get in the harvest more quickly than Jones and his men could do."

Reading Strategy

Evaluate Details Are the details that showed the main characters as animals convincing, or do you start to question the animals' abilities and characteristics?

_____
_____
_____
_____
_____
_____
_____
_____
_____
_____
_____
_____
_____
_____
_____
_____
_____
_____
_____
_____
_____
_____
_____
_____
_____
_____
_____
_____
_____
_____

MARK IT UP

Are you allowed to write in your novel? If so, then mark up the pages as you read, or reread, to help with your note-taking. Develop a shorthand system, including symbols, that works for you. Here are some ideas:

Underline = important idea

Bracket = text to quote

Asterisk = just what you were looking for

Checkmark = might be useful

Circle = unfamiliar word or phrase to look up

▶ **BIG Idea**

Our World and Beyond How have the pigs established their power and leadership?

Mark up the excerpt, looking for evidence of how it expresses the Big Idea.

NOVEL EXCERPT: CHAPTER 3

Napoleon took no interest in Snowball's committees. He said that the education of the young was more important than anything that could be done for those who were already grown up. It happened that Jessie and Bluebell had both whelped soon after the hay harvest, giving birth between them to nine sturdy puppies. As soon as they were weaned, Napoleon took them away from their mothers, saying that he would make himself responsible for their education. He took them up into a loft which could only be reached by a ladder from the harness-room, and there kept them in such seclusion that the rest of the farm soon forgot their existence.

The mystery of where the milk went to was soon cleared up. It was mixed every day into the pigs' mash. The early apples were now ripening, and the grass of the orchard was littered with windfalls. The animals had assumed as a matter of course that these would be shared out equally; one day, however, the order went forth that all the windfalls were to be collected and brought to the harness-room for the use of the pigs. At this some of the other animals murmured, but it was no use. All the pigs were in full agreement on this point, even Snowball and Napoleon. Squealer was sent to make the necessary explanations to the others.

"Comrades!" he cried. "You do not imagine, I hope, that we pigs are doing this in a spirit of selfishness and privilege? Many of us actually dislike milk and apples. I dislike them myself. Our sole object in taking these things is to preserve our health. Milk and apples (this has been proved by Science, comrades) contain substances absolutely necessary to the well-being of a pig. We pigs are brainworkers. The whole management and organisation of this farm depend on us. Day and night we are watching over your welfare. It is for your sake that we drink that milk and eat those apples. Do you know what would happen if we pigs failed in our duty? Jones would come back! Yes, Jones would come back! Surely, comrades," cried Squealer almost pleadingly, skipping from side to side and whisking his tail, "surely there is no one among you who wants to see Jones come back?"

Now if there was one thing that the animals were completely certain of, it was that they did not want Jones back. When it was put to them in this light, they had no more to say. The importance of keeping the pigs in good health was all too obvious. So it was agreed without further argument that the milk and the windfall apples (and also the main crop of apples when they ripened) should be reserved for the pigs alone.

Use the Cornell Note-Taking system to take notes on the excerpt at the left. Record your notes, Reduce them, and then Recap (summarize) them.

Record

_____
_____
_____
_____
_____
_____
_____
_____
_____
_____
_____
_____
_____
_____
_____
_____
_____
_____
_____
_____
_____
_____
_____
_____
_____

Recap

_____
_____
_____
_____
_____
_____
_____

Reduce

Try the following approach as you reduce your notes.

ASK QUESTIONS

Write any questions you have about the novel. Do you have to go to an outside source to find the answers?

_____
_____
_____
_____
_____
_____
_____
_____
_____
_____
_____
_____
_____
_____
_____
_____
_____
_____
_____
_____
_____

Respond and Think Critically

1. Describe how the Rebellion takes place. How does the animals' behavior during the Rebellion suggest both human and animal characteristics? [Interpret]

_____

_____

_____

_____

2. How do the pigs gain the rights to the cow's milk? Why do the other animals allow this to occur? What does this event suggest about the power hierarchy on the farm? [Infer]

_____

_____

_____

_____

3. What technique does Orwell use to cast doubt on the likelihood of a successful revolution? [Analyze]

_____

_____

_____

_____

4. Characterize Snowball as a leader. Do you think his reaction to the stable boy's death is the appropriate reaction to have during a revolution? [Evaluate]

_____

_____

_____

_____

5. **Our World and Beyond** How do the pigs initially establish themselves as the rightful leaders of Animal Farm? [Interpret]

_____

_____

_____

_____

APPLY BACKGROUND
Reread Introduction to the Novel on pages 300–301. How did that information help you understand or appreciate what you read in the novel?

_____

_____

_____

_____

_____

_____

_____

_____

_____

_____

_____

_____

_____

_____

_____

_____

_____

_____

_____

_____

_____

_____

_____

_____

_____

_____

_____

_____

_____

_____

_____

_____

_____

Literary Element Allegory

In what way do the events in these chapters reflect the rise of Stalin and the beginnings of the Russian Revolution? [Connect]

_____

_____

_____

_____

_____

_____

_____

_____

_____

_____

Reading Strategy Evaluate Details

In your opinion, does Orwell create believable characters and settings in *Animal Farm*? [Evaluate]

_____

_____

_____

_____

_____

_____

_____

_____

_____

_____

_____

Vocabulary Practice

Identify the context clues in the following sentences that help you determine the meaning of each boldfaced vocabulary word.

1. When they're not able to find enough food to survive, some animals resort to **cannibalism**.

   _____

2. Instead of being easy to solve, the riddle turned out to be **cryptic**.

   _____

3. After finding out that he got into his first choice college, Robert was so excited that he **gamboled** around his room.

   _____

4. She was embarassed by her **ignominious** conduct at the debate tournament; she shamefully ridiculed one of her opponents.

   _____

5. The world-renowned athlete seemed to be **indefatigable**, or untiring.

   _____

Academic Vocabulary

Initially, the humans doubted that the animals could **sustain** *the farm and their livelihoods, but the animals vowed to prove them wrong.* Using context clues, try to figure out the meaning of the word *sustain* in the sentence above. Write your guess below. Then check it in a dictionary.

_____

_____

_____

_____

_____

_____

_____

Writing

Write a Log The animals recognize the Battle of the Cowshed as a pivotal moment in the Revolution. What effects did the battle have on the animals, individually and as a group? Write a short battle log describing the events and evaluating the animals' behavior. Share your battle log with a partner and compare your evaluations of the events and the effects on the animals.

Jot down some notes here first.

_____
_____
_____
_____
_____
_____
_____
_____
_____
_____
_____
_____
_____
_____
_____
_____
_____
_____
_____
_____
_____
_____
_____
_____
_____
_____
_____

Speaking and Listening

Oral Interpretation

Assignment While addressing a serious topic on one level, the plot of *Animal Farm*, when taken literally, is also quite humorous. With a partner, reread two passages and then identify how Orwell creates humor.

Prepare With a partner, choose two scenes or passages that you find especially funny. Determine who will read and who will interpret each scene.

Discuss The reader of the first passage should read clearly and expressively. After the reading, the interpreter should explain how Orwell created humor in that particular passage. Together, fill in a graphic organizer like the one below.

Humorous comment or situation	Orwell's technique

When you finish the first passage, continue with your reading and discussion of the second passage.

Perform Read one excerpt aloud to the class, and briefly explain how Orwell created humor in these two passages. Make sure you read loudly and clearly, using your voice to emphasize the humorous moments in the chosen passage.

Evaluate Write a paragraph in which you assess the effectiveness of your interpretation and partner work.

Connect to the Literature

How would you feel if the rules for correct behavior kept changing?

Have a Discussion

In a small group, discuss some methods people have for persuading others to follow particular rules of behavior. Consider ways in which this persuasion relies on bias and manipulation of information.

Build Background

Power Struggle

In Chapters 5 through 7, the battle for power between Snowball and Napoleon comes to its climax. In Soviet history, a similar battle raged between two very different men, Leon Trotsky and Joseph Stalin. Stalin exercised power through regulations and rules. As its leader, he controlled the Communist Party bureaucracy. Trotsky had proven himself a masterful military strategist and inspirational leader during the Russian Civil War. He wanted to limit government power. The two also disagreed about how to industrialize and whether to focus on Soviet or worldwide socialism. Stalin took control in 1925, and he kept this control largely through tactics of terror. Large portraits of Stalin were placed around the country to remind the people of the dictator's control.

NOVEL NOTEBOOK
Keep a special notebook to record entries about the novels that you read this year.

WRITE THE CAPTION
Write a caption for the image below, using information in Build Background.

_____
_____
_____
_____
_____
_____
_____
_____
_____
_____
_____
_____
_____
_____
_____
_____
_____
_____
_____
_____
_____
_____
_____
_____
_____
_____
_____
_____

Set Purposes for Reading

▶ **BIG Idea** **Our World and Beyond**

In what ways are you influenced by others and by institutions around you (for example, media, government, school)? Do you consider yourself a free-thinker, or are your beliefs and opinions shaped by these external forces?

In these chapters, Napoleon begins to secretly rewrite the rules upon which Animalism was founded. As you read, think about how he and the other pigs are exploiting the other animals. How do they justify their unequal rations and powers? Why are the other animals so willing to accept these justifications?

Literary Element Dialogue

Dialogue is conversation between characters in a literary work. Dialogue brings characters to life by revealing their personalities and by showing what they are thinking and feeling as they react to other characters. Dialogue can also create mood, advance the plot, and develop theme.

In an allegory, look closely at what is being said and what is being implied. By "reading between the lines," you can identify allusions being made and discover the author's social commentary.

As you read, keep track of the inferences you make as you read the character's dialogue. What do these reveal about Orwell's attitude toward socialism? Use the graphic organizer on the next page to help you "read between the lines."

Reading Strategy Analyze Motivation

Motivation is the stated or implied reason or cause for a character's actions. Motivation can be revealed through a character's speech or actions, or through suggestions made by the narrator.

As you read, try to determine what motivation each animal has for their behavior on the farm. You may find it helpful to use a graphic organizer like the one below.

Character	Action	Motivation

Vocabulary

canvas [kan´vəs]
v. to request support
Michelle knew she needed to canvas her school in order to get enough votes to be elected freshman class president.

dynamo [dī´nə mō]
n. electric generator
When the power goes out, a dynamo can be a lifesaver.

embolden [em bōld´ən]
v. to instill with courage
He knew that if won his division at Saturday's regional debate competition, the win would embolden him during the state competition next month.

malignity [mə lig´nə tē]
n. an example of evil behavior
The killing of those who opposed his leadership is just one example of a malignity during Stalin's rule.

manouever [mə nōō´vər]
(U.S.: maneuver)
n. strategy to gain a particular aim
The boat's captain knew he need to perform a tricky manouever to avoid hitting the approaching whale.

Orwell's characters and narrator use language to communicate hidden agendas. Sometimes Orwell hints that language should be carefully questioned, other times it's up to the reader to notice. As you read Chapters 5 through 7, complete the chart below by filling in some examples of manipulative communication. Then state what you think the language really means. Use as many boxes as you need. You may paraphrase the passages from the text.

The Words

	What They Really Mean
In future all questions relating to the working of the farm would be settled by a special committee of pigs presided over by himself.	Napoleon is going to make all the decisions from now on.

Literary Element

Dialogue What impression do you get of Squealer from this speech?

_____
_____
_____
_____
_____
_____
_____
_____
_____
_____
_____
_____
_____
_____
_____
_____
_____
_____
_____
_____
_____
_____
_____
_____
_____
_____
_____
_____
_____

NOVEL EXCERPT: CHAPTER 7

Napoleon decreed that there should be a full investigation into Snowball's activities. With his dogs in attendance he set out and made a careful tour of inspection of the farm buildings, the other animals following at a respectful distance. At every few steps Napoleon stopped and snuffed the ground for traces of Snowball's footsteps, which, he said, he could detect by the smell. He snuffed in every corner, in the barn, in the cow-shed, in the henhouses, in the vegetable garden, and found traces of Snowball almost everywhere. He would put his snout to the ground, give several deep sniffs, and exclaim in a terrible voice, "Snowball! He has been here! I can smell him distinctly!" and at the word "Snowball" all the dogs let out blood-curdling growls and showed their side teeth.

The animals were thoroughly frightened. It seemed to them as though Snowball were some kind of invisible influence, pervading the air about them and menacing them with all kinds of dangers. In the evening Squealer called them together, and with an alarmed expression on his face told them that he had some serious news to report.

"Comrades!" cried Squealer, making little nervous skips, "a most terrible thing has been discovered. Snowball has sold himself to Frederick of Pinchfield Farm, who is even now plotting to attack us and take our farm away from us! Snowball is to act as his guide when the attack begins. But there is worse than that. We had thought that Snowball's rebellion was caused simply by his vanity and ambition. But we were wrong, comrades. Do you know what the real reason was? Snowball was in league with Jones from the very start! He was Jones's secret agent all the time. It has all been proved by documents which he left behind him and which we have only just discovered. To my mind this explains a great deal, comrades. Did we not see for ourselves how he attempted—fortunately without success—to get us defeated and destroyed at the Battle of the Cowshed?"

The animals were stupefied. This was a wickedness far outdoing Snowball's destruction of the windmill. But it was some minutes before they could fully take it in. They all remembered, or thought they remembered, how they had seen Snowball charging ahead of them at the Battle of the Cowshed, how he had rallied and encouraged them at every turn, and how he had not paused for an instant even when the pellets from Jones's gun had wounded his back. At first it was a little difficult to see how this fitted in with his being on Jones's side. Even Boxer, who seldom asked questions, was puzzled. He lay down, tucked his fore hoofs beneath him, shut his eyes, and with a hard effort managed to formulate his thoughts.

"I do not believe that," he said. "Snowball fought bravely at the Battle of the Cowshed. I saw him myself. Did we not give him 'Animal Hero, First Class,' immediately afterwards?"

"That was our mistake, comrade. For we know now—it is all written down in the secret documents that we have found—that in reality he was trying to lure us to our doom."

"But he was wounded," said Boxer. "We all saw him running with blood."

"That was part of the arrangement!" cried Squealer. "Jones's shot only grazed him. I could show you this in his own writing, if you were able to read it. The plot was for Snowball, at the critical moment, to give the signal for flight and leave the field to the enemy. And he very nearly succeeded—I will even say, comrades, he *would* have succeeded if it had not been for our heroic Leader, Comrade Napoleon. Do you not remember how, just at the moment when Jones and his men had got inside the yard, Snowball suddenly turned and fled, and many animals followed him? And do you not remember, too, that it was just at that moment, when panic was spreading and all seemed lost, that Comrade Napoleon sprang forward with a cry of 'Death to Humanity!' and sank his teeth in Jones's leg? Surely you remember *that*, comrades?" exclaimed Squealer, frisking from side to side.

Now when Squealer described the scene so graphically, it seemed to the animals that they did remember it. At any rate, they remembered that at the critical moment of the battle Snowball had turned to flee. But Boxer was still a little uneasy.

"I do not believe that Snowball was a traitor at the beginning," he said finally. "What he has done since is different. But I believe that at the Battle of the Cowshed he was a good comrade."

"Our Leader, Comrade Napoleon," announced Squealer, speaking very slowly and firmly, "has stated categorically—categorically, comrade—that Snowball was Jones's agent from the very beginning—yes, and from long before the Rebellion was ever thought of."

"Ah, that is different!" said Boxer. "If Comrade Napoleon says it, it must be right."

"That is the true spirit, comrade!" cried Squealer, but it was noticed he cast a very ugly look at Boxer with his little twinkling eyes. He turned to go, then paused and added impressively: "I warn every animal on this farm to keep his eyes very wide open. For we have reason to think that some of Snowball's secret agents are lurking among us at this moment!"

Literary Element

Dialogue What do these exchanges reveal about how the pigs are able to brainwash the other animals into believing the stories that they make up?

_____

_____

_____

_____

_____

_____

_____

_____

_____

_____

_____

_____

_____

_____

_____

_____

_____

_____

_____

_____

_____

_____

_____

_____

_____

_____

_____

_____

_____

_____

Reading Strategy

Analyze Motivation What is Snowball's motivation to build a windmill on Animal Farm land?

_____

_____

_____

_____

_____

_____

_____

_____

_____

_____

_____

_____

_____

_____

_____

_____

_____

_____

_____

_____

_____

_____

_____

_____

_____

_____

_____

_____

NOVEL EXCERPT: CHAPTER 5

Apart from the disputes over the windmill, there was the question of the defence of the farm. It was fully realised that though the human beings had been defeated in the Battle of the Cowshed they might make another and more determined attempt to recapture the farm and reinstate Mr. Jones. They had all the more reason for doing so because the news of their defeat had spread across the countryside and made the animals on the neighbouring farms more restive than ever. As usual, Snowball and Napoleon were in disagreement. According to Napoleon, what the animals must do was to procure firearms and train themselves in the use of them. According to Snowball, they must send out more and more pigeons and stir up rebellion among the animals on the other farms. The one argued that if they could not defend themselves they were bound to be conquered, the other argued that if rebellions happened everywhere they would have no need to defend themselves. The animals listened first to Napoleon, then to Snowball, and could not make up their minds which was right; indeed, they always found themselves in agreement with the one who was speaking at the moment.

At last the day came when Snowball's plans were completed. At the Meeting on the following Sunday the question of whether or not to begin work on the windmill was to be put to the vote. When the animals had assembled in the big barn, Snowball stood up and, though occasionally interrupted by bleating from the sheep, set forth his reasons for advocating the building of the windmill. Then Napoleon stood up to reply. He said very quietly that the windmill was nonsense and that he advised nobody to vote for it, and promptly sat down again; he had spoken for barely thirty seconds, and seemed almost indifferent as to the effect he produced. At this Snowball sprang to his feet, and shouting down the sheep, who had begun bleating again, broke into a passionate appeal in favour of the windmill. Until now the animals had been about equally divided in their sympathies, but in a moment Snowball's eloquence had carried them away. In glowing sentences he painted a picture of Animal Farm as it might be when sordid labour was lifted from the animals' backs. His imagination had now run far beyond chaff-cutters and turnip-slicers. Electricity, he said, could operate threshing machines, ploughs, harrows, rollers, and reapers and binders, besides supplying every stall with its own electric light, hot and cold water, and an electric heater. By the time he had finished speaking, there was no doubt as to which way the vote would go. But just at this moment Napoleon stood up and, casting a peculiar sidelong look at Snowball, uttered a high-pitched whimper of a kind no one had ever heard him utter before.

At this there was a terrible baying sound outside, and nine enormous dogs wearing brass-studded collars came bounding into the barn. They dashed straight for Snowball, who only sprang from his place just in time to escape their snapping jaws. In a moment he was out of the door and they were after him. Too amazed and frightened to speak, all the animals crowded through the door to watch the chase. Snowball was racing across the long pasture that led to the road. He was running as only a pig can run, but the dogs were close on his heels. Suddenly he slipped and it seemed certain that they had him. Then he was up again, running faster than ever, then the dogs were gaining on him again. One of them all but closed his jaws on Snowball's tail, but Snowball whisked it free just in time. Then he put on an extra spurt and, with a few inches to spare, slipped through a hole in the hedge and was seen no more.

Silent and terrified, the animals crept back into the barn. In a moment the dogs came bounding back. At first no one had been able to imagine where these creatures came from, but the problem was soon solved: they were the puppies whom Napoleon had taken away from their mothers and reared privately. Though not yet full-grown, they were huge dogs, and as fierce-looking as wolves. They kept close to Napoleon. It was noticed that they wagged their tails to him in the same way as the other dogs had been used to do to Mr. Jones.

Napoleon, with the dogs following him, now mounted on to the raised portion of the floor where Major had previously stood to deliver his speech. He announced that from now on the Sunday-morning Meetings would come to an end. They were unnecessary, he said, and wasted time. In future all questions relating to the working of the farm would be settled by a special committee of pigs, presided over by himself. These would meet in private and afterwards communicate their decisions to the others. The animals would still assemble on Sunday mornings to salute the flag, sing *Beasts of England*, and receive their orders for the week; but there would be no more debates.

In spite of the shock that Snowball's expulsion had given them, the animals were dismayed by this announcement. Several of them would have protested if they could have found the right arguments. Even Boxer was vaguely troubled. He set his ears back, shook his forelock several times, and tried hard to marshal his thoughts; but in the end he could not think of anything to say. Some of the pigs themselves, however, were more articulate.

Reading Strategy

Analyze Motivation What are Napoleon's true motivations for ending the Sunday-morning Meetings?

_____

_____

_____

_____

_____

_____

_____

_____

_____

_____

_____

_____

_____

_____

_____

_____

_____

_____

_____

_____

_____

_____

_____

_____

_____

_____

_____

_____

_____

_____

MARK IT UP

Are you allowed to write in your novel? If so, then mark up the pages as you read, or reread, to help with your note-taking. Develop a shorthand system, including symbols, that works for you. Here are some ideas:

Underline = important idea

Bracket = text to quote

Asterisk = just what you were looking for

Checkmark = might be useful

Circle = unfamiliar word or phrase to look up

▶ BIG Idea

Our World and Beyond Why is it that the animals on Animal Farm can be so easily influenced by Napoleon?

Mark up the excerpt, looking for evidence of how it expresses the Big Idea.

NOVEL EXCERPT: CHAPTER 6

It was about this time that the pigs suddenly moved into the farmhouse and took up their residence there. Again the animals seemed to remember that a resolution against this had been passed in the early days, and again Squealer was able to convince them that this was not the case. It was absolutely necessary, he said, that the pigs, who were the brains of the farm, should have a quiet place to work in. It was also more suited to the dignity of the Leader (for of late he had taken to speaking of Napoleon under the title of "Leader") to live in a house than in a mere sty. Nevertheless, some of the animals were disturbed when they heard that the pigs not only took their meals in the kitchen and used the drawing-room as a recreation room, but also slept in the beds. Boxer passed it off as usual with "Napoleon is always right!", but Clover, who thought she remembered a definite ruling against beds, went to the end of the barn and tried to puzzle out the Seven Commandments which were inscribed there. Finding herself unable to read more than individual letters, she fetched Muriel.

"Muriel," she said, "read me the Fourth Commandment. Does it not say something about never sleeping in a bed?"

With some difficulty Muriel spelt it out.

"It says, 'No animal shall sleep in a bed with sheets,'" she announced finally.

Curiously enough, Clover had not remembered that the Fourth Commandment mentioned sheets; but as it was there on the wall, it must have done so. And Squealer, who happened to be passing at this moment, attended by two or three dogs, was able to put the whole matter in its proper perspective.

"You have heard then, comrades," he said, "that we pigs now sleep in the beds of the farmhouse? And why not? You did not suppose, surely, that there was ever a ruling against beds? A bed merely means a place to sleep in. A pile of straw in a stall is a bed, properly regarded. The rule was against sheets, which are a human invention. We have removed the sheets from the farmhouse beds, and sleep between blankets. And very comfortable beds they are too! But not more comfortable than we need, I can tell you, comrades, with all the brainwork we have to do nowadays. You would not rob us of our repose, would you, comrades? You would not have us too tired to carry out our duties? Surely none of you wishes to see Jones back?"

The animals reassured him on this point immediately, and no more was said about the pigs sleeping in the farmhouse beds. And when, some days afterwards, it was announced that from now on the pigs would get up an hour later in the mornings than the other animals, no complaint was made about that either.

Use the Cornell Note-Taking system to take notes on the excerpt at the left. Record your notes, Reduce them, and then Recap (summarize) them.

Record

_____

_____

_____

_____

_____

_____

_____

_____

_____

_____

_____

_____

_____

_____

_____

_____

_____

_____

_____

_____

_____

_____

_____

Recap

_____

_____

_____

_____

_____

Reduce

Try the following approach as you reduce your notes.

TO THE POINT
Write a few key ideas.

_____

_____

_____

_____

_____

_____

_____

_____

_____

_____

_____

_____

_____

_____

_____

_____

_____

_____

_____

_____

_____

_____

Respond and Think Critically

1. What happens to Snowball during the meeting about the windmill? What events in Soviet history does this scene suggest? [Infer]

_____

_____

_____

_____

2. Identify three ways that Napoleon tries to solidify his leadership position on the farm. How does the process of decision-making on the farm change under Napoleon's leadership? [Conclude]

_____

_____

_____

3. How does Orwell compare _Animal Farm_ under Napoleon's leadership, to its exploited state under Farmer Jones's rule? What attitude about totalitarian government do you think Orwell conveys? [Infer]

_____

_____

_____

4. Do you think it's fair that those who are more educated or more skilled—like the pigs in _Animal Farm_—have more influence in decision-making? Consider how decisions are made in your community, state, or in the nation. [Connect]

_____

_____

_____

5. **Our World and Beyond** In their own unique world, the animals reveal how far some are willing to go to achieve fame and power. While we know that Orwell intended for his readers to make connections to Soviet leaders like Stalin, are there any other historical or contemporary figures you know who have been known to go too far in order to secure power? [Connect]

_____

_____

_____

_____

APPLY BACKGROUND
Reread Build Background on page 315. How did that information help you understand or appreciate what you read in the novel?

_____

_____

_____

_____

_____

_____

_____

_____

_____

_____

_____

_____

_____

_____

_____

_____

_____

_____

_____

_____

_____

_____

_____

_____

_____

_____

Literary Element   Dialogue

What happens each time the sheep start bleating,
"Four legs good, two legs bad!"? [Analyze]

_____

_____

_____

_____

_____

_____

_____

_____

_____

_____

_____

_____

Reading Strategy   Analyze Motivation

What is Boxer's motivation for consistently working
hard and putting in even longer hours than he needs
to? [Infer]

_____

_____

_____

_____

_____

_____

_____

_____

_____

_____

_____

_____

_____

Vocabulary Practice

Write the vocabulary word that correctly completes
each sentence. If none of the words fits the sentence,
write "none."

canvas	malignity
dynamo	manoeuvre
embolden	

1. The chess master's final _____
   allowed him to win the match.

2. When their power went out during the storm,
   the Smiths were glad that they had kept their
   old _____.

3 An act of terrorism is an extreme
   _____.

4. The telephone company wanted to offer additional
   _____, but they weren't sure that
   people would want to buy them.

5. The presidential candidates knew it was important
   to _____ as many states as possible
   if they wanted to win the election.

6. The dictator did not want to _____
   his subjects; if he did, he was afraid that
   they would speak their minds and try to revolt
   against him.

7. The melting glaciers are already threatening the
   _____ of native wildlife.

Academic Vocabulary

In these chapters of Animal Farm, some of the
fundamental _rules of Animalism are mysteriously_
altered. In the preceding sentence, fundamental
means "basic or underlying." Think about those rules,
and complete the following sentence:

_____

_____

_____, _one of the_ **_fundamental_** _rules of_
Animalism, was changed to _____

_____

_____.

Writing

Write a List What do you think of the way Napoleon runs the farm? Would you support his leadership? Imagine you are a newcomer to the farm. Write a list of talking points that you would use if you were going to craft a political speech advocating either support for or opposition to Napoleon's views and methods. In your list, include the specific examples you would use to support each talking point.

Jot down some notes here first.

_____
_____
_____
_____
_____
_____
_____
_____
_____
_____
_____
_____
_____
_____
_____
_____
_____
_____
_____
_____
_____
_____
_____
_____

Research and Report
Visual/Media Presentation

Assignment Governments, like businesses, need to convey a particular image to their citizens and to other nations in the world. They use public relations experts to craft that image and communicate it through electronic and print media, word of mouth, and specific policies. Present examples of public relations media or images that craft a positive image of your home country or city, and discuss why you think these pieces are created.

Get Ideas Craft a question to help guide your research. For example, what public relations media or images are currently being used to present a positive image of _____? On a chart like the one below, make a list of potential sources that you can use as you conduct your research.

Potential Source	Information I might find there

Research Use both print resources and the Internet to conduct your research. You might also consider contacting the public relations coordinator in your town. As you collect information, make sure to make copies of the images/media that you want to include in your presentation and record the source information for each piece.

Prepare Create a media presentation of the information you have found. Consider using presentation software such as Powerpoint to help you develop a professional-looking report. Your presentation should also include a discussion of why these specific images/media were created and what effect they have on public opinion of your country or city. At the end of your presentation, comment on how your research relates to what Napoleon does in the novel.

Present Share your media presentation with the class. Use appropriate and effective eye contact, tone of voice, and body language.

Connect to the Literature

Do you think revolution is worth the upheaval and damage it inevitably causes? Can it bring about real and lasting change? Why or why not?

Conduct a Debate

With a partner, identify and discuss factors that a government can modify (such as policies) and those that it cannot (such as climate conditions). Consider also whether there are elements to the human condition so basic that no revolution can change them.

Build Background

Allies and Enemies

Napoleon wants the farm to have greater contact with the outside world. Joseph Stalin had similar visions for the Soviet Union. During the 1930s, he was torn between allying himself with Western capitalist nations or with Adolf Hitler's fascist German government. The Soviet propaganda machine defiled each "enemy" in turn as Stalin shifted allegiances. In 1939 Stalin pledged himself to Hitler by signing a "non-aggression pact." Hitler broke his promise and invaded the Soviet Union in 1941. The Soviets then became allies with the West. At first, Hitler had great success against Stalin's less modern armies. Ultimately, the Soviet army turned the tide with the Battle of Stalingrad, though the city was nearly destroyed and hundreds of thousands of Soviets killed.

NOVEL NOTEBOOK

Keep a special notebook to record entries about the novels that you read this year.

SUMMARIZE

Summarize in one sentence the most important idea(s) in Build Background.

_____

_____

_____

_____

_____

_____

_____

_____

_____

_____

_____

_____

_____

_____

_____

_____

_____

_____

_____

_____

_____

_____

_____

_____

_____

_____

_____

_____

Set Purposes for Reading

▶ **BIG Idea** **Our World and Beyond**

Have you ever traveled to a country that has a completely different culture than your own? Often, it is not until we are removed from our own culture that we can begin to see it more objectively and to reevalute our own societal and personal belief systems.

As Orwell brings his discussion of leadership and government on Animal Farm to a close in these chapters, what ideas do you think he wants you to consider about your own society?

Literary Element   Moral

A **moral** is a practical lesson about right and wrong conduct. The moral can either be stated directly or implied.

Authors use both **satire** and **irony** to highlight the morals of their stories. Satire uses humor to ridicule the follies of people or societies. Irony refers to a discrepany between appearance and reality. **Dramatic irony** refers to a situation in which the reader knows more than the characters do.

As you read, try to determine what lessons Orwell is trying to convey through the final resolution of characters and situations.

Reading Strategy   Connect to Contemporary Issues

To **connect to contemporary issues** is to make links between the issues and situations in a literary work and similar issues and situations that occur in today's world.

When reading works that have an unusual or unfamiliar setting, it is important to consider how the events in the story relate to issues in the real world. For example, a recent film production of *Animal Farm* established connections between the situations the animals encountered and the situation in modern Russia.

As you read, record at least three significant issues or problems that the chapters raise. After you finish reading, note issues from today's world that relate to each issue in the story. You may find it helpful to use a graphic organizer like the one below. The graphic organizer on the next page can also help you organize issues from the book that relate to contemporary issues.

Vocabulary

demeanor [di mē´nər]
n. outward manner
The teacher had such a kind demeanor that students could not help liking him.

devotees [dev´ə tēz´]
n. ardent followers
The devotees of the Australian pop singer attended all of her concerts.

interment [in tur´mənt]
n. the act of burial
After the funeral service at the church, we traveled to the cemetary, his place of interment.

machinations [mak´ə nā´shəns]
n. scheming actions
His secret machinations ended up getting him in trouble with the police.

taciturn [tas´ə turn´]
adj. not inclined to talking
Some authors are rather taciturn; they prefer to write in solitude, not to talk in public forums.

Issue/Problem in Novel

Contemporary Issue/Problem

As Napoleon takes over leadership of the farm, a new social and political structure emerges. This restructuring brings about many changes in power and privilege among the animals, and it mirrors many of the social, political and economic changes that occur in countries around the world when leadership changes hands. As you read, record each major change that occurs on Animal Farm, then identify a contemporary situation that mirrors this change.

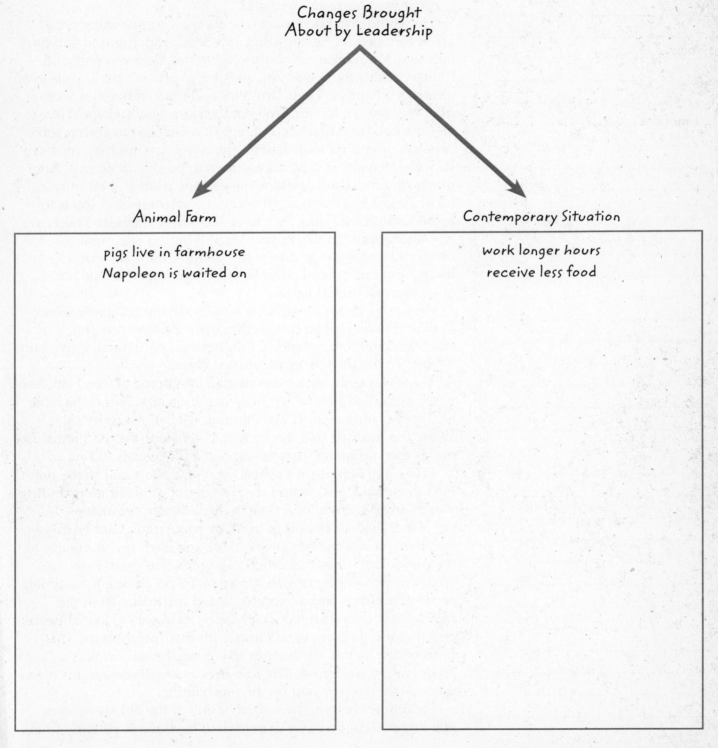

Changes Brought
About by Leadership

Animal Farm

pigs live in farmhouse
Napoleon is waited on

Contemporary Situation

work longer hours
receive less food

Literary Element

Moral How is Mr. Pilkington's assertion here ironic and satiric? How does this satire highlight the moral of *Animal Farm*?

_____
_____
_____
_____
_____
_____
_____
_____
_____
_____
_____
_____
_____
_____
_____
_____
_____
_____
_____
_____
_____
_____
_____
_____
_____
_____
_____
_____

NOVEL EXCERPT: CHAPTER 10

He believed that he was right in saying that the lower animals on Animal Farm did more work and received less food than any animals in the county. Indeed, he and his fellow-visitors today had observed many features which they intended to introduce on their own farms immediately.

He would end his remarks, he said, by emphasising once again the friendly feelings that subsisted, and ought to subsist, between Animal Farm and its neighbours. Between pigs and human beings there was not, and there need not be, any clash of interests whatever. Their struggles and their difficulties were one. Was not the labour problem the same everywhere? Here it became apparent that Mr. Pilkington was about to spring some carefully prepared witticism on the company, but for a moment he was too overcome by amusement to be able to utter it. After much choking, during which his various chins turned purple, he managed to get it out: "If you have your lower animals to contend with," he said, "we have our lower classes!" This *bon mot* set the table in a roar; and Mr. Pilkington once again congratulated the pigs on the low rations, the long working hours, and the general absence of pampering which he had observed on Animal Farm.

And now, he said finally, he would ask the company to rise to their feet and make certain that their glasses were full. "Gentlemen," concluded Mr. Pilkington, "gentlemen, I give you a toast: To the prosperity of Animal Farm!"

There was enthusiastic cheering and stamping of feet. Napoleon was so gratified that he left his place and came round the table to clink his mug against Mr. Pilkington's before emptying it. When the cheering had died down, Napoleon, who had remained on his feet, intimated that he too had a few words to say.

Like all of Napoleon's speeches, it was short and to the point. He too, he said, was happy that the period of misunderstanding was at an end. For a long time there had been rumours— circulated, he had reason to think by some malignant enemy— that there was something subversive and even revolutionary in the outlook of himself and his colleagues. They had been credited with attempting to stir up rebellion among the animals on neighbouring farms. Nothing could be further from the truth! Their sole wish, now and in the past, was to live at peace and in normal business relations with their neighbours. This farm which he had the honour to control, he added, was a co-operative enterprise. The title-deeds, which were in his own possession, were owned by the pigs jointly.

He did not believe, he said, that any of the old suspicions still lingered, but certain changes had been made recently in the routine of the farm which should have the effect of promoting confidence still further. Hitherto the animals on the farm had had a rather foolish custom of addressing one another as "Comrade." This was to be suppressed. There had also been a very strange custom, whose origin was unknown, of marching every Sunday morning past a boar's skull which was nailed to a post in the garden. This, too, would be suppressed, and the skull had already been buried. His visitors might have observed, too, the green flag which flew from the masthead. If so, they would perhaps have noted that the white hoof and horn with which it had previously been marked had now been removed. It would be a plain green flag from now onwards.

He had only one criticism, he said, to make of Mr. Pilkington's excellent and neighbourly speech. Mr. Pilkington had referred throughout to "Animal Farm." He could not of course know— for he, Napoleon, was only now for the first time announcing it—that the name "Animal Farm" had been abolished. Henceforward the farm was to be known as "The Manor Farm"—which, he believed, was its correct and original name.

"Gentlemen," concluded Napoleon, "I will give you the same toast as before, but in a different form. Fill your glasses to the brim. Gentlemen, here is my toast: To the prosperity of The Manor Farm!"

There was the same hearty cheering as before, and the mugs were emptied to the dregs. But as the animals outside gazed at the scene, it seemed to them that some strange thing was happening. What was it that had altered in the faces of the pigs? Clover's old dim eyes flitted from one face to another. Some of them had five chins, some had four, some had three. But what was it that seemed to be melting and changing? Then, the applause having come to an end, the company took up their cards and continued the game that had been interrupted, and the animals crept silently away.

But they had not gone twenty yards when they stopped short. An uproar of voices was coming from the farmhouse. They rushed back and looked through the window again. Yes, a violent quarrel was in progress. There were shoutings, bangings on the table, sharp suspicious glances, furious denials. The source of the trouble appeared to be that Napoleon and Mr. Pilkington had each played an ace of spades simultaneously.

Twelve voices were shouting in anger, and they were all alike. No question, now, what had happened to the faces of the pigs. The creatures outside looked from pig to man, and from man to pig, and from pig to man again; but already it was impossible to say which was which.

Literary Element

Moral What does the final sentence of *Animal Farm* reveal about the moral Orwell wanted his readers to understand?

_____

_____

_____

_____

_____

_____

_____

_____

_____

_____

_____

_____

_____

_____

_____

_____

_____

_____

_____

_____

_____

_____

_____

_____

_____

_____

_____

_____

_____

_____

Reading Strategy

Connect to Contemporary Issues
Why is Napoleon's belief that the windmill is strong enough to withstand an attack flawed? Does his attitude remind you of any current political leaders toward avowed "enemies" or other threatening situations?

_____
_____
_____
_____
_____
_____
_____
_____
_____
_____
_____
_____
_____
_____
_____
_____
_____
_____
_____
_____
_____
_____
_____
_____
_____

NOVEL EXCERPT: CHAPTER 8

The very next morning the attack came. The animals were at breakfast when the look-outs came racing in with the news that Frederick and his followers had already come through the five-barred gate. Boldly enough the animals sallied forth to meet them, but this time they did not have the easy victory that they had had in the Battle of the Cowshed. There were fifteen men, with half a dozen guns between them, and they opened fire as soon as they got within fifty yards. The animals could not face the terrible explosions and the stinging pellets, and in spite of the efforts of Napoleon and Boxer to rally them, they were soon driven back. A number of them were already wounded. They took refuge in the farm buildings and peeped cautiously out from chinks and knot-holes. The whole of the big pasture, including the windmill, was in the hands of the enemy. For the moment even Napoleon seemed at a loss. He paced up and down without a word . . .

Meanwhile Frederick and his men had halted about the windmill. The animals watched them, and a murmur of dismay went round. Two of the men had produced a crowbar and a sledge hammer. They were going to knock the windmill down.

"Impossible!" cried Napoleon. "We have built the walls far too thick for that. They could not knock it down in a week. Courage, comrades!"

But Benjamin was watching the movements of the men intently. The two with the hammer and the crowbar were drilling a hole near the base of the windmill. Slowly, and with an air almost of amusement, Benjamin nodded his long muzzle.

"I thought so," he said. "Do you not see what they are doing? In another moment they are going to pack blasting powder into that hole."

Terrified, the animals waited. It was impossible now to venture out of the shelter of the buildings. After a few minutes the men were seen to be running in all directions. Then there was a deafening roar. The pigeons swirled into the air, and all the animals, except Napoleon, flung themselves flat on their bellies and hid their faces. When they got up again, a huge cloud of black smoke was hanging where the windmill had been. Slowly the breeze drifted it away. The windmill had ceased to exist!

At this sight the animals' courage returned to them. The fear and despair they had felt a moment earlier were drowned in their rage against this vile, contemptible act. A mighty cry for vengeance went up, and without waiting for further orders they charged forth in a body and made straight for the enemy. This time they did not heed the cruel pellets that swept over them like hail. It was a savage, bitter battle. The men fired again and again, and, when the animals got to close quarters, lashed out with their sticks and their heavy boots. A cow, three sheep, and two geese were killed, and nearly everyone was wounded. Even Napoleon, who was directing operations from the rear, had the tip of his tail chipped by a pellet. But the men did not go unscathed either. . . . They saw that they were in danger of being surrounded. Frederick shouted to his men to get out while the going was good, and the next moment the cowardly enemy was running for dear life. The animals chased them right down to the bottom of the field, and got in some last kicks at them as they forced their way through the thorn hedge.

They had won, but they were weary and bleeding. Slowly they began to limp back towards the farm. The sight of their dead comrades stretched upon the grass moved some of them to tears. And for a little while they halted in sorrowful silence at the place where the windmill had once stood. Yes, it was gone; almost the last trace of their labour was gone! Even the foundations were partially destroyed. And in rebuilding it they could not this time, as before, make use of the fallen stones. This time the stones had vanished too. The force of the explosion had flung them to distances of hundreds of yards. It was as though the windmill had never been.

As they approached the farm Squealer, who had unaccountably been absent during the fighting, came skipping towards them, whisking his tail and beaming with satisfaction. And the animals heard, from the direction of the farm buildings, the solemn booming of a gun.

"What is that gun firing for?" said Boxer.

"To celebrate our victory!" cried Squealer.

"What victory?" said Boxer. His knees were bleeding, he had lost a shoe and split his hoof, and a dozen pellets had lodged themselves in his hind leg.

"What victory, comrade? Have we not driven the enemy off our soil—the sacred soil of Animal Farm?"

"But they have destroyed the windmill. And we had worked on it for two years!"

"What matter? We will build another windmill. We will build six windmills if we feel like it. You do not appreciate, comrade, the mighty thing that we have done. The enemy was in occupation of this very ground that we stand upon. And now— thanks to the leadership of Comrade Napoleon—we have won every inch of it back again!"

"Then we have won back what we had before," said Boxer.

Reading Strategy

Connect to Contemporary Issues
George Orwell intended this passage to refer to the Battle of Stalingrad. What battle or conflict that you have studied does this passage call to mind?

_____

_____

_____

_____

_____

_____

_____

_____

_____

_____

_____

_____

_____

_____

_____

_____

_____

_____

_____

_____

_____

_____

_____

_____

_____

_____

▶ **BIG Idea**

Our World and Beyond What is the fate of Animalism?

Mark up the excerpt, looking for evidence of how it expresses the Big Idea.

NOVEL EXCERPT: CHAPTER 9

And finally there was a tremendous baying of dogs and a shrill crowing from the black cockerel, and out came Napoleon himself, majestically upright, casting haughty glances from side to side, and with his dogs gambolling round him.

He carried a whip in his trotter.

There was a deadly silence. Amazed, terrified, huddling together, the animals watched the long line of pigs march slowly round the yard. It was as though the world had turned upside-down. Then there came a moment when the first shock had worn off and when, in spite of everything—in spite of their terror of the dogs, and of the habit, developed through long years, of never complaining, never criticising, no matter what happened—they might have uttered some word of protest. But just at that moment, as though at a signal, all the sheep burst out into a tremendous bleating of—

"Four legs good, two legs *better*! Four legs good, two legs *better*! Four legs good, two legs *better*!"

It went on for five minutes without stopping. And by the time the sheep had quieted down, the chance to utter any protest had passed, for the pigs had marched back into the farmhouse.

Benjamin felt a nose nuzzling at his shoulder. He looked round. It was Clover. Her old eyes looked dimmer than ever. Without saying anything, she tugged gently at his mane and led him round to the end of the big barn, where the Seven Commandments were written. For a minute or two they stood gazing at the tarred wall with its white lettering.

"My sight is failing," she said finally. "Even when I was young I could not have read what was written there. But it appears to me that that wall looks different. Are the Seven Commandments the same as they used to be, Benjamin?"

For once Benjamin consented to break his rule, and he read out to her what was written on the wall. There was nothing there now except a single Commandment. It ran:

ALL ANIMALS ARE EQUAL

BUT SOME ANIMALS ARE MORE EQUAL THAN OTHERS

After that it did not seem strange when next day the pigs who were supervising the work of the farm all carried whips in their trotters.

Use the Cornell Note-Taking system to take notes on the excerpt at the left. Record your notes, Reduce them, and then Recap (summarize) them.

Record

_____

_____

_____

_____

_____

_____

_____

_____

_____

_____

_____

_____

_____

_____

_____

_____

_____

_____

_____

_____

_____

_____

_____

_____

Recap

_____

_____

_____

_____

_____

_____

Reduce

Try the following approach as you reduce your notes.

MY VIEW
Write down your thoughts on the excerpt.

_____

_____

_____

_____

_____

_____

_____

_____

_____

_____

_____

_____

_____

_____

_____

_____

_____

_____

_____

Respond and Think Critically

1. What dealings does Napoleon have with Frederick and Pilkington? How does the battle over the windmill affect the animals? What events from Soviet history is Orwell highlighting? [Infer]

_____

_____

_____

_____

2. What changes are made to the Fifth and Sixth Commandments? How is the entire list of Commandments ultimately refashioned? What point is Orwell making about the role of communication in Soviet society? [Analyze]

_____

_____

_____

_____

3. In Chapter 10 the pigs begin to walk on two legs. In your opinion is this evolution a sign of progress? Explain. [Evaluate]

_____

_____

_____

_____

4. Some critics believe that, at the end of the book, Orwell suggests that the pigs and human political leaders are interchangeable. Do you think most government rulers are interchangeable? How might power change those who have it? Explain. [Connect]

_____

_____

_____

_____

5. **Our World and Beyond** Why do you think Orwell chose to place this story in an unrealistic setting? [Infer]

_____

_____

_____

_____

APPLY BACKGROUND
Reread Meet the Author on page 302. How did that information help you understand or appreciate what you read in the novel?

_____

_____

_____

_____

_____

_____

_____

_____

_____

_____

_____

_____

_____

_____

_____

_____

_____

_____

_____

_____

_____

_____

_____

_____

_____

_____

_____

_____

_____

_____

_____

_____

Literary Element **Moral**

How does dramatic irony help to establish the morals presented in *Animal Farm*? Give at least two examples to support your response. [Analyze]

_____

_____

_____

_____

_____

_____

_____

_____

_____

_____

_____

Reading Strategy **Connect to Contemporary Issues**

What modern situations or figures come to your mind as you consider the characters and situations in this novel? [Connect]

_____

_____

_____

_____

_____

_____

_____

_____

_____

_____

Vocabulary Practice

Identify whether each set of paired words have the same or the opposite meaning.

1. **demeanor** and deportment

_____

2. **devoteees** and opposition

_____

3. **interment** and burial

_____

4. **machinations** and conspiracies

_____

5. **taciturn** and garrulous

_____

Academic Vocabulary

The animals were amazed to see Napoleon **emerge** *from the farmhouse walking on two, not four, legs.* Using context clues, try to figure out the meaning of the boldfaced word in the sentence above. Write your guess below. Then check it in a dictionary.

_____

_____

_____

_____

_____

_____

_____

_____

_____

_____

_____

_____

Writing

Write a Profile Analyze the descriptions of Napoleon's physical and behavioral characteristics in Chapters 9 and 10. On a separate sheet of paper, use these details to write a profile of Napoleon for Animal Farm's local newspaper.

Jot down some notes here first.

_____
_____
_____
_____
_____
_____
_____
_____
_____
_____
_____
_____
_____
_____
_____
_____
_____
_____
_____
_____
_____
_____
_____
_____
_____
_____
_____
_____

Research and Report
Literary Criticism
Assignment Evaluate literary criticism about Orwell's work and write a short response in which you explain whether you agree or disagree that the criticism applies to *Animal Farm*. Present the response to the class.

Prepare Read the following quotation about Orwell's work by critic Robert A. Lee:

The beast fable is in many ways the ideal form in which to articulate attack [on social injustice].
The presence of beasts provides a readymade vehicle for the tenor of the hatred in this essentially metaphorical mode.
From Orwell's Fiction.

Some literary criticism may include unfamiliar words or words with unfamiliar connotations. Look up *articulate* and *tenor* to be sure you know what they mean in this context.

Determine your position. Craft a thesis statement about your position, and gather details from the story to support your argument.

Report When you present your response, make eye contact, speak loudly and clearly, and maintain good posture to reflect confidence. Use an appropriate tone of voice to enhance emotional and logical appeals. All this will help as you try to persuade your audience to agree with your point of view.

Evaluate Write a paragraph evaluating your report. When your classmates present, offer oral feedback on their performances.

Animal Farm

The following questions refer to the Related Readings in Glencoe's *Literature Library* edition of this novel. Support your answers with details from the text. Write your answers on a separate sheet of paper, but jot down some notes first on the lines provided.

The Last Word
Matthew Arnold

In your opinion, would Arnold and Orwell have agreed about the possibility of successful social revolution? Is Arnold's purpose in writing "The Last Word" the same as or different from Orwell's purpose in writing *Animal Farm*? Use elements of both the poem and the novel to support your answers. How do these writers' thoughts compare with your own? Explain your answer.

_____

_____

_____

_____

The Freedom of the Press
George Orwell

How does reading Orwell's preface affect your interpretation of *Animal Farm*?

_____

_____

_____

_____

_____

from Leaves from a Russian Diary – and Thirty Years After
Pitirim A. Sorokin

What advice do you think Sorokin would give the animals for dealing with the oppression in *Animal Farm*? Support your answers with examples from the reading.

_____

_____

_____

_____

_____

Inquisitive Nature Wins Swine Credit for Smarts
from *USA Today*

In your opinion, are the pigs in *Animal Farm* more intelligent than all the other animals? What qualities enabled them to lead the others? Give examples from the novel to support your answer.

_____

_____

_____

_____

from Aesop's Fables
adapted by Jack Zipes

Why do you think Orwell chose to use animals as the characters for his story?

_____

_____

_____

_____

LITERATURE EXCERPT: The Golden Kite, the Silver Wind

"This cannot go on," said the faint voice. "Our people do nothing but rebuild our cities to a different shape every day, every hour. They have no time to hunt, to fish, to love, to be good to their ancestors and their ancestors' children."

"This I admit," said the mandarins of the towns of the Cage, the Moon, the Spear, the Fire, the Sword and this, that, and other things.

"Carry us into the sunlight," said the voice.

The old men were borne out under the sun and up a little hill. In the late summer breeze a few very thin children were flying dragon kites in all the colors of the sun, and frogs and grass, the color of the sea and the color of coins and wheat.

The first Mandarin's daughter stood by his bed.

"See," she said.

"Those are nothing but kites," said the two old men.

"But what is a kite on the ground?" she said. "It is nothing. What does it need to sustain it and make it beautiful and truly spiritual?"

"The wind, of course!" said the others.

"And what do the sky and the wind need to make *them* beautiful?"

"A kite, of course—many kites, to break the monotony, the sameness of the sky. Colored kites, flying!"

"So," said the Mandarin's daughter. "You, Kwan-Si, will make a last rebuilding of your town to resemble nothing more nor less than the wind. And we shall build like a golden kite. The wind will beautify the kite and carry it to wondrous heights. And the kite will break the sameness of the wind's existence and give it purpose and meaning. One without the other is nothing. Together, all will be beauty and cooperation and a long and enduring life."

Whereupon the two mandarins were so overjoyed that they took their first nourishment in days, momentarily were given strength, embraced, and lavished praise upon each other, called the Mandarin's daughter a boy, a man, a stone pillar, a warrior, and a true and unforgettable son. Almost immediately they parted and hurried to their towns, calling out and singing, weakly but happily.

And so, in time, the towns became the Town of the Golden Kite and the Town of the Silver Wind. And harvestings were harvested and business tended again, and the flesh returned, and disease ran off like a frightened jackal.[1] And on every night of the year the inhabitants in the Town of the Kite could hear the good clear wind sustaining them. And those in the Town of the Wind could hear the kite singing, whispering, rising, and beautifying them.

"So be it," said the Mandarin in front of his silken screen.

---

1. A *jackal* is a small doglike animal. The jackal has long been connected with superstitions about death and evil spirits.

Compare the novel you have just read to the literature selection at the left, which is excerpted from "The Golden Kite, the Silver Wind" by Ray Bradbury in *Glencoe Literature*. Then answer the questions below.

Compare & Contrast

1. Allegory What comment do Bradbury and Orwell make about what initially motivates most leaders?

_____

_____

_____

_____

_____

_____

_____

2. Dialogue Who ultimately provides the most sensible advice to the two mandarins? In what way are the animals prevented from giving advice to their leaders?

_____

_____

_____

_____

_____

_____

3. Moral What is the moral of this story? How does this compare with the moral of *Animal Farm*?

_____

_____

_____

_____

_____

_____

_____

WRITE ABOUT IT

Briefly discuss why the two mandarins call the mandarin's daughter "a boy, a man, a stone pillar." How is such name-calling used in *Animal Farm?*

Jot down some notes here first.

_____

_____

_____

_____

_____

_____

_____

_____

_____

_____

_____

_____

_____

_____

_____

_____

_____

_____

_____

_____

_____

_____

_____

_____

_____

_____

_____

Editorial

Offer a Solution In *Animal Farm*, Orwell offered a frightening statement about the ways in which Stalin manipulated the Russian citizens during the Russian Revolution. Unfortunately, this issue continues to exist today, even outside the political arena: many workers in a variety of fields are abused by management. Write an editorial in which you offer a solution to this problem and justify why your solution is appropriate.

Prewrite Fill in a chart with evidence that supports your solution. Make another chart with opposing arguments and evidence to refute those arguments.

Solution	
Argument (unionization allows for strength in numbers)	Evidence
labor strikes have been successful at bringing about change	

Opposing Argument	Counter-Evidence
In the past, union leaders have grown wealthy at their members' expense	

Draft Begin your editorial by presenting your solution, or thesis. Your body paragraphs should all have topic sentences related to the thesis. Use evidence from your chart as support. Cite the page numbers for quotations. Address opposing arguments in a separate paragraph. Conclude by restating your thesis.

Revise Exchange papers with a partner. Evaluate each other's editorial. Is the recommended solution logical and well-supported? Does the essay refute potential counter-arguments? Does the essay include persuasive techniques? Revise your essay based on the comments you receive.

Edit and Proofread Edit your writing so that it expresses your thoughts effectively and is well organized. Carefully proofread for grammar, punctuation, and spelling errors.

UNDERSTAND THE TASK

- When you **argue** in a persuasive essay, you use logic or reason to try to influence a reader's ideas or actions.

Grammar Tip

Italics

In addition to identifying titles of books, plays, films, etc., italics can also be used to emphasize a certain idea or to call out a special concept that might otherwise be in quotation marks.

EXAMPLE: When Nicholas Copernicus published *On the Revolution of Heavenly Spheres*, he put in motion a period of scientific inquiry now referred to as the *Scientific Revolution*.